Helping Children Cope with Trauma

Helping Children Cope with Trauma bridges theory and practice in examining emerging approaches to enhancing resilience and treating traumatized children. Adopting a child-centered perspective, it highlights the importance of the synergy between individual, family, community and social interventions for recovery from post traumatic stress.

Consisting of chapters written by an international range of contributors, the book is presented in three sections, reflecting the ecological circles of support that facilitate healthy development in the face of traumatic circumstances. Section 1, *Individual*, addresses the impact of exposure to trauma and loss on post-traumatic adaptation, focusing on biological aspects, attachment patterns, emotion regulation and aggressive behavior in children. Section 2, *Family*, looks at the concept of family resilience, the impact of trauma on playfulness in toddlers and parents, innovative models for working with children traumatized by war, domestic violence and poverty, and describes the challenges faced by refugee families in the light of intergenerational transmission of trauma. Section 3, *Community*, broadly explores the concept of community resilience and preparedness, the centrality of the school in the community during times of war and conflict, post-traumatic distress and resilience in diverse cultural contexts and the impact of trauma work on mental health professionals who live and work in shared traumatic realities. The book concludes with a theoretical discussion of the concept of "survival mode" as an organizing principle for understanding post traumatic phenomena.

Helping Children Cope with Trauma will provide mental health professionals, child welfare workers, educators, child development experts and researchers with a thorough understanding of the needs of children after trauma and how those needs may best be met.

Ruth Pat-Horenczyk is a clinical psychologist and Director of Child and Adolescent Clinical Services at the Temmy and Albert Latner Israel Center for the Treatment of Psychotrauma at Herzog Hospital in Jerusalem. She is also Adjunct Associate Professor at the Paul Baerwald School of Social Work and Social Welfare at the Hebrew University of Jerusalem.

Danny Brom is a clinical psychologist, the Founding Director of the Israel Center for the Treatment of Psychotrauma at Herzog Hospital in Jerusalem, and Adjunct Associate Professor at the Paul Baerwald School of Social Work and Social Welfare at the Hebrew University of Jerusalem. He is former director of the Dutch Institute for Psychotrauma (IVP), the Netherlands.

Juliet M. Vogel is a clinical psychologist and has been associated with the North Shore-Long Island Jewish Health System in Manhasset, New York for more than 20 years. She was previously the Director of Training for the Division of Trauma Psychiatry, and is currently an associate professor at the Hofstra North Shore-LIJ School of Medicine at Hofstra University.

Helping Children Cope with Trauma

Individual, family and community perspectives

Edited by Ruth Pat-Horenczyk, Danny Brom and Juliet M. Vogel

 Routledge
Taylor & Francis Group

LONDON AND NEW YORK

First published 2014
by Routledge
27 Church Road, Hove, East Sussex, BN3 2FA

and by Routledge
711 Third Avenue, New York, NY 10017

Routledge is an imprint of the Taylor & Francis Group, an informa business

© 2014 Ruth Pat-Horenczyk, Danny Brom and Juliet M. Vogel

British Library Cataloguing in Publication Data
A catalogue record for this book is available from the British Library

Library of Congress Cataloging in Publication Data
Helping children cope with trauma : individual, family and community perspectives / edited by Ruth Pat-Horenczyk, Danny Brom, Juliet M. Vogel. — First Edition.
  pages cm
1. Psychic trauma in children – Treatment. 2. Post-traumatic stress disorder in children – Treatment. I. Pat-Horenczyk, Ruth. II. Brom, D. III. Vogel, Juliet M.
RJ506.P66H43 2014
618.92'8521–dc23

2013022988

ISBN: 978-0-415-50455-3 (hbk)
ISBN: 978-0-415-50456-0 (pbk)
ISBN: 978-1-315-85775-6 (ebk)

Typeset in Times New Roman
by RefineCatch Ltd, Bungay, Suffolk

MIX
Paper from
responsible sources
FSC
www.fsc.org   FSC® C013604

Printed and bound by CPI Group (UK) Ltd, Croydon, CR0 4YY

In loving memory of
Baruch Patt
Zvi Brom
Anita Vogel Sklarsky

Contents

Concluding comments   241

Editors

Ruth Pat-Horenczyk is Director of Child and Adolescent Clinical Services at Herzog Hospital's ICTP in Jerusalem, Israel, and an Adjunct Associate Professor at the School of Social Work and Social Welfare at the Hebrew University of Jerusalem. She is a clinical psychologist who received her PhD from the Hebrew University and completed her post-doctoral training at the University of California in San Diego. Subsequently, she was involved in clinical research and teaching in several areas of behavioral medicine, such as sleep and eating disorders. Dr. Pat-Horenczyk has published a variety of articles and book chapters in the field of child trauma, and has appeared at numerous international conferences to present her clinical work and research findings. Recently, she has co-edited, with Drs. Brom and Ford, the book *Treating Traumatized Children: Risk, resilience and recovery* (Routledge, 2009). Her research topics focus on risk and protective factors for childhood posttraumatic stress disorder (PTSD), preparedness and resilience, relational trauma and posttraumatic growth. In the last few years, she has been conducting a nationwide screening project aimed at identification of posttraumatic distress among schoolchildren and developing evidenced-based interventions and treatments.

Danny Brom is Founding Director of the ICTP at Herzog Hospital in Jerusalem. Dr. Brom has worked in the field of traumatic stress since 1979 in the Netherlands and was the Director of the Dutch Institute of Psychotrauma from 1985 until 1988. In 1989, he was appointed Director of the Latner Institute for the Study of Social Psychiatry and Psychotherapy at Herzog Hospital. In addition, he was Director of Research of Amcha, the National Israeli Center for the Psychosocial Support of Survivors of the Holocaust and the Second Generation from 1994 until 2000. Dr. Brom has taught at the Hebrew University of Jerusalem since 1998 in the Department of Clinical Psychology, and, in 2010, was appointed Adjunct Associate Professor at its Paul Baerwald School of Social Work and Social Welfare. Dr. Brom has published numerous books and articles on psychological trauma and PTSD. He published the first controlled outcome study on brief therapy for PTSD in 1989, *Journal of Consulting and Clinical Psychology*. He has co-edited *The Trauma of*

Terrorism: Sharing Knowledge and Shared Care, an International Handbook (Haworth Maltreatment and Trauma Press, 2005) with Yael Danieli and Joe Sills; and *Treating Traumatized Children: Risk, Resilience and Recovery* (Routledge, 2009) with Ruth Pat-Horenczy and Julian D. Ford. Currently, his main effort goes to bridging the gap between scientific data and the development of service provision in the community.

Juliet M. Vogel has a doctorate in developmental psychology from Harvard University and respecialization training in child and family clinical psychology from Michigan State University. She has been affiliated with the North Shore-LIJ Health System in metropolitan New York City for more than 20 years and currently is an associate professor at the Hofstra North Shore-LIJ School of Medicine at Hofstra University. She has served as Training Director for North Shore-LIJ's Division of Trauma Psychiatry and the Rosen Family Wellness Center for Law Enforcement and Military Personnel and Their Families (2007–2009) and as Director of Child Psychology Training for the North Shore Hospital Division of Child and Adolescent Psychiatry (1997–2007). Her trauma work has included chairing a taskforce on children's psychological responses to disasters for the child section, Division of Clinical Psychology, American Psychological Association; its report, co-authored by Eric Vernberg, was published as a pair of papers, 'Part 1: Children's psychological responses to disasters' and 'Part 2: Interventions with children after disasters', in the *Journal of Clinical Child Psychology* in 1993. She was project director of several programs for children and families affected by the September 11 terrorist attacks. Since 2001, she has been involved with the National Child Traumatic Stress Network (NCTSN), including the treatment development site at North Shore-LIJ (2001–2009) and national workgroups that developed adaptations of psychological First Aid for schools and for community religious professionals. She has served as a consultant for the NCTSN's Terrorism and Disaster Center at the University of Oklahoma Health Sciences Center.

Contributors

Naomi L. Baum, PhD, is a psychologist and Director of the Resilience Unit at the ICTP, Jerusalem. She has created and implemented resilience-building programs for those exposed to trauma, both man-made and natural. She has been a consulting psychologist for schools and has taught courses in psychology at the university level.

Richard A. Bryant, PhD, is an Australian Research Council (ARC) Laureate Fellow, a Scientia Professor of Psychology, University of New South Wales, and Director of the Traumatic Stress Unit, Westmead Hospital, Australia. His research has focused on acute psychological responses to trauma. He has identified some of the key biological and cognitive markers of risk for PTSD, developed screening tools for identifying people who are at high risk for PTSD, conducted the major early interventions trials for PTSD and studied neural networks of PTSD.

Esther Cohen, PhD, is a professor and the former Head of the Graduate Program for Child-Clinical Psychology at the Hebrew University of Jerusalem. She is an accredited supervisor in Clinical Psychology, Developmental Psychology and Family Therapy. She combines research with clinical work with families and consulted in New York City in the aftermath of 9/11.

Sarale Cohen, PhD, is Professor Emeritus at the University of California, Los Angeles (UCLA). She is currently a professional volunteer at the ICTP, Jerusalem. Dr. Cohen received her PhD from UCLA. She is a developmental psychologist and worked in the Child Development Division of the Pediatric Department of UCLA's School of Medicine. Her research focused on biological and social risk factors in childhood and adolescence for cognitive, social and emotional development.

Katie Dawson, PhD, is a postdoctoral Fellow at the University of New South Wales, Australia and a clinical psychologist. She completed her PhD in Aceh, Indonesia, exploring the applicability of western-based cognitive models of PTSD in children exposed to natural disaster and conflict. She works in a clinical and research capacity at the Traumatic Stress Unit at Westmead

Hospital, New South Wales, serving refugee communities. She is also a private clinical consultant for the Centre of Clinical Therapy in Sydney.

Rachel Dekel, PhD, is an associate professor and Head of the Louis and Gabi Weisfeld School of Social Work at Bar-Ilan University in Israel. She is interested in exploring the consequences of direct and indirect continuous exposure to traumatic events. She is particularly interested in the study of individuals who have experienced secondary exposure to traumatic events. Her research has examined spouses of former veterans and prisoners of war, children of fathers with PTSD and therapists who have treated victims of terrorism.

Elisa van Ee, MSc, LLM, is a clinical psychologist at Foundation Centrum '45, the Dutch institute for specialized diagnosis and treatment of psychotrauma, and has worked mainly with refugee families. Her PhD project focuses on the impact of parental war trauma on the development of young children. In her work, she aims to combine the different perspectives of psychology and law to reach a more holistic approach in the treatment of traumatization.

Julian D. Ford, PhD, is Professor of Psychiatry at the University of Connecticut School of Medicine. He directs the Child Trauma Clinic and Center for Trauma Response Recovery and Preparedness. Dr. Ford developed the TARGET (Trauma Affect Regulation: Guide for Education and Therapy) treatment for adults and children. He has co-edited three books – *Treating Traumatized Children: Risk, Resilience and Recovery* (Routledge, 2009), the *Encyclopedia of Psychological Trauma* (Wiley, 2008) and *Treating Complex Traumatic Stress Disorders: An Evidence-Based Guide* (Guilford Press, 2009 – and authored the textbook *Posttraumatic Stress Disorder: Scientific and Professional Dimensions* (Elsevier/Academic Press, 2009).

Rebecca S. Ginat, BA in Psychology and English (Media and Rhetoric) from the University of Illinois at Chicago (UIC). She currently works in the Resilience Unit at the ICTP and has worked in psychology labs at UIC and the Hebrew University.

Damion J. Grasso, PhD, is an assistant professor in the Department of Psychiatry at the University of Connecticut School of Medicine. Dr. Grasso's research focuses on violence exposure in children and adolescents, with the overarching goal of enhancing protective resources towards reducing risk of trauma-related psychopathology and maladaptive developmental outcomes.

Carolyn A. Greene, PhD, is an assistant professor in the Department of Psychiatry at the University of Connecticut School of Medicine. She is a licensed clinical psychologist specializing in the treatment of traumatic stress disorders and problems of emotion regulation with children, adolescents and families.

Daniel Hamiel, PhD, is Professional Director of the School Resilience Program at the Donald J. Cohen & Irving B. Harris Center for Trauma and Disaster

Intervention (the Cohen-Harris Center). Since the 2006 Lebanon War, he has developed and was involved in empirical testing of a pioneering model for a teacher-delivered classroom program focusing on child resilience. In addition, he directed the nationwide training of hundreds of school personnel counselors, psychologists and teachers, within a national pilot program on urban preparedness.

Judith Harel, DSc, has a doctorate in medical sciences from the Israeli Institute of Technology and is an active clinician, researcher and teacher. She is Professor of Clinical Psychology and Head of the Clinical-Educational Psychology track at the University of Haifa in Israel. She is also a Supervisor in Clinical and Developmental Psychology and was Chief Psychologist at the Child Development Center of the Bnai Zion Medical Center in Haifa. She and colleagues developed a well-recognized mother–child and father–child psychotherapy model, dyadic therapy.

Emily E. Haroz, MA, is a doctoral student in the Department of Mental Health at Johns Hopkins Bloomberg School of Public Health. Her research includes the role of resilience in mental health prevention and treatment programs for children and improvement in measurement techniques for crosscultural mental health research.

Rebecca S. Hock is a PhD candidate in the Department of Mental Health at Johns Hopkins Bloomberg School of Public Health. Her research focuses on mental health in under-served populations globally, with a particular interest in family factors influencing risk and resilience in youth.

Mark J. D. Jordans, PhD, is a child psychologist and works as Head of Research for HealthNet TPO, a Dutch aid agency that works on health care in areas disrupted by war or disasters. He is also an honorary senior lecturer at the London School of Hygiene and Tropical Medicine, where he teaches the MSc course in global mental health. He is co-founder of and advisor to TPO Nepal, one of the country's leading mental health NGOs.

Hanna Kaminer, DSc, is a clinical and developmental psychologist. She received her DSc from the Technion-Israel Institute of Technology. She has been the director of the Psychological and Developmental Clinic in the Haifa District Health Office of the Ministry of Health, Israel for the last 20 years. She lectures at Haifa University and teaches courses in mother–child, father–child psychotherapy to mental health professionals specializing in early childhood all over the country.

Jeremy C. Kane, MPH, is a doctoral student in the Department of Mental Health at Johns Hopkins Bloomberg School of Public Health. His research interests include the effects of migration on mental health and the development and evaluation of children's mental health services in post-conflict settings.

Rolf J. Kleber, PhD, is Professor of Psychotraumatology in the Department of Clinical and Health Psychology at Utrecht University and Head of Research for the Arq Psychotrauma Expert Group. He was a lecturer at the University of California, Irvine, and has also held academic positions at several Dutch universities. His research and teaching fields encompass conceptual issues concerning traumatic stress, general processes of coping with trauma, effective trauma-focused interventions, (late) sequelae of war and disasters and crosscultural aspects of health and illness.

Nathaniel Laor, MD, PhD, is Professor of Psychiatry and Philosophy at Tel Aviv University, Israel, and Clinical Professor at the Yale Child Study Center. He directs the Tel Aviv-Brull Community Mental Health Center and the Cohen-Harris Center's resilience unit. He developed an ecological-systemic child-oriented model for urban resilience and disaster preparedness. Since 2010, he has served in Israel's Ministry of Defense as Professional Director of the national urban preparedness program.

Trudy Mooren, PhD, works as a clinical psychologist in Foundation Centrum '45 through which she is involved in the treatment of families after severe incidents or episodes of interpersonal violence, such as occur during war, oppression, migration and military service. The program she coordinates for traumatized families involves the implementation, training and study of the effects of a mentalization-based multifamily therapeutic approach.

Orit Nuttman-Shwartz, PhD, is an associate professor, Founder and Head of the School of Social Work at Sapir College, Israel, and chairperson of the Israeli National Council for Social Work. Her research focuses on personal and social trauma, group work and therapy and life transitions and occupational crises. Working near the Israeli border, she also studies the effects of continuous exposure to threat on individuals, communities and organizations.

Betty Pfefferbaum, MD, JD, is Director of the Terrorism and Disaster Center of the NCTSN, a network of centers across the United States focused on improving services and the standard of care for traumatized children. She has worked in the disaster field for more than 15 years.

Laura C. Pratchett, PsyD, is Assistant Clinical Professor of Psychiatry at Mount Sinai Medical Center, New York, and a clinical psychologist in the PTSD Clinic and team leader of the Transitions Clinic for returning veterans at the James J. Peters VA Medical Center, also in New York. Dr. Pratchett has authored papers and book chapters on the consequences of trauma, including childhood trauma, and biological and psychological risk factors for PTSD, as well as treatment for trauma-related illness.

Sarit Schramm has an MA in educational psychology and clinical child psychology from the Hebrew University. She works at the ICTP, where she is in charge of the building emotion and affect regulation (BEAR) program for children. In addition, she is currently an intern in educational psychology in Jerusalem, Israel.

Anat Shoshani, PhD, is an assistant professor at the School of Psychology of the Interdisciplinary Center (IDC) Herzliya, a private university in Israel. Dr. Shoshani received her PhD in clinical psychology from Tel Aviv University. Her clinical experience includes working in hospitals, public clinical centers and as a private practitioner. She serves as Academic Director of MAYTIV, a center for research and practice in positive psychology that was established as part of the School of Psychology in IDC Herzliya.

Phyllis R. Silverman, PhD, SMHyg, MSW, is a resident scholar at the Brandeis University Women's Study Research Center. She was Co-Principal Investigator and Project Director of the Massachusetts General Hospital/Harvard Child Bereavement Study. Her books include *Widow to Widow: How the bereaved help one another* (Brunner-Routledge, 2004) and *Never Too Young to Know: Death in children's lives* (Oxford University Press, 1999).

Michelle Slone, PhD, is Professor of Psychology at Tel Aviv University, Israel. She is currently Head of the Child Clinical Graduate Program at the university, and a member of the governing council of its Adler Center for Research in Child Development and Psychopathology. Her research interests include the effects of political violence and conflict on children, resilience and its promotion, primary and secondary intervention and cultural issues of mental disorders.

Smadar Spirman, MA, MSW, is a social worker who specialized in urban planning, served as Associate Director of the Cohen-Harris Center. She also directed the Tel Aviv Emergency Treatment Services. Following the 1991 missile attacks on Tel Aviv, she developed a model for multi-systemic response to municipal emergencies, and was Deputy Director of the pilot national program on urban preparedness.

Lesley Sternin, MSW, LCSW, is Director of the Child Trauma Training Institute, a program of Parents Places, Jewish Family and Children's Services, San Francisco, that works to ensure the best possible care for traumatized children by training mental health professionals in early intervention.

Wietse A. Tol, PhD, is the Dr. Ali and Rose Kawi Assistant Professor at the Department of Mental Health of Johns Hopkins Bloomberg School of Public Health in Baltimore and Senior Advisor for the Dutch aid agency HealthNet TPO. His research focuses on preventive mental health interventions in populations experiencing adversity in low- and middle-income countries.

Amy Weiss, MS, LMFT, is a licensed marriage and family therapist and the Child Training Director of Parents Place, San Francisco, a program of Jewish family and children's services. She oversees the Child Trauma Training Institute and has presented widely on identifying and treating trauma in young children.

Zeev Wiener, MD, is a family physician and a psychiatrist. He is the Director of Community Interventions at the Cohen-Harris Center and Deputy Director of the Day Hospital, Tel Aviv-Brull Community Mental Health Center. He is an instructor of primary care professionals in community psychiatry and Program Director of the School for the Study of Trauma, Preparedness, and Community Resilience established by the Cohen-Harris Center.

Leo Wolmer, MA, is a clinical psychologist, Director of Research at the Cohen-Harris Center and Director of Assessment for the national pilot program on urban preparedness. Following the 1999 earthquake in Turkey, he developed and empirically tested a pioneering model for a teacher-delivered classroom program focusing on trauma, transforming the role of the teacher into one of educator and "clinical mediator."

Victoria Yeh, BS, graduated from Harvard University in 2012 with a BS in psychology. She researched at the ICTP while studying at the Hebrew University of Jerusalem. She is currently studying Arabic and teaching English in Amman, Jordan, as a Fulbright US student Fellow.

Rachel Yehuda, PhD, is Professor of Psychiatry and Neuroscience at Mount Sinai School of Medicine and the Mental Health Patient Care Center Director at the James J. Peters VA Medical Center in New York. She has authored several hundred papers, chapters and books on the neurobiology, neuroendocrinology and molecular biology of traumatic stress in diverse populations. She has numerous federal grants for her research, and has won awards nationally and internationally for her scientific advances. She has received honorary professorships from Max Planck Institute of Psychiatry in Munich, Germany, and Leiden University in the Netherlands.

Preface

We would like to have our children grow up without trauma in their lives. "Trauma" and "children" are words we would not like to see on the same page. Yet, trauma and chronic stress impact both children and adults and the cumulative nature of chronic stress or allostatic load of trauma, takes a great toll on mental and physical health.

The major aims of *Helping Children Cope with Trauma* are to bridge theory and practice and to provide updated and innovative theoretical and clinical conceptualizations and research into posttraumatic distress and resilience. We address the impact of trauma on children using a socialecological system framework (Bronfenbrenner, 1979), viewing the development of individual children within the context of the family, community and society in which the children live and grow, and in which they experience and recover from trauma. As Masten (2001) noted, the traumas that children experience often impact not only their individual development, but the systems that support and protect them as well.

The collective personal motivation of the editors of this book is based on a background colored by a family history of the Holocaust and emigration, as well as a parallel history of coping, resilience, altruism and success. Although we grew up in three continents and diverse sociopolitical contexts, we have come together with the motivation of preventing or reducing the suffering of children who have been victimized by the way adults manage the world.

We developed our theoretical thinking on the basis of the centrality of attachment in both healthy and pathological child development. The fact that children are embedded in multiple circles of support is one of the underlying premises of this book. Psychodynamic and cognitive theories of trauma have enriched our understanding of the inner experience of traumatized children. Judith Herman (1992) had a tremendous impact on our thinking about trauma and the complex relationship between societal forces, feminism and the willingness of society to confront and recognize the sources of trauma. The past 20 years have added rich experiences of looking at trauma through its impact on the body, the way the body keeps the memory, and how the body can play a pivotal role in recovery from trauma.

Three decades of clinical experience have taught us the importance and long-term consequences of childhood trauma. We also realize the crucial importance of developing a continuity of services, integrating clinical and community interventions and recognizing the synergy between the various ecological systems. We have discovered how fruitful crosscultural collaboration can be and how much we can learn from the discourse between different cultures and languages of trauma.

As trauma and resilience research continues to evolve, the importance of multiple levels of analysis is evident. This includes the biological impact of psychological trauma and its impact on individual self-regulation, as reflected in discussions of "survival mode." The importance of family support for resilience is well documented. However, it can be difficult for families to provide support for members if the family's own functioning is significantly compromised by trauma. Just as there is now a considerable consensus about the factors that contribute to individual resilience, there is also an emerging consensus regarding what makes a family resilient. At times, the difficulties are based on community issues, and resilience can be fostered by intervening at a community level.

Helping Children Cope with Trauma is based on the assertion that adopting a socio-ecological perspective may advance the effectiveness of interventions for recovery from post traumatic distress and enhance resilience. It is intended to provide clinicians, educators, community workers, public policy makers and researchers with a deeper understanding of the needs of children after trauma and possible ways of meeting these needs.

The book is divided into three sections, focusing respectively on the individual, the family and the community. In addition to theoretical background, most of the chapters include a detailed description of an applied aspect of the field, such as:

- *a model of clinical or community intervention* for post trauma response and building resilience, including examples of implementation;
- *research design and evidence* for post trauma responses of young children and families, or the effectiveness of clinical and community interventions;
- *clinical case studies* illustrating individual or group intervention with traumatized children, families or communities.

Section I of this book focuses on individual factors that influence coping with trauma. Chapter 1, by Laura Pratchett and Rachel Yehuda, presents insights into the biological impact of early trauma and describes how trauma in childhood can increase the risk for later trauma and the development of PTSD. It integrates cutting-edge research on the neurobiology of PTSD, including genetic, epigenetic and neuroendocrine studies, and lays the foundation for understanding the complex pathways from childhood trauma to adult PTSD.

In Chapter 2, Carolyn Greene, Damion Grasso and Julian Ford take on the challenge of defining emotion regulation, its normative and impaired development and its centrality in complex childhood trauma. They further elucidate how trauma can shift the brain away from learning mode to hypervigilant survival mode.

The chapter concludes with a description of a therapeutic intervention for developing reflective self-awareness to restore "learning mode" and capacity for emotion regulation.

Ruth Pat-Horenczyk, Victoria Yeh, Sarale Cohen and Sarit Schramm explore the impact of exposure to violence on aggressive behavior in children and adolescents from the individual, family, community and cultural perspectives in Chapter 3. They present a comprehensive review of the multidisciplinary literature on the complex relationship between trauma and aggression in childhood, with the aim of understanding the mechanisms by which the exposure to violence can lead to increased aggressive behavior in children. The authors propose trauma- and resilience-informed recommendations for intervention programs aimed at the reduction and prevention of aggressive behavior in children.

The last chapter in this section deals with childhood bereavement and traumatic loss. Naomi Baum, Rebecca Ginat and Phyllis Silverman (Chapter 4) argue that it is important to understand the grieving process in a developmental framework, and that using a trauma lens can help identify and address trauma issues when they are present in a child's loss. They provide two case examples: the clinical treatment of a child who experienced the traumatic loss of a sibling, and a community group intervention program for children and their caregivers to facilitate the grieving process and promote resilience after bereavement.

In Section II, the focus shifts to the family and dealing with child trauma in a family context. In Chapter 5, Juliet Vogel and Betty Pfefferbaum provide an overview of current perspectives on family resilience—the family's ability to withstand or overcome adversities, including the ability to support individual members. They describe the central roles of the meaning the family makes of adversity as well as the family's coping strategies and the resources to which the family has access. They discuss the relevance of family belief systems, organization, communication and problem solving and the ways that these affect resilience at times of significant stress.

Esther Cohen (Chapter 6) provides a theoretical framework for using a play-based preventive intervention for young children and their mothers who live in circumstances of ongoing political violence (rocket and mortar attacks). She then describes in detail an innovative intervention for mothers and young children, highlighting the centrality of play and playfulness in mother–child interaction and in creating a sense of safety.

In Chapter 7, Judith Harel and Hanna Kaminer describe an Israeli model for dyadic therapy (the "Haifa dyadic therapy") and discuss its application for treating post-traumatic stress in war-traumatized children. This psychodynamic relationship-focused model aims at the restoration of mentalization and reflective functioning as a way to facilitate the co-construction of a post-trauma narrative, which creates new meanings for the traumatic experience and contains the child's fears and wishes.

In Chapter 8, Lesley Sternin and Amy Weiss discuss the use of a "home visiting" application of the child–parent psychotherapy model developed by Alicia

Lieberman and Patricia Van Horn (2005, 2008). Sternin and Weiss provide clinical examples showing how home visits are used as a vehicle for assessment and therapeutic change with high-risk families affected by domestic violence and poverty. The challenges of creating therapeutic space in the home, maintaining flexible boundaries and taking care of safety issues are discussed.

Elisa van Ee, Trudy Mooren and Rolf Kleber (Chapter 9) describe the challenges to parenting for refugees who are dealing with their own trauma histories as well as a range of issues involved in refugee status. They then describe a study of the interaction between refugee parents and their young children (born in the Netherlands) and a multi family intervention designed to reduce the likelihood of intergenerational transmission of trauma and to support the emotional availability of refugee parents to their children.

Section III focuses on the community/societal level. Laor and colleagues (Chapter 10) broadly discuss the concept of community resilience, as well as the role of preparedness. They describe the rationale for the "Cohen-Harris model of urban resilience" and its four components (population, education, health/mental health and information) as implemented in 18 Israeli cities.

Michelle Slone and Anat Shoshani (Chapter 11) describe a model developed in Israel for building resilience in schools. The authors argue that since present-day wars extend beyond the traditional battlefields and affect whole communities, empowering schools is the optimal way of creating a community support system for children.

Wietse Tol, Emily Haroz, Rebecca Hock, Jeremy Kane and Mark Jordans (Chapter 12) discuss the importance of focusing on protective factors and processes in the development of intervention programs for traumatized children. They give examples from community work focusing on resilience with war-affected children in Palestine and northern Uganda.

In Chapter 13, Katie Dawson and Richard Bryant present a theoretical model of children's responses to disaster and conflict in the context of Islam. They highlight the importance of adapting cognitive models of childhood traumatic stress to diverse cultural environments and discuss the example of children in a strictly Islamic, non-Western setting. They present qualitative data and lessons learned from children exposed to a tsunami.

The community section concludes with a chapter by Rachel Dekel and Orit Nuttman-Shwartz (Chapter 14), which focuses on the mental health professionals who live and work in shared traumatic reality. They used focus group methodology to explore the implications of the dual roles of being a helping professional and parent while living and working in an area that is under frequent rocket attack (in southern Israel).

The book concludes with a theoretical look at the concept of survival mode as an organizing principle for understanding post traumatic phenomena. This chapter (Chapter 15) by Danny Brom explains some basic mechanisms in human survival responses and reviews several of the issues that are discussed in this book in the framework of "survival mode theory."

References

Bronfenbrenner, U. (1979). *The ecology of human development: Experiments by nature and design.* Cambridge, MA: Harvard University Press.

Herman, J. L. (1992). *Trauma and recovery.* New York, NY: Basic Books.

Lieberman, A. F., & Van Horn, P. (2005). *Don't hit my mommy!: A manual for child–parent psychotherapy with young witnesses of family violence.* Washington, D.C.: ZERO TO THREE.

Lieberman, A. F., & Van Horn, P. (2008). *Psychotherapy with infants and young children: Repairing the effects of stress and trauma on early attachment.* New York, NY: Guilford Press.

Masten, A. S. (2001). Ordinary magic: Resilience processes in development. *American Psychologist, 56*(2), 227–238.

Acknowledgements

Editing a book is a joint effort between many people. First of all, we want to thank the authors that have worked with us and have been generous in sharing their knowledge and being patient with the editors. We acknowledge that all authors are committed to their social network and that writing often takes away from time with family, friends and community, who all deserve our gratefulness. Special appreciation goes to our colleagues and friends at the ICTP of Herzog Hospital, with whom we learn, brainstorm, cope with common challenges and keep growing and developing, both personally and professionally.

Our exceptionally talented editor, Dr. Naomi Goldblum, deserves all praise. Her ability to integrate both critical reading of content and rigorous and careful language editing has made her an indispensable asset for editing this book. We appreciate the opportunity that Routledge has provided us to again be part of their prestigious publications, and Joanne Forshaw and Susannah Frearson for their guidance, flexibility and professional expertise.

Our families are a source of constant and continual support and love. These strong attachments are the basis of our curiosity, enthusiasm and ability to create new connections. We deeply appreciate the reflective space they granted us.

Figures

Figure 5.1 originally appeared in Patterson, J. M. (1988), Families experiencing stress: I. The Family Adjustment and Adaptation Response Model: II. Applying the FAAR Model to health-related issues for intervention and research, *Family Systems Medicine*, *6*(2), 202–237, and is reproduced here by kind permission of the American Psychological Association.

Figure 12.1 originally appeared in Tol, W. A., Barbui, C., Galappatti, A., Silove, D., Betancourt, T. S., Souza, R., Golaz, A. and van Ommeren, M. (2011), Mental health and psychosocial support in humanitarian settings: Linking practice and research, *Lancet*, *378*(9802), 1581–1591, and is reproduced here by kind permission of Elsevier.

Section 1

Individual

Chapter I

Developmental trauma from a biophysical perspective

Laura C. Pratchett and Rachel Yehuda

Introduction

Higher rates of childhood trauma (usually defined as chronic and repeated episodes of maltreatment, abuse or neglect, as opposed to single exposures to accidents or disasters) have been found among adults with posttraumatic stress disorder (PTSD) than among similarly exposed individuals who did not develop PTSD (Bremner, Southwick, Johnson, Yehuda, & Charney, 1993; Cloitre, Scarvalone, & Difede, 1997; Follette, Polusny, & Milbeck, 1994; Lang et al., 2008; Rodriguez, Ryan, Vande Kemp, & Foy, 1997; Zlotnick, 1997). Also, among adults who report childhood trauma, rates of PTSD are generally found to range from 72% to 100% (Lindberg & Distad, 1985; Rodriguez et al., 1997), often due to subsequent trauma exposure. These observations support the idea that exposure to childhood trauma is a risk factor for PTSD following trauma in adulthood. Moreover, developmental trauma appears to increase the likelihood of trauma exposure in adulthood, which may lead to the development of PTSD (Brewin, Andrews, & Valentine, 2000; Nishith, Mechanic, & Resick, 2000; Widom, 1999; for a review, see Classen, Palesh, & Aggarwal, 2005). Though not a necessary prerequisite for PTSD in adulthood, developmental trauma is therefore considered a potent risk factor for it.

In recent years, investigation of the biological correlates of childhood trauma has revealed similarities to those found in association with adult PTSD. In particular, the neurobiology of childhood trauma is similar to that of adult PTSD, raising the question of whether the neurobiology of adult PTSD reflects this risk. In this chapter, we evaluate the contribution of developmental trauma to some of the alterations in the hypothalamic–pituitary–adrenal (HPA) axis associated with PTSD. Advances in our understanding of the molecular biology of PTSD also allow us to consider a variety of mechanisms, such as genetic and epigenetic processes, including developmental programming, that may form the foundation for the biological changes observed following both exposure to childhood trauma and the development of PTSD (de Kloet, Joels, & Holsboer, 2005; Jovanovic & Ressler, 2010; Seckl, 2008; Yehuda & Bierer, 2008, 2009; Yehuda & LeDoux, 2007).

Neuroendocrine alterations in PTSD

The HPA axis has been a focus of study in PTSD because of the central role it plays in the neuroendocrine response to acute stress, including responses to fear, which would fit the current conceptualizations of precipitants of PTSD. In response to provocation, the stress response of the HPA axis involves the secretion of corticotropin-releasing hormone (CRH), which activates the release of adrenocorticotropic hormone (ACTH). ACTH, in turn, stimulates the release of glucocorticoids (GCs)—in particular, cortisol in humans—which are essential for the restoration of the biological homeostasis necessary for adaptation and recovery (McEwen, 2002; de Kloet et al., 2005). While older studies focused on hormone release, there has been increased emphasis on receptors and other compounds that affect hormone binding and steroid metabolism, as well as the genes underlying these processes.

The first published study of PTSD illustrated lower levels of basal cortisol in veterans with PTSD than among veterans with other psychiatric diagnoses (Mason, Giller, Kosten, Ostroff, & Podd, 1986). This observation was unexpected in light of numerous findings of elevated cortisol in individuals with both chronic stress and depression (Holsboer, 2003; Strohle & Holsboer, 2003). However, this finding has been replicated in numerous other studies that have substantially increased our understanding of the neuroendocrinology of PTSD. To summarize these many reports, studies of the HPA axis in PTSD revealed a profile in which CRH levels are increased (Bremner et al., 1997; Baker et al., 1999) while levels of cortisol are often lower than in controls (e.g., Bremner, Vermetten, & Kelley, 2007; Thaller, Vrkljan, Hotujac, & Thakore, 1999; Vythilingam et al., 2010; Yehuda et al., 1990; Yehuda, Teicher, Trestman, Levengood, & Siever, 1996). Increased cortisol suppression in response to dexamethasone (DEX), a synthetic GC, has also been repeatedly observed, suggesting increased sensitivity of glucorticoid receptors (GRs), and reflecting enhanced negative feedback inhibition (for a review, de Kloet et al., 2006; Yehuda, 2002, 2009). In PTSD, then, the HPA axis is dysregulated in a way that suggests an increased cortisol signaling capacity, so that lower GC levels efficiently suppress the HPA axis, leading to reduced levels of cortisol, which may contribute to increased sympathetic activation (de Kloet et al., 2005; Raison & Miller, 2003; Yehuda, 2002). Thus, although cortisol levels at baseline may be lower, the enhanced responsiveness of GR—the major regulatory elements of the HPA axis—may render the individual hyperresponsive to some types of provocations.

Neuroendocrine alterations associated with childhood trauma

Neuroendocrine alterations in adults with PTSD who report childhood trauma

Results of studies of adults diagnosed with PTSD who report a history of childhood trauma have been somewhat conflicting, but this may reflect the fact that childhood trauma is also a risk factor for depression, which has some hormonal similarities with PTSD (e.g., CRH) but also some differences from it (e.g., cortisol). Lemieux and Coe (1995) observed significantly higher cortisol, norepinephrine (noradrenaline) and epinephrine (adrenaline) levels in women with PTSD than in women without it, among a sample of women who reported childhood sexual abuse. The subjects in that study who reported abuse also tended to be more obese, particularly if they had PTSD, which might be one of the factors contributing to higher ambient hormone levels. In comparison, Bremner et al. (2003) found lower cortisol levels among women with both reported abuse and current PTSD than among those who did not have PTSD, whether or not they reported childhood abuse. However, the ACTH response to CRH administration was blunted in women with PTSD only, in comparison to the women who did not report abuse, while no such differences were observed in comparison to abused women without PTSD. Lower cortisol levels (and higher cortisol pulsatility) was also observed by Bremner et al. (2007) in women with PTSD and a history of childhood abuse compared to women without PTSD, whether or not they reported abuse. Thus, there are some similarities in the observed HPA axis abnormalities associated with PTSD due to childhood abuse and adult traumatization, and certainly target hormones such as cortisol and norepinephrine are impacted. However, further work is needed to understand the differences and discover whether they are associated with factors such as comorbidity with depression or type of trauma, the period of development when the trauma(s) occurred and the longitudinal course from childhood trauma to adulthood. It is of particular interest that these studies also show that HPA axis dysfunction may be associated with a history of childhood abuse even in the absence of PTSD.

Neuroendocrine alterations in traumatized children

There are studies that have attempted to clarify the association between childhood abuse and HPA-axis dysfunction by removing longitudinal elements as a variable and studying children with recent abuse and maltreatment. As is the case in individuals with adult trauma and PTSD, low levels of cortisol have been observed in some groups of traumatized children: those in foster care due to maltreatment (Bruce, Fisher, Pears, & Levine, 2009; Gunnar & Vazquez, 2001); those being raised in Romanian orphanages under presumably deprived, if not previously abusive, conditions (Carlson & Earls, 1997); sexually abused girls (King, Mandansky, King, Fletcher, & Brewer, 2001); children suffering from the loss of family members or their home at the epicenter of a devastating earthquake (Goenjian et al., 1996); and children who have experienced peer victimization or witnessed violence (Kliewer, 2006). In addition, low cortisol levels have been observed among children with a more general history of trauma (Bevans, Cerbone, & Overstreet, 2008). However, multiple studies have found elevated morning cortisol in maltreated children (reviewed in Tarullo & Gunnar, 2006). Despite a trend for low cortisol in physically abused children, Cicchetti and Rogosch (2001) found elevated cortisol levels in children who had suffered both physical and sexual abuse, and De Bellis et al. (2000) found that both cortisol and catecholamines were higher in maltreated children with PTSD than in normal control subjects. Interestingly, a recent study that followed sexually abused children longitudinally from age 6 to age 30 demonstrated a progressive attenuation in cortisol activity starting in adolescence, with significantly lower levels of cortisol appearing only in early adulthood (Trickett, Noll, Susman, Shenk, & Putnam, 2010).

Neuroendocrine alterations in adults reporting childhood trauma

Other attempts to better clarify and understand the complex biological responses to trauma have focused on adults without PTSD who report a history of childhood abuse. Blunted diurnal variation of cortisol has been identified among women with a reported history of childhood physical or sexual abuse (Brewer-Smyth & Burgess, 2008; Weissbecker, Floyd, Dedert, Salmon, & Sephton, 2006) and among adults who were adopted in childhood following extreme abuse or neglect (van der Vegt, van der Ende, Kirschbaum, Verhulst, & Tiemeier, 2009). Increased ACTH responses to the administration of CRH have been observed in women with histories of childhood abuse (Newport, Heim, Bonsall, Miller, & Nemeroff, 2004). Attenuated cortisol response to either a stress test or DEX was reported in association with severe childhood maltreatment (Carpenter et al., 2007; MacMillan et al., 2009), emotional neglect (Watson et al., 2007), emotional abuse (Carpenter et al., 2009) and sexual abuse (Stein, Yehuda, Koverola, & Hanna, 1997; Newport et al., 2004), suggesting similarities in negative feedback inhibition in the HPA as is observed in PTSD. However, some studies have suggested that HPA axis dysregulation as a consequence of childhood abuse is present only in adults with depression (Heim, Plotsky, & Nemeroff, 2004; Heim, Newport, Mletzko, Miller, & Nemeroff, 2008). The exact nature of the relationship between childhood trauma and HPA axis dysfunction is thus complex and unclear. What does seem clear is childhood trauma is associated with HPA axis dysfunction, which, at least for some individuals, may reflect the kind of dysfunction observed among individuals with PTSD subsequent to adult trauma. The fluctuating directionality of the findings may reflect the cross-sectional nature of biological studies. Indeed, findings showing extreme high or low HPA axis activity may reflect a system that is more dynamic or hyperresponsive (Yehuda et al., 1996).

HPA axis dysfunction as a risk for adult PTSD

Although prospective longitudinal studies are required to delineate the mechanisms and associations involved in the progression from childhood trauma to biological changes and adult PTSD, the previous literature offers one plausible hypothesis— that early life trauma produces HPA axis sensitization, which serves as the risk factor for PTSD in the face of later trauma. Indeed, the inconsistencies in the literature may reflect the complexity of how environmental events shape biological responses to stress. Clearly, there may be many significant contributors, including the nature of the trauma, the point in development when the event occurred, the nature of the child's parental attachment and countervailing resilience and coping mechanisms.

This would be consistent with our current understanding of the nature of low cortisol as a risk factor for PTSD. Although cortisol findings in PTSD were initially interpreted as reflecting pathophysiology of the disorder resulting from trauma exposure and/or chronic symptoms, data from prospective longitudinal studies have raised the possibility that low cortisol levels reflect pre-traumatic predictors of PTSD. For example, several prospective longitudinal studies have demonstrated that lower cortisol levels in the acute aftermath of trauma were associated with either the subsequent development of PTSD or the risk factor of prior trauma exposure (Delahanty, Raimonde, & Spoonster, 2000; McFarlane, Atchison, & Yehuda, 1997; Resnick, Yehuda, Pitman, & Foy, 1995; Yehuda, McFarlane, & Shalev, 1998). Low cortisol levels at the time of the trauma could compromise the inhibition of stress-induced biologic responses to trauma, such as catecholamines, resulting in prolonged physiological arousal and distress, leading to PTSD (Yehuda, 2002). The idea that reduced cortisol levels might reflect HPA dysfunction associated with pre-exposure vulnerability provides a plausible explanation for discrepant observations in PTSD. Cortisol levels may be low only in PTSD associated with specific pre-exposure risk factors. The previously discussed literature on neuroendocrine findings associated with childhood trauma suggests that this may be one such risk factor.

The role of genes in risk for HPA alterations to trauma

Looking even earlier for risk factors, there is increasing interest in the role of genetic factors in predicting HPA axis alterations to developmental trauma. This is a relevant issue because not all individuals exposed to childhood trauma show HPA axis alterations. The most convincing evidence for an association between genetic factors and PTSD has been observations from twin studies of a greater prevalence of PTSD among monozygotic twins of PTSD positive probands (reviewed in Afifi, Asmundson, Taylor, & Jang, 2010). True and colleagues (1993) first demonstrated that the risk for developing PTSD among combat veterans after trauma exposure was significantly greater for the non-combat exposed co-twin among monozygotic than among dizygotic twins of PTSD-affected probands. More recently, PTSD was also found more often in monozygotic twins of individuals with PTSD in a civilian population (Stein, Jang, Taylor, Vernon, & Livesley, 2002).

Genetic factors can play a role in a variety of ways. One such role could be genotyping (the specific genetic make-up in terms of allele composition of cells or individuals). In this regard, one gene that has been of particular interest to researchers is FKBP5, due to its role in regulating the cortisol-binding affinity of GRs. The activity of this gene is directly associated with GR responsiveness, with underactivity causing greater binding of cortisol to the GR and increasing sensitivity, and overactivity causing less cortisol binding (i.e., reduced sensitivity). The FKBP5 gene has been found to be associated with altered cortisol reactivity— and accompanying increased self-reported anxiety—to a stressor in healthy (non-psychiatric) individuals (Ising et al., 2008).

In one large study of inner-city adults (in which the majority had experienced at least one childhood or adulthood trauma), four single nucleotide polymorphisms (SNPs) in the FKBP5 gene, including two potentially functional SNPs, were observed to interact with the severity of child abuse (but not other kinds of childhood trauma) to predict the severity of adult PTSD (Binder et al., 2008). Impressively, this gene-by-environment interaction remained significant when severity of depression, age, gender, levels of adult trauma and genetic ancestry were controlled for. Further analyses in a subsample of participants showed that people who carried the risk alleles and had PTSD also had enhanced GR sensitivity, as measured by the dexamethasone suppression test (DST)—a test designed to assess the individual cortisol response to DEX administration. This is an important finding supporting the hypothesized risk associated with the gene. Specific polymorphisms of FKBP5 have also been studied for their influence on HPA axis dysfunction in PTSD (Mehta et al., 2011). This study found an association with one FKBP5 polymorphism and decreased baseline cortisol in PTSD—another important finding supporting the hypothesized risk associated with the gene.

More recently, the same four FKBP5 SNPs were genotyped in a large, mixed-race sample of 1,143 European Americans and 1,284 African Americans (Xie et al., 2010). Among African Americans who did not report childhood abuse, one SNP was associated with lower levels of PTSD. Among those who did report childhood abuse, this same genotype was associated with higher levels of PTSD. This pattern of results was not observed in the European Americans in this sample.

In the study of genetic risk, both gene and environment are relevant, in that the presence of a specific gene could contribute to an individual's response to the environmental exposure—in this case, developmental trauma (reviewed in Mehta & Binder, 2012). One cross-sectional study of gene x environment (GxE) interactions examined two polymorphisms of CRHR1—a gene that regulates binding to the CRH receptor—in a sample of 129 Caucasian adults. Among those participants who reported childhood abuse, the risk allele of CRHR1 was associated with elevated cortisol responses to the DST (Tyrka et al., 2009), a finding that corresponds with observations that the risk allele of this gene interacts with child abuse to predict adult depression (Binder et al., 2004; Bradley et al., 2008; Grabe et al., 2010). From a neuroendocrinologic standpoint, comparable CRH elevations have been noted in both PTSD and depression, so these findings certainly indicate a role for this particular gene in the risk for specific HPA axis dysfunction following developmental trauma.

Risk of gene expression associated with developmental trauma and PTSD

Another way that genetic factors can play a role in the risk for PTSD following developmental trauma is in gene expression—the process by which genetic information is used to synthesize functional genetic products such as proteins or RNA. Gene expression was investigated in a recent study that used genome-wide microarray analysis to identify genes of interest for PTSD in the aftermath of 9/11 in New York (Yehuda et al., 2009). Once again, FKBP5 was implicated. A sample of 20 Caucasians with PTSD was randomly selected from a large epidemiological sample and matched to a comparison group of 20 Caucasians without PTSD on age, gender and severity of exposure to the events of 9/11. Analysis of the expression profiles revealed 25 probe sets expressed differently in the PTSD and the control group (who were similarly exposed but did not develop PTSD). Some of the genes identified are known to be involved in signal transduction as well as brain and immune cell function. In particular, the PTSD group expressed lower levels of STAT5B, a direct inhibitor of GR, found to be down-regulated in PTSD. This is notable because a down-regulation in STAT5B could contribute to higher activity of GRs. Of particular interest to this discussion, the proportion of individuals reporting childhood trauma was higher in the PTSD group than in the non-PTSD group.

When the analysis was restricted to subjects with current PTSD only ($n = 15$), compared to the 20 subjects exposed to the 9/11 events but without PTSD mentioned above, 24 genes were identified. In this analysis, FKBP5 gene expression was significantly lower in the subjects with PTSD (i.e., consistent with enhanced glucocorticoid responsiveness), using two probe sets. Additionally, there were alterations in the expression of STAT5B (a direct inhibitor of GR) and major histocompatibility complex Class II gene, which is compatible with the assumption of abnormally reduced cortisol levels, as expression of this gene family is stimulated by glucocorticoids (Chauhan, Leach, Kunz, Bloom, & Miesfeld, 2003; Schwiebert, Schleimer, Radka, & Ono, 1995). Regression analyses indicated that when cortisol, PTSD severity, total lifetime traumatic events and childhood trauma were entered in the model, only cortisol emerged as a significant predictor of FKBP5 expression. Thus, although this study investigated gene expression associated with adult trauma, the findings provide further support for the possible role of FKBP5 in some of the observed neuroendocrine alterations associated with PTSD. They may further elucidate the nature of the genetic risk for such alterations following childhood trauma, in terms of its association with cortisol dysregulation, in particular.

Epigenetic mechanisms as a risk for PTSD

More recent attention to epigenetic processes—heritable functional modifications to gene expression that do not involve a change in the underlying DNA sequence—has opened the door to investigations of whether epigenetics factors can contribute to the potential risk for the development of HPA axis alterations observed in developmental trauma (and thus for PTSD). Indeed, there have been some observations of PTSD risk factors that are difficult to explain with classic genetic models, but are suggestive of epigenetic mechanisms. For example, in a sample of adult children of Holocaust survivors, cortisol and GR alterations in association with PTSD risk were more often linked with maternal than paternal PTSD (Yehuda et al., 2007). Furthermore, the prevalence of PTSD was greater in offspring who reported maternal PTSD than in those who reported paternal PTSD (Yehuda, Bell, Bierer, & Schmeidler, 2008). The finding that this risk is greater in association with maternal than with paternal PTSD may implicate an epigenetic mechanism via either early rearing or *in utero* transmission. In related research, which investigated the children of women exposed to the events of 9/11, the trimester of maternal exposure and the factor of whether or not the mothers developed PTSD following the event had varying effects on cortisol and behavioral measures in the children (Yehuda et al., 2005).

Developmental programming involves the enduring effects of early environmental events, including those that occur *in utero*, on tissue structure and function, which subsequently affect psychological, behavioral and neuroendocrine processes in the adult (Barker, 2002; de Boo & Harding, 2006; McMillen & Robinson, 2005). This occurs when the hormonal reactions of a pregnant woman to stressful events are transmitted through the placenta to the fetus and result in a "recalibration" of GC responsiveness in the child (Levitt, Lindsay, Holmes, & Seckl, 1996; Shoener, Baig, & Page, 2006; Welberg, Seckl, & Holmes, 2000). However, attention has recently been drawn to the question of whether GC or GR programming can also occur from postnatal exposure, either mediated through maternal care or occurring directly in response to environmental events (Seckl & Meaney, 2006; Weaver et al., 2004). In animal models, postnatal events producing epigenetic alterations have been implicated in at least some changes in GR gene expression (Weaver et al., 2007). Further supporting the role of GR programming in some of the neuroendocrine alterations observed following developmental trauma, a recent study of brain tissue in suicide victims showed epigenetic alterations of NR3C1 promoter, a glucocorticoid receptor (GCR) gene, in individuals with a history of child abuse (McGowan et al, 2009).

The observations from both animal and human studies of epigenetic mechanisms make it possible to define the pathways by which environmental risk factors might directly alter GR expression, thus forming a basis for individual differences in endocrine function and, perhaps, vulnerability. It is particularly intriguing to speculate about the extent to which epigenetic changes explain not only changes in GR responsiveness, but also the gene expression profiles for FKBP5 in PTSD.

Clinical implications

In general, it is the presence of psychopathology that prompts mental health intervention. However, the conclusion that childhood trauma has consequences that lay the biological foundation of risk for subsequent PTSD supports the idea of a preventive model of intervention. Ideally, the prevention of childhood abuse would be the ultimate outcome, and therefore interventions targeted at it would be the most effective. To this end, treatments that focus on parent training have been developed, and there is some evidence for their effectiveness in reducing the rates of childhood abuse in targeted families (Chaffin et al., 2004; Peterson, Tremblay, Ewigman, & Saldana, 2003). One obvious limitation of such an approach is that it depends on identifying and engaging at-risk families. In addition, a recent review of early childhood primary prevention programs concluded that the evidence base for such interventions remains weak (Reynolds, Mathieson, & Topitzes, 2009), and so secondary prevention programs need to be considered.

The issue of prescribing psychotropic medications to children is a complex one, and few would argue that there must be clear benefits to justify such an intervention. In the absence of specific psychopathology, psychopharmacologic intervention for purposes of prevention is unlikely to gain favor. It is simply not clear how medication would prevent future pathology. However, there is some recent evidence that family-based interventions targeting behavioral change in children can alter HPA axis functioning (Brotman et al., 2007; Fisher, Gunnar, Chamberlain, & Reid, 2000), and a recent study linked the changes in HPA reactivity to treatment-induced changes in behavior (O'Neal et al., 2010). There is a growing body of literature that supports interventions such as parent–child interaction therapy (Chaffin et al., 2004), child–parent psychotherapy (Lieberman & Van Horn, 2008) and trauma-focused CBT (Cohen, Mannarino, & Deblinger, 2006), which focus on the parent–child relationship as a vehicle for addressing the emotional and behavioral consequences of childhood abuse. Efforts to establish efficacy have, understandably, focused on children presenting with emotional and behavioral disturbances that already meet levels defined as pathological. However, a preventive approach to treatment necessitates that interventions for abused children should not simply focus on treating PTSD or other defined disorders, but should view their goal as changing the trajectory from childhood trauma to potential subsequent PTSD by addressing sub-threshold symptoms and other behavioral and emotional sequelae. Longitudinal studies that assess the effectiveness of these treatments in preventing the development of adult PTSD are still necessary.

Conclusions

The literature on neuroendocrine responses to developmental trauma, when combined with recent observations from genetic and epigenetic research, has begun to lay a foundation for an understanding of the complex pathways involved in linking childhood trauma and adult PTSD. Specifically, it seems possible that the basis for the risk that childhood trauma presents for adult PTSD involves a genetic predisposition for neuroendocrine alterations that are modulated by the experience of such developmental trauma. Genetic background may contribute to biological response to trauma, and more recent observations suggest that

DNA function can also be modified by such exposure to these events through epigenetic pathways; the environment might also be the cause of transient or enduring changes in molecular pathways. All these factors likely combine to determine susceptibility versus resilience and are therefore an appropriate target for preventive interventions.

References

Afifi, T. O., Asmundson, G. J. G., Taylor, S., & Jang, K. L. (2010). The role of genes and environment on trauma exposure and posttraumatic stress disorder symptoms: A review of twin studies. *Clinical Psychology Review, 30*(1), 101–112.

Baker, D. G., West, S. A., Nicholson, W. E., Ekhator, N. N., Kasckow, J. W., Hill, K. K., et al. (1999). Serial CSF corticotropin-releasing hormone levels and adrenocortical activity in combat veterans with posttraumatic stress disorder. *American Journal of Psychiatry, 156*(986), 585–588.

Barker, D. J. P. (2002). Fetal programming of coronary heart disease. *Trends in Endocrinology Metabolism, 13*(9), 364–368.

Bevans, K., Cerbone, A., & Overstreet, S. (2008). Relations between recurrent trauma exposure and recent life stress and salivary cortisol among children. *Development and Psychopathology, 20*(1), 257–272.

Binder, E. B., Bradley, R. G., Liu, W., Epstein, M. P., Deveau, T. C., Mercer, K. B., et al. (2008). Association of FKBP5 polymorphisms and childhood abuse with risk of posttraumatic stress disorder symptoms in adults. *JAMA: Journal of the American Medical Association, 299*(11), 1291–1305.

Binder, E. B., Salyakina, D., Lichtner, P., Wochnik, G. M., Ising, M., Putz, B., et al. (2004). Polymorphisms in FKBP5 are associated with increased recurrence of depressive episodes and rapid response to antidepressant treatment. *National Genetics, 36*(12), 1319–1325.

Bradley, R. G., Binder, E. B., Epstein, M. P., Tang, Y., Nair, H. P., Liu, W., et al. (2008). Influence of child abuse on adult depression: Moderation by the corticotropin-releasing hormone receptor gene. *Archives of General Psychiatry, 65*(2), 190–200.

Bremner, J. D., Licinio, J., Darnell, A., Krystal, J. H., Owens, M. J., Southwick, S. M., et al. (1997). Elevated CSF corticotropin-releasing factor con-centrations in posttraumatic stress disorder. *American Journal of Psychiatry, 154*(5), 624–629.

Bremner, J. D., Southwick, S. M., Johnson, D. R., Yehuda, R., & Charney, D. S. (1993). Childhood physical abuse and combat-related posttraumatic stress disorder in Vietnam veterans. *American Journal of Psychiatry, 150*(2), 235–239.

Bremner, D., Vermetten, E., & Kelley, M. E. (2007). Cortisol, dehydroepiandrosterone, and estradiol measured over 24 hours in women with childhood sexual abuse-related posttraumatic stress disorder. *Journal of Nervous and Mental Disease, 195*(11), 919–927.

Bremner, J. D., Vythilingam, M., Anderson, G., Vermetten, E., McGlashan, T., Heninger, G., et al. (2003). Assessment of the hypothalamic-pituitary-adrenal axis over a 24-hour diurnal period and in response to neuroendocrine challenges in women with and without childhood sexual abuse and posttraumatic stress. *Biological Psychiatry, 54*(7), 710–718.

Brewer-Smyth, K., & Burgess, A. W. (2008). Childhood sexual abuse by a family member, salivary cortisol, and homicidal behavior of female prison inmates. *Nursing Research, 57*(3), 166–174.

Brewin, C. R., Andrews, B., & Valentine, J. D. (2000). Meta-analysis of risk factors for posttraumatic stress disorder in trauma-exposed adults. *Journal of Consulting and Clinical Psychology, 68*(5), 748–766.

Brotman, L. M., Gouley, K. K., Huang, K. Y., Kamboukos, D., Fratto, C., & Pine, D. S. (2007). Effects of psychosocial family-based preventive intervention on cortisol response to a social challenge in preschoolers at high risk for antisocial behavior. *Archives of General Psychiatry, 64*(10), 1172–1179.

Bruce, J., Fisher, P. A., Pears, K. C., & Levine, S. (2009). Morning cortisol levels in preschool-aged foster children: Differential effects of maltreatment type. *Developmental Psychobiology, 51*(1), 14–23.

Carlson, M., & Earls, F. (1997) Psychological and neuroendocrinological sequelae of early social deprivation in institutionalized children in Romania. *Annals of the New York Academy of Sciences, 807*(1), 419–428.

Carpenter, L. L., Carvalho, J. P., Tyrka, A. R., Wier, L. M., Mello, A. F., Mello, M. F., et al. (2007). Decreased adrenocorticotropic hormone and cortisol responses to stress in healthy adults reporting significant childhood maltreatment. *Biological Psychiatry, 62*(10), 1080–1087.

Carpenter, L. L., Tyrka, A. R., Ross, N. S., Khoury, L., Anderson, G. M., & Price, L. H. (2009). Effect of childhood emotional abuse and age on cortisol responsivity in adulthood. *Biological Psychiatry, 66*(1), 69–75.

Chaffin, M., Silovsky, J. F., Funderburk, B., Valle, L. A., Brestan, E. V., Balachova, T., et al. (2004). Parent–child interaction therapy with physically abusive parents: Efficacy for reducing future abuse reports. *Journal of Consulting and Clinical Psychology, 72*(3), 500–510.

Chauhan, S., Leach, C. H., Kunz, S., Bloom, J. W., & Miesfeld, R. L. (2003). Glucocorticoid regulation of eosinophil gene expression. *Journal of Steroid Biochemical Molecular Biology, 84*(4), 441–452.

Cicchetti, D., & Rogosch, F. A. (2001). Diverse patterns of neuroendocrine activity in maltreated children. *Developmental Psychopathology, 13*(3), 677–693.

Classen, C. C., Palesh, O. G., & Aggarwal, R. (2005). Sexual revictimization: A review of the empirical literature. *Trauma, Violence & Abuse, 6*(2), 103–129.

Cloitre, M., Scarvalone, P., & Difede, J. (1997). Posttraumatic stress disorder, self- and interpersonal dysfunction among sexually retraumatized women. *Journal of Traumatic Stress, 10*(3), 437–452.

Cohen, J. A., Mannarino, A. P., & Deblinger, E. (2006). *Treating trauma and traumatic grief in children and adolescents.* New York, NY: Guilford Press.

De Bellis, M. D., Clark, D. B., Beers, S. R., Soloff, P. H., Boring, A. M., Hall, J., et al. (2000). Hippocampal volume in adolescent-onset alcohol use disorders. *American Journal of Psychiatry, 157*(5), 737–744.

de Boo, H. A., & Harding J. E. (2006). The developmental origins of adult disease (Barker) hypothesis. *Australian and New Zealand Journal of Obstetrics and Gynaecology, 46,* 4–14.

de Kloet, E. R., Joels, M., & Holsboer, F. (2005). Stress and the brain: From adaption to disease. *Natural Reviews: Neuroscience, 6*(6), 463–475.

de Kloet, C. S., Vermetten, E., Geuze, E., Kavelaars, A., Heijnen, C. J., & Westenberg, H. G. M. (2006). Assessment of HPA-axis function in posttraumatic stress disorder: Pharmacological and non-pharmacological challenge tests, a review. *Journal of Psychiatry Research, 40*(6), 50–67.

Delahanty, D. L., Raimonde, A. J., & Spoonster, E. (2000). Initial posttraumatic urinary cortisol levels predict subsequent PTSD symptoms in motor vehicle accident victims. *Biological Psychiatry, 48*(9), 940–947.

Fisher, P. A., Gunnar, M. R., Chamberlain, P., & Reid, J. B. (2000). Prevention intervention for maltreated preschool children: Impact on children's behavior, neuroendocrine activity, and foster parent functioning. *Journal of the American Academy & Adolescent Psychiatry, 39*(11), 1356–1364.

Follette, V. M., Polusny, M. M., & Milbeck, K. (1994). Mental health and law enforcement professionals: Trauma history, psychological symptoms, and impact of providing service to child sexual abuse survivors. *Professional Psychology: Research and Practice, 25*(3), 275–282.

Goenjian, A. K., Yehuda, R., Pynoos, R. S., Steinberg, A. M., Tashjian, M., Yang, R. K., et al. (1996). Basal cortisol, dexamethasone suppression of cortisol, and MHPG in adolescents after the 1988 earthquake in Armenia. *American Journal of Psychiatry, 153*(7), 929–934.

Grabe, H. J., Schwahn, C., Appel, K., Mahler, J., Schulz, A., Spitzer, C., et al. (2010). Childhood maltreatment, the corticotropin-releasing hormone receptor gene and adult depression in the general population. *American Journal of Medical Genetics, Part B, 153*(8), 1483–1493.

Gunnar, M. R., & Vazquez, D. M. (2001). Low cortisol and flattening of expected daytime rhythm: Potential indices of risk in human development. *Development and Psychopathology, 13*(3), 515–538.

Heim, C., Newport, D. J., Mletzko, T., Miller, A. H., & Nemeroff, C. B. (2008). The link between childhood trauma and depression: Insights from HPA axis studies in humans. *Psychoneuroendocrinology, 33*(6), 693–710.

Heim, C., Plotsky, P. M., & Nemeroff, C. B. (2004). Importance of studying the contributions of early adverse experience to neurobiological findings in depression. *Neuropsychopharmacology, 29*(4), 641–648.

Holsboer, F. (2003). Corticotropin-releasing hormone modulators and depression. *Current Opinion in Investigational Drugs, 4*(1), 46–50.

Ising, M., Depping, A. M., Siebertz, A., Lucae, S., Unschuld, P. G., Kloiber, S., et al. (2008). Polymorphisms in the FKBP5 gene region modulate recovery from psychosocial stress in healthy controls. *European Journal of Neuroscience, 28*(2), 389–398.

Jovanovic, T., & Ressler, K. J. (2010). How the neurocircuitry and genetics of fear inhibition may inform our understanding of PTSD. *American Journal of Psychiatry, 167*(6), 648–662.

King, J. A., Mandansky, D., King, S., Fletcher, K. E., & Brewer, J. (2001), Early sexual abuse and low cortisol. *Psychiatry and Clinical Neurosciences, 55*(1), 71–74.

Kliewer, W. (2006). Violence exposure and cortisol responses in urban youth. *International Journal of Behavioral Medicine, 13*(2), 109–120.

Lang, A. J., Aarons, G. A., Gearity, J., Laffaye, C., Satz, L., Dresselhaus, T. R., et al. (2008). Direct and indirect links between childhood maltreatment, posttraumatic stress disorder, and women's health. *Behavioral Medicine, 33*(4), 125–135.

Lemieux, A. M., & Coe, C. L. (1995). Abuse-related posttraumatic stress disorder: Evidence for chronic neuroendocrine activation in women. *Psychosomatic Medicine, 57*(2), 105–115.

Levitt, N. S., Lindsay, R. S., Holmes, M. C., & Seckl, J. R. (1996). Dexamethasone in the last week of pregnancy attenuates hippocampal glucocorticoid receptor gene expression and elevates blood pressure in the adult offspring in the rat. *Neuroendocrinology*, *64*(6), 412–418.

Lieberman, A. F., & Van Horn, P. (2008). *Psychotherapy with infants and young children: Repairing the effects of stress and trauma on early attachment*. New York, NY: Guilford Press.

Lindberg, F. H., & Distad, L. J. (1985). Post-traumatic stress disorders in women who experienced childhood incest. *Child Abuse & Neglect*, *9*(3), 329–334.

McEwen, B. S. (2002). The neurobiology and neuroendocrinology of stress: Implications for post-traumatic stress disorder from a basic science perspective. *The Psychiatric Clinics of North America*, *25*(2), 469–494.

McFarlane, A. C., Atchison, M., & Yehuda, R. (1997). The acute stress response following motor vehicle accidents and its relation to PTSD. *Annals of the New York Academy of Sciences*, *821*, 437–441.

McGowan, P. O., Sasaki, A., D'Alessio, A. C., Dymov, S., Labonté, B., Szyf, M., et al. (2009). Epigenetic regulation of the glucocorticoid receptor in human brain associates with childhood abuse. *Natural Neuroscience*, *12*(3), 342–348.

MacMillan, H. L., Georgiades, K., Duku, E. K., Shea, A., Steiner, M., Niec, A., et al. (2009). Cortisol response to stress in female youths exposed to childhood maltreatment: Results of the youth mood project. *Biological Psychiatry*, *66*(1), 62–68.

McMillen, I. C., & Robinson, J. S. (2005). Developmental origins of the metabolic syndrome: Prediction, plasticity, and programming. *Physiological Reviews*, *85*(2), 571–633.

Mason, J. W., Giller, E. L., Kosten, T. R., Ostroff, R. B., & Podd, L. (1986). Urinary free-cortisol levels in posttraumatic stress disorder patients. *Journal of Nervous Mental Diseases*, *174*(3), 145–149.

Mehta, D., & Binder, E. B. (2012). Gene x environment vulnerability factors for PTSD: The HPA-axis. *Neuropharmacology*, *62*(2), 654–662.

Mehta, D., Gonik, M., Klengel, T., Rex-Haffner, M., Menke, A., Rubel, J., et al. (2011). Using polymorphisms in FKBP5 to define biologically distinct subtypes of posttraumatic stress disorder: Evidence from endocrine and gene expression studies. *Archives of General Psychiatry*, *68*(9), 901–910.

Newport, D. J., Heim, C., Bonsall, R., Miller, A. H., & Nemeroff, C. B. (2004). Pituitary-adrenal responses to standard and low-dose dexamethasone suppression tests in adult survivors of child abuse. *Biological Psychiatry*, *55*(1), 10–20.

Nishith, P., Mechanic, M. B., & Resick, P. A. (2000). Prior interpersonal trauma: The contribution to current PTSD symptoms in female rape victims. *Journal of Abnormal Psychology*, *109*(1), 20–25.

O'Neal, C. R., Brotman, L. M., Huang, K.-Y., Gouley, K. K., Kamboukos, D., Calzada, E. J., et al. (2010). Understanding relations among early family environment, cortisol response, and child aggression via a prevention experiment. *Child Development*, *81*(1), 290–305.

Peterson, L., Tremblay, G., Ewigman, B., & Saldana, L. (2003). Multilevel selected primary prevention of child maltreatment. *Journal of Consulting and Clinical Psychology*, *71*(3), 601–612.

Raison, C. L., & Miller, A. H. (2003). When not enough is too much: The role of insufficient glucocorticoid signaling in the pathophysiology of stress-related disorders. *American Journal of Psychiatry*, *160*(9), 1554–1565.

Resnick, H. S., Yehuda, R., Pitman, R K., & Foy, D. W. (1995). Effect of previous trauma on acute plasma cortisol level following rape. *American Journal of Psychiatry, 152*(11), 1675–1677.

Reynolds, A. J., Mathieson, L. C., & Topitzes, J. W. (2009). Do early childhood interventions prevent child maltreatment? A review of research. *Child Maltreatment, 14*(2), 182–206.

Rodriguez, N., Ryan, S. W., Vande Kemp, H., & Foy, D. W. (1997). Posttraumatic stress disorder in adult female survivors of child sexual abuse: A comparison study. *Journal of Consulting and Clinical Psychology, 65*(1), 53–59.

Schwiebert, L. M., Schleimer, R. P., Radka, S. F., & Ono, S. J. (1995). Modulation of MHC Class II expression in human cells by dexamethasone. *Cell Immunology, 165*(1), 12–19.

Seckl, J. R. (2008). Glucocorticoids, developmental "programming" and the risk of affective dysfunction. *Progress in Brain Research, 167,* 17–31.

Seckl, J. R., & Meaney, M. J. (2006). Glucocorticoid "programming" and PTSD risk. *Annals of the New York Academy of Sciences, 1071*(1), 351–378.

Shoener, J. A., Baig, R., & Page, K. C. (2006). Prenatal exposure to dexamethasone alters hippocampal drive on hypothalamic-pituitary-adrenal axis activity in adult male rats. *American Journal of Physiology: Regulatory, Integrative, and Comparative Physiology, 290*(5), 1366–1373.

Stein, M. B., Jang, K. L., Taylor, S., Vernon, P. A., & Livesley, W. J. (2002). Genetic and environmental influences on trauma exposure and posttraumatic stress disorder symptoms: A twin study. *American Journal of Psychiatry, 159*(10), 1675–1681.

Stein, M. B., Yehuda, R., Koverola, C., & Hanna, C. (1997). Enhanced dexamethasone suppression of plasma cortisol in adult women traumatized by childhood sexual abuse. *Biological Psychiatry, 42*(8), 680–686.

Strohle, A., & Holsboer, F. (2003). Stress responsive neurohormones in depression and anxiety. *Pharmacopsychiatry, 36*(3), 207–214.

Tarullo, A. R., & Gunnar, M. R. (2006). Child maltreatment and the developing HPA axis. *Hormones and Behavior, 50*(4), 632–639.

Thaller, V., Vrkljan, M., Hotujac, L., & Thakore, J. (1999). The potential role of hypocortisolism in the pathophysiology of PTSD and psoriasis. *Collegium Antropologicum, 23*(2), 611–619.

Trickett, P. K., Noll, J. G., Susman, E. J., Shenk, C. E., & Putnam, F. W. (2010). Attenuation of cortisol across development for victims of sexual abuse. *Developmental Psychopathology, 22*(1), 165–175.

True, W. R., Rice, J., Eisen, S. A., Heath, A. C., Goldberg, J., Lyons, M. J., et al. (1993). A twin study of genetic and environmental contributions to liability for posttraumatic stress symptoms. *Archives of General Psychiatry, 50*(4), 257–264.

Tyrka, A. R., Price, L. H., Gelernter, J., Schepker, C., Anderson, G. M., & Carpenter, L. L. (2009). Interaction of childhood maltreatment with the corticotropin-releasing hormone receptor gene: Effects on hypothalamic-pituitary-adrenal axis reactivity. *Biological Psychiatry, 66*(7), 681–685.

van der Vegt, E. J., van der Ende, J., Kirschbaum, C., Verhulst, F. C., & Tiemeier, H. (2009). Early neglect and abuse predict diurnal cortisol patterns in adults: A study of international adoptees. *Psychoneuroendocrinology, 34*(5), 660–669.

Vythilingam, M., Gill, J. M., Luckenbaugh, D. A., Gold, P. W., Collin, C., Bonne, O., et al. (2010). Low early morning plasma cortisol in posttraumatic stress disorder is associated with co-morbid depression but not with enhanced glucocorticoid feedback inhibition. *Psychoneuroendocrinology*, *35*, 442–450.

Watson, S., Owen, B. M., Gallagher, P., Hearn, A. J., Young, A. H., & Ferrier, I. N. (2007). Family history, early adversity and the hypothalamic-pituitary-adrenal (HPA) axis: Mediation of the vulnerability to mood disorders. *Neuropsychiatric Disorder and Treatment*, *3*(5), 647–653.

Weaver, I. C., Cervoni, N., Champagne, F. A., D'Alessio, A. C., Sharma, S., Seckl, J. R., et al. (2004). Epigenetic programming by maternal behavior. *Journal of Neuroscience*, *7*(8), 847–854.

Weaver, I. C., D'Alessio, A. C., Brown, S. E., Hellstrom, I. C., Dymov, S., Sharma, S., et al. (2007). The transcription factor nerve growth factor-inducible protein a mediates epigenetic programming: Altering epigenetic marks by immediate-early genes. *Journal of Neuroscience*, *27*(7), 1756–1768.

Weissbecker, I., Floyd, A., Dedert, E., Salmon, P., & Sephton, S. (2006). Childhood trauma and diurnal cortisol disruption in fibromyalgia syndrome. *Psychoneuroendocrinology*, *31*(3), 312–324.

Welberg, L. A., Seckl, J. R., & Holmes, M. C. (2000). Inhibition of 11beta-hydroxysteroid dehydrogenase, the foeto-placental barrier to maternal glucocorticoids, permanently programs amygdala GR mRNA expression and anxiety-like behaviour in the offspring. *European Journal of Neuroscience*, *12*(3), 1047–1054.

Widom, C. S. (1999). Posttraumatic stress disorder in abused and neglected children grown up. *American Journal of Psychiatry*, *156*(8), 1223–1229.

Xie, P., Kranzler, H. R., Poling, J., Stein, M. B., Anton, R. F., Farrer, L. A., et al. (2010). Interaction of FKBP5 with childhood adversity on risk for post-traumatic stress disorder. *Neuropsychopharmacology*, *35*(8), 1684–1692.

Yehuda, R. (2002). Post-traumatic stress disorder. *New England Journal of Medicine*, *346*(2), 108–112.

Yehuda, R. (2009). Status of glucocorticoid alterations in post-traumatic stress disorder. *Annals of the New York Academy of Sciences*, *1179*(1), 56–69.

Yehuda, R., Bell, A., Bierer, L. M., & Schmeidler, J. (2008). Maternal, not paternal, PTSD is related to increased risk for PTSD in offspring of Holocaust survivors. *Journal of Psychiatric Research*, *42*(13), 1104–1111.

Yehuda, R., & Bierer, L. M. (2008). Transgenerational transmission of cortisol and PTSD risk. *Progress in Brain Research*, *167*, 121–135.

Yehuda, R., & Bierer, L. M. (2009). The relevance of epigenetics to PTSD: implications for the DSM-V. *Journal of Traumatic Stress*, *22*(5), 427–434.

Yehuda, R., Cai, G., Golier, J. A., Sarapas, C., Galea, S., Ising, M., et al. (2009). Gene expression patterns associated with posttraumatic stress disorder following exposure to the World Trade Center attacks. *Biological Psychiatry*, *66*(7), 708–711.

Yehuda, R., Engel, S. M., Brand, S. R., Seckl, J., Marcus, S. M., & Berkowitz, G. S. (2005). Transgenerational effects of posttraumatic stress disorder in babies of mothers exposed to World Trade Center attacks during pregnancy. *Journal of Clinical Endocrinology and Metabolism*, *90*(7), 4115–4118.

Yehuda, R., & LeDoux, J. (2007). Response variation following trauma: A translational neuroscience approach to understanding PTSD. *Neuron*, *56*(1), 19–32.

Yehuda, R., McFarlane, A. C., & Shalev, A. Y. (1998). Predicting the development of posttraumatic stress disorder from the acute response to a traumatic event. *Biological Psychiatry*, *44*(12), 1305–1313.

Yehuda, R., Southwick, S. M., Nussbaum, G., Wahby, V., Giller, E. L., & Mason, J. W. (1990). Low urinary cortisol excretion in patients with posttraumatic stress disorder. *Journal of Nervous and Mental Disorders, 178*(6), 366–369.

Yehuda, R., Teicher, M.H.,Seckl, J.R., Grossman, R.A., Morris, A., Bierer, L.M (2007). Parental Posttraumatic Stress Disorder as a Vulnerability Factor for Low Cortisol Trait in Offspring of Holocaust Survivors. *Archive of General Psychiatry, 64*(9), 1040–1048.

Yehuda, R., Teicher, M. H., Trestman, R. L., Levengood, R. A., & Siever, L. J. (1996). Cortisol regulation in posttraumatic stress disorder and major depression: A chronobiological analysis. *Biological Psychiatry, 40*(2), 79–88.

Zlotnick, C. (1997). Posttraumatic stress disorder (PTSD), PTSD comorbidity, and childhood abuse among incarcerated women. *Journal of Nervous Mental Diseases, 185*(12), 761–763.

Chapter 2

Emotion regulation in the wake of complex childhood trauma

Carolyn A. Greene, Damion J. Grasso and Julian D. Ford

Children with complex emotional and behavioral problems often have complex histories of victimization, including physical, sexual and emotional abuse, domestic and community violence, and separation from, abandonment by or impairment of key caregivers. The resultant combination of traumatic, alienating and demoralizing experiences therefore has been described as "complex trauma" (Courtois, 2008). In recent years, our understanding of the substantial impact that complex trauma has on children's development has grown, and it has become clear that the reactions of victims of repeated and extensive childhood trauma often do not fit well into the traditional *Diagnostic and Statistical Manual of Mental Disorders* (4th ed.) posttraumatic stress disorder (PTSD) symptom triad of re-experiencing, avoidance and hyperarousal (Courtois, 2008). In fact, no single psychiatric diagnosis or combination of diagnoses can account for the cluster of symptoms frequently associated with a history of complex trauma (D'Andrea, Ford, Stolbach, Spinazzola, & van der Kolk, 2012). Rather, the sequelae of complex trauma in childhood are more likely to be problems associated with self-regulation and interpersonal relatedness that manifest as difficulties with emotion regulation, somatization, attention, impulse control, dissociation, interpersonal relationships and self-attributions (Cook et al., 2005; D'Andrea et al., 2012).

Early childhood is a critical period of rapid neuronal growth and shaping, during which the child acquires the building blocks of psychological and biological development. Thus, the brain is particularly susceptible during this period to being altered by experience, particularly interpersonal experience (Ford, 2009; see also Brom, Chapter 15 of this volume). Development in early childhood takes place primarily within the caregiving environment. If caregivers are able to consistently provide safety and security, the child can focus on exploring and mastery. However, when interpersonal victimization experiences occur within this caregiving environment, the child is instead oriented toward anticipating, preventing or protecting him- or herself against potential or actual danger. This shift from a brain focused on learning to a brain focused on survival interrupts the essential neuronal growth and impairs the child's development of the biopsychosocial competences that are at the core of self-regulation and interpersonal relatedness (Ford, 2009). Preoccupation with safety and survival is fundamentally incompatible with the development of secure emotional bonds, even with caregivers who are consistently empathic and responsive (Cicchetti & Toth, 1995). Moreover, the survival-focused child not only may feel insecure with caregivers, but also with her or his own core self—specifically, with internal emotion states. The capacity to trust, utilize and modulate emotions thus may be severely underdeveloped when a young child experiences complex trauma (Bariola, Gullone, & Hughes, 2011; Zeman, Cassano, Perry-Parrish, & Stegall, 2006). Indeed, there is growing evidence that early life complex trauma places children at risk for severe emotion dysregulation (Cicchetti & Toth, 2005; Kim & Cicchetti, 2010).

In this chapter, we first define emotion regulation and review various types of emotion regulation strategies. Second, we discuss factors that contribute to its normative development, including the impact of the caregiving context on the development of children's emotion regulation competence. Next, we consider how exposure to interpersonal violence influences the development of emotion regulation by shifting the brain's orientation from learning to survival. Finally, we present a case example to show how enhancing emotion regulation can be integral to the effective treatment for children with complex trauma histories.

Defining emotion regulation

Defining emotion regulation has proven to be a difficult challenge. The term "emotion regulation" is variously used to refer to the inhibition, enhancement, delay or maintenance of emotion and the coherence of emotion and emotional responses (e.g., facial expressions) by processes that are either volitional and deliberate or involuntary or automatic (Gross & Thompson, 2007). Calkins (2010) provides a useful framework for emotion regulation: "those behaviors, skills, and strategies, whether conscious or unconscious, automatic or effortful, that serve to modulate, inhibit, and enhance emotional experiences and expressions" (p. 92). As such, emotion regulation is an essential link between situational social demands and context, individual experience and development, and the formulation and achievement of personal goals. This is why emotion dysregulation is associated with behavioral dysregulation, problems with social relationships and psychopathology (Southam-Gerow & Kendall, 2002; Suveg, Southam-Gerow, Goodman, & Kendall, 2007).

Emotion regulation may occur before the emotions are consciously recognized (antecedent-focused approaches to dealing with situational influences and allocating attentional resources; Gross & Thompson, 2007). Situational-based emotion regulation involves *selecting into* a particular situation in advance or *modifying* aspects of an existing situation. For example, Tommy is a teenager who wants to visit his dying grandfather in the hospital, but expects this will be extremely emotionally upsetting. He selects the situation by picking a time when there will be no other visitors, and asking his mother to accompany him. He also modifies the situation during the visit by sitting close to his mother and leaving when he feels himself starting to cry. Selecting or modifying situations necessitates matching current actions and contexts to those involved in past significant emotion experiences. This may sound easy, but it is not, given the well-demonstrated bias to under- or overestimate past and future emotional responses (Gilbert, Pinel, Wilson, Blumberg, & Wheatley, 1998; Gross & Thompson, 2007; Kahneman, 2000) and wrongly estimate the short- and long-term costs and benefits of decisions to select into or modify situations (Gross & Thompson, 2007).

Another antecedent approach to emotion regulation is by either decreasing or increasing one's allocation of attentional resources (distraction and concentration, respectively). Consider the following example. Ella, Tommy's 10-year-old sister, becomes upset when visiting her dying grandfather. Seeing her grandfather hooked up to scary-looking apparatuses and looking very ill frightened her greatly. Without realizing it, Ella shifted her gaze from her grandfather to a vase of flowers on the windowsill. The flowers reminded her of the ones she often picked in the field behind her house. This *distraction* buffered the sadness and fear Ella felt during the visit. She was able to allocate fewer attentional resources to the distressing stimuli and more towards incongruent stimuli. Studies have shown that, even in young children, shifting attention away from negative stimuli results in less distress in the moment, whereas maintaining attention enhances distress (Crockenberg & Leerkes, 2004; Johnson, Posner, & Rothbart, 1991). Distraction can also take an imaginal form, such as visualizing. Distracters need not be emotionally or motivationally salient, as the flowers were for Ella, nor do they have to be tangibly present (e.g., imaginal visualization, "daydreaming"). Neuroimaging studies have shown that when people try to decrease their emotional reactions to an unpleasant picture, they often shift their gaze to irrelevant or non-emotional parts of an unpleasant picture—and, as they do so, brain areas involved in emotion processing become less activated (Dunning & Hajcak, 2009; van Reekum et al., 2007). Distraction also may take the form of dissociative immersion or, especially among survivors of complex trauma, pathological/structural dissociation (Lanius et al., 2010).

The opposite of distraction as an emotion regulation strategy, *concentration*, occurs when emotional responses are enhanced because attention is directed towards emotional aspects of stimuli (Wegner & Bargh, 1997). This might happen intentionally or unintentionally, due to biases or predispositions to allocate more attention to emotional aspects of a situation. There may be ethological survival value in selectively attending to affective stimuli in one's environment (Izard, 2009). There are also individual differences in how much attention a person allocates to stimuli with positive or negative valence. An attentional bias toward negative or threat-related information has been linked to depression, anxiety and PTSD (Yiend, 2010).

A second domain of emotion regulation involves actively modifying one's emotion reactions, cognitively, physiologically or behaviorally, rather than the situation eliciting the emotions. Let us return to our example of Ella. At her grandfather's funeral, Ella stood by her mother and cried. She kept visualizing her grandfather the way she last saw him: gaunt, pale and bruised. She thought of him lying in the coffin with a pained look on his face, fraught with despair that he would be forever underground. When she started to cry harder, Ella's mother whispered to her that grandpa was in a better place—doing what he loved the most, which was traveling. This allowed Ella to think of her grandfather's death as a ticket for endless travel around the world. She pictured him somewhere in France, sad that he had to say goodbye to his family, but pleased with what was to come. When Ella shifted her thinking from imagining her grandfather in the ground, devastated by his own death, to her grandfather traveling somewhere in France, excited by this new opportunity, she was implementing *cognitive change*, or reappraising the situation in a way that changed its emotional significance (Gross & Thompson, 2007). One may do this by altering how one thinks about what is happening in a situation, or thinking about how competent one believes oneself to be to manage the situation (Gross & Thompson, 2007). In Ella's case, her mother encouraged this shift, which reflects one way parental support may help children learn how to cope with stress.

Alternatively, emotion regulation may involve suppressing or modifying behavioral or physiological reactions (Gross & Thompson, 2007). For example, Tommy stood on the other side of his mother at the funeral with a blank expression on his face. He felt very much like crying; however, he used behavioral tactics to resist crying, such as biting his tongue, squeezing his fists and taking long deep breaths. While *emotion suppression* is functional in the short term, there is evidence that it is maladaptive in the long term (Hayes, Luoma, Bond, Masuda, & Lillis, 2006). In addition, studies examining physiological correlates of emotion suppression have identified a paradoxical effect, such that participants instructed to suppress their emotional response to emotional stimuli exhibited increased sympathetic nervous system activation (e.g., heart rate, systolic and diastolic blood pressure; Campbell-Sills, Barlow, Brown, & Hoffmann, 2006; Feldner, Zvolensky, Stickle, Bonn-Miller, & Leen-Feldner, 2006; Gross & Levenson, 1997; Hopp, Rohrmann, Zapf, & Hodapp, 2010; Tull, Jakupcak, & Roemer, 2010). Thus, attempts to conceal one's emotional responses *on the outside* appear to result in increased physiological arousal, which is maintained even after the emotional stimuli are no longer applicable (Campbell-Sills et al., 2006; Feldner et al., 2006). Another line of work suggests that emotion suppression in one context may result in a *rebound* effect in another context, so that the emotional distress returns to negatively impact subsequent functioning (Richards & Gross, 2000; Salters-Pedneault, Tull, & Roemer, 2004). In effect, one may show increased sensitivity to subsequent stimuli that may be less emotionally salient (e.g., suppression of anger during a disagreement enhancing one's sensitivity to subsequent anger cues; Tull et al., 2010).

The development of emotion regulation

The development of emotion regulation is dependent upon both the psycho-biological development of the child and the reliable support of a primary caregiver who can teach, model and otherwise socialize their child's understanding and regulation of emotion.

Psychobiological development

The rapid development of the young child's brain provides the foundation for the development of the core components of emotion regulation (Lewis, 2005), particularly in the limbic system (Ford, 2009). This region of the central nervous system focuses sustained attention and triggers automatic (via the brainstem and hypothalamus) and conscious (via the cortex) responses based on the emotional significance of perceptual and memory information (via the amygdala; Milad et al., 2007), and coordinates these responses based on the overall context, including past experiences (episodic memory) and current circumstances (via the hippocampus; Bremner, 2008). Therefore, as these regions develop, children gain the neurological capacity for selective and sustained attention, concentration and executive function that is necessary to recognize and modulate their emotional responses and reallocate attentional resources; the cognitive capacity to process and communicate their experiences, engage in cognitive change and effectively problem-solve to select or modify situations; and the behavioral control needed to modulate their impulses.

Initially, infants predominantly regulate their emotions using automatic responses such as crying (attempts to modify the situation by recruiting help), sucking (response modulation) or averting gaze (allocation of attention). Equally important are caregivers' more direct strategies at altering environmental stimuli that elicit emotions (situation selection) and providing soothing for distress or eliciting positive emotions (response modulation; Eisenberg, Spinrad, & Eggum, 2010). As language develops, so does the child's ability to label emotions, to think themselves through difficult emotional situations or reactions and to seek comfort and support from caregivers and peers.

Support from caregivers

As children move into the elementary school years and beyond, they become more adept at selecting and utilizing cognitive and behavioral strategies appropriate to the situation to cope with and manage their emotions (Zeman et al., 2006). Caregivers (and, later, peers) play a vital role by modeling how to recognize and select or modify situations, thoughts, body states and behaviors so as to maintain an optimal level of awareness and intensity of emotion states (Bariola et al., 2011; Bowlby, 1982; Eisenberg, Cumberland, & Spinrad, 1998; Mikulincer, Shaver, & Pereg, 2003; Morris, Silk, Steinberg, Myers, & Robinson, 2007; Stocker, Richmond, Rhoades, & Kiang, 2007; Valiente, Lemery-Chalfant, & Reiser, 2007; Volling, McElwain, Notaro, & Herrera, 2002; Waters et al., 2010). Caregivers who provide the safety and responsiveness that characterize secure attachment are usually able to do so because they themselves are emotionally regulated, thereby modeling the adaptive expression and management of emotional experiences (Bariola et al., 2011). Ultimately, emotion regulation enables children to explore the world around them, seeking an optimal balance of novel and familiar experiences, and incorporating and mastering new skills and competences.

Conversely, emotion socialization is more likely to be impaired within child–caregiver relationships characterized by an insecure or disorganized attachment or a family environment including stressors (e.g., marital dissatisfaction, parent depressive symptoms, high job constraints and low satisfaction), aggression or chaotic patterns of interaction (Morris et al., 2007; Repetti, Taylor, & Seemant, 2002). Specifically, a harsh or unsupportive caregiver response to emotion is more likely to occur within an insecure attachment system, increases child distress and contributes to the development of emotional suppression (Shipman et al., 2007), deficits in emotion understanding (Pears & Fisher, 2005) and less adaptive distress coping (Compas, Connor-Smith, Saltzman, Thomsen, & Wadsworth, 2001). In stressful family environments, caregivers may be unavailable or too dysregulated themselves to provide their children with the supportive, empathic responses to their emotional distress that are necessary for them to learn adaptive ways to manage their negative affective states (Kim & Cicchetti, 2010), and they are apt to model reactive or helpless emotional responses (Shipman et al., 2007; Valiente et al., 2007). Family stress (marital dissatisfaction, home chaos, parental depressive symptoms, job role satisfaction) also has been found to be associated with lower levels of supportive responses and higher levels of nonsupportive responses by mothers and fathers to their children's negative emotions (Nelson, O'Brien, Blankson, Calkins, & Keane, 2009).

Since there is much empirical support for the role of both the caregiver and the family setting on children's development of emotion regulation, it is not surprising that disruptions within these systems due to experiencing complex trauma also have a significant impact on the socialization of children's emotion regulatory abilities. For example, the emotional socialization of mothers who physically maltreated their children was found to mediate the relationship between maltreatment and children's adaptive emotion regulation (Shipman et al., 2007). Maltreating mothers provided less validation and emotion coaching than non-maltreating mothers in response to their children in emotionally arousing situations. Maltreated children demonstrated fewer adaptive emotion regulation strategies and greater emotion dysregulation than non-maltreated children.

Interestingly, the nature of the attachment system may be an important factor in the outcomes associated with maltreatment. Maltreated children are more likely to have insecure and atypical attachments with their caregivers than non-maltreated children (Cicchetti & Toth, 1995; Cook et al., 2005), and these inadequate bonds have been found to mediate the relationship between abuse and psychological distress (Shapiro & Levendosky, 1999). Conversely, a secure attachment can be a protective factor that helps to promote resiliency in the face of traumatic experiences (Shapiro & Levendosky, 1999). In a study of maltreated and non-maltreated children, Alink and colleagues (2009) found that the mother–child relationship quality buffered the impact of maltreatment (physical, sexual and/or emotional abuse and neglect) on emotion regulation. That is, while maltreated children scored lower on a measure of emotion regulation than non-maltreated children, this relationship was true only for children with an insecure attachment style. For securely attached children, maltreatment was unrelated to emotion regulation. A secure relationship thus may provide sufficient safety and security to sustain—or restore—the capacity to regulate emotions through exploring and learning, despite the threat posed by maltreatment.

Complex trauma: Dysregulated emotion and maladaptive emotion regulation strategies

Complex trauma in childhood fosters the development of brain networks that operate in the service of automatic processes organized by the stress response system (i.e., the "survival brain"): dysregulated information processing, biased towards perceiving threat in the environment; and maladaptive emotion regulation strategies, motivated by harm avoidance. This becomes the foundation for how the child perceives, conceptualizes and responds to the self, others and the world, and is maintained by lasting, but not necessarily irreversible, changes in the function of key brain areas (neural/neurochemical activity within and between these areas) and structure (the volume and integrity of these areas). Thus, the "survival brain" is fixated on automatic, nonconscious scanning for and escape from threats, which fundamentally alters information processing and emotion regulation (Ford, 2009).

When an individual with a brain operating in survival mode transitions from an adverse environment to a favorable one, information processing and emotion regulation strategies important for surviving adversity may persist and compromise functioning in the new environment. Thus, protective neural and behavioral responses to traumatic experiences in effect become stabilized in the form of chronic biological, emotional and mental hyperarousal, and the entrenched belief that survival is in jeopardy, from which the person is unable to disengage (Lewis, 2005). Children functioning in survival mode are thus inherently prone to emotion dysregulation.

Numerous studies have documented a variety of associated emotion regulation difficulties, including the impaired ability to identify and label one's own emotional responses and bodily sensations (i.e., alexithymia), which is critical to self-regulation (Cloitre, Scarvalone, & Difede, 1997; McLean, Toner, Jackson, Desrocher, & Stuckless, 2006; Zlotnick et al., 1996). Studies have shown a correlation between the degree of alexithymia, the severity of child maltreatment and trauma-related symptoms, and the number of trauma types experienced (Cloitre, Cohen, & Koenen, 2006; Zlotnick, Mattia, & Zimmerman, 2001). Alexithymia has also been associated with emotional numbing (Frewen et al., 2008) and attachment-related problems (Hall, Geher, & Brackett, 2004) in trauma-exposed individuals, as well as with dissociation and depersonalization in children with complex trauma presentations (Sayar, Kose, Grabe, & Topbas, 2005). Above and beyond the lack of awareness of one's thoughts, feelings and behaviors, complex trauma involves a core deficiency in reflective self-awareness—the ability to be consciously aware of and able to modulate emotional and bodily feelings, thoughts and actions. Furthermore, without the capacity to observe one's own physical sensations, thinking and associated emotion processes, it is not feasible to seek or to create new knowledge (i.e., experience-dependent learning), but only to react to experiences with automatic, chaotic and fixated perceptions, thoughts and actions ("experience-expectant" reactivity) (Lewis, 2005).

Consider the example of Manny, a 14-year-old foster youth who underwent terrible physical and emotional abuse at the hands of his biological father and lost his mother to drugs. Manny has been in the foster care system for eight years of his life and has had a total of ten failed placements. While the placements start off okay, after about six months Manny's behavior in the home and relationship with his foster family begins to slide downhill. Manny presents with clinical symptoms of posttraumatic stress, mood instability, oppositionality and anger. He has been seen by numerous counselors, psychologists and psychiatrists during his time in foster care. Although Manny is a boy who yearns to be part of a family and to become close to people he can call "Mom" and "Dad," when relationships do become more personal, Manny experiences a flood of mixed emotions, including fear, sadness, anxiety, confusion, anger and compassion. Emotions associated with past memories emerge, along with emotions linked to his experiences with the family. During this emotionally labile period, Manny exhibits a range of increased disruptive behaviors, including breaking household rules, being disruptive in school, social withdrawal and risk behaviors such as drinking alcohol and staying out later than he is supposed to. While Manny is familiar with this futile pattern of sabotaging his foster placements, he feels powerless to change it because he does not know why it happens and cannot make sense of his emotional experience. At most, Manny realizes that he is bored and angry, and, when asked to justify his behavior, he claims that he acts the way he does because there is something fundamentally wrong or different about him.

Manny has not had much success with the in-home counseling he receives. In fact, he despises it and often avoids sessions by not coming home. When he is home, he often pulls his hooded sweatshirt over his face and refuses to talk. His reason is that "all *they* want to talk about is the abuse," and he neither sees the need for it, nor knows how to tolerate or understand the extreme distress that he feels when he perceives himself to be forced to "wallow in the past." It is likely that Manny's brain is hypersensitive to negative stimuli and quickly overwhelmed and incapacitated by the high demand for resources (allostatic load; Danese & McEwen, 2011) elicited by emotional cues. His problem is one of biological/ cognitive capacity, but this is not necessarily an inborn deficit and may more plausibly be due to the intensive allocation of resources required by his brain being in survival mode much of the time. As a result, he finds it difficult to tolerate negative emotions (lower distress tolerance) and tends to rely on avoidant emotion regulation, which is associated with less positive outcomes (Briere & Rickards, 2007; Tull, Jakupcak, McFadden, & Roemer, 2007). These strategies include intentionally avoiding situations that may elicit negative or strong emotions, modifying situations to avoid experiencing negative emotions, actively suppressing emotional responses, and unhealthy distractions. These are also individuals for whom threat is highly salient—who allocate more attention to threat and respond more strongly to perceived threat in the environment (Pine et al., 2005; Pollak & Tolley-Schell, 2003). Individuals whose brains are in survival mode often use antecedent-focused strategies (situation selection and modification) that function to avoid external stimuli (behavioral avoidance) and internal experiences (experiential avoidance of thoughts, feelings, memories, physical sensations) which provoke memories of past traumas. Experiential and behavioral avoidance mediate several trauma-related symptoms (Marx & Sloan, 2002; Polusny, Rosenthal, Aban, & Follette, 2004) and are strong predictors of the development of PTSD (Plumb, Orsillo, & Luterek, 2004; Shenk, Putnam, & Noll, 2012). Moreover, avoidant behavior often impedes one's ability to habituate to and process the trauma memory on one's own, as well as during targeted treatment (Shenk et al., 2012; Trusz, Wagner, Russo, Love, & Zatzick, 2011). Although avoidance appears superficially to be a conscious choice—both to the survivor of the complex trauma and to observers such as parents, teachers or therapists—it may be better understood as an involuntary consequence of a brain operating in survival mode as a result of over-learned hypervigilance. This shift in perspective may have substantial implications for formulating intervention strategies for prevention and treatment.

Response-based strategies using distraction from negative emotions and reminders of the trauma may take the form of impulsive and high-risk behavior (Bergen, Martin, Richardson, Allison, & Roeger, 2003; Brown, Houck, Hadley, & Lescano, 2005), alcohol or other substance abuse (Dorard, Berthoz, Phan, Corcos, & Bungener, 2008), sexualized behavior (Pithers, Gray, Busconi, & Houchens, 1998) and habitual or reactive self-harm, including cutting, picking and head-banging (Van der Kolk, Perry, & Herman, 1991). While these behaviors indeed have multiple determinants, the evidence points to avoidance through distraction as being at least partially responsible for survivors of complex trauma. Theories about the functional significance of deliberate self-harm propose that it allows the individual to escape or provides relief from unwanted emotions (Brown, Comtois, & Linehan, 2002; Chapman, Gratz, & Brown, 2006). Estimates of the lifetime prevalence of self-harm behavior among individuals with PTSD exceed 50% (Cloitre, Koenen, Cohen, & Han, 2002). One line of thought regarding the mechanism by which self-harm facilitates emotional avoidance involves distraction through physical stimulation—a shift from emotional pain to physical pain (Chapman et al., 2006). Similarly, sexualized behavior in traumatized children may also provide a means of escape from distress through physical stimulation, except that here the shift is from emotional pain to physical arousal (Gilgun, 2006).

In the same vein, alcohol and substance abuse in the wake of trauma may function to distract individuals from unwanted emotional experiences by altering their physiological and cognitive-emotional state (Carver, Scheier, & Weintraub, 1989; Folkman & Moskowitz, 2004; Stewart, Pihl, Conrod, & Dongier, 1998). Abuse of alcohol and other substances is highly comorbid with trauma-related psychopathology (Kessler, Sonnega, Bromet, & Hughes, 1995), and is particularly associated with symptoms of posttraumatic avoidance (Shipherd, Stafford, & Tanner, 2005). Finally, high-risk, thrill-seeking behavior can function as a diversion from emotional distress by shifting attention towards highly arousing and motivationally significant stimuli and activities (Laye-Gindhu & Schonert-Reichl, 2005). Engaging in these behaviors places a strong demand on attentional resources, preoccupies motivation systems (i.e., appetitive, defensive), and results in neurochemical and physiological changes and altered cognitive and emotional states that temporarily subdue emotional distress. Furthermore, individuals with a brain in survival mode tend to be inflexible in their utilization of emotion regulation strategies (Gratz & Roemer, 2004), which means that they are incapable of adapting to the range of possible situations, and the degree of inflexibility appears to be associated with the severity of trauma-related symptoms (Tull et al., 2007).

Manny's "aggressive," "oppositional" and substance-using behaviors can be understood as both an expression of and an attempt to cope with emotional distress. Such behaviors serve the function of selecting and modifying the situation (e.g., leading other people to avoid him or engage with him) and altering emotion-related reactions (e.g., suppressing awareness of or providing a distraction or temporary relief from disturbing emotions). He also bangs his head against the wall of his bedroom on occasion. Once, after a rather heated argument with his foster parents, Manny made the impulsive decision to go into the medicine cabinet and swallow his foster mother's medications. Later, when asked about it, Manny claimed not to know why he did it—just that it seemed like the only thing he could do at that moment. For many victimized youths, suicidal acts or gestures may seem to be the only way to express their distress or the only solution to coping with their negative emotions. Moreover, the risk of suicidal behavior increases substantially as the number of childhood victimization experiences increase (Dube et al., 2001).

Manny's caregivers described other times when he appeared to "shut down" and tune the world out following reminders of past abuse. Emotion suppression— the suppression of both the emotional state and its expression—is associated with PTSD symptoms in trauma-exposed individuals (Moore, Zoellner, & Mollenholt, 2008), as is a general lack of emotional acceptance (Tull et al., 2007). In experimental studies, participants instructed to suppress emotional expression during the presentation of emotional stimuli (Gross & Levenson, 1997) and during a carbon dioxide challenge (Feldner et al., 2006) paradoxically exhibit increased physiological arousal. In one study, participants with mood or anxiety disorders were instructed to either suppress or *accept* emotion during a distressing film clip (Campbell-Sills et al., 2006). Emotion suppression resulted in greater physiological arousal compared to acceptance when participants were recovering from emotional distress (Campbell-Sills et al., 2006). In PTSD, emotion suppression has been found to interfere with therapeutic exposure interventions and delay or compromise the habituation that is typically observed during and following several iterations of successful trauma memory exposure (Foa & Kozak, 1986).

Manny's interpersonal difficulties are partly attributable to emotion-based distortions in how he perceives social interactions. Manny appears not to trust anyone, and to perceive any attention as an attack. Manny has deep-rooted beliefs that others are only out for themselves and that friendly gestures are fake and driven by ulterior motives. He also feels highly vulnerable and inferior around people—that he is not worth others' compassion. These cognitive schemas can be understood both as the product of attachment insecurity developed in reaction to his father's unpredictable and violent behavior, and as initially protective but currently maladaptive and involuntary emotion regulation strategies (i.e., distraction, suppression, self-soothing).

When operating in survival mode, children like Manny seem to be unwilling or unable to think clearly (or at all) or make responsible choices. Moreover, their beliefs and actions serve to maintain and intensify their emotional distress and PTSD symptoms (Brewin & Holmes, 2003; Ehlers, Mayou, & Bryant, 2003; Foa, Ehlers, Clark, Tolin, & Orsillo, 1999; LoSavio et al., in preparation). Yet, from an emotion regulation perspective, they are actively and resiliently attempting to tolerate and manage extreme distress. They are dysregulated not because they are unmotivated, incapable or unintelligent, but because they are prioritizing survival over any other goal. And they are usually the last person to recognize this, because operating in survival mode has become second nature. Or, they may be well aware that they are operating on the basis of principles such as "the best defense is a good offense" or "do unto others before they do unto you," but they see no better alternative in the face of the emotional turmoil created by their traumatic experiences.

The shift from survival to learning mode

Although *survival* conditioning during critical periods of child development may have pervasive and persistent effects on the brain structures and functions that underlie emotion regulation, these alterations are neither inherently permanent nor unchangeable. Interventions geared toward strengthening core abilities to engage in reflective self-awareness in the service of *learning* from emotions can shift the brain from survival into learning mode. While existing treatments for trauma-related psychopathology, such as trauma-focused cognitive behavioral therapy (CBT), recognize the importance of emotion regulation and teach valuable coping and relaxation skills, they do not systematically incorporate a curriculum informed by theories of emotion and emotion regulation.

Therapies with the strongest research evidence base for the treatment of adults (Cahill, Rothbaum, Resick, & Follette, 2009) and children (Saxe, MacDonald, & Ellis, 2007) with PTSD (i.e., prolonged exposure, cognitive processing therapy, trauma-focused CBT, and eye movement desensitization and reprocessing) are designed to help clients to process trauma memories in order to reduce avoidance and associated re-experiencing, emotional numbing and hyperarousal symptoms. Although children and adults with complex trauma histories have been shown to benefit from these therapies, poor outcomes have been associated with high levels of anger, guilt and shame, or aggression and conduct problems (Cohen, Berliner, & Mannarino, 2010), suggesting that it is important to enhance their ability to address emotion dysregulation.

A recent meta-analysis of therapy outcome studies with adult survivors of childhood sexual abuse concluded that CBT was superior to other therapies for anxiety, depression and other internalizing problems, but not for problems associated with more severe emotion dysregulation (Harvey & Taylor, 2010). Thus, some adult clients with trauma histories, especially those who experienced violence or maltreatment in childhood, may respond best to therapy if emotion regulation problems are directly addressed (Cloitre et al., 2010). Indeed, in a pilot study aimed at evaluating the importance of emotion regulation skills as a treatment target in psychotherapy, Berking et al. (2008) found that emotion regulation training enhanced the effectiveness of CBT-based treatments for patients in an inpatient unit. In particular, acceptance, tolerance and active modification of negative emotions were strongly associated with mental health and treatment outcomes. If the clinical picture is complicated by the presence of comorbid disorders—particularly, addictive (Ford, Russo, & Mallon, 2007), dissociative (Nijenhuis & van der Hart, 2011), somatoform (van Dijke, Ford, et al., 2010) or Axis II personality disorders (van Dijke, van der Hart, et al., 2010) or severe mental illness (e.g., psychotic or bipolar disorders; Ford & Fournier, 2007))—emotion regulation skills can be essential for enabling clients to achieve sufficient stability to benefit from any therapy. With clients who are willing or actively seeking to work through trauma memories therapeutically, building competence in emotion regulation also is often recommended as a first step (Cohen, Bukstein, et al., 2010; Cook, Schnurr, & Foa, 2004).

Trauma Affect Regulation: Guide for Education and Therapy (TARGET)

TARGET is an example of a therapeutic intervention for restoring posttraumatic emotion regulation. It is a manualized, evidence-based treatment and prevention intervention for youth and adults that incorporates psychoeducation and behavioral exercises designed to enhance adaptive emotion recognition and expression, cognitive reappraisal of emotion-related beliefs and arousal modulation prior to, during or instead of trauma memory processing. TARGET begins with psychoeducation, which explains emotional, behavioral, school and relational problems as the result of a shift in the brain's interconnections between an "alarm center" (a colloquial description of the amygdala) with information retrieval ("filing") and executive functions ("thinking center") systems (colloquial descriptions of the hippocampus and the medial and dorsolateral prefrontal cortex, respectively). This biological model provides a de-stigmatizing rationale for overcoming dysregulation by strengthening the "filing" and "thinking" centers and resetting the brain's "alarm"; that is, shifting from a *survival* brain to a *learning* brain.

TARGET then engages the individuals in learning a seven-step sequence for focused thinking that draws on skills taught in CBT, mindfulness and meditative therapies, as well as experiential psychotherapies. The goal is not to modify the learner's thinking, but to demonstrate to each learner how she or he is capable of intentionally using the ability to think systematically and clearly to achieve a balanced emotional state—that is, moderate arousal, engagement and hopefulness—as opposed to emotion states of excessive arousal or dissociation, detachment or preoccupation, and shame, hostility or hopelessness that can result from unsafe environments. The focusing skills are summarized in an easily learned acronym, "FREEDOM":

- *focusing* the mind on one thought that the learner chooses based on his or her core values and hopes;
- *recognizing* current triggers for "alarm" reactions;
- distinguishing alarm-driven ("reactive") versus adaptive ("main") *emotions*;
- thoughts (*evaluations*);
- goal *definitions*;
- behavioral *options*; and
- *making* a contribution to the world by regulating "alarm reactions."

A structured FREEDOM practice exercise template distinguishes between alarm reactions and emotionally regulated responses, and shows how to use *both* of these types of emotion to learn from and explore life, rather than just survive. The FREEDOM skills also can be applied to trauma memory processing.

Clinical case

Manny was referred for "trauma therapy" by his probation officer after he was arrested for assaulting a peer at school. His foster parents felt unable to break through his defiance, and unsafe with his aggressive and defiant behavior. Manny entered therapy with the same dismissive, angry presentation. He said he had been in therapy "forever" and "it doesn't help." He also firmly stated that he would not talk about the abuse. Manny's therapist reassured him that he would not have to talk about his worst memories. Rather, they would be learning skills to deal with extreme stress reactions that were happening in his life *right now*. She began by asking him to identify what his goals were, validating his feelings and concerns and re-framing them with positive goals as necessary. She then explained that the best way to prevent extreme stress reactions that interfere with these goals is to turn down the alarm in his brain so that he will be better able to think clearly even when under stress. Manny, while still maintaining emotional distance and skepticism, spontaneously said that he found this mildly interesting.

The TARGET framework thus provided a bridge for the therapist to engage Manny by aligning with his intrinsic motivations and validating his concerns and perspective. He related quickly to a description of how the brain and body react to normal and extreme stress, and how the alarm in his brain (the amygdala) signals the "fight–flight–freeze" response that prepares his body to survive danger. Manny appreciated the idea that his brain had become so proficient at protecting him from the abuse that the alarm was now stuck in the "on" position, reacting to small stressors as if they were dangerous and making his body gear up or shut down. His foster parents were provided with this same information in a parallel session. Both Manny and the parents raised the same question: "How do you turn down an alarm that's gotten stuck?"

At the next session, Manny's therapist began to teach him the first of the seven FREEDOM steps designed to help him turn down his alarm: focusing. She taught him how to slow down, focus his mind on one thought of his choosing and check his stress level and feelings of personal control. The therapist explained how these simple steps could enable him to engage his thinking center and turn down his alarm. Manny quickly understood this metaphorical way of explaining how he could use his brain to stop and think instead of reacting.

The next FREEDOM step that Manny and his therapist discussed was recognizing triggers. Helping Manny identify and understand the situations, people, places or other stimuli that activate his brain's alarm and generate automatic physical and emotional feelings, thoughts, perceptions and behavioral reactions was the first step in helping him learn how to prepare for and manage alarm reactions. Manny was able to recognize that, in addition to specific reminders of his past abuse, close personal relationships also activated his alarm, due to his history of being hurt by the people who were close to him. These triggers were also discussed with Manny's foster parents. In addition, the therapist helped them understand how their fear of losing Manny was a trigger for their own stress reactions. Through this step, Manny and his parents were able improve their emotion regulation skills by consciously allocating their attention to stress triggers instead of trying to avoid recognizing or suppress reactions to them.

The remaining FREEDOM skills were designed to continue to build Manny's and his foster parents' ability to engage the brain's thinking and filing centers. These skills include evaluating emotions, thoughts and goals so as to identify and distinguish those that are reactive (generated by the alarm) from those that reflect one's main values, hopes and goals, as well as defining one's goals and finding positive options. Applying these skills to Manny's situation involved helping him recognize reactive thoughts and goals (e.g., "I want to make them feel as bad as I do") and balancing these with the main goals that reflect his hopes for what he really wants to achieve in his life (e.g., "I deserve to be a member of this family"), and then finding positive options to allow him to achieve goals consistent with his values (such as treating his foster parents with respect) and distinguishing them from his reactive options (e.g., disregarding house rules). Manny (and his parents) realized that, when they were acting primarily on the basis of alarm reactions, they were missing the opportunity to make choices based upon their deeper values and goals. In Manny's terms,

> My alarm gets angry and tells me to do stuff to get payback or not let anyone think I'm weak, but I'm smarter and stronger when I use my thinking center to figure out what I really want. I thought I had to be angry all the time, and I felt stupid, like I must be really messed up to be that way. But I'm not that way when I do the SOS first.

During work on the final FREEDOM step—making a contribution—Manny's therapist helped him to see that, now that he knew how to turn down his alarm enough so that he was not responding to every situation as if he was being "dissed" or as if it was a life-or-death emergency, he was really very smart. She helped him see that he actually was a very caring and respectful person, not just a "mad, bad boy" as he and many others in his life had believed or feared. As a result, he was able to become closer to his foster parents, enjoy their company and earn their respect and trust, and, in this way, he was making a positive difference in their lives and his own.

Conclusion

Emotion regulation begins with experience-dependent brain development early in life, when the key experiences are security with caregivers and rewarding exploration of the world (of both external environment and the internal environment of one's body). Complex trauma directly interferes with this crucial development by shifting the brain into hypervigilant survival mode. Recovery from complex trauma therefore involves a shift from survival-based reactivity to learning-focused emotion regulation. That shift is possible when the individual (and support persons and service providers) are helped to understand emotional and behavioral problems as the inherent cost of operating in survival mode, thus allowing survivors to regain their innate emotion regulation capacities. As Manny so articulately captured the challenge:

> I couldn't stop being angry until I knew what was going on in my brain that was making me angry, and that I could use my brain to start really thinking. I wasn't stupid, I just didn't know how to use my brain. Now I do, and it works great!

References

Alink, L. R. A., Cicchetti, D., Kim, J., & Rogosch, F. A. (2009). Mediating and moderating processes in the relation between maltreatment and psychopathology: Mother-child relationship quality and emotion regulation. *Journal of Abnormal Child Psychology*, *37*(6), 831–843.

Bariola, E., Gullone, E., & Hughes, E. K. (2011). Child and adolescent emotion regulation: The role of parental emotion regulation and expression. *Clinical Child and Family Psychology Review*, *14*(2), 198–212. doi: 10.1007/s10567-011-0092-5

Bergen, H. A., Martin, G., Richardson, A. S., Allison, S., & Roeger, L. (2003). Sexual abuse and suicidal behavior: A model constructed from a large community sample of adolescents. *Journal of the American Academy of Child & Adolescent Psychiatry*, *42*(11), 1301–1309. doi: 10.1097/01.chi.0000084831.67701.d6

Berking, M., Wupperman, P., Reichardt, A., Pejic, T., Dippel, A., & Znoj, H. (2008). Emotion-regulation skills as a treatment target in psychotherapy. *Behaviour Research and Therapy*, *46*(11), 1230–1237.

Bowlby, J. (1982). Attachment and loss: Retrospect and prospect. *American Journal of Orthopsychiatry*, *52*(4), 664–678.

Bremner, J. D. (2008). Hippocampus. In G. Reyes, J. D. Elhai & J. D. Ford (Eds.), *Encyclopedia of psychological trauma* (pp. 313–315). Hoboken, NJ: Wiley.

Brewin, C. R., & Holmes, E. A. (2003). Psychological theories of posttraumatic stress disorder. *Clinical Psychology Review*, Special Issue: Post Traumatic Stress Disorder, *23*(4), 339–376.

Briere, J., & Rickards, S. (2007). Self-awareness, affect regulation, and relatedness: Differential sequels of childhood versus adult victimization experiences. *Journal of Nervous and Mental Disease*, *195*(6), 497–503.

Brown, L. K., Houck, C. D., Hadley, W. S., & Lescano, C. M. (2005). Self-cutting and sexual risk among adolescents in intensive psychiatric treatment. *Psychiatric Services*, *56*(2), 216–218. doi: 10.1176/appi.ps.56.2.216

Brown, M. Z., Comtois, K. A., & Linehan, M. M. (2002). Reasons for suicide attempts and nonsuicidal self-injury in women with borderline personality disorder. *Journal of Abnormal Psychology*, *111*(1), 198–202.

Cahill, S. P., Rothbaum, B. O., Resick, P. A., & Follette, V. M. (2009). Cognitive-behavioral therapy for adults. In E. B. Foa, T. M. Keane, M. J. Friedman & J. A. Cohen (Eds.), *Effective treatments for PTSD: Practice guidelines from the International Society for Traumatic Stress Studies* (2nd ed., pp. 139–222). New York, NY: Guilford Press.

Calkins, S. D. (2010). Commentary: Conceptual and methodological challenges to the study of emotion regulation and psychopathology. *Journal of Psychopathology and Behavioral Assessment*, *32*(1), 92–95.

Campbell-Sills, L., Barlow, D. H., Brown, T. A., & Hoffmann, S. G. (2006). Effects of suppression and acceptance on emotional responses of individuals with anxiety and mood disorders. *Behaviour Research and Therapy*, *44*(9), 1251–1263.

Carver, C. S., Scheier, M. F., & Weintraub, J. K. (1989). Assessing coping strategies: A theoretically based approach. *Journal of Personality and Social Psychology*, *56*(2), 267–283.

Chapman, A. L., Gratz, K. L., & Brown, M. Z. (2006). Solving the puzzle of deliberate self-harm: The experiential avoidance model. *Behaviour Research and Therapy*, *44*(3), 371–394. doi: 10.1016/j.brat.2005.03.005

Cicchetti, D., & Toth, S. L. (1995). A developmental psychopathology perspective on child abuse and neglect. *Journal of the American Academy of Child & Adolescent Psychiatry, 34*(5), 541–565.

Cicchetti, D., & Toth, S. L. (2005). Child maltreatment. *Annual Review of Clinical Psychology, 1*(1), 409–438.

Cloitre, M., Cohen, L. R., & Koenen, K. C. (2006). *Treating survivors of childhood abuse: Psychotherapy for the interrupted life*. New York: Guilford.

Cloitre, M., Koenen, K. C., Cohen, L. R., & Han, H. (2002). Skills training in affective and interpersonal regulation followed by exposure: A phase-based treatment for PTSD related to childhood abuse. *Journal of Consulting & Clinical Psychology, 70*(5), 1067–1074.

Cloitre, M., Scarvalone, P., & Difede, J. (1997). Posttraumatic stress disorder, self- and interpersonal dysfunction among sexually retraumatized women. *Journal of Traumatic Stress, 10*(3), 437–452.

Cloitre, M., Stovall-McClough, K. C., Nooner, K., Zorbas, P., Cherry, S., Jackson, C. L., et al. (2010). Treatment for PTSD related to childhood abuse: A randomized controlled trial. *The American Journal of Psychiatry, 167*(8), 915–924. doi: 10.1176/appi.ajp.2010.09081247

Cohen, J. A., Berliner, L., & Mannarino, A. (2010). Trauma focused CBT for children with co-occurring trauma and behavior problems. *Child Abuse & Neglect, 34*(4), 215–224. doi: 10.1016/j.chiabu.2009.12.003

Cohen, J. A., Bukstein, O., Walter, H., Benson, S. R., Chrisman, A., Farchione, T. R., et al. (2010). Practice parameter for the assessment and treatment of children and adolescents with posttraumatic stress disorder. *Journal of the American Academy of Child & Adolescent Psychiatry, 49*(4), 414–430.

Compas, B. E., Connor-Smith, J. K., Saltzman, H., Thomsen, A. H., & Wadsworth, M. E. (2001). Coping with stress during childhood and adolescence: Problems, progress, and potential in theory and research. *Psychological Bulletin, 127*(1), 87–127.

Cook, A., Spinazzola, J., Ford, J., Lanktree, C., Blaustein, M., Cloitre, M., et al. (2005). Complex trauma in children and adolescents. *Psychiatric Annals, 35*(5), 390–398.

Cook, J., Schnurr, P. P., & Foa, E. B. (2004). Bridging the gap between posttraumatic stress disorder research and clinical practice: The example of exposure therapy. *Psychotherapy: Theory, Research, Practice, Training, 41*(4), 374–387.

Courtois, C. A. (2008). Complex trauma, complex reactions: Assessment and treatment. *Psychological Trauma: Theory, Research, Practice, and Policy, S*(1), 86–100. doi: 10.1037/1942-9681.s.1.86

Crockenberg, S., & Leerkes, E. (2004). Infant and maternal behaviors regulate infant reactivity to novelty to predict anxious behavior at 2.5 years. *Developmental Psychology, 40*(6), 1123–1132.

D'Andrea, W., Ford, J. D., Stolbach, B., Spinazzola, J., & van der Kolk, B. A. (2012). Understanding interpersonal trauma in children: Why we need a developmentally appropriate trauma diagnosis. *American Journal of Orthopsychiatry, 82*(2), 187–200.

Danese, A., & McEwen, B. S. (2011). Adverse childhood experiences, allostasis, allostatic load, and age-related disease. *Physiology & Behavior, 106*(1). doi: 10.1016/j.physbeh.2011.08.019

Dorard, G., Berthoz, S., Phan, O., Corcos, M., & Bungener, C. (2008). Affect dysregulation in cannabis abusers: A study in adolescents and young adults. *European Child & Adolescent Psychiatry, 17*(5), 274–282. doi: 10.1007/s00787-007-0663-7

Dube, S. R., Anda, R. F., Felitti, V. J., Chapman, D. P., Williamson, D. F., & Giles, W. H. (2001). Childhood abuse, household dysfunction, and the risk of attempted suicide throughout the life span: Findings from the Adverse Childhood Experiences Study. *JAMA: Journal of the American Medical Association, 286*(24), 3089–3096. doi: 10.1001/jama.286.24.3089

Dunning, J. P., & Hajcak, G. (2009). See no evil: Directing visual attention within unpleasant images modulates the electrocortical response. *Psychophysiology, 46*(1), 28–33.

Ehlers, A., Mayou, R. A., & Bryant, B. (2003). Cognitive predictors of posttraumatic stress disorder in children: Results of a prospective longitudinal study. *Behaviour Research and Therapy, 41*(1), 1–10.

Eisenberg, N., Cumberland, A., & Spinrad, T. L. (1998). Parental socialization of emotion. *Psychological Inquiry, 9*(4), 241–273. doi: 10.1207/s15327965pli0904_1

Eisenberg, N., Spinrad, T. L., & Eggum, N. D. (2010). Emotion-related self-regulation and its relation to children's maladjustment. *Annual Review of Clinical Psychology, 6*(1), 495–525. doi: 10.1146/annurev.clinpsy.121208.131208

Feldner, M. T., Zvolensky, M. J., Stickle, T. R., Bonn-Miller, M. O., & Leen-Feldner, E. W. (2006). Anxiety sensitivity-physical concerns as a moderator of the emotional consequences of emotion suppression during biological challenge: An experimental test using individual growth curve modeling. *Behaviour Research and Therapy, 44*(2), 249–272.

Foa, E. B., Ehlers, A., Clark, D. M., Tolin, D. F., & Orsillo, S. M. (1999). The posttraumatic cognitions inventory (PTCI): Development and validation. *Psychological Assessment, 11*(3), 303–314.

Foa, E. B., & Kozak, M. J. (1986). Emotional processing of fear: Exposure to corrective information. *Psychological Bulletin, 99*(2), 20–35.

Folkman, S., & Moskowitz, J. T. (2004). Coping: Pitfalls and promise. In S. T. Fiske, D. L. Schacter & C. Zahn-Waxler, *Annual Review of Psychology* (Vol. 55, pp. 745–774). Palo Alto, CA: Annual Reviews.

Ford, J. D. (2009). Neurobiological and developmental research: Clinical implications. In C. A. Courtois, J. D. Ford & J. L. Herman (Eds.), *Treating complex traumatic stress disorders: An evidence-based guide* (pp. 31–58). New York, NY: Guilford Press.

Ford, J. D., & Fournier, D. (2007). Psychological trauma and post-traumatic stress disorder among women in community mental health aftercare following psychiatric intensive care. *Journal of Psychiatric Intensive Care, 3*(1), 27–34. doi: 10.1017/s1742646407001094

Ford, J. D., Russo, E. M., & Mallon, S. D. (2007). Integrating treatment of posttraumatic stress disorder and substance use disorder. *Journal of Counseling and Development, 85*(4), 475–489.

Frewen, P. A., Lanius, R. A., Dozois, D. J. A., Neufeld, R. W., Pain, C., Hopper, J. W., et al. (2008). Clinical and neural correlates of alexithymia in posttraumatic stress disorder. *Journal of Abnormal Psychology, 117*(1), 171–181.

Gilbert, D. T., Pinel, E. C., Wilson, T. D., Blumberg, S. J., & Wheatley, T. P. (1998). Immune neglect: A source of durability bias in affective forecasting. *Journal of Personality and Social Psychology, 75*(3), 617–638.

Gilgun, J. F. (2006). Children and adolescents with problematic sexual behaviors: Lessons from research on resilience. In R. Longo & D. Prescott (Eds.), *Current perspectives on working with sexually aggressive youth and youth with sexual behavior problems* (pp. 383–394). Holyoke, MA: NEARI Press.

Gratz, K. L., & Roemer, L. (2004). Multidimensional assessment of emotion regulation and dysregulation: Development, factor structure, and initial validation of the Difficulties in Emotion Regulation Scale. *Journal of Psychopathology and Behavioral Assessment, 26*(1), 41–54.

Gross, J. J., & Levenson, R. W. (1997). Hiding feelings: The acute effects of inhibiting negative and positive emotion. *Journal of Abnormal Psychology, 106*(1), 95–103.

Gross, J. J., & Thompson, R. A. (2007). Emotion regulation: Conceptual foundations. In J. J. Gross (Ed.), *Handbook of emotion regulation* (pp. 3–24). New York, NY: Guilford Press.

Hall, S. E. K., Geher, G., & Brackett, M. A. (2004). The measurement of emotional intelligence in children: The case of reactive attachment disorder. In G. Geher (Ed.), *Measuring emotional intelligence: Common ground and controversy* (pp. 199–217). Hauppauge, NY: Nova Science Publishers.

Harvey, S. T., & Taylor, J. E. (2010). A meta-analysis of the effects of psychotherapy with sexually abused children and adolescents. *Clinical Psychology Review, 30*(5), 517–535. doi: 10.1016/j.cpr.2010.03.006

Hayes, S. C., Luoma, J. B., Bond, F. W., Masuda, A., & Lillis, J. (2006). Acceptance and commitment therapy: Model, processes, and outcomes. *Behavior Research and Therapy, 44*(1), 1–25.

Hopp, H., Rohrmann, S., Zapf, D., & Hodapp, V. (2010). Psychophysiological effects of emotional dissonance in a face-to-face service interaction. *Anxiety, stress, and coping, 23*(4), 399–414. doi: 10.1080/10615800903254091

Izard, C. E. (2009). Emotion theory and research: Highlights, unanswered questions, and emerging issues. In S. T. Fiske, D. L. Schacter & C. Zahn-Waxler, *Annual Review of Psychology* (Vol. 60, pp. 1–25). Palo Alto, CA: Annual Reviews.

Johnson, M., Posner, M. I., & Rothbart, M. K. (1991). Components of visual orienting in early infancy: Contingent learning, anticipatory looking, and disengaging. *Journal of Cognitive Neuroscience, 3*(4), 335–344.

Kahneman, D. (2000). Experienced utility and objective happiness: A moment-based approach. In D. Kahneman & A. Tversky (Eds.), *Choices, values, and frames* (Chapter 37). Cambridge: Cambridge University Press.

Kessler, R. C., Sonnega, A., Bromet, E., & Hughes, M. (1995). Posttraumatic stress disorder in the National Comorbidity Survey. *Archives of General Psychiatry, 52*(12), 1048–1060.

Kim, J., & Cicchetti, D. (2010). Longitudinal pathways linking child maltreatment, emotion regulation, peer relations, and psychopathology. *Journal of Child Psychology and Psychiatry, 51*(6), 706–716.

Lanius, R. A., Vermetten, E., Loewenstein, R. J., Brand, B., Schmahl, C., Bremner, J. D., et al. (2010). Emotion modulation in PTSD: Clinical and neurobiological evidence for a dissociative subtype. *The American Journal of Psychiatry, 167*(6), 640–647.

Laye-Gindhu, A., & Schonert-Reichl, K. A. (2005). Nonsuicidal self-harm among community adolescents: Understanding the "whats" and "whys" of self-harm. *Journal of Youth and Adolescence, 34*(5), 447–457. doi: 10.1007/s10964-005-7262-z

Lewis, M. D. (2005). Self-organizing individual differences in brain development. *Developmental Review, 25*(3–4), 252–277.

LoSavio, S., Grasso, D., Moser, J. S., Hajcak, G., Simons, R., Foa, E. B., et al. (in preparation). *Maladaptive cognitions prospectively predict severity of posttraumatic stress following trauma exposure.* University of Delaware, Delaware.

Marx, B. P., & Sloan, D. M. (2002). The role of emotion in the psychological functioning of adult survivors of childhood sexual abuse. *Behavior Therapy*, *33*(4), 563–577.

McLean, L. M., Toner, B., Jackson, J. F., Desrocher, M., & Stuckless, N. (2006). The relationship between childhood sexual abuse, complex post-traumatic stress disorder and alexithymia in two outpatient samples: Examination of women treated in community and institutional clinics. *Journal of Child Sexual Abuse*, *15*(3), 1–17.

Mikulincer, M., Shaver, P. R., & Pereg, D. (2003). Attachment theory and affect regulation: The dynamics, development, and cognitive consequences of attachment-related strategies. *Motivation and Emotion*, *27*(2), 77–102.

Milad, M. R., Wright, C. I., Orr, S. P., Pitman, R. K., Quirk, G. J., & Rauch, S. L. (2007). Recall of fear extinction in humans activates the ventromedial prefrontal cortex and hippocampus in concert. *Biological Psychiatry*, *62*(5), 446–454.

Moore, S. A., Zoellner, L. A., & Mollenholt, N. (2008). Are expressive suppression and cognitive reappraisal associated with stress-related symptoms? *Behaviour Research and Therapy*, *46*(9), 993–1000.

Morris, A. S., Silk, J. S., Steinberg, L., Myers, S. S., & Robinson, L. R. (2007). The role of the family context in the development of emotion regulation. *Social Development*, *16*(2), 361–388. doi: 10.1111/j.1467-9507.2007.00389.x

Nelson, J. A., O'Brien, M., Blankson, A. N., Calkins, S. D., & Keane, S. P. (2009). Family stress and parental responses to children's negative emotions: Tests of the spillover, crossover, and compensatory hypotheses. *Journal of Family Psychology*, *23*(5), 671–679. doi: 10.1037/a0015977

Nijenhuis, E. R. S., & van der Hart, O. (2011). Dissociation in trauma: a new definition and comparison with previous formulations. *Journal of Trauma and Dissociation*, *12*(4), 416–445.

Pears, K. C., & Fisher, P. A. (2005). Emotion understanding and theory of mind among maltreated children in foster care: Evidence of deficits. *Development & Psychopathology*, *17*(1), 47–65.

Pine, D. S., Mogg, K., Bradley, B. P., Montgomery, L., Monk, C. S., McClure, E., et al. (2005). Attention bias to threat in maltreated children: Implications for vulnerability to stress-related psychopathology. *The American Journal of Psychiatry*, *162*(2), 291–296. doi: 10.1176/appi.ajp.162.2.291

Pithers, W. D., Gray, A., Busconi, A., & Houchens, P. (1998). Children with sexual behavior problems: Identification of five distinct child types and related treatment considerations. *Child Maltreatment*, *3*(4), 384–406. doi: 10.1177/1077559598003004010

Plumb, J. C., Orsillo, S. M., & Luterek, J. A. (2004). A preliminary test of the role of experiential avoidance in post-event functioning. *Journal of Behavior Therapy and Experimental Psychiatry*, *35*(3), 245–257.

Pollak, S. D., & Tolley-Schell, S. A. (2003). Selective attention to facial emotion in physically abused children. *Journal of Abnormal Psychology*, *112*(3), 323–338. doi: 10.1037/0021-843x.112.3.323

Polusny, M. A., Rosenthal, M. Z., Aban, I., & Follette, V. M. (2004). Experiential avoidance as a mediator of the effects of adolescent sexual victimization on negative adult outcomes. *Violence and Victims*, *19*(1), 109–120.

Repetti, R. L., Taylor, S. E., & Seemant, T. E. (2002). Risky families: Family social environments and the mental and physical health of offspring. *Psychological Bulletin*, *128*(2), 330–366.

Richards, J. M., & Gross, J. J. (2000). Emotion regulation and memory: The cognitive costs of keeping one's cool. *Journal of Personality and Social Psychology, 79*(3), 410–424.

Salters-Pedneault, K., Tull, M. T., & Roemer, L. (2004). The role of avoidance of emotional material in the anxiety disorders. *Applied and Preventive Psychology, 11*(2), 95–114.

Saxe, G., MacDonald, H., & Ellis, H. (2007). Psychological approaches for children with PTSD. In E. B. Foa, M. J. Friedman, T. M. Keane & P. A. Resick (Eds.), *Handbook of PTSD: Science and practice* (pp. 359–375). New York, NY: Guilford Press.

Sayar, K., Kose, S., Grabe, H. J., & Topbas, M. (2005). Alexithymia and dissociative tendencies in an adolescent sample from Eastern Turkey. *Psychiatry and Clinical Neurosciences, 59*(2), 127–134. doi: 10.1111/j.1440-1819.2005.01346.x

Shapiro, D. L., & Levendosky, A. A. (1999). Adolescent survivors of childhood sexual abuse: The mediating role of attachment style and coping in psychological and interpersonal functioning. *Child Abuse & Neglect, 23*(11), 1175–1191.

Shenk, C. E., Putnam, F. W., & Noll, J. G. (2012). Experiential avoidance and the relationship between child maltreatment and PTSD symptoms: Preliminary evidence. *Child Abuse & Neglect, 36*(2), 118–126. doi: 10.1016/j.chiabu.2011.09.012

Shipherd, J. C., Stafford, J., & Tanner, L. R. (2005). Predicting alcohol and drug abuse in Persian Gulf War veterans: What role do PTSD symptoms play? *Addictive Behaviors, 30*(3), 595–599. doi: 10.1016/j.addbeh.2004.07.004

Shipman, K. L., Schneider, R., Fitzgerald, M. M., Sims, C., Swisher, L., & Edwards, A. (2007). Maternal emotion socialization in maltreating and non-maltreating families: Implications for children's emotion regulation. *Social Development, 16*(2), 268–285. doi: 10.1111/j.1467-9507.2007.00384.x

Southam-Gerow, M., & Kendall, P. C. (2002). Emotion regulation and understanding: Implications for child psychopathology and therapy. *Clinical Psychology Review, 22*(2), 189–222.

Stewart, S. H., Pihl, R. O., Conrod, P., & Dongier, M. (1998). Functional associations among trauma, PTSD, and substance-related disorders. *Addictive Behaviors, 23*(6), 797–812.

Stocker, C. M., Richmond, M. K., Rhoades, G. K., & Kiang, L. (2007). Family emotional processes and adolescents' adjustment. *Social Development, 16*(2), 310–325. doi: 10.1111/j.1467-9507.2007.00386.x

Suveg, C., Southam-Gerow, M. A., Goodman, K. L., & Kendall, P. C. (2007). The role of emotion theory and research in child therapy development. *Clinical Psychology: Science and Practice, 14*(4), 358–371. doi: doi:10.1111/j.1468-2850.2007.00096.x

Trusz, S. G., Wagner, A. W., Russo, J., Love, J., & Zatzick, D. F. (2011). Assessing barriers to care and readiness for cognitive behavioral therapy in early acute care PTSD interventions. *Psychiatry: Interpersonal and Biological Processes, 74*(3), 207–223. doi: 10.1521/psyc.2011.74.3.207

Tull, M. T., Jakupcak, M., McFadden, M. E., & Roemer, L. (2007). The role of negative affect intensity and the fear of emotions in posttraumatic stress symptom severity among victims of childhood interpersonal violence. *Journal of Nervous and Mental Disease, 195*(7), 580–587.

Tull, M. T., Jakupcak, M., & Roemer, L. (2010). Emotion suppression: A preliminary experimental investigation of its immediate effects and role in subsequent reactivity to novel stimuli. *Cognitive Behaviour Therapy, 39*(2), 114–125. doi: 10.1080/16506070903280491

Valiente, C., Lemery-Chalfant, K., & Reiser, M. (2007). Pathways to problem behaviors: Chaotic homes, parent and child effortful control, and parenting. *Social Development, 16*(2), 249–267. doi: 10.1111/j.1467-9507.2007.00383.x

Van der Kolk, B. A., Perry, J. C., & Herman, J. L. (1991). Childhood origins of self-destructive behavior. *The American Journal of Psychiatry, 148*(12), 1665–1671.

van Dijke, A., Ford, J. D., van der Hart, O., van Son, M., van der Heijden, P., & Buhring, M. (2010). Affect dysregulation in borderline personality disorder and somatoform disorder: Differentiating under- and over-regulation. *Journal of Personality Disorders, 24*(3), 296–311.

van Dijke, A., van der Hart, O., Ford, J. D., van Son, M., van der Heijden, P., & Buhring, M. (2010). Affect dysregulation and dissociation in borderline personality disorder and somatoform disorder: Differentiating inhibitory and excitatory experiencing states. *Journal of Trauma and Dissociation, 11*(4), 424–443.

van Reekum, C. M., Johnstone, T., Urry, H. L., Thurow, M. E., Schaefer, H. S., Alexander, A. A., et al. (2007). Gaze fixations predict brain activation during the voluntary regulation of picture-induced negative affect. *NeuroImage, 36*(3), 1041–1055.

Volling, B. L., McElwain, N. L., Notaro, P. C., & Herrera, C. (2002). Parents' emotional availability and infant emotional competence: Predictors of parent–infant attachment and emerging self-regulation. *Journal of Family Psychology, 16*(4), 447–465. doi: 10.1037/0893-3200.16.4.447

Waters, S. F., Virmani, E. A., Thompson, R. A., Meyer, S., Raikes, H. A., & Jochem, R. (2010). Emotion regulation and attachment: Unpacking two constructs and their association. *Journal of Psychopathology and Behavior Assessment, 32*(1), 37–47. doi: 10.1007/s10862-009-9163-z

Wegner, D. M., & Bargh, J. A. (1997). Control and automaticity in social life. In D. T. Gilbert, S. T. Fiske & G. Lindzey (Eds.), *Handbook of social psychology*. Boston, MA: McGraw-Hill.

Yiend, J. (2010). The effects of emotion on attention: A review of attentional processing of emotional information. *Cognition & Emotion, 24*(1), 3–47. doi: 10.1080/02699930903205698

Zeman, J., Cassano, M., Perry-Parrish, C., & Stegall, S. (2006). Emotion regulation in children and adolescents. *Journal of Developmental and Behavioral Pediatrics, 27*(2), 155–168.

Zlotnick, C., Mattia, J. I., & Zimmerman, M. (2001). The relationship between posttraumatic stress disorder, childhood trauma and alexithymia in an outpatient sample. *Journal of Traumatic Stress, 14*(1), 177–188.

Zlotnick, C., Zakriski, A. L., Shea, M. T., Costello, E., Begin, A., Pearlstein, T., et al. (1996). The long-term sequelae of sexual abuse: Support for a complex posttraumatic stress disorder. *Journal of Traumatic Stress, 9*(2), 195–205.

Chapter 3

The impact of exposure to violence on aggression in children and adolescents

What can be learned from the trauma and resilience perspective?

Ruth Pat-Horenczyk, Victoria Yeh, Sarale Cohen and Sarit Schramm

Exposure to violence and subsequent aggression and violent behavior in children and youth is a worldwide public health problem (WHO, 2010). Alarming evidence is accumulating about the long-term impact of the trauma of exposure to violence on children's development and mental health (Buka, Stichick, Birdthistle, & Earls, 2001). Much attention has been paid to internalizing problems, such as anxiety, depression, post traumatic stress symptoms and post-traumatic stress disorder (PTSD). Less attention has been given to externalizing problems, such as aggressive behavior and conduct disorders. Nonetheless, there is a growing body of research literature indicating a link between exposure to violence and aggressive behavior in children and adolescents. Research has documented the impact of different types of violence, including child abuse, domestic and interpersonal violence, community violence and enemy violence. Virtually all published research has shown that exposure to violence potentiates aggression in children (Dodge, Bates & Pettit, 1990; Orue et al., 2011) and adolescents (Barroso et al., 2008; Flannery, Singer, & Wester, 2001; Kaya, Bilgin & Singer, 2011). Both witnessing violence (when the child is the observer) and victimization (when the child is the victim) have been shown to intensify children's and adolescents' aggressive behavior (Flannery, Wester, & Singer, 2004; O'Keefe, 1994). Co-occurrence or "dual exposure" has generally been found to be most deleterious (Hughes, 1988; Moylan et al., 2009). Further, younger children are more susceptible to the effects of family violence than older children (Sternberg, Lamb, Guterman, & Abbott, 2006).

The field has moved from an emphasis on describing cases of exposure to violence, to studies of the link between exposure and aggression and then to studies of risk and protective factors (Evans, Davies, & DiLillo, 2008). Exposure to violence poses a major social problem that may lead to a cycle of events perpetuating escalating levels of violent behavior. Increasing effort has been directed toward developing intervention programs for reducing and preventing aggression in children and adolescents. However, to date, there has been little emphasis on how a trauma and resilience informed perspective can inform and potentially benefit such programs.

Based on the premise that exposure to violence is potentially traumatic, this chapter addresses the complex relationship between exposure to violence and aggressive behavior in children and adolescents from a perspective of trauma and resilience. We first present theoretical views about the link between exposure to violence and aggression in children and adolescents. Second, we present recommendations for intervention programs to reduce aggression and violence based on these theoretical views. We will also suggest how these intervention programs can benefit from a trauma and resilience perspective.

Theoretical views

In this section, we present some physiological, emotional, cognitive and social views that propose possible paths or mechanisms by which exposure to violence may lead to aggressive behavior in children and adolescents. We discuss various ecological systems, including the individual, the family, the school, the community and the national/cultural systems. We begin with the individual system, discussing neurophysiological research which shows that exposure to trauma results in a constellation of biological changes in the neural and endocrine systems. Other approaches to the individual system view aggression against the self and others as a result of difficulties in emotional regulation and impulse control (Kereteš, 2006). Cognitive models focus on the processes that shape children's thoughts about the use of violence and contribute to aggression scripts. Family and parenting constructs are described, as well as social learning theories that address the ways in which social learning, socializing factors and normative beliefs affect children's functioning in the community through the development of their identity structures and the concept of self. These, in turn, can lead to the construction of worldviews and nationalistic ideas. Each of these theoretical approaches is described more fully below.

Individual and family

Physiological

Empirical evidence shows that exposure to trauma results in a constellation of biological changes in neural and endocrine systems. These changes then become important mediators in the relationship between exposure to violence and post-traumatic distress and aggressive behavior (Allwood & Bell, 2008; Ruchkin, Henrich, Jones, Vermeiren, & Schwab-Stone, 2007; Schore, 2003a). Trauma during early childhood, when the brain is quite plastic, may lead to permanent effects on brain development, thus making young children especially vulnerable (Beckman, 2004).

Research on child maltreatment shows that right brain development is impaired as a result of trauma (Shin et al., 1999; van der Kolk, 2005). The right hemisphere is closely linked to the autonomic, limbic and arousal systems and is thus responsible for processing emotion, social interaction and the stress response (Schore, 2002). The right brain plays a vital role in inhibitory and controlling functions associated with the expression of aggression, such as the control of spontaneously evoked emotional responses, the regulation of "primary emotions" (Ross, Homan, & Buck, 1994) and the ability to use affect regulation. The prefrontal cortex controls higher executive functions, such as judgment, reasoning, decision-making and the control of impulses. However, it is also one of the last brain regions to mature (Giedd, 2004) and is thus strongly affected by trauma during childhood and adolescence.

In keeping with these neurophysiological findings, Perry, Perry, and Rasmussen (1986) found that aggressive children reported more difficulty in inhibiting impulses than nonaggressive children. Punamäki (2009) also concluded that impulsive and aggressive behavior results from the lack of inhibitory processes and deficits in regulating aggressive impulses. When the prefrontal cortex is impaired by early childhood trauma, it cannot assess the appropriate level of threat, leaving the child in a defense-driven response state (Morgan & LeDoux, 1995) throughout childhood and into adulthood. More specifically, the "fight or flight" response of the sympathetic nervous system is triggered too often and/or incorrectly by perceptions of threat or danger. These triggers may also be activated by sensory stimulation, such as the color of the room where the traumatic experience occurred (van der Kolk & Fisler, 1994). Because responses to stimuli are driven more by impulsive limbic system and brain stem activity than by the higher cortical regions that govern decision-making (Heide & Solomon, 2006), the traumatized child or adolescent is unable to regulate their affective reactions. Physiological hyperarousal may last for years after the experience of trauma. A lack of habituation of the startle response, in addition to heightened skin conductance, has been documented in numerous groups that have been exposed to various types of trauma. These studies have been conducted hours to years after the traumatic incident in groups of children (Ornitz & Pynoos, 1989), and also among adults, such as Gulf War veterans (Morgan, Grillon, Southwick, Davis, & Charney, 1996) and civilians exposed to other types of traumatic events (Shalev et al., 2000).

Dysregulation of the endocrine system is also strongly implicated in the development of post-traumatic symptoms (Yehuda, Lowy, Southwick, Shaffer, & Giller, 1991). The hypothalamic–pituitary–adrenal (HPA) axis regulates cortisol, abnormal levels of which have been associated with child maltreatment, in both young victims and adult survivors (Schore, 2003b). Empirical evidence suggests that, as time passes, a trauma survivor's body adapts to high cortisol levels by decreasing its output. Eventually, cortisol levels become too low to respond to stressors, prompting survivors to adopt ineffective coping strategies and leaving them vulnerable to stressors. Abnormal endogenous opioid function has also been found post-trauma. Endogenous opioids are known to facilitate the capacity to gain emotional and psychological distance (Pitman, van der Kolk, Orr, & Greenberg, 1990; van der Kolk, Greenberg, Orr, & Pitman, 1989).

In summary, exposure to traumatic events limits the ability of higher-order cortical regions to regulate the intensity and duration of affect. The extremely heightened, prolonged physiological reactivity caused by the disruption of this top-down influence renders the individual anxious, hyperalert and easily startled. Abnormal neurotransmitter function and cortisol activity also contribute to the core symptoms of PTSD, including hypervigilance, exaggerated startle response, irritability and outbursts of anger, which, in turn, may give rise to increased aggression (U.S. Department of Veterans Affairs, 2007).

Emotional

Children who are in a frequent traumatized state of hyperarousal, fear and possibly anger are unable to effectively recognize and process environmental cues to properly guide their behavioral responses (Dodge, Pettit, Bates, & Valente, 1995). Studies have shown that high physiological arousal, combined with anger and fear, distorts perceptions. Evolutionary pressures have led humans to react more strongly and quickly to negative stimuli because emotions such as anger and fear are associated with life-threatening situations. Such immediate behavioral responses may be beneficial for survival, but are disadvantageous for suppressing aggressive responses (Cacioppo & Gardner, 1999). In addition, a negative affective state biases the individual towards retrieval of negative emotional memories (Power & Dalgleish, 1997), further feeding the current state.

The link between impulsive behavior and emotional desensitization in traumatized children has been the focus of several studies (e.g., Moradi, Neshat-Doost, Taghavi, Yule, & Dalgleish, 1999). Impulsivity has been implicated in fostering aggression by lowering response control and impairing the inhibition of aggressive responses (Vigil-Colet & Codorniu-Raga, 2004). Through repeated exposure to a stimulus, children build up tolerance to the distress response, which results in decreased neurophysiological reactivity. Although this buildup of tolerance is useful for the systematic desensitization treatment of phobias and other fear or anxiety disorders (Wolpe, 1973), desensitization to violence and conflict may actually increase aggressive behavior. A substantial body of empirical evidence has documented the desensitizing effects of television, video games and other types of media violence on children (Molitor & Hirsch, 1994). In a trauma-inducing environment such as a conflict zone, children witness repeated episodes of violence and this exposure may gradually elicit less and less of an emotional reaction. Eventually, the use of violence by the child may also induce a blunted emotional response, which decreases the likelihood that aggressive behavior will be internally censored.

Huesmann's (1988, 1998) social-cognitive information-processing model attempts to explain the effect of desensitization to violence on aggressive behavior.

If consideration of potential violence causes the child to experience negative affect and arousal, then the child is likely to discard the idea. However, if the idea of violence causes the child less arousal and consequently less distress, then the child is more likely to contemplate aggression for solving social problems. In other words, exposure to high levels of violence causes emotional and cognitive desensitization to violence in some children. This numbing limits immediate psychological distress, increasing the risk of aggressive responses (Ng-Mak, Salzinger, Feldman, & Stueve, 2004).

Relatively little research has addressed the seemingly incongruous connection between the two post-traumatic symptom categories of hyperarousal and desensitization. How can a child be hypersensitive to stimuli while experiencing emotional and physiological numbing? Studies of children with a history of trauma and post-traumatic symptomatology have provided preliminary evidence that emotional numbing develops after the exhaustion of cognitive and emotional resources, a result of prolonged physiological hyperarousal (Weems, Saltzman, Reiss, & Carrion, 2003).

In sum, although the relationship between desensitization and hyperarousal is still unclear, a sizeable body of empirical evidence has indicated that physiology and affect play central roles in the relationship between exposure to trauma and aggressive behavior. Treatments for PTSD that target emotional regulation have often been effective (Cloitre, Koenen, Cohen, & Han, 2002), further suggesting the mediating role of affect regulation in the association between trauma and aggression.

Cognitive

Aggressive children display narrow, biased problem-solving strategies due to deficits in processing social interactions, especially in attending to and encoding relevant social cues (Dodge et al., 1990). Research has suggested that physiological and emotional arousal impairs problem-solving abilities (Lochman & Lenhart, 1993). Studies using modified versions of the Stroop task have discovered that PTSD victims take longer to identify words that seem threatening (Bryant & Harvey, 1995) or are associated with the traumatic incident they experienced (Foa, Feske, Murdock, Kozak, & McCarthy, 1991; Kaspi, McNally, & Amir, 1995). Due to their increased arousal and ineffective emotional regulation, traumatized children are unable to use their emotions as guides for appropriate actions (van der Kolk & Fisler, 1994). Accordingly, studies have shown that, although aggressive and nonaggressive boys produce the same number of effective first solutions to hypothetical situations, nonaggressive boys produce a greater number of effective alternative solutions (Evans & Short, 1991) and aggressive boys produce a greater number of aggressive solutions (Asarnow & Callan, 1985).

The basic cognitive steps taken to encode and process social information in the selection of an internal script that guides social behavior have been described in Huesmann and Kirwil's (2007) model. These cognitive processes also occur in traumatized children whose cognitive processing capabilities are still developing, molded by a traumatic environment. Internal scripts highlighting aggressive responses are processed through a combination of "the subject's current emotional state, coupled with both the objective properties of the current stimulus situation and the evaluative cognitions cued by the stimulus situation" (Huesmann & Eron, 1992, p. 146).

Children enter a social situation with a pre-existing emotional state that affects their cognitive processing. When they process information in a state of high physiological arousal, they may consider an aggressive behavioral response appropriate more often than they would in a lower state of physiological arousal. Furthermore, Huesmann (1988) suggests that "recent environmental stimuli may also directly trigger conditioned emotional reactions and may cue the retrieval of cognitions that define the current emotional state" (p. 16). The author proposes that the sight of an "enemy" triggers both physiological arousal and negative thoughts associated with the "enemy," leading the child to interpret their physiological arousal as anger. The second step is evaluation of situational cues. Depending on children's emotional state and cognitive history, they may attend to certain cues over others. They may selectively encode more threatening cues from peers if they feel anxious, for example, and pay less attention to cues indicating prosocial orientation. Research has shown that aggressive children rely more on their affective state and past experience than on the facts when analyzing situations (Dodge & Tomlin, 1987). When compared to nonaggressive adolescents, aggressive adolescents scan less for information and thus encode fewer cues when analyzing situations (Slaby & Guerra, 1988).

Hostile intent plays a significant role in the next step of the social-cognitive information-processing model (Dodge, 2006). The moral judgment literature has explored the importance of determining the other person's intention when regulating aggressive responses to negative outcomes. A child analyzes a social situation by determining whether or not an outcome was purposefully caused by the actions of the peer. If a child determines that the peer has caused an unfavorable outcome *intentionally*, the response is more likely to be retaliatory aggression. If the child determines that the peer acted *accidentally*, then the affected child is more likely to inhibit aggressive responses, regardless of what actually happened (Dodge, 1980). Dodge's study presented children with a frustrating social situation including a peer who exhibited hostile, benign or ambiguous intent. Though both aggressive and nonaggressive boys responded more aggressively in situations involving hostile intent than in situations involving benign intent, aggressive boys responded more aggressively than nonaggressive boys in situations of ambiguous intent—*as if* the peer had acted with hostile intent (Dodge, 1980).

A significant body of research on hostile intent has shown that, when a traumatized child is presented with a situation of ambiguous provocation and asked to interpret the actor's intention, a number of factors may lead the child to attribute hostile intent to the actor and ignore situational information, thus increasing the likelihood of an aggressive behavioral response (Punamäki, 2009; Shahinfar, Kupersmidt, & Matza, 2001). There are several factors that explain hostile attributional biases among traumatized children. First of all, past experiences in an environment filled with violent conflict have taught these children that the world is a mean place. Children exposed to traumatic events develop feelings of mistrust that persist through adolescence and adulthood (Crawford & Wright, 2007). Physiological hyperarousal resulting from trauma compounds these feelings of mistrust and renders traumatized children hypervigilant, with an intensified perception of threat and danger (Punamäki, 2009). Traumatized children also have difficulties in recognizing emotions and thus may fail to recognize distress and fear in others. Instead, they may interpret the behavior of others as threatening or dominating and respond aggressively (Fisher & Blair, 1998). A child living in a conflict zone, suffering from post traumatic distress and anxiety, may, when faced with an ambiguous situation, tend to perceive more threatening negative cues. Graham and Hudley (1994) found that priming for the intentionality of negative situational outcomes caused both aggressive and nonaggressive boys to be equally extreme in assigning hostile intent, while aggressive boys assigned more hostile intent in conditions without such priming.

After a child has made attributions of hostile intent, they construct a goal for a behavioral response and retrieve a script to guide their behavior. Research has suggested that growing up in a violent, unstable environment not only limits exposure to behaviorally competent, prosocial scripts (Dodge et al., 1990), but also increases the likelihood that children will employ aggressive scripts, which are more accessible from memory (Huesmann & Eron, 1989). Once aggressive scripts have been learned through experienced or witnessed violence, they become resistant to change. As a result of continuous exposure to trauma, these aggressive scripts are reinforced and new aggressive scripts are learned.

Aggressive scripts are easier to retrieve than more complex and less direct problem-solving strategies (Huesmann, 1988). Due to the availability of aggressive scripts, traumatized children may skip steps in the cognitive processing of flexible, nonaggressive response strategies, going directly from stimulus to behavioral response without pausing to thoroughly evaluate their scripts. Indeed, in a study measuring hostile intent, Dodge and Newman (1981) found that their sample of aggressive boys took significantly less time to respond than nonaggressive boys.

The attractiveness of a script is influenced by its potential repercussions. Children suffering from post-traumatic distress may have difficulty considering long-term repercussions. Foreshortened sense of the future is a symptom of PTSD (Adler, Kunz, Chua, Rotrosen, & Resnick, 2004; Husain, Allwood, & Bell, 2008). A traumatized child who has a difficult time visualizing the future is more willing to engage in aggressive behavior (Huesmann & Eron, 1989). Aggression may have immediate positive consequences, such as gaining a toy, but will also incur negative long-term consequences, such as being ostracized by peers and gaining an unfavorable reputation.

"Future orientation provides the grounds for setting goals, planning, exploring options and making commitments that guide the person's behavior and development course" (Seginer, 2008, p. 272). A traumatized child with an impaired sense of future orientation is more likely to engage in impulsive, aggressive behavior. Factors such as efficacy and internalized social norms have an enormous impact on a child's evaluation of behavioral scripts and their decision on whether or not to engage in aggressive behavior (Huesmann & Eron, 1989).

In summary, each of these perspectives may help understand the phenomenon of exposure to violence and aggression on the individual level. The social-cognitive information-processing model indicates the different points at which a child's traumatic experience and distress can influence their decision to engage in aggressive behavior. Physiological and emotional arousal can not only impair problem-solving abilities, but also provide additional negative meaning to the assessment of situational cues. Feelings of mistrust and fear derived from past experiences can bias a traumatized child's perception and interpretation of situational cues. Lastly, aggressive responses that produce unfavorable outcomes may end up increasing a child's frustration, causing him or her to engage in more aggression. Children who are able to avoid or combat the negative effects of trauma exposure on cognitive processing—narrow, biased, inaccurate or rigid problem-solving—are able to function better despite exposure to violent conflict (Qouta, Punamäki & El-Sarraj, 2008).

Family and parenting

The association between children's exposure to maltreatment, domestic violence and interpersonal violence, on the one hand, and their subsequent aggressive behavior, on the other, has been widely substantiated in various groups of children and adolescents. A meta-analysis of 60 studies indicated an effect size of .47 between childhood exposure to domestic violence and externalizing symptoms (Evans et al., 2008). The question is what the mediators and moderators of this relationship might be. Parenting has been identified as a major factor to consider in investigating the link between domestic violence and aggressive behavior, and the importance of relevant aspects in the parent–child relationship is generally accepted. A study of interpersonal aggression in adolescents and parental mediators indicated parental monitoring practices were directly associated with less aggression and also had an indirect effect that was mediated by the adolescents achieving better anger control skills (Griffin, Scheier, Botvin, Diaz, & Mille, 1999). There is much to be learned about mediators that can guide interventions to improve parent–child relationships. Five chapters in this book (5–9) address the issue of parenting and helping trauma victims. Although none of the chapters specifically address ways of reducing aggressive behavior, the methods outlined are directed at improving the parent–child relationship, which appears to be an effective way of reducing maladaptive and aggressive behavior.

Community

The concept of self in a societal context interacts with cognitive processes to shape children's thoughts about the use of violence. Factors that play a particular mediating role in the association between trauma and aggression in children include social learning, normative beliefs and the socialization process.

Social learning

A child forms cognitions about the legitimacy of aggressive behavior by observing and interpreting the behavior of others (Huesmann & Kirwil, 2007). Environments in which aggression and violence tend to occur are often associated with a rise in aggressive behavior in youth (Dawes, 1990). A child who witnesses violence every day in their household or on the streets eventually comes to the conclusion that violence is common, mundane and even inevitable. After continual exposure, violence becomes less aversive. This cognitive desensitization can promote coping, but also lowers children's inhibitions against aggressive behavior (Huesmann, 1998). A child's environment may also reinforce the use of aggression through social learning. If a child is exposed to violence and observes that it seems to work for the aggressor, they will likely be encouraged to increase their aggressive behavior. Dodge et al. (1995) have found that, in cases of physical abuse by the parents, the abused children believed that aggressive behavior could lead to rewards. In Crittenden and Ainsworth's (1989) research on child maltreatment, previous witnessing of severe violence significantly predicted children's notions about the consequences of aggressive behavior. In other words, children who witnessed more severe violence were more certain that use of violence would result in a better outcome. Studies have found that youths who had previously been victims of severe violence were more likely to endorse aggression as a social response (Shahinfar et al., 2001).

Bandura's social learning theory proposes that aggressive scripts are developed and reinforced in early childhood through the processes of observational and enactive learning (Bandura, 1973). In a traumatic environment such as an abusive home, or during violent conflict and war, children have many opportunities to acquire new scripts for aggression by observing the aggressive behavior of others. Research has found that children who have witnessed violence commonly engage in fantasy rehearsal of the violent experience (Eth & Pynoos, 1985; Guerra, Huesmann, & Spindler, 2003) and that children synthesize new behaviors and new forms of aggression from observed models of behavior (Bandura, 1978). Furthermore, the more closely the child identifies with the aggressor, the more likely it is that they will encode the aggressive script (Huesmann, 1988).

Children also engage in enactive learning by acting out aggressive scripts through trial and error. These experiences allow children to become acquainted with both positive and negative consequences of their behavior. A child may first resort to physical aggression only after verbal negotiation fails to solve the problem; with time, they learn that aggression works when nonaggression does not (Huesmann & Eron, 1989). Aggressive behavior may escalate or even generalize to a larger number of social situations with continued rehearsal. If pushing worked this time, will punching or kicking work even better next time? Enactive learning creates a self-perpetuating cycle of escalating violence as continued rehearsal of aggressive scripts results in desensitization to violence, prompting further aggression. In addition, a child who engages in aggressive behavior will influence their own environment by creating conditions that expose the child to new scenes of violence, leading to observation of more aggression and prompting additional aggressive behavior.

Aggressive children develop an ineffective way of dealing with others through their aggressive behavior, and the interpersonal problems caused by their aggression exacerbate their poor relationship skills (Egeland, Yates, Appleyard, & van Dulmen, 2002). Aggressive behavior often detracts from a child's social and academic achievements. Unwarranted aggression (Dodge, 1980) may have deleterious effects on children's educational achievements and popularity, and these effects can sometimes serve as negative consequences that prompt children to inhibit their aggressive behavior. However, the same consequences may also serve to frustrate them. Such children feel that the way their peers treat them justifies their use of aggression, which creates a "self-perpetuating spiral of increased hostile attributions, aggressive behavior and social rejection" (Dodge, 1980, p. 169).

Normative beliefs

Normative beliefs are a fundamental part of a child's worldview. Internal norms about violence govern a child's idea of appropriate behaviors in various situations and interact with cognitive processes to influence children's aggression (Guerra et al., 2003). A sizeable body of empirical research has supported the association between normative beliefs about aggression and actual aggressive behavior among various groups, such as elementary school-aged children (Dodge, Laird, Lochman, & Zelli, 2003), adolescents (Crane-Ross, Tisak, & Tisak, 1998) and ethnically diverse elementary (Guerra, Huesmann, Tolan, Van Acker, & Eron, 1995) and middle school-aged children (Bellmore, Witkow, Graham, & Juvonen, 2005). Beliefs about aggression and other violations of conventional rules fall into three domains: (a) beliefs about acceptability, (b) beliefs about expected outcomes for self and (c) beliefs about effects on others (Crane-Ross et al., 1998). Studies have suggested that the normalization of violence mediates the relationship between exposure to violence and aggressive behavior (Ozkol, Zucker, & Spinazzola, 2011). Indeed, children who believe that violence is an acceptable way to solve conflicts are more likely to be aggressive (Barkin, Kreiter, & DuRant, 2001). Furthermore, aggressive children tend to expect favorable outcomes following aggressive behavior and evaluate outcomes of violence as interpersonally and instrumentally positive (Gellman & Delucia-Waack, 2006). Other research has shown that aggressive children expect that aggressive behavior will "produce tangible rewards . . . increase self-esteem, and . . . reduce aversive treatment" (Pakaslahti, 2000, p. 472). Aggression may also be partly justified when compared to the anticipated costs of nonaggression or timidity; an adolescent may choose to engage in a physical confrontation rather than suffer victimization, humiliation and abuse (Bandura, 1978). Aggressive adolescents, as compared to nonaggressive ones, also expect fewer negative consequences of aggressive acts (Slaby & Guerra, 1988). Lastly, aggressive children believe that aggression raises one's self-esteem and social image and that victims both deserve the violence inflicted upon them and do not suffer unduly (Gellman & Delucia-Waack, 2006). An additional important factor is children's confidence in their ability to perform an aggressive act. A frustrated, angry child who believes that they are capable of executing aggressive behavior is more likely to follow through with violent behavior than a child feeling similar unpleasant emotions but with a lower level of self-efficacy.

National

Group social identity

An adolescent's group identity provides motivation, emotion and meaning, and affects social constructs such as worldviews and nationalistic ideas. Since maintenance of group identity is important, individuals constantly strive to maintain a positive group identity. The salience of group identity increases when group differences are highlighted (Tajfel, 1982), and intergroup conflict arises when individuals attempt to "maintain or achieve superiority over an out-group" (Tajfel & Turner, 1979, p. 41). Intergroup differences become especially polarized between "good" and "bad" in situations of political oppression and violence (Fanon, 1979). The importance of group identity in adolescence is manifested in the need to belong to a group in order to gain respect (Dawes, 1990). The importance of belonging may be intertwined with use of violence in that "it is an element of belonging to the group, I'm part of the group so I'm violent, I'm violent therefore I'm part of the group" (Africa Youth for Peace and Development executive director Philip Bangura, quoting a young activist in Dari, 2011, p. 87).

Ethnic violence

In an environment of intergroup conflict, youths perceive events through the filter of ethnic identity (Tajfel & Turner, 1986), which, according to Phinney (1990), is comprised of three main elements: (a) a feeling of belonging or attachment to the group, (b) participation in group behaviors or practices and (c) exploration of commitment to ethnic group identity. Researchers have suggested that the correlation between exposure to ethnic violence and aggression towards the out-group may be moderated by the individual level of commitment to the in-group (Dubow, Huesmann, & Boxer, 2009).

Ethnic violence is an ongoing issue for children and adolescents in many parts of the world. Dubow et al. (2009) conceptualize ethnic violence as comprising forms of violence sanctioned by various influential political and social bodies based on a history of conflict between ethnic groups. They argue that the effects of observing or experiencing ethnic violence are different from the effects of observing or experiencing other kinds of violence, due to the persistence and multiple channels involved in the experiences of ethnic violence (direct experience, hearing about incidents of others close to one and through the media).

Although most of the research regarding the outcomes of exposure to enemy violence in youths focuses on posttraumatic stress symptoms, there is some evidence showing increased aggressive behavior among children exposed to war and military violence. For example, Qouta and El-Sarraj (1992) found that, of the children they studied during the first Palestinian uprising (*intifada*) in Gaza, 38% developed aggressive behavior. Barber (2008) reported that significant numbers of Palestinian and Bosnian adolescents exposed to enemy violence agreed with the statement, "I am more violent."

An Israeli study (Wang et al., 2006) investigated the reactions of 2- to 4-year-old children who were exposed to terrorist attacks during the second Palestinian *intifada*, distinguishing the various kinds of exposure to traumatic events. They found that toddlers who were directly exposed to terrorist attacks, as compared to those who were indirectly exposed, had more emotional and behavioral problems, such as externalizing (e.g., aggressive behaviors), internalizing (e.g., withdrawal) and anxiety symptoms. Other research with schoolchildren and adolescents has found a positive correlation between exposure to enemy violence and the resulting post traumatic distress, as well as a variety of behavioral and emotional problems, including aggressive behavior (Pat-Horenczyk et al., 2007).

Post-war societies are often characterized by social tolerance, normalization and internalization of violence. Dari (2011) discusses how disarmament, demobilization and rehabilitation programs paid Sierra Leonean youths to disarm and gave them skills training after the war ended. Because the armed youths who had carried out violent acts during the war were rewarded with money and training programs, other youths received the message that violence is a valuable societal mechanism and that violence pays. According to one interviewee in Dari's (2011) study, "People fearing you is respect, fear is respect as during the war" (GOAL–Sierra Leone, Disadvantaged Children and Youth project coordinator Michael Thompson, in Dari, 2011, p. 86). During war, societies value characteristics associated with aggressiveness, such as heroism and risk-taking. After war, those who perpetrated violence often become heroes and are rewarded with success, influence and admiration.

Trauma and resilience informed recommendations for interventions

The theoretical approaches described in the previous section of this chapter have important implications for clinical and community interventions. We urge that the trauma aspect of the exposure to violence be considered in the treatment plan. Attribution of aggressive behavior to post traumatic reaction is very rare (van der Kolk & Andrea, 2010); this may lead to treatment of the symptom (the aggressive behavior) rather than the cause of the problem (exposure to trauma), thus lowering the efficacy of such interventions. A perspective informed by studies of trauma and resilience is proposed as the basis for effective violence reduction intervention programs. Such a perspective includes the consideration of risk and protective factors, strengths and vulnerabilities, as well as the emerging understanding of the mechanisms by which the trauma of exposure to violence may lead to increased aggressive behavior in children.

Reduction of aggression was addressed in a report on violence and health published by the World Health Organization (WHO, 2010, p. 3). Seven guidelines for creating programs to reduce aggression were outlined: (a) developing safe, stable and nurturing relationships between children and their parents and caregivers; (b) developing life skills in children and adolescents; (c) reducing the availability and harmful use of alcohol; (d) reducing access to guns, knives and pesticides; (e) promoting gender equality to prevent violence against women; (f) changing cultural and social norms that support violence; and (g) victim identification, care and support programs.

In line with these recommendations by the WHO, we briefly present interventions that focus on three major strategies: (a) enhancing parent–child relationships, (b) developing self-regulation skills in children and adolescents and (c) early identification of children and adolescents who have been exposed to violence. Further, we suggest that the interventions should be used at the individual, family, community (e.g., schools) and national levels. Most important, the interventions presented all target both trauma and aggression as major factors acting in synergy, in line with the evidence reviewed above.

Over the past several decades, many intervention programs aimed at reducing violence and aggression have been developed and implemented, with varying degrees of success. Thus, it is critical to identify the programs for which there is the best possible evidence of efficacy in reducing or preventing youth violence (Massetti et al., 2011). According to a report of the surgeon general of the United States (Office of the Surgeon General (U.S.), 2001), the most effective youth violence prevention programs are comprehensive and evidence based, and they involve simultaneous action at the school, family and community levels. One major attempt to identify effective treatment programs is the Blueprints for Healthy Youth Development initiative (formerly, Blueprints for Violence Prevention; see www.colorado.edu/cspv/blueprints), developed to serve as a resource for communities and others trying to make informed choices about youth violence and drug abuse programming. Blueprints currently lists 11 prevention and intervention programs that meet a strict scientific standard of program effectiveness as model programs, and another 22 that have produced promising results based on rigorous evaluation but need further replication (Center for the Study and Prevention of Violence, 2004). Whereas some of the programs were designed especially for violence prevention, others, such as programs aimed at early developmental stages and promoting positive parent–child relationships, also had an effect on violence prevention (Greenwood, 2006). In general, a review of evidence-based programs for the reduction of aggressive behavior indicates little emphasis on trauma, whether as a precipitating or as a mediating factor.

Along with prevention programs for aggressive behavior, there has been a growing interest in interventions that both mitigate the effects of trauma and build resilience to better cope with adversities. The RAND Corporation published a report titled "How Schools Can Help Students Recover from Traumatic Experiences," focusing on long-term recovery (Jaycox, Morse, Tanielian, & Stein, 2006). Of the 24 programs reviewed, the only program geared at exposure to violence is the Safe Harbor program (U.S. Department of Justice, 2003). This comprehensive school-based victim-assistance and violence-prevention program addresses violence, victimization and associated trauma. It includes counseling, workshops, school-wide campaigns, peer-leadership development and outreach to parents, staff and community. The counseling component is intended to relieve behavioral and/or psychological issues students may be experiencing, such as acting out, depression and other symptoms in students who have been exposed to violence. The Safe Harbor program is unusual, as few other existing trauma interventions focus on exposure to violence.

Individual and family level

Regulative abilities

The emerging literature stresses the impact of trauma on regulative abilities in various domains, including regulation of physiological arousal (e.g., hyperarousal), cognitive regulation (e.g., executive functioning), emotional regulation (e.g., anger) and interpersonal regulation (e.g., aggressive behavior). It is thus imperative that trauma-informed interventions aimed at reducing aggression include active components for enhancing self-regulation. This approach needs to address self-regulation in various domains through psychoeducation, experiential exercises and creating synergy between practicing relaxation, mindfulness and cognitive, emotional and interpersonal regulation.

An example of a skills program for enhancing the ability to regulate emotion and affect was recently introduced and piloted in Singapore with children living in children's homes. The Building Emotion and Affect Regulation (BEAR) program (Pat-Horenczyk, Bar-Halpern et al., 2012) aims at enhancing regulation abilities in the physiological, cognitive, emotional and social domains among children affected by trauma. The BEAR program is comprised of group sessions in which the children practice identification of emotions, expression and modulation of affect, alternative scripts and enhancing flexibility and creativity. Preliminary evidence from implementation of this program in children's homes in Singapore indicates the importance of practicing the central concepts of self-regulation and skills on a regular basis so that they can be assimilated into the daily routine (Pat-Horenczyk, Schramm, & Bar-Halpern, 2012).

Strengthening the parent–child relationship

It is important to identify exposure to violence even before children turn 3 years old, as this offers a chance for early intervention (Tremblay, 2006), and it is known that young children are more susceptible to violence than older children (Sternberg et al., 2006). Recent research on young children exposed to enemy violence, both in the USA and in Israel, has shown the severe impact of ongoing exposure to terrorism and missile attacks on young children's behavior (Chemtob et al., 2010; Pat-Horenczyk, & Achituv et al., 2012; Pat-Horenczyk et al., in press). These studies have led to the development of programs for both treating posttraumatic distress in young children and mothers and building resilience in early childhood.

One recent Israeli example of a parenting program is "Make Room for Play" (Cohen, Pat-Horenczyk, & Haar-Shamir, in press). Based on the premise that play and playfulness can contribute to resilience, the preventive group-intervention program "Make Room for Play" was designed for mothers and their toddlers living under the chronic stress of recurrent missile attacks in Israel. This is a program for strengthening parent–child attachment and joint play as a way to enhance coping with the continual threat of enemy violence. The major objective of the program is to bolster children's resilience by enhancing co-regulation of arousal and increasing playful interactions with their parents (see Chapter 6 in this book). This increased ability to regulate emotions may lead to better emotional control and reduction of impulsive and aggressive behavior.

Community level

School-based interventions

School-based programs have been developed to identify post traumatic distress in children and provide a range of interventions, from treatment of post traumatic symptoms for affected students (clinical interventions) to building resilience for the entire school (universal intervention) (Pat-Horenczyk et al., 2011). There are also group programs in schools and community groups that are intended to build protective factors against exposure to violence. Peer involvement and support appear to be important change mechanisms involved in the extinguishing of aggressive behavior, with programs involving peer mediation showing especially promising results (Garrard & Lipsey, 2007). In addition to the effective psychoeducational component for reduction of aggression that has been implemented in most programs for reduction of violence (Horne, Stoddard, & Bell, 2007), there is growing interest in the inclusion of prosocial activities as an effective way of preventing aggression.

Programs that foster social and competency skills have been effective in violence prevention, and are particularly effective in early childhood (Office of the Surgeon General (U.S.), 2001). Successful social development programs also need to focus on competency and social skills, such as anger management, improving social skills and resolving conflicts, so as to reduce aggressive and antisocial behavior. For example, there is evidence that high prosocial values are negatively associated with aggressive behavior (Valiente & Eisenberg, 2006). Further, children who have failed to adopt prosocial values and norms have difficulty making decisions that include other people's needs, feelings and rights (Hastings, Zhan-Waxler, Robinson, Usher, & Bridges, 2000; Ludwig & Pittman, 1999). Children exposed to trauma develop feelings of mistrust that may persist through adolescence and adulthood (Crawford & Wright, 2007), making them more prone to use aggressive behavior. Research has suggested that growing up in a violent, unstable environment also limits exposure to behaviorally competent, prosocial scripts (Dodge et al., 1990). Recent support for this view comes from Şahin (2012), whose results show the efficacy of empathy training programs on preventing bullying in primary schools. Therefore, interventions focusing on cognitive restructuring, prosocial scripts, strengthening social support, enhancing the ability for empathy and encouraging altruistic behavior are suggested as effective program components for reducing aggressive behavior in children.

National level

It takes a village to raise a child (Clinton, 1996). A child is nested in a family, which is nested in a community, which is nested in a culture. A possible important direction for violence reduction involves broad national and international campaigns. One such program aimed specifically at violence reduction is the "City Without Violence" initiative conducted throughout Israel (see http://www.cwv.gov.il/English/Pages/default.aspx). The program focuses on dealing with a broad range of antisocial behavior—including violence, delinquency and crime—in local communities. The program's aim is to enhance the residents' sense of personal security by combining five circles of activity: (a) law enforcement, (b) education, (c) regulation of youth recreational time, (d) the welfare of those affected by violence and (e) presentation of the program to the general public. The guiding principles focus on a number of policies: zero tolerance towards violence; effective, unambiguous responses; extensive cooperation among all relevant authorities in the city; strengthening municipal sovereignty and the rule of law; creating an accepted, city-wide, unified language on the subject; and many others.

The program is currently being implemented in 80 cities and municipalities throughout Israel. However, this campaign may further benefit from a perspective based on studies of trauma and resilience.

A similarly successful program is the Community Initiative to Reduce Violence (CIRV), an initiative founded in 2008 aimed at reduction of gang violence across Glasgow. The CIRV's approach focuses on deterrence, bringing together partners from different fields such as justice, government and the community. Two years after the program began, reports indicated a drop of almost 50% in violent offences by gang members who had signed up to CIRV (see http://www.actiononviolence. co.uk/CIRV).

Consistent with these attempts, WHO recently published a Global Campaign for Violence Prevention "Plan of Action for 2012–2020" (Butchart, Mikton, & Kieselbach, 2012) prepared by WHO's Prevention of Violence Team on behalf of the Violence Prevention Alliance—that aims to unify international efforts to prevent violence and to set priorities for interventions. Its first aim is to "prioritize violence prevention within the global public health agenda," followed by recommendations to establish "foundations for on-going violence prevention efforts" and to implement evidence-informed programs for families, enhancing life skills, teaching social norms and addressing the risk of alcohol abuse (Butchart et al., 2012, p. 3).

From our clinical experience in the field of trauma and resilience, the success of such comprehensive intervention models is heavily dependent on the ability to coordinate, plan continuity of services and create a unified language and synergy among the various ecological systems. A perspective based on studies of trauma and resilience can be useful in understanding the link between exposure to violence and aggressive behavior, as well as aiding in the implementation of intervention programs. Based on the known advantages of a comprehensive ecological model (Bronfenbrenner, 1979), it is time to integrate an approach based on studies of trauma and resilience with programs to reduce exposure to violence and create synergy among the individual, family, community and national levels.

In conclusion, the association between exposure to trauma and violence and aggression in children is a complex one. In this chapter, we called attention to the potential role of trauma in the development of aggressive behavior and discussed moderating and mediating factors leading to aggressive behavior. We acknowledge that not all trauma leads to aggressive behavior and not all aggression is rooted in trauma. Furthermore, traumatized children do not necessarily externalize or internalize aggression. Some children are resilient and show remarkable ability to cope and adapt despite even heavy exposure to violence and trauma. Resilience factors such as secure attachment, optimism and self-efficacy are possible mediators that allow children to process their experiences, create meaning and rise above their personal experiences. After exposure to violence, trajectories of both aggressive and resilient behavior in children remain a challenge to be explored in future research.

References

Adler, L. A., Kunz, M., Chua, H. C., Rotrosen, J., & Resnick, S. G. (2004). Attention-deficit/hyperactivity disorder in adult patients with posttraumatic stress disorder (PTSD): Is ADHD a vulnerability factor? *Journal of Attention Disorders*, *8*(1), 11–16.

Allwood, M. A., & Bell, D. J. (2008). A preliminary examination of emotional and cognitive mediators in the relations between violence exposure and violent behaviors in youth. *Journal of Community Psychology*, *36*(8), 989–1007.

Asarnow, J. R., & Callan, J. W. (1985). Boys with peer adjustment problems: Social cognitive processes. *Journal of Consulting and Clinical Psychology*, *53*(1), 80–87.

Bandura, A. (1973). *Aggression: A social learning analysis*. Englewood Cliffs, NJ: Prentice-Hall.

Bandura, A. (1978). Social learning theory of aggression. *Journal of Communication*, *28*(3), 12–29.

Barber, B. K. (2008). Contrasting portraits of war: Youths' varied experiences with political violence in Bosnia and Palestine. *International Journal of Behavioral Development*, *32*(4), 298–309.

Barkin, S., Kreiter, S., & DuRant, R. H. (2001). Exposure to violence and intentions to engage in moralistic violence during early adolescence. *Journal of Adolescence*, *24*(6), 777–789.

Barroso, C. S., Peters, R. J., Kelder, S., Conroy, J., Murray, N., & Orpinas, P. (2008). Youth exposure to community violence: Association with aggression, victimization, and risk behaviors. *Journal of Aggression, Maltreatment & Trauma*, *17*(2), 141–155.

Beckman, M. (2004). Neuroscience: Crime, culpability, and the adolescent brain. *Science*, *305*(5684), 596–599.

Bellmore, A. D., Witkow, M. R., Graham, S., & Juvonen, J. (2005). From beliefs to behavior: The mediating role of hostile response selection in predicting aggression. *Aggressive Behavior*, *31*(5), 453–472.

Bronfenbrenner, U. (1979). *The ecology of human development: Experiments by nature and design*. Cambridge, MA: Harvard University Press.

Bryant, R. A., & Harvey, A. G. (1995). Processing threatening information in posttraumatic stress disorder. *Journal of Abnormal Psychology*, *104*(3), 537–541.

Buka, S. L., Stichick, T. L., Birdthistle, I., & Earls, F. J. (2001). Youth exposure to violence: Prevalence, risks, and consequences. *American Journal of Orthopsychiatry*, *71*(3), 298–310.

Butchart, A., Mikton, C., & Kieselbach, B.; World Health Organization (WHO). (2012). Violence Prevention Alliance (VPA) & Global Campaign for Violence Prevention (GCVP): Plan of Action for 2012–2020 [online]. Geneva, Switzerland, 21 May 2012. Retrieved from http://www.who.int/violence_injury_prevention/violence/global_campaign/gcvp_plan_of_action.pdf

Cacioppo, J. T., & Gardner, W. L. (1999). Emotion. In J. T. Spence, J. M. Darley & D. J. Foss, *Annual Review of Psychology* (Vol. 50, pp. 191–214). Palo Alto, CA: Annual Reviews.

Center for the Study and Prevention of Violence (2004). Blueprints for violence prevention: overview and model programs. Boulder, CO. Retrieved from www.colorado.edu/cspv/blueprints/index.html

Chemtob, C. M., Nomura, Y., Rajendran, K., Yehuda, R., Schwartz, D., & Abramovitz, R. (2010). Impact of maternal posttraumatic stress disorder and depression following exposure to the September 11 attacks on preschool children's behavior. *Child Development, 81*(4), 1129–1141.

Clinton, H. R. (1996). *It takes a village: And other lessons children teach us.* New York, NY: Simon and Schuster.

Cloitre, M., Koenen, K. C., Cohen, L. R., & Han, H. (2002). Skills training in affective and interpersonal regulation followed by exposure: A phase-based treatment for PTSD related to childhood abuse. *Journal of Consulting and Clinical Psychology, 70*(5), 1067–1074.

Cohen, E., Pat-Horenczyk, R., & Haar-Shamir, D. (in press). Making room for play: An empirically-informed intervention for toddlers and families under rocket fire. *Journal of Clinical Social Work.*

Crane-Ross, D., Tisak, M. S., & Tisak, J. (1998). Aggression and conventional rule violation among adolescents: Social reasoning predictors of social behavior. *Aggressive Behavior, 24*(5), 347–365.

Crawford, E., & Wright, M. O. (2007). The impact of childhood psychological maltreatment on interpersonal schemas and subsequence experiences of relationship aggression. *Journal of Emotional Abuse, 7*(2), 93–116.

Crittenden, P. M., & Ainsworth, M. D. S. (1989). Child maltreatment and attachment theory. In D. Cicchetti (Ed.), *Child maltreatment: Theory and research on the causes and consequences of child abuse and neglect* (pp. 432–463). New York, NY: Cambridge University Press.

Dari, E. (2011). Embedded violence and youth: The transmission and perpetuation of violence in post-war Sierra Leone (Master's thesis, University of St Andrews). Retrieved from International Relations Theses collection, University of St Andrews Digital Repository, St Andrews University Library.

Dawes, A. (1990). The effects of political violence on children: A consideration of South African and related studies. *International Journal of Psychology, 25*(1), 13–31.

Dodge, K. A. (1980). Social cognition and children's aggressive behavior. *Child Development, 51*(1), 162–170.

Dodge, K. A. (2006). Translational science in action: Hostile attributional style and the development of aggressive behavior problems. *Development and Psychopathology, 18*(3), 791–814.

Dodge, K. A., Bates, J. E., & Pettit, G. S. (1990). Mechanisms in the cycle of violence. *Science, 250*(4988), 1678–1683.

Dodge, K. A., Laird, R., Lochman, J. E., & Zelli, A. (2003). Multidimensional latent-construct analysis of children's social information processing patterns: Correlations with aggressive behavior problems. *Psychological Assessment, 14*(1), 60–73.

Dodge, K. A., & Newman, J. P. (1981). Biased decision-making processes in aggressive boys. *Journal of Abnormal Psychology, 90*(4), 375–379.

Dodge, K. A., Pettit, G. S., Bates, J. E., & Valente, E. (1995). Social information-processing patterns partially mediate the effect of early physical abuse on later conduct problems. *Journal of Abnormal Psychology, 104*(4), 632–643.

Dodge, K. A., & Tomlin, A. M. (1987). Utilization of self-schemas as a mechanism of interpretational bias in aggressive children. *Social Cognition, 5*(3), 280–300.

Dubow, E. F., Huesmann, L. R., & Boxer, P. (2009). A social-cognitive-ecological framework for understanding the impact of exposure to persistent ethnic-political violence on children's psychosocial adjustment. *Clinical Child and Family Psychology Review, 12*(2), 113–126.

Egeland, B., Yates, T., Appleyard, K., & van Dulmen, M. (2002). The long-term consequences of maltreatment in the early years: A developmental pathway model to antisocial behavior. *Children's Services: Social Policy, Research, and Practice*, *5*(4), 249–260.

Eth, S., & Pynoos, R. S. (Eds.). (1985). *Post-traumatic stress in children*. Washington D.C.: American Psychiatric Press.

Evans, S. E., Davies, D., & DiLillo, D. (2008) Exposure to domestic violence: A meta-analysis of child and adolescent outcomes. *Aggression and Violent Behavior*, *13*(2), 131–140.

Evans, S. W., & Short, E. J. (1991). A qualitative and serial analysis of social problem-solving in aggressive boys. *Journal of Abnormal Child Psychology*, *19*(3), 331–340.

Fanon, F. (1979). *The wretched of the earth*. New York, NY: Grove Press.

Fisher, L., & Blair, R. J. R. (1998). Cognitive impairment and its relationship to psychopathic tendencies in children with emotional and behavioral difficulties. *Journal of Abnormal Child Psychology*, *26*(6), 511–519.

Flannery, D. J., Singer, M. I., & Wester, K. L. (2001). Violence exposure, psychological trauma, and suicide risk in a community sample of dangerously violent adolescents. *Journal of the American Academy of Child and Adolescent Psychiatry*, *40*(4), 435–442.

Flannery, D. J., Wester, K. L., & Singer, M. I. (2004). Impact of exposure to violence in school on child and adolescent mental health and behavior. *Journal of Community Psychology*, *32*(5), 559–573.

Foa, E. B., Feske, U., Murdock, T. B., Kozak, M. J., & McCarthy, P. R. (1991). Processing of threat-related information in rape victims. *Journal of Abnormal Psychology*, *100*(2), 156–162.

Garrard, W. M., & Lipsey, M. W. (2007). Conflict resolution education and antisocial behavior in U. S. schools: A meta-analysis. *Conflict Resolution Quarterly 25*(1), 9–38.

Gellman, R. A., & Delucia-Waack, J. L. (2006). Predicting school violence: A comparison of violent and nonviolent male students on attitudes towards violence, exposure to violence, and PTSD symptomatology. *Psychology in the Schools*, *43*(5), 591–598.

Giedd, J. N. (2004). Structural magnetic resonance imaging of the adolescent brain. *Annals of the New York Academy of Sciences*, *1021*, 105–109.

Graham, S., & Hudley, C. (1994). Attributions of aggressive and nonaggressive African-American male early adolescents: A study of construct accessibility. *Developmental Psychology*, *30*(3), 365–373.

Greenwood, P. W. (2006). Cost-effective violence prevention through targeted family interventions. *Annals of the New York Academy of Sciences*, *1036*(1), 201–214.

Griffin, K. W., Scheier, L. M., Botvin, G. J., Diaz, T., & Mille, N. (1999). Interpersonal aggression in urban minority youth: Mediators of perceived neighborhood, peer, and parental influences. *Journal of Community Psychology*, *27*(3), 281–298.

Guerra, N. G., Huesmann, L. R., & Spindler, A. J. (2003). Community violence exposure, social cognition, and aggression among urban elementary school children. *Child Development*, *74*(5), 1561–1576.

Guerra, N. G., Huesmann, L. R., Tolan, P. H., Van Acker, R., & Eron, L. (1995). Stressful events and individual beliefs as correlates of economic disadvantage and aggression among urban children. *Journal of Consulting and Clinical Psychology*, *63*(4), 518–528.

Hastings, P. D., Zhan-Waxler, C., Robinson, J., Usher, B., & Bridges, D. (2000). The development of concern for others in children with behavior problems. *Developmental Psychology*, *36*(5), 531–546.

Heide, K. M. & Solomon, E. P. (2006). Biology, childhood trauma, and murder: Rethinking justice. *International Journal of Law and Psychiatry*, *29*(3), 220–223.

Horne, A. M., Stoddard, J. L., & Bell, C. D. (2007). Group approaches to reducing aggression and bullying in school. *Group Dynamics: Theory, Research, and Practice*, *11*(4), 262–271.

Huesmann, L. R. (1988). An information processing model for the development of aggression. *Aggressive Behavior*, *14*(1), 13–44.

Huesmann, L. R. (1998). The role of social information processing and cognitive schemas in the acquisition and maintenance of habitual aggressive behavior. In R. G. Green & E. I. Donnerstein (Eds.), *Human aggression: Theories, research and implications for policy* (pp. 73–109). New York, NY: Academic Press.

Huesmann, L. R., & Eron, L. D. (1989). Individual differences and the trait of aggression. *European Journal of Personality*, *3*(2), 95–106.

Huesmann, L. R., & Eron, L. D. (1992). Childhood aggression and adult criminality. In J. McCord (Ed.). *Facts, frameworks, and forecasts: Advances in criminological theory* (Vol. 3, pp. 137–156). New Brunswick, NJ: Transaction Publishers.

Huesmann, L. R., & Kirwil, L. (2007). Why observing violence increases the risk of violent behavior by the observer. In D. J. Flannery, A. T. Vazsonyi & I. D. Waldman (Eds.), *The Cambridge handbook of violent behavior and aggression* (pp. 545–570). New York, NY: Cambridge University Press.

Hughes, H. M. (1988). Psychological and behavioral correlates of family violence in child witnesses and victims. *American Journal of Orthopsychiatry*, *58*(1), 77–90.

Husain, S. A., Allwood, M. A., & Bell, D. J. (2008). The relationship between PTSD symptoms and attention problems in children exposed to the Bosnian War. *Journal of Emotional and Behavioral Disorders*, *16*(1), 52–62.

Jaycox, L. H., Morse, L. K., Tanielian, T. L., & Stein, B. D. (2006). *How schools can help students recover from traumatic experiences: A tool-kit for supporting long-term recovery*. Santa Monica, CA: Rand Gulf States Policy Institute. Retrieved from http://site.ebrary.com/id/10225473

Kaspi, S. P., McNally, R. J., & Amir, N. (1995). Cognitive processing of emotional information in posttraumatic disorder. *Cognitive Therapy and Research*, *19*(4), 433–444.

Kaya, F., Bilgin, H., & Singer, M. I. (2011). Contributing factors to aggressive behaviors in high school students in Turkey. *The Journal of School Nursing*, *28*(1), 56–69.

Kereteš, G. (2006). Children's aggressive and prosocial behavior in relation to war exposure. *International Journal of Behavioral Development*, *30*(3), 227–239.

Lochman, J. E., & Lenhart, L. A. (1993). Anger coping intervention for aggressive children: Conceptual models and outcome effects. *Clinical Psychology Review*, *13*(8), 785–805.

Ludwig, K. B. & Pittman, J. F. (1999). Adolescent prosocial values and self-efficacy in relation to delinquency, risky sexual behavior, and drug use. *Youth & Society*, *30*(4), 461–482.

Massetti, G. M., Vivolo, A. M., Brookmeyer, K., DeGue, S., Holland, K. M., Holt, M. K., et al. (2011). Preventing youth violence perpetration among girls. *Journal of Women's Health*, *20*(10), 1415–1428.

Molitor, F., & Hirsch, K. W. (1994). Children's toleration of real-life aggression after exposure to media violence: A replication of the Drabman and Thomas studies. *Child Study Journal*, *24*(3), 191–208.

Moradi, A. R., Neshat-Doost, H. T., Taghavi, R., Yule, W., & Dalgleish, T. (1999). Performance of children of adults with PTSD on the Stroop color-naming task: A preliminary study. *Journal of Traumatic Stress*, *12*(4), 663–671.

Morgan, C. A. III, Grillon, C., Southwick, S. M., Davis, M., & Charney, D. S. (1996). Exaggerated acoustic startle reflex in Gulf War veterans with posttraumatic stress disorder. *The American Journal of Psychiatry*, *153*(1), 64–68.

Morgan, M. A., & LeDoux, J. E. (1995). Differential acquisition of dorsal and ventral medial prefrontal cortex to the acquisition and extinction of conditioned fear in rats. *Behavioral Neuroscience*, *109*(4), 681–688.

Moylan, C. A., Herrenkohl, T. I., Sousa, C., Tajima, E. A., Herrenkohl, R. C., & Russo, M. J. (2009). The effects of child abuse and exposure to domestic violence on adolescent internalizing and externalizing behavior problems. *Journal of Family Violence*, *25*(1), 53–63.

Ng-Mak, D. S., Salzinger, S., Feldman, R. S., & Stueve, C. A., (2004). Pathologic adaptation to community violence among inner-city youth. *American Journal of Orthopsychiatry*, *74*(2), 196–208.

Office of the Surgeon General (U.S.). (2001). Youth violence: A report of the surgeon general. Rockville, MD: U.S. Department of Health and Human Services.

O'Keefe, M. (1994). Linking marital violence, mother-child/father-child aggression, and child behavior problems. *Journal of Family Violence*, *9*(1), 63–78.

Ornitz, E. M., & Pynoos, R. S. (1989). Startle modulation in children with posttraumatic stress disorder. *American Journal of Psychiatry*, *146*(7), 866–870.

Orue, I., Bushman, B. J., Calvete, E., Thomaes, S., de Castro, B. O., & Hutteman, R. (2011). Monkey see, monkey do, monkey hurt: Longitudinal effects of exposure to violence on children's aggressive behavior. *Social Psychological and Personality Science*, *2*(4), 432–437.

Ozkol, H., Zucker, M., & Spinazzola, J. (2011). Pathways to aggression in urban elementary school youth. *Journal of Community Psychology*, *39*(6), 733–748.

Pakaslahti, L. (2000). Children's and adolescents' aggressive behavior in context: The development and application of aggressive problem solving strategies. *Aggression and Violent Behavior*, *5*(5), 467–490.

Pat-Horenczyk, R., Abramovitz, R., Peled, O., Brom, D., Daie, A., & Chemtob, C. M. (2007). Adolescent exposure to recurrent terrorism in Israel: Posttraumatic distress and functional impairment. *American Journal of Orthopsychiatry*, *77*(1), 76–85.

Pat-Horenczyk, R., Achituv, M., Kagan-Rubenstein, A., Khodabakhsh, A., Brom, D. & Chemtob, C. M. (2012). Growing up under fire: Building resilience in young children and parents exposed to ongoing missile attacks. *Journal of Child & Adolescent Trauma*, *5*(4), 303–314.

Pat-Horenczyk, R., Brom, D., Baum. N., Benbenishty, R., Schiff, M. & Astor, R. A. (2011). A city-wide school-based model for addressing the needs of children exposed to terrorism and war. In V. Ardino (Ed.) *Post-traumatic syndromes in childhood and adolescence* (pp. 243–254). New York, NY: Wiley/Blackwell.

Pat-Horenczyk, R., Ziv, Y., Asulin-Peretz, L., Achituv, M., Cohen, S. & Brom, D. (in press). Relational trauma in times of political violence: Continuous traumatic stress vs. past trauma. *Peace and Conflict: Journal of Peace Psychology*.

Pat-Horenczyk, R., Bar-Halpern, M., Schramm, S., Miron, T., Asulin-Peretz, L., Achituv, M., et al. (2012). BEAR: Building Emotion and Affect Regulation. An intervention protocol and a facilitator guide. Jerusalem: Israel Center for the Treatment of Psychotrauma.

Pat-Horenczyk, R., Schramm, S., & Bar-Halpern, M. (2012). Report on the BEAR Project conducted with the Ministry of Community Development, Youth and Sports (MCYS), Singapore.

Perry, D. G., Perry, L. C., & Rasmussen, P. (1986). Cognitive social learning mediators of aggression. *Child Development, 57*(3), 700–711.

Phinney, J. S. (1990). Ethnic identity in adolescents and adults: Review of research. *Psychological Bulletin, 108*(3), 499–514.

Pitman, R. K., van der Kolk, B. A., Orr, S. P., & Greenberg, M. S. (1990). Naloxone-reversible analgesic response to combat-related stimuli in posttraumatic stress disorder: A pilot study. *Archives of General Psychiatry, 47*(6), 541–544.

Power, M., & Dalgleish, T. (1997). *Cognition and emotion: From order to disorder.* Hove, Sussex: Psychology Press.

Punamäki, R.-L. (2009). War and military violence and aggressive development: Child, family and social preconditions. In B. K. Barber (Ed.), *Adolescents and war: How youth deal with political violence* (pp. 62–80). New York, NY: Oxford University Press.

Qouta, S., & El-Sarraj, E. (1992). Curfew and children's mental health. *Journal of Psychological Studies, 4*, 13–18.

Qouta, S., Punamäki, R. L., & El-Sarraj, E. (2008). Child development and family mental health in war and military violence: The Palestinian experience. *International Journal of Behavioral Development, 32*(4), 310–321.

Ross, E. D., Homan, R. W., & Buck, R. (1994). Differential hemispheric lateralization of primary and social emotions: Implications for developing a comprehensive neurology for emotions, repression, and the subconscious. *Neuropsychiatry, Neuropsychology, and Behavioral Neurology, 7*(1), 1–19.

Ruchkin, V., Henrich, C. C., Jones, S. M., Vermeiren, R., & Schwab-Stone, M. (2007). Violence exposure and psychopathology in urban youth: The mediating role of posttraumatic stress. *Journal of Abnormal Child Psychology, 35*(4), 578–593.

Şahin, M. (2012). An investigation into the efficiency of empathy training program on preventing bullying in primary schools. *Children and Youth Services Review, 34*(7), 1325–1330.

Schore, A. N. (2002). Dysregulation of the right brain: A fundamental mechanism of traumatic attachment and the psychopathogenesis of posttraumatic stress disorder. *Australian and New Zealand Journal of Psychiatry, 36*(1), 9–30.

Schore, A. N. (2003a). *Affect dysregulation and disorders of the self.* New York, NY: W. W. Norton.

Schore, A. N. (2003b). Early relational trauma, disorganized attachment, and the development of a predisposition to violence. In M. F. Solomon & D. J. Siegel (Eds.), *Healing trauma: Attachment, mind, body, and brain* (Chapter 3). New York, NY: W. W. Norton.

Seginer, R. (2008). Future orientation in times of threat and challenge: How resilient adolescents construct their future. *International Journal of Behavioral Development, 32*(4), 272–282.

Shahinfar, A., Kupersmidt, J. B., & Matza, L. S. (2001). The relation between exposure to violence and social information processing among incarcerated adolescents. *Journal of Abnormal Psychology, 110*(1), 136–141.

Shalev, A. Y., Peri, T., Brandes, D., Freedman, S., Orr, S. P., & Pitman, R. K. (2000). Auditory startle response in trauma survivors with posttraumatic stress disorder: A prospective study. *American Journal of Psychiatry, 157*(2), 255–261.

Shin, L. M., McNally, R. J., Kosslyn, S. M., Thompson, W. L., Rauch, S. L., Alpert, N. M., et al. (1999). Regional cerebral blood flow during script-driven imagery in childhood sexual abuse-related PTSD: A PET Investigation. *The American Journal of Psychiatry, 156*(4), 575–584.

Slaby, R. G., & Guerra, N. G. (1988). Cognitive mediators of aggression in adolescent offenders: I. Assessment. *Developmental Psychology, 24*(4), 580–588.

Sternberg, K. J., Lamb, M. E., Guterman, E., & Abbott, C. B. (2006). Effects of early and later family violence on children's behavior problems and depression: A longitudinal, multi-informant perspective. *Child Abuse & Neglect, 30*(3), 283–306.

Tajfel, H. (1982). Social psychology of intergroup relations. In M. R. Rosenzweig & L. W. Porter, *Annual Review of Psychology* (Vol. 33, pp. 1–39). Palo Alto, CA: Annual Reviews.

Tajfel, H., & Turner, J. C. (1979). An integrative theory of intergroup conflict. In W. G. Austin & S. Worchel (Eds.), *The social psychology of intergroup relations* (pp. 33–47). Monterey, CA: Brooks/Cole.

Tajfel, H., & Turner, J. C. (1986). The social identity theory of intergroup behavior. In S. Worchel & W. G. Austin (Eds.), *Psychology of intergroup relations* (pp. 7–24). Chicago, IL: Nelson-Hall.

Tremblay, R. E. (2006). Prevention of youth violence: Why not start at the beginning? *Journal of Abnormal Child Psychology, 34*(4), 480–486.

United States Department of Veterans Affairs. (2007). DSM criteria for PTSD. In National Center for PTSD [online], United States Department of Veterans Affairs. July 5, 2007. Retrieved from http://www.ptsd.va.gov/professional/pages/dsm-iv-tr-ptsd.asp

U.S. Department of Justice. (2003). Safe harbor: A school-based victim assistance/violence prevention program. *OVC Bulletin* [online], January 2003. Safe Horizon, New York; Office for Victims of Crime, Office of Justice Programs, U.S. Department of Justice. Retrieved from: http://www.ojp.usdoj.gov/ovc/publications/bulletins/safehabor_2003/193464.pdf (accessed February 2013).

Valiente, C. Eisenberg, N. (2006). Parenting and children's adjustment: The role of children's emotion regulation. In D. K. Snyder, J. Simpson, J. N. Hughes (Eds.), *Emotion regulation in couples and families: Pathways to dysfunction and health* (pp. 123–142). Washington, DC: American Psychological Association. doi: 10.1037/11468006.

van der Kolk, B. A. (2005). Developmental trauma disorder. *Psychiatric Annals, 35*(5), 401–409.

van der Kolk, B. A., & Andrea, W. D. (2010). Towards a developmental trauma disorder diagnosis for childhood interpersonal trauma. In R. A., Lanius, E., Vermetten & C., Pain (Eds.), *The impact of early life trauma on health and disease. The hidden epidemic* (pp. 57–68). Cambridge University Press.

van der Kolk, B. A., & Fisler, R. E. (1994). Childhood abuse and neglect and loss of self-regulation. *Bulletin of the Menninger Clinic, 58*(2), 145.

van der Kolk, B. A., Greenberg, M. S., Orr, S. P., & Pitman, R. K. (1989). Endogenous opioids, stress induced analgesia, and posttraumatic stress disorder. *Psychopharmacology Bulletin, 25*(3), 417–421.

Vigil-Colet, A. & Codorniu-Raga, M. J. (2004). Aggression and inhibition deficits, the role of functional and dysfunctional impulsivity. *Personality and Individual Differences*, *37*(7), 1431–1440.

Wang, Y., Nomura, Y., Pat-Horenczyk, R., Doppelt, O., Abramovitz, R., Brom, D., et al. (2006). Association of direct exposure to terrorism, media exposure to terrorism, and other trauma with emotional and behavioral problems in preschool children. *Annals of the New York Academy of Sciences*, *1094*(1), 363–368.

Weems, C. F., Saltzman, K. M., Reiss, A. L., & Carrion, V. G. (2003). A prospective test of the association between hyperarousal and emotional numbing in youth with a history of traumatic stress. *Journal of Clinical Child and Adolescent Psychology*, *32*(1), 166–171.

Wolpe, J. (1973). *The practice of behavior therapy* (2nd ed.). Oxford: Pergamon.

World Health Organization. (2010). *Violence prevention: The evidence*. Department of Violence and Injury Prevention and Disability, World Health Organization; Centre for Public Health, WHO Collaborating Centre for Violence Prevention, Liverpool John Moores University, UK. Geneva, Switzerland: WHO Press. Available at: http://apps. who.int/iris/bitstream/10665/77936/1/9789241500845_eng.pdf

Yehuda, R., Lowy, M. T., Southwick, S. M., Shaffer, D., & Giller, E. L. (1991). Lymphocyte glucocorticoid receptor number in posttraumatic stress disorder. *American Journal of Psychiatry*, *148*(4), 499–504.

Chapter 4

Childhood bereavement and traumatic loss

*Naomi L. Baum, Rebecca S. Ginat
and Phyllis R. Silverman*

When a child loses a significant person in his or her life, this can impact both the child's developmental trajectory, affecting their psychological wellbeing, as well as their life circumstances, which may alter greatly. Whether or not the loss is objectively classified as a traumatic loss, the interplay between grief and trauma is ever-present in all situations of the death of a significant attachment figure such as a parent. Even when a person's death is anticipated after a long illness, the subjective reaction of family members may be one of shock and disbelief, and is often accompanied by symptoms that we might consider post traumatic. When a child loses a family member, particularly a parent, this death will necessarily be shocking, no matter how long it has been anticipated or how well prepared the child is. Due to the nature of young children's cognitive ability, their preparedness and ability to project into the future are limited. Understanding children's loss of significant family members in cases of both normal and traumatic grief reactions can help to suggest appropriate community interventions and treatment approaches, which can help both the children and their families at this critical juncture.

Acceptance of loss as an inevitable part of life lies at the root of our understanding of bereavement and grief. The need to categorize and describe stages and phases of grief derives from our need for control in a situation, which is, by its nature, more out of control than anything else. Understanding children's grief reactions as part of a normal, albeit painful, process will help to pave the way for interventions that are not the specific bailiwick of the "grief professional" or the mental health professional, but can be utilized in schools, places of worship and community centers. The normative acceptance of loss and grief will go a long way toward helping those who have experienced loss and are grieving to receive support and understanding. However, support and empathy alone may not be sufficient for all kinds of loss, particularly those that may be more traumatic.

In this chapter we explore the effects of early loss on children and consider appropriate interventions for helping them during this difficult time. We begin with an overview of normative grieving, as a means for discussing more complex forms of grief. Traumatic grief and complicated grief are two such forms. Traumatic grief refers to a loss that occurs under traumatic circumstances, which may be either subjective or objective. Complicated grief involves prolonged grief reactions accompanied by impairment in daily functioning. While the term "traumatic grief" is useful for understanding children's reactions and planning interventions, we use the term "complicated grief" more cautiously, to avoid the overmedicalization of a life event and to address specific needs that may interfere with normal childhood development. In this chapter, we will conclude with two case studies—one a clinical intervention and the second a community intervention—to provide examples of how children who are experiencing loss can be helped.

While the loss of a parent is an exceptional event in the life of a child, it is more common than one might think. The U.S. Social Security Administration (2000) estimates that 4% of children in the United States experience the loss of a parent before the age of 18, leaving approximately 1.9 million children under the age of 18 orphaned (Children's Bereavement Center of South Texas, 2008). While there are no reliable estimates, it can be assumed that many more children lose a sibling, grandparent or peer before age 10 (Batts, 2004). In the United Kingdom, it has been estimated that 40 children are bereaved each day as a consequence of the death of a parent (Lowton & Higginson, 2003).

While the death of a family member affects everyone, the world changes immeasurably for children in particular when they lose a parent—and, the younger the children, the more radically their life will be impacted. From living arrangements to who makes their lunch in the morning, a world that was once safe and familiar can appear foreign, uncertain and unstable (Green & Connolly, 2009). While adults realize that life will go on even following terrible loss, children typically do not have this perspective (Silverman, 2000). It is often hard for a child to imagine how life *can* go on, when so much has changed in his or her life as result of bereavement. These changes include shifting relationships in their family, community and with friends, and also frequently include changes in economic circumstances (Auman, 2007; Silverman, 2000).

When a child loses a significant family member, be it parent or sibling, they must deal not only with their own loss, but that of their surviving parent(s) as well. In addition, there may be significant feelings of rivalry, guilt and/or resentment, which may be difficult to acknowledge at this time (Auman, 2007). Research has shown that the way a surviving parent (or parents) handles his or her own grief has a large impact on the child's overall functioning following the loss (Wolchik, Ma, Tein, Sandler, & Ayers, 2008). Parents and caregivers who are able to maintain greater continuity with life prior to the loss, and lower levels of disruption in their child's day-to-day life, can prevent maladaptive coping styles, including emotional dysregulation, in their children (Luecken, Kraft, Appelhans, & Enders, 2009). Furthermore, particularly with the loss of a parent, the surviving parent becomes "the repositories of memory, of family history, and of continuity in the family" (Silverman, 2000, p.109). The surviving parent's openness to discussing the loss of the deceased with their children, and thus mediating the child's own grief experience, is paramount (Packman, Horsley, Davies, & Kramer, 2006).

There is no one normal way to grieve following the loss of a loved one. This cannot be underscored enough, and it can provide reassurance for parents and children who are grieving to know that there is a range of normative responses (Silverman, 2000; Worden, 1996). The term "uncomplicated bereavement" has been used (Cohen & Mannarino, 2004; Cohen, Mannarino, Greenberg, Padlo, & Shipley, 2002) to refer to the normative grieving process, offering a spectrum of reactions experienced by children and adults following the death of a loved one. Many of these normative reactions share characteristics with symptoms of clinical depression. They may include sadness, difficulty sleeping, loss of appetite, lack of interest in day-to-day activities and difficulty concentrating (Mannarino & Cohen, 2011). The current literature views uncomplicated grieving as a process that leads to a resolution, with the time required for such resolution typically left unspecified (Breen & O'Connor, 2007; Wortman & Silver, 1989). For some, it may be a matter of months, while for others it may be years, but, in either case, the loss will accompany both children and adults for a lifetime. Adults show great variance in both the way they grieve and the time it takes for this process to unfold. To better understand children's grieving process, it is imperative to look at the age variable to understand how children experience the loss of a loved one.

Children under the age of two often suffer separation anxiety, and mirror the distress expressed by their caregiver (Himebauch, Arnold, & May, 2008; Lieberman, Compton, Van Horn, & Ghosh Ippen, 2003). Some researchers suggest that three- to four-year olds and young adolescents are particularly at risk for developing depression, anxiety, withdrawal and other grief symptoms (Abdelnoor & Hollins, 2004). Very young children do not grasp the finality and irreversibility of death, repeatedly asking when the deceased will return (Cohen & Mannarino, 2011). Many researchers refer to this as a kind of "magical thinking" (Cohen et al., 2002; Green & Connolly, 2009). An additional form of magical thinking in young children is that death can be caused by thoughts or words, often leading them to blame themselves for the loss of their loved one and experiencing the resultant guilt (Green & Connolly, 2009; Himebauch et al., 2008). Furthermore, limited verbal communication skills at this age may make children's grief appear to be both scattered and fleeting (Green & Connolly, 2009) and can make it difficult for children to articulate what they are feeling (Griffith, 2003; Lieberman et al., 2003).

Children aged six to eight may experience anxiety, depressive symptoms, regressive behavior and physical complaints after a significant loss (Black, 2005; Himebauch et al., 2008). This is considered normative and part of the bereavement process. Though children at this age know that death is permanent, they tend to view themselves as immortal. Bereaved children in this age group often express a fear of death, particularly the likelihood that death may befall others with whom the child is close (Himebauch et al., 2008). If Mom could die, what is to prevent Dad from dying as well? In the case of bereavement inside the family, children may also feel awkward or conspicuous when comparing their own family to intact families and experience the stigma of being different (Green & Connolly, 2009).

As children mature and move into the 8–12 age range, they develop a more adult view of death, knowing that it is permanent and will ultimately happen to everyone, including themselves. Children of this age often intellectualize their loss and approach it cognitively. They may want to know physical details of the death, perhaps because talking about feelings is more difficult for them or as an attempt to gain some mastery or comprehension in a situation that is, by its very nature, incomprehensible. It is also common for children of this age to want to know details about religious and cultural issues surrounding death (Himebauch et al., 2008).

Adolescents aged 12–18 are often concerned about the existential implications of death. Behaviorally, bereaved adolescents may participate in high-risk activities, challenging their own mortality through drug or alcohol use or precocious sexual behavior (Himebauch et al., 2008; Black, 2005). This high-risk behavior is similar to that found in adolescents exposed to trauma (Pat-Horenczyk et al., 2007). One potential way of understanding this reaction is to consider that the adolescent who has experienced an uncontrollable event—the loss of a loved one—wants to regain a sense of control in their life by deciding which dangerous or risky situations they expose themselves to. Adolescents may also have a strong emotional reaction, like their younger counterparts, and they too may have difficulty identifying and expressing their feelings (Himebauch et al., 2008). To hazard a generalization, we might say that talking about sad and difficult feelings is not something that most individuals in Western culture have learned to do easily. Adults are not particularly good models for children or adolescents in this regard, and it is not surprising that they have trouble communicating about their loss on an emotional level.

Some researchers have divided adolescence into two categories—younger adolescents (12–14 years old) and older adolescents (15–17 years old)—stating that younger adolescents are likely to react with indifference and egocentric behavior towards the death of a parent or sibling while their older counterparts will be more inclined to express thoughtfulness and empathy (Black, 2005). However, both present with similar symptoms such as high-risk behavior and difficulty expressing strong emotions.

Lichtenthal, Cruess and Prigerson (2004) note that, while the normative reactions of grief are varied in both their characteristics and duration, even uncomplicated grief "involve[s] suffering and frequently involves functional impairment" (p. 642), which may be confused with pathology and clinical diagnosis. It is important to reiterate that, while grieving is painful, it is not pathological but a normal life cycle process. There has been much discussion in the psychiatric community, and over the course of several editions of the *Diagnostic and Statistical Manual of Mental Disorders* (*DSM*), about the dividing line between uncomplicated or normative grief and complicated grief reactions. Uncomplicated bereavement, which was listed in the *DSM-III*, is not found in the *DSM-IV-TR*, where bereavement is listed under "Other conditions that may be a focus of attention" (American Psychiatric Association, 2000). Some see the current listing as promising, as it provides recognition that "grief symptoms may warrant clinical attention," while not diagnosing all grief reactions as clinical depression (Lichtenthal et al., 2004, p. 642). With the latest revision of *DSM-V*, there have been significant discussions about the removal of the bereavement exclusion in diagnosing depression. There has been an outcry regarding over-medicalizing a natural process by removing this exclusion (Friedman, 2012), which the *DSM-V* has responded to by including several notes that attempt to distinguish between grief and clinical depression (Society for Humanistic Psychology, 2011). This move is of great concern to those in the bereavement field who are eager to underscore the range of normal reactions to grief, which include depression.

While the debate about normative and complicated grief continues, it is clear to all that grief can have strong and lasting effects on children. Studies that have looked at grieving children often compare them to their non-grieving peers. Not surprisingly, the bereaved children were found to have higher levels of emotional disturbance and symptoms for up to 2 years following the death of a parent (Auman, 2007; Cerel, Fristad, Verducci, Weller, & Weller, 2006; Worden, 1996) when compared to their non-bereaved peers. Childhood symptoms of bereavement may present as withdrawal, anxiety, alarm, panic, loss of concentration, apathy, insomnia, psychosomatic symptoms, irritability, stress and family problems (Abdelnoor & Hollins, 2004). Long-term symptoms following the loss of a close family member may include those related to depression (Auman, 2007; Brent, Melhelm, Donohoe, & Walker, 2009). Silverman & Worden (1992) found that children who had psychological problems following the death of a parent often came from families where these problems tended to exist before the death.

While we have argued so far that there is a wide range of grief reactions that can be considered normative, and that symptoms may be varied and endure for long periods of time, the issue of complicated bereavement or grief should also be considered. Much research has been conducted in the past decade on complicated bereavement and grief in adults (Auman, 2007; Brown et al., 2008; Cohen & Mannarino, 2004; Holland, 2008; Horowitzet et al., 1997; Rosner, Pfoh, & Kotoučová, 2011; Zhang, El-Jawahri, & Prigerson, 2006), and complicated grief has been proposed for inclusion in the *DSM-V* (Lichtenthal et al., 2004). Auman (2007) defines complicated bereavement, which used to be called "pathological" grief (see Buglass, 2010), as a difficulty in "completing" the grief process. We have used the word "completing" with quotation marks here because we take issue with the notion that the grief process is ever completed. As stated above, it is the belief of the authors that the loss accompanies the bereaved throughout their lifetime, and, while accommodations are made, there is never a completion. It is interesting to note the shift of viewpoints about prolonged grief from "pathology" to a "complication," which underscores the complex nature of this entity. But what constitutes complicated bereavement or grief? Is it a function of time, number of symptoms or something else?

Complicated bereavement and grief has been studied almost exclusively in adults. However, one study (Melhelm, Moritz, Walker, Shear, & Brent, 2007) has found complicated grief in children and adolescents as well. In a sample of 129 children who had lost a parent through suicide, accident or sudden natural death, Melhelm et al. found initial evidence of complicated grief in children and adolescents (aged 7–18). Complicated grief was also shown to be correlated with functional impairment after controlling for clinical disorders such as posttraumatic stress disorder (PTSD) and depression, supporting the hypothesis that complicated grief is unique to these disorders.

Unlike complicated grief, childhood traumatic grief (CTG) has been the focus of several studies in the past decade. While some have likened CTG to complicated grief (Goodman & Brown, 2008), we would like to suggest that the notion of "childhood traumatic grief" is a descriptive term that can help plan a course of treatment without making a judgment as to whether the grief reaction is normative or complicated. As the term "traumatic grief" suggests, a child may suffer from CTG following a death that is either objectively or subjectively perceived as traumatic (Cohen et al., 2002). The word "subjective" should be stressed, as it is a child's *perception* of the suddenness/shock of losing a loved one that is the truest reflection of whether or not the death was traumatic. Even when a parent dies from a chronic terminal condition, the loss may be unexpected if the child has failed to comprehend that the illness would result in certain death (Mannarino & Cohen, 2011).

For children affected by traumatic grief, trauma symptoms may interfere with the child's ability to go through the grieving process (Auman, 2007; Brown et al., 2008; Cohen & Mannarino, 2004; Cohen & Mannarino, 2011). Such symptoms may include intrusive and distressing thoughts about the trauma, nightmares, memories and images, which are often triggered by trauma reminders (Cohen et al., 2002). To help children who experience trauma symptoms during the grieving process, one must first focus on treating and processing these symptoms before addressing the grief reaction (Cohen, Mannarino, & Knudsen, 2004; McClatchey, Vonk, & Palardy, 2009; Cohen & Mannarino, 2004).

There have been questions about whether CTG is simply another name for PTSD (Brown et al., 2008; Melhelm et al., 2007), or whether it can be classified as a separate disorder. In an open treatment study by Layne et al. (2001), Bosnian youths ($N = 55$) who had lost loved ones in the country's civil war received a trauma- and grief-focused treatment intervention. The study found that youngsters who received this treatment had significantly fewer PTSD and CTG symptoms. In contrast, youths who received only the trauma-focused treatment, and did not complete the grief components, had significantly lower levels of PTSD. Though the CTG symptoms of the youngsters in this group were fewer than at the start, they did not decrease as much as the group that completed both the grief- and the trauma-focused treatment. These results were reinforced in a study by Cohen et al. (2004), who found that PTSD and CTG symptoms in children significantly decreased in a trauma-focused intervention, while only

CTG symptoms decreased in a grief-focused intervention. Both studies give credence to the idea that traumatic symptoms are distinct from grief reactions and should be treated differentially. This important distinction has considerable implications for developing an intervention program for children who have experienced traumatic loss, and offers intriguing avenues of exploration for researchers, educators and parents working with such children.

In conclusion, while the grieving process is a normal one in the wake of common life cycle events such as illness and death, using a trauma lens to address some, if not most, of the loss experience may add an important dimension to the intervention programs available. In addition, this trauma lens may enable us to acknowledge a range of symptoms that may have hitherto gone unnoticed and untreated in children. Focusing on children, a traditionally underserved population (particularly with bereavement and traumatic loss), we have chosen to highlight, below, two case studies that describe interventions. The first is a clinical intervention specifically targeting an adolescent who experienced a traumatic loss, and the second is a community intervention designed to facilitate coping with general bereavement issues of children and families. Both of these interventions illustrate responses created out of the need to address childhood bereavement and grief, which may or may not have a traumatic origin, and help both adults and children navigate the rocky terrain of loss.

Clinical intervention

Case study: Treatment of sibling loss

The importance of addressing features of both the trauma and the loss is illustrated by the case of A., who was referred to our treatment center (the Israel Center for the Treatment of Psychotrauma) after the accidental, traumatic death of her twin sister on a school outing. A. (identifying details have been changed), who was ten years old at the time of the loss, presented with symptoms of withdrawal, anxiety, difficulty concentrating in school and at home and a general change in behavior. On intake, A. readily talked about the loss of her twin sister and described the circumstances in detail. She described her inability to concentrate, intrusive thoughts and pictures concerning the dead sibling and anxiety for the wellbeing of other family members.

With the parents' approval, a treatment contract was drawn up with the child. The contract stated that we would first concentrate on processing the traumatic event that caused the death of the sibling, utilizing evidence-informed treatment methods that included elements of narrative therapy, exposure therapy and eye movement desensitization and reprocessing (EMDR) therapy. At the conclusion of this phase of treatment, we would enter the second phase of treatment, which would focus on grieving and loss.

The first stage of treatment consisted of approximately twelve sessions. The first few sessions focused on building resources of relaxation, safety and emotional regulation, as well as a trusting relationship with the therapist. During this time, the outline of the traumatic event was transcribed into a series of chapters, creating an outline of the order of the event and setting the stage for the next segment of work.

During the second phase of treatment A. drew one picture at each session, depicting the event described in the chapter heading. While she initially said that she didn't like to draw, when she was asked to illustrate the first chapter, she jumped right in and exhibited no resistance for the remainder of the treatment sessions. When the drawing was complete a SUDs (subjective units of distress, generally rated on a scale of 0 to 10) level was assessed and the therapist asked A. to look at the picture and describe what was happening. After she completed the description, she was asked to look at the picture and "butterfly tap" (an EMDR bi-lateral stimulation technique often used with children) for a minute. An additional SUDs level was assessed. If the SUDs level continued to be elevated, more processing was done until it dropped. Additional tools of guided imagery, particularly the "safe place," were used to complete the session and help A. return to a comfortable state in both her body and her emotions.

At each subsequent session, the therapist and child reviewed the chapters that had been completed, allowing for a retelling of the traumatic story, the creation of a coherent narrative and the reprocessing of the event, with continued exposure to the traumatic material. A. participated willingly throughout the treatment sessions, and seemed eager both to tell the story and to reach a sense of completion. She described a reduction of intrusive dreams and pictures, as well as less anxiety, during this period of time.

While the traumatic event was being addressed, A.'s parents were invited for two meetings to explain the treatment, update them on the progress of the treatment and get a better understanding of the child's functioning at home and at school. The parents reported symptom reduction and improved behavior on the part of the child during this time.

When all the chapters of the traumatic event had been processed, and the "book" was completed, the next stage of treatment commenced. This stage, referred to as the grief-focused stage, involved the expression of feelings of longing and sadness, and discussions of ways to memorialize the lost sibling. This stage lasted only a few sessions, as both the family and the child were already heavily invested in memorializing the lost sibling and were satisfied that they had much opportunity in their lives for this part of the process. In our understanding of the wide range of normative reactions to grief, this child and family were actively involved in grieving, were able to share feelings and thoughts about their loss and did not seem unduly stuck in the process. Some issues involving school performance remained and A. was referred for follow-up with the school guidance counselor after the counselor was apprised of the work that had been completed.

This case demonstrates the importance of processing the trauma before focusing on the bereavement. It was only after working through the trauma that A. was able to allow herself to fully experience the sadness and feelings of loss for her twin sister. Since each part of the process was given the required time and attention, the tangle of emotions that included, among other things, horror, guilt, sadness and loss, began to disentangle, allowing for processing, accommodation and containment.

Community intervention

The Children's Room

The Children's Room (TCR) in Arlington, Massachusetts, was established in 1993, based on the model of the Dougy Center for Grieving Children, located in Portland, Oregon. (Founded in 1982, the Dougy Center provides support for children, parents or surrogate caregivers of children grieving a death.) Today, TCR has more than 180 children and teens enrolled in their peer support program. It is based on an understanding of the broad range of normative experiences in the grieving process, and the importance of social supports during this time. TCR fills an important need for families of various backgrounds who are experiencing grief as a result of the death of a parent or sibling, in a context that normalizes the grief experience of each family. Normalization is a key factor, as so often grieving families are told that there must be something "wrong" with them if they are still grieving after a week, a month or a year.

While some of the children at TCR have experienced particularly traumatic loss, such as losing a parent to suicide, children are not treated differentially depending on their type of loss. Rather, peer groups provide the children and adolescents with support during the grieving process. Participants have usually lost an immediate family member, and typically come to TCR following the death of a parent or sibling. One of the ground rules of TCR is that a family is only admitted to the program if the child or children know what happened. They don't necessarily need to know all the details surrounding the death, but it is important for them to know the larger picture; for example, in the case of a parental suicide, that the death was self-inflicted. If the surviving parent does not know how to tell the child about it, the professional staff will help him or her do so before the family is admitted to the program. The groups meet every other week for an hour and a half, and, while participants are welcome in a group for as long as they would like to remain, typical participation ranges anywhere from one to three years. Parent(s) or guardian(s) accompany the children and meet in their own group, parallel to the youngsters' groups.

Each group is facilitated by a trained volunteer. These volunteers have completed 32 hours of training on theoretical models of grieving, child development, reflective practice and group facilitation. The volunteers are supervised by a professional staff member. The facilitators themselves are often drawn to the center because of their own experiences of loss as either a child or an adult.

The groups are formed into subgroups by age, based on a developmental understanding of the grieving process (a group for 3 to 5 year olds, an elementary school-aged group, a tween/teen group and an adult group), though family members all attend their respective groups on the same afternoon or evening. Children and teens typically start with an opening circle in which they share their names and the name of the family member who died. This is followed by an activity or discussion about an aspect of the grief process. Activities may include art, music, play or poetry, which serve as a means of grief expression, memory sharing, feeling exploration and/or self-care. While sharing is part of the small group process, the children are never pressured to speak during these small group sessions. After the group, the children disperse and choose various play activities that are offered at TCR.

The adult groups, which are run parallel to the youngsters' groups and are also facilitated by trained volunteers, aim to create a safe space where parents or primary caregivers can discuss the challenges and developmental implications of raising bereaved children. The adults also discuss their own grief and the many changes in their lives. At the end of each session, all of the small groups join together for a closing ceremony in a big circle. This serves as a time for making announcements (such as birthdays and anniversaries of death), welcoming new families and saying goodbye to families or volunteers who are leaving. It also symbolically helps families rejoin after having been separated for the session.

While the peer support groups form the heart of TCR, additional services include the Teen Performance Troupe, made up of bereaved teens who create and perform an original show about grief in their lives; a Parent Education series, a free six-part psychoeducational series on "Parenting while Grieving"; individual family consultations; free monthly drop-in discussion groups on grieving families for "Children's Room alumni" adults; a referral system to local grief support services and programs; and lectures and training programs for teachers, parent–teacher organizations and counselors.

TCR has also been involved in traumatic deaths in communities where innocent children and adults have been injured or killed by gang violence. The professional staff of TCR has facilitated groups in these communities with the goal of recreating a feeling of safety in both the homes and the community. The TCR group is a first step in that direction. The participants learn breathing skills to help them relax and regain a feeling of self-regulation that is often disturbed by the traumatic event. They are also taught to use journals as well as play to express their feelings. Sharing feelings and listening to each other creates a feeling of group solidarity and safety. Unfortunately, it must be recognized that the group has limited ability to actually make the community safe.

Conclusion

The picture we have painted throughout this chapter highlights the importance of understanding the normative nature of the grieving process within a developmental framework to better help children and families during times of loss. Adding the lens of trauma or traumatic loss can help professionals to better understand children and families and to further refine the delivery of services for them during this difficult and challenging time.

References

Abdelnoor, A., & Hollins S. (2004). The effect of childhood bereavement on secondary school performance. *Educational Psychology in Practice, 20*(1), 43–54.

American Psychiatric Association. (2000). *Diagnostic and statistical manual of mental disorders* (4th ed., rev.). Washington, D.C.: Author.

Auman, M. J. (2007). Bereavement support for children. *The Journal of School Nursing, 23*(1), 34–39.

Batts, J. (2004). *Death and grief in the family: Tips for parents* [Brochure]. Bethesda, MD: National Association of School Psychologists.

Black, S. (2005). When children grieve: How teachers and counselors can reach out to bereaved students. *American School Board Journal, 192*(8), 28–30.

Brent, D., Melhelm, N., Donohoe, M. B., Walker, M. (2009). The incidence and course of depression in bereaved youth 21 months after the loss of a parent to suicide, accident, or sudden natural death. *American Journal of Psychiatry, 166*(7), 786–794.

Breen, L. J., & O'Connor, M. (2007). The fundamental paradox in the grief literature: A critical reflection. *OMEGA, 55*(3), 199–218.

Brown, E. J., Amaya-Jackson, L., Cohen, J., Handel, S., Thiel De Bocanegra, H., Zatta, E., et al. (2008). Childhood traumatic grief: A multi-site empirical examination of the construct and its correlates. *Death Studies, 32*(10), 899–923.

Buglass, E. (2010). Grief and bereavement theories. *Nursing Standard, 24*(41), 44–47.

Cerel, J., Fristad, M. A., Verducci, J., Weller, R. A., & Weller, E. B. (2006). Childhood bereavement: Psychopathology in the 2 years postparental death. *Journal of the American Academy of Child and Adolescent Psychiatry, 45*(6), 681–690.

Children's Bereavement Center of South Texas. (2008). *2008 Report to our community* [Online]. Retrieved from http://www.cbcst.org/docs/AnnualReport.pdf

Cohen, J. A., & Mannarino, A. P. (2004). Treatment of childhood traumatic grief. *Journal of Clinical Child and Adolescent Psychology, 33*(4), 819–831.

Cohen, J. A., & Mannarino, A. P. (2011). Supporting children with traumatic grief: What educators need to know. *School Psychology International, 32*(2), 117–131.

Cohen, J. A., Mannarino, A. P., Greenberg, T., Padlo, S., & Shipley, C. (2002). Childhood traumatic grief: Concepts and controversies. *Trauma, Violence & Abuse, 3*(4), 307–327.

Cohen, J. A., Mannarino, A. P., & Knudsen, K. (2004). Treating childhood traumatic grief: A pilot study. *Journal of the American Academy of Child and Adolescent Psychiatry, 43*(10), 1225–1233.

Friedman, R. A. (2012). Grief, depression, and the DSM-5. *The New England Journal of Medicine, 366*(20), 1855–1857.

Goodman, R. F., & Brown, E. J. (2008). Service and science in times of crisis: Developing, planning, and implementing a research program for children traumatically bereaved after 9/11. *Death Studies, 32*(2), 154–180.

Green, E. J., & Connolly, M. E. (2009). Jungian family sandplay with bereaved children: Implications for play therapists. *International Journal of Play Therapy, 18*(2), 84–98.

Griffith, T. (2003). Assisting with the "big hurts, little tears" of the youngest grievers: Working with three-, four-, and five-year-olds who have experienced loss and grief because of death. *Illness, Crisis & Loss, 11*(3), 217–225.

Himebauch, A., Arnold, R. M., & May, C. (2008). Grief in children and developmental concepts of death #138. *Journal of Palliative Medicine, 11*(2), 242–243.

Holland, J. (2008). How schools can support children who experience loss and death. *British Journal of Guidance & Counseling, 36*(4), 411–424.

Horowitz, M. J., Siegel, B., Holen, A., Bonanno, G. A., Milbrath, C., & Stinson, C. H. (1997). Diagnostic criteria for complicated grief disorder. *American Journal of Psychiatry, 154*(7), 904–910.

Layne, C. M., Pynoos, R. S., Saltzman, W. R., Arslanagic, B., Black, M., Savjak, N., et al. (2001). Trauma/grief-focused group psychotherapy: School-based postwar intervention with traumatized Bosnian adolescents. *Group Dynamics: Theory, Research, and Practice, 5*(4), 277–290.

Lichtenthal, W. G., Cruess, D. G., & Prigerson, H. G. (2004). A case for establishing complicated grief as a distinct mental disorder in DSM-V. *Clinical Psychology Review, 24*(6), 637–662.

Lieberman, A. F., Compton, N. C., Van Horn, P., & Ghosh Ippen, C. (2003). *Losing a parent to death in the early years: Guidelines for the treatment of traumatic bereavement in infancy and early childhood.* Washington, D.C.: Zero to Three Press.

Lowton, K., & Higginson, I. J. (2003). Managing bereavement in the classroom: A conspiracy of silence? *Death Studies, 27*(8), 717–741.

Luecken, L. J., Kraft, A., Appelhans, B. M., & Enders, C. (2009). Emotional and cardiovascular sensitization to daily stress following childhood parental loss. *Developmental Psychology, 45*(1), 296–302.

Mannarino, A. P., & Cohen, J. A. (2011). Traumatic loss in children and adolescents. *Journal of Child & Adolescent Trauma, 4*(1), 22–33.

McClatchy, I. S., Vonk, M. E., & Palardy, G. (2009). The prevalence of childhood traumatic grief: A comparison of violent/sudden and expected loss. *OMEGA, 59*(4), 309–323.

Melhelm, N. M., Moritz, G., Walker, M., Shear, M. K., & Brent, D. (2007). Phenomenology and correlates of complicated grief in children and adolescents. *Journal of the American Academy of Child and Adolescent Psychiatry, 46*(6), 493–499.

Packman, W., Horsley, H., Davies, B., & Kramer, R. (2006). Sibling bereavement and continuing bonds. *Death Studies, 30*(9), 817–841.

Pat-Horenczyk, R., Peled, O., Miron, T., Brom, D., Villa, Y., & Chemtob, C. M. (2007). Risk-taking behaviors among Israeli adolescents exposed to recurrent terrorism: Provoking danger under continuous threat? *The American Journal of Psychiatry, 164*(1), 66–72.

Rosner, R., Pfoh, G., & Kotoučová, M. (2011). Treatment of complicated grief. *European Journal of Psychotraumatology, 2*, 1–10.

Silverman, P. R. (2000). *Never too young to know: Death in children's lives.* New York, NY: Oxford University Press.

Silverman, P. R., & Worden, J. W. (1992). Children's reactions in the early months after the death of a parent. *American Journal of Orthopsychiatry, 62*(1), 93–104.

Society for Humanistic Psychology. (2011, October 22). Open letter to the DSM-5 Task Force and the American Psychiatric Association. Posted by B. Robbins to http://societyforhumanisticpsychology.blogspot.co.uk/2011/10/open-letter-to-dsm-5-task-force-and.html

U.S. Social Security Administration (2000). Intermediate assumptions of the 2000 trustees report. Washington, DC: Office of the Chief Actuary of the Social Security Administration.

Wolchik, S. A., Ma, Y., Tein, J.-Y., Sandler, I. N., & Ayers, T. S. (2008). Parentally bereaved children's grief: Self-system beliefs as mediators of the relations between grief and stressors and caregiver-child relationship quality. *Death Studies*, *32*(7), 597–620.

Worden, J. W. (1996). *Children and grief: When a parent dies*. New York, NY: Guilford Press.

Wortman, C. B., & Silver, R. C. (1989). The myths of coping with loss. *Journal of Consulting and Clinical Psychology*, *57*(3), 349–357.

Zhang, B., El-Jawahri, A., & Prigerson, H. G. (2006). Update on bereavement research: Evidence-based guidelines for the diagnosis and treatment of complicated bereavement. *Journal of Palliative Medicine*, *9*(5), 1188–1203.

Section II

Family

Chapter 5

Family resilience after disasters and terrorism

Examining the concept[1]

Juliet M. Vogel and Betty Pfefferbaum

Disasters and acts of terrorism challenge the coping resources of individuals, families and communities. Most individuals cope well or show good psychological recovery in the aftermath of such adverse events. Information is more limited and more mixed for families and communities, beyond the clear finding that post-disaster family and social relationships have an impact on individual functioning (see Bonanno, Brewin, Kaniasty, & La Greca, 2010).

Functioning well in spite of adversity or overcoming the effects of adversity is referred to as "resilience." This concept initially was applied primarily to individuals, particularly children, who function well in spite of growing up under adverse circumstances (e.g., Rutter, 1985; Werner, 1984). However, the concept also has been applied to families (e.g., Patterson, 2002a; Walsh, 2006) and larger social systems, including communities (Landau & Saul, 2004; Norris, Stevens, Pfefferbaum, Wyche, & Pfefferbaum, 2008; Pfefferbaum & Klomp, 2013). This chapter addresses the concept of family resilience and its relevance to understanding the functioning of families after disasters and acts of terrorism.

The conceptualization of family resilience, although fairly recent, builds not only on work on individual resilience, but also on two long-standing traditions of family work—a family therapy tradition of focusing on family strengths, which dates back to the early 1980s (see Walsh, 2002, 2006), and a family research tradition focusing on models of family stress and coping (e.g., Hill, 1949, 1958; McCubbin & Patterson, 1983a, b). In this chapter, we provide a brief description of precursors that have influenced the development of current views of family resilience. We then introduce two major theoretical models of family resilience by (a) Froma Walsh (e.g., 1996, 2006), developed from the family therapy/family strengths perspective, and (b) Joan Patterson (1995; 2002a, b), working from a tradition of family research on stress and coping.

These authors have written for somewhat different audiences, with Walsh writing primarily for practitioners intervening with families who are under stress, while Patterson has addressed both research issues and some practical implications, primarily for medical personnel working with families in which a child has a disability. Walsh and Patterson agree on many of the key elements involved in family resilience, although with some differences in organization as well as differences that appear to reflect their primary audiences and goals.

In the third and fourth sections of the chapter, we discuss themes in the family resilience work by Walsh and Patterson as a basis for a framework for considering family resilience in the aftermath of disasters and acts of terrorism. The third section describes general issues in conceptualizing family resilience; the fourth, key factors that contribute to family resilience. We conclude with a summary and recommendations for future directions in applying this concept to research and applied work after disasters.

We will recommend that, in examining the family context of child functioning, it is important not only to look for associations between levels of child and parent symptoms, but also to consider the impact of key family-level variables. In addition, we argue that family functioning is an important outcome in its own right. Finally, it is important to examine and address factors from other ecosystem levels (e.g., community factors) that influence families' ability to function adaptively in the aftermath of major stressors such as disasters.

Perspectives on psychological resilience in individuals and families: A brief historical summary

Individual resilience

The research tradition that led to the concept of individual resilience began approximately 40 years ago, initially focusing on groups of children who showed "normal" development in spite of growing up in high-risk circumstances— children of schizophrenic mothers (Anthony, 1987; Garmezy, 1987) and children raised in poverty or with other risk factors for adverse outcomes (e.g., Garmezy 1987; Rutter, 1979, 1985; Werner, 1984). At first, these children were labeled "stress resistant" or "invulnerable," but, with time, the label shifted to "resilient."

There was also a shift from viewing resilience as a fixed characteristic of a subset of at-risk individuals to viewing it in transactional terms as a process reflecting interactions between individuals and their environments (e.g., Wright & Masten, 2005). One of the factors in this shift was the observation in longitudinal studies (e.g., Werner, 1993) of shifts in functioning over time, including good subsequent functioning for some individuals who earlier had not been judged to be resilient. A search for risk and protective factors revealed a shortlist of factors that emerged across studies as contributing to resilience (see Masten, 2001; Werner, 2005). Notably, this list includes not only individual characteristics such as intelligence and temperament, but also relationship variables—particularly, the presence of a supportive adult within or outside of one's family. There also has been a shift to a broader focus—considering adults' resilience and applying the concept of resilience to multiple system levels (Masten & Obradovic, 2008).

Family resilience: Contributions from a family therapy perspective

Like the early work in developmental psychopathology, early theories of family therapy emphasized ways in which family functioning could put the development or mental health of its members at risk. By the 1980s, this perspective began to change, with an increased focus on exploring family strengths as key ingredients in a family's ability to overcome adversities. Froma Walsh has worked within this tradition since the early 1980s, and has made major contributions to the concept of family resilience from a family therapy perspective (e.g., Walsh, 1996, 2006). Other contributions from this perspective are also discussed in Becvar (2013).

Writing primarily for practitioners working with families under stress, Walsh has emphasized the role of three categories of factors in family resilience: (a) belief systems, (b) family organization and (c) family communication/problem solving. She has elaborated in detail on these factors (Walsh, 2006), which are discussed further below.

Family stress and coping research: Evolution of a model of family resilience

Family sociology research led to the development in the second half of the twentieth century of models describing how families cope with highly stressful events. By the 1990s, these models were applied to address family resilience, and new models were proposed. In this section, we describe three key models within the evolution of this work.

The ABC-X model

Reuben Hill's (1958) ABC-X model provided a foundation from which subsequent models of family stress and coping have evolved. The ABC-X model was developed to describe how some families come to be in crisis after a major stressor such as wartime separation of service members from their families or natural disasters such as tornadoes, floods or hurricanes. Hill described a family crisis (X) as resulting from the interaction of a major stressor (A) with the family's crisis-meeting resources (B) and the meaning the family makes of the event (C). The "A" event is external, but one for which the family is not adequately prepared. The hardships caused by this event are likely to differ from family to family, but are conceptualized as part of the stressor. A key aspect of this model is that the family's interpretation of the stressor and appraisal of their resources to cope with it determine whether the family will become overwhelmed and experience a crisis. Hill noted that there is often a "roller-coaster" adaptation course, with the temporal patterns of difficulties in functioning, recovery and reorganization likely to differ depending, in part, on the type of stressor.

The Double ABCX model

Hamilton McCubbin and Joan Patterson's (1983a, b) Double ABCX model built on Hill's work, but emphasized that most crises that overwhelm families create a cascade of events and adaptations over time after the initial stressor. McCubbin and Patterson proposed that family outcomes are influenced by four factors that occur subsequent to the initial crisis, which they labeled with double letters. There is typically a pileup of stressors and secondary adversities (which they labeled the "aA factor"). The resources (their "bB factor") available to deal with the stressors and adversities, as well as meanings/appraisals ("cC factor"), also change over time. Finally, their model adds and emphasizes coping strategies/skills. Coping draws on the appraisals and resources and leads to the outcome, which is described as falling on a continuum of adaptive to maladaptive functioning. Coping has both cognitive and behavioral components. Its goals can be reducing stressors, managing hardships, maintaining the family system and morale, acquiring/developing new resources and/or implementing structural changes in the family to meet the new demands.

The extended recovery after Hurricane Katrina (see Abramson, Park, Stehling-Ariza, & Redlener, 2010) provides a relevant example for the Double ABCX model. The post-disaster pileup of stressors and secondary adversities began with the direct impact of the storm, but additional difficulties then arose, some as by-products of attempts to cope with the storm impact (e.g., issues resulting from temporary relocation). In addition, some families had pre-existing strains, defined by McCubbin and Patterson as residuals from attempts to address earlier issues (e.g., tensions about role allocation) that complicated post-hurricane coping efforts. Interacting with each of these were normative family life cycle issues, such as the need to provide care for young children, deal with adolescents' strivings for independence and launch them into the world or care for frail elderly relatives. For example, many parents' return to work after Katrina was hindered by the reduced availability of childcare. College planning for many adolescents was disrupted by a "lost" high school senior year during which schooling was disrupted; and, because of family needs, some youths questioned their earlier decision to leave home to attend college (Osofsky, Osofsky, & Harris, 2007). Family coping meant dealing with these issues and their impact on the family, often redefining family goals and accessing relevant resources. The resources available after the disaster included the family's pre-existing resources as well as additional resources recruited from within and outside the family, such as support from their extended family, as well as the disaster relief provided by the American Red Cross and the U.S. Federal Emergency Management Agency.

The Family Adjustment and Adaptation Response (FAAR) model

At the same time that they introduced the Double ABCX model, McCubbin and Paterson (1983a) also presented the Family Adjustment and Adaptation

Response (FAAR) model to describe changes families experience in the process of coping with a crisis event. According to the FAAR model, most families try to deal with stress by making minimal changes in established patterns of functioning, a strategy labeled "adjustment." However, dealing adequately with major crises often ultimately requires major family changes, labeled "adaptation." McCubbin and Patterson discuss that adaptation takes place on individual, family and community levels, and that functioning at the family level is influenced by demands and resources from the other two.

The concept of resilience per se was not discussed in the original presentation of the Double ABCX and FAAR models. However, Patterson (1988) has further developed the FAAR model and has described family resilience as reflecting crisis adaptation (Patterson, 1995, 2002a, b). She now depicts the FAAR model as a set of balance beams with demands on one side, capabilities (i.e., coping strategies plus resources from both inside and outside the family) on the other and "family meanings" mediating the degree of balance between the two (see Figure 5.1). As noted above, *adjustment* is involved when there is a minor imbalance between demands/stressors and capabilities (resources and coping strategies), so that the family can deal with the stresses using existing resources and strategies with minimal need for change in family functioning. A different set of processes, *adaptation*, occurs when family appraisal indicates that current resources are not adequate for coping with the stressors. This leads to a crisis and necessitates significant changes to restore balance. This can be done by reducing stressors or by developing new coping mechanisms or resources (from within or outside the family). It also can involve reappraisal to gain new perspectives on how to view the stressors and one's coping mechanisms and resources, so that they will be more adequate to fit the current situation.

Conceptualizing family resilience: General issues

In this section, we define basic terms and discuss key factors described by both Walsh and Patterson. We then discuss how Patterson's FAAR model provides a framework for organizing these factors that is likely to be useful for both research and applied work.

What is family resilience?

Walsh describes family resilience as follows:

> The concept of family resilience goes beyond a contextual view of individual resilience to a family-system level of assessment and intervention, focusing on *relational resilience* in the family as a functional unit. A family-systems perspective enables us to understand the mediating influence of family processes in surmounting crisis or prolonged hardship. How a family confronts and manages a disruptive experience, buffers stress, effectively reorganizes,

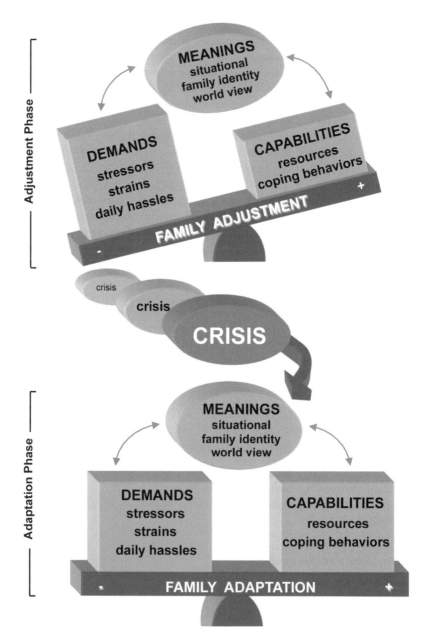

Figure 5.1 The Family Adjustment and Adaptation Response model (from Patterson, 1988).

and moves forward with life will influence immediate and long-term adaptation for all family members and for the family unit.

(1996, p. 265)

Although primarily referring to resilience as a process, Walsh nevertheless sometimes has referred to resilience as "a relational hardiness" (2006, p. 3). This reflects a perspective that a family can build strengths that will facilitate—but not guarantee—adaptive coping with future stressors. Thus, she states, "A particular solution to a presenting problem may not be relevant to future problems, but in building *processes for resilience*, families become more resourceful in dealing with unforeseen problems and averting crises" (2006, p. 25).

Consistent with the initial description by Walsh presented above, Patterson defines family resilience as "doing well in the face of adversity" (2002a, p. 350) and "an ongoing, often emergent process in families and not a stable trait. Family resilience is similar to family regenerative power, particularly when good outcomes follow significant risk situations confronting a family" (2002b, p. 237).

Under what circumstances should effective coping be labeled "resilience"?

There is agreement that effective coping or recovery after extraordinary stressors such as major disasters and acts of terrorism (the focus of this chapter) should be classified as resilient. However, perspectives differ regarding the range of stressors in the face of which effective functioning should be considered resilient.

Patterson (2002a) advocates following the position of individual resilience theorists Masten and Coatsworth (1998) that resilience pertains to (a) coping well in spite of ongoing adversity, (b) overcoming the impact of a major stressful event (such as a disaster) or (c) a combination of both. In contrast, writing primarily for practitioners, Walsh proposes that her family resilience approach is relevant for all instances in which clinicians intervene with families overwhelmed by their current stressors. "Challenges may range from expectable strains of normative life-cycle transitions such as retirement, divorce, or remarriage, to a sudden job loss or untimely death of a key family member" (Walsh, 1996, p. 261). Nevertheless, the two positions do not differ as sharply as initially seems the case. Walsh (2006, p. 13) states that "stressful life events are more likely to affect functioning adversely when they are unexpected, when a condition is severe or persistent, when multiple stressors generate cumulative effects" or when events are "off time or out of sync with chronological or social expectations." Patterson (2002a) notes that "normative" transitions at times can lead to a cascade of adversities, especially when the transitions are out of sequence, and thus would constitute or create significant risk. Also, if a family has few resources to deal with a normative transition, this is more likely to cause significant difficulty. "Thus, there is no clear rule that competence in managing normative demands could not be characterized as resilience" (Patterson, 2002a, p. 356).

What outcomes would demonstrate family resilience?

Both Walsh (2006) and Patterson (2002a) identify the ability to support the functioning of the family's members, including appropriate nurturance of children, as one aspect of resilience. Indeed, it is well established that the presence of supportive adult relationships is an important contributor to individual resilience in children (e.g., Rutter, 1985; Werner, 1993). But family resilience involves more. Walsh (1996, 2006) emphasizes that family resilience concerns the family's coping and adaptation as a functional unit. Similarly, Patterson (2002a, b) emphasizes that family resilience must be assessed in terms of family-level outcomes. She also notes the interplay not only between family and individual functioning, but also between family and community functioning. In disaster research, the interaction of levels has been demonstrated in terms of risk (rather than resilience) research in impoverished neighborhoods after Hurricane Katrina. In a longitudinal study, community-level variables such as post-hurricane lack of neighborhood safety were shown to impact children's functioning through their influence on parental functioning (Abramson et al., 2010).

For Walsh (2006, p. 8), a judgment of resilience requires that families "heal from painful wounds, take charge of their lives, and go on to live fully and love well." Patterson (2002a) has proposed that resilience be judged in terms of ability to fulfill one or more of four basic functions of families: (a) family formation and membership (which includes keeping the family intact after a severe stressor or loss), (b) education and nurturance of the young, (c) taking care of vulnerable members and (d) economic support of members. The difference in emphasis again appears to reflect the difference between a clinical and family sociology/research perspective, with the clinical one taking into account the affective variables that separate families fulfilling basic functions, but in a joyless way, from those more fully going on with their lives. However, from both perspectives, it is a complex matter to develop criteria to determine if an appropriate level of functioning has been met so that a family can be judged resilient.

One important suggestion by Patterson (2002a) is that which criteria are most important for a specific situation may be an empirical question. For example, in her area of expertise—dealing with children with chronic illness—a major criterion is the family's ability to care for the ill child; however, an additional important criterion over time is the nurturance of all members, even when much of the family's resources must be focused on the needs of the one who is ill or disabled.

The importance of developmental context

Both Walsh and Patterson consider the developmental context—family life cycle development combined with the individual development of family members—as influencing family needs and family functioning in the face of adversity. Walsh

(2006) and Patterson (2002a) note that adaptive processes that work at one stage of development may not work at other stages. Similarly, both of them (Walsh, 2006; Patterson 2002a) note that optimal family functioning in terms of variables such as cohesion varies, depending on the developmental stage of the family and its members. Consistent with this, McCubbin and McCubbin (1988) summarize results from a large survey study by themselves and others which indicated that the presence of strong family routines and valuing of routines, while protective under stress, were less frequent for families with adolescents than those with younger children.

Finally, both objective stressors and belief systems that influence the appraisal of stressors may change with family development. Bromet and Litcher-Kelly (2002) provide a striking example of an interaction among stage-specific family development issues, characteristics of a specific disaster and the role of belief systems to provide unique sets of challenges/risk factors. After the Three Mile Island nuclear accident, a high rate of persistent anxiety in mothers of infants or very young preschool children was associated with enduring beliefs about the dangerousness of the nuclear plant and worry about their children's health (and their own), even though there was no objective increase in health problems due to the disaster. Instead, these findings probably reflect knowledge of the high risk from radiation for young children, about which there had been warnings at the time of the accident.

The importance of cultural context

Both Walsh (2006) and Patterson (2002a, p. 356) point out that family process research on family relational patterns has been conducted predominantly with Caucasian, middle-class families in the United States, underscoring the need for caution in applying the findings to other groups. For example, the normative degree of family cohesion varies by culture. Socioeconomic and minority status can be relevant to family beliefs and resources as well.

Family explanations of adversity play an important role in subsequent adaptation. In addition to being influenced by family history, including intergenerational history, explanations of adversity are often affected by cultural factors. Indeed, Reiss and Oliveri (1991) describe a method of assessing community views on adversities in relatively homogeneous communities; they argue that these community views play an important role in appraisals by individual families.

McCubbin, McCubbin, Thompson and Thompson (1998) and McCubbin and McCubbin (2013) have elaborated on cultural differences that could influence response to stressors such as disasters. These include whether responsibility for issues within a family is seen as lying primarily within the individual family (as for much of Western society), or with a larger group, such as an extended family or tribe, as in Native (Hawaiian, Indian) subgroups in the United States. Another set of factors that can influence family coping and beliefs after disasters concerns the importance for some groups of attachment to a particular place or to the land.

There also are differences in views on whether functioning of the individual or that of the family and community get higher priority.

Boss (2002, Chapter 8) has pointed out that cultural beliefs and family values at times can contribute to maladaptive appraisals and responses. She tells of a couple whose baby was born with severe disabilities. The couple belonged to a prayer group that emphasized a "just world" belief system and told them that they must be at fault for their baby's problems—a view they accepted, which led to very high levels of guilt and stress.

The importance of historical context

Families' prior experiences in dealing with adversity may affect their appraisal of their capability to deal with a new stressor such as a disaster. How families think about major stressors/challenges is also influenced by prior generations' experiences and coping methods. Both types of prior experience may be reflected in family stories. Finally, the historical era in which a family develops can influence its functioning and values. For example, individuals raised during the Great Depression in the United States learned lessons about frugality that they often carried through their lifetime (Elder, 1974), influencing the families they formed.

The importance of examining stressors and adaptation over time

Both Walsh (2003) and Patterson (e.g., McCubbin & Patterson, 1983a) note that the impact of most overwhelming stressors unfolds over time, often with secondary adversities resulting from the original stressor, or with a pileup of other stressors interacting with the original stressor over time. Families that ultimately function well may follow different temporal patterns of adaptation over time as a function of both their specific situational adversities and the family's resources and coping (Walsh, 2003; McCubbin & Patterson, 1983a). For an attempt to map patterns of family coping and adaptation over time after Hurricane Katrina, see Knowles, Sasser, & Garrison (2009).

Loss and ambiguous loss

Disasters and incidents of terrorism are often accompanied by loss—of family members, of property and even, at times, of a community. Loss of family members can challenge belief systems and disrupt family organization and functioning. Pauline Boss (e.g., 2004) has emphasized the heightened challenges that occur under circumstances of ambiguous loss. These include situations in which a member is physically absent and his or her return uncertain, as well as situations in which a member is present but unable to perform prior functions, as in cases of disability. Nevertheless, the same factors are thought to contribute to resilience, which often is observed (see Boss, 2004, for dealing with ambiguous loss after the 9/11 terrorist attacks). Although Boss refers primarily to ambiguous loss of people, in the aftermath of disasters there may also be ambiguity about loss of "place," when there is uncertainty about return to damaged homes or rebuilding in a damaged area, and this also contributes to stress and difficulty in making readjustments.

Key processes in family resilience

Meaning making and belief systems

Family belief systems are the family's shared assumptions, including appraisal of adversity and their capacity to deal with it, as well as more general assumptions about the family and the world. Across theorists, meaning making and belief systems are seen as playing a central role in family coping and resilience.

Walsh (2006, Chapter 2) and Patterson (2005) both discuss the important role of having or developing a perspective that provides hope, but within a framework that has a basis in reality. This is described by Walsh as "mastering the art of the possible" and by Patterson as "optimism grounded in reality." Patterson discusses the idea that sometimes family resilience involves shifting positions on what is a "good" outcome and focusing on a positive aspect of a situation (e.g., in her research with families in which a child has a disability, shifting from a focus on finding a cure to finding the positives in the disabled member and the family's responses).

Both Walsh and Patterson consider the family's belief in pulling together and having members support each other in the face of adversity a resilience factor. Finally, both discuss the importance of relating one's perspective to a spiritual belief system or a worldview larger than the family, which may or may not be a religious perspective.

Both Walsh (2006) and Patterson (McCubbin & Patterson, 1983a) suggest that it is an important part of resilient beliefs that the family develops a sense of coherence, a concept based on the work of Antonovsky (1979, 1988), who found that, on an individual level, survivors of overwhelming stressors such as the Holocaust did better if they could develop a view that the world is comprehensible, manageable and coherent (that their life is part of a coherent system), which he called a "sense of coherence." Antonovsky (1988; Antonovsky & Sourani, 1988) also supported studying the relevance of the concept for families. McCubbin and Patterson (1983a) noted that developing a family sense of coherence after a major stressor such as a disaster may involve a balance between trust in the family and trust in others.

Patterson (1988; Patterson & Garwick, 1994) has reviewed a range of theoretical discussions about family worldviews and suggested five dimensions as emerging from the combined work, dimensions consistent with her own work with families of medically fragile children. Consistent with the factors discussed above, these are the degree to which the family (a) has shared goals or a shared sense of purpose, (b) sees the family unit as part of something larger and members see themselves as part of the family unit, (c) has optimism grounded in reality, (d) has the ability to live in present circumstances and adjust expectations accordingly (e.g., tolerating the need to adjust some expectations for functioning under disaster conditions) and (e) can balance personal/family control with trust in others.

Walsh provides an example of a resilient family's beliefs in the aftermath of "ethnic cleansing" in Kosovo. She quotes an interview with a surviving member of a family in which five men had been murdered. The interview reflects religious faith, commitment to surviving family members and a perspective that providing a future for children is a way of honoring their dead relatives:

> *The surviving son in the family replied*: "We are all believers. One of the strengths in our family is from Allah. Having something to believe has helped very much."
> INTERVIEWER: "What do you do to keep faith strong?"
> SON: "I see my mother as our 'spring of strength'. . . to see someone who has lost five family members—it gives us strength just to see her. We must think about the future and what we can accomplish. This is what keeps us strong. What will happen to him *(pointing to his 5-year-old nephew)* if I am not here? If he sees me strong, he will be strong. If I am weak, he will become weaker than me."
> INTERVIEWER: "What do you hope your nephew will learn about the family as he grows up?"
> SON: "The moment when he will be independent and helping others and the family—for him, it will be like seeing his father and grandfather and uncles alive again."
>
> (Becker, Sargent, & Rolland, 2000, p. 29;
> as quoted by Walsh, 2013, p.78)

Both Patterson and Walsh note that a crisis or disaster can lead people to question their worldview, contributing to disequilibrium, at least initially. In other cases, the family may need to revise counterproductive beliefs, such as when belief in a "just world" leaves a family "stuck," focusing on guilt and shame.

Family organization

Assumptions about how families should function are part of family belief systems and are labeled "family identity" in Patterson's FAAR model. These beliefs may or may not be stated or even reach conscious awareness, but they tend to be reflected in the family's routines and rituals.

Although there are cultural differences in family organization, Walsh and Patterson agree on the importance of providing continuity of family routines and rituals to the extent possible, but with flexibility to take new realities into account (which Walsh labels "bouncing forward"). Regarding the importance of routines and continuity, a mother from the Rockaway Peninsula of New York City cited the role of family routines in her family's recovery from "Superstorm Sandy." She reported that they were relocated for eight weeks before they could return to living in their home. She described that it was after they moved back, when she put her "daily board" of the family's activities back up and resumed preparing family dinners, that her family (including three youngsters) went back to normal functioning, even though the house was still undergoing repairs.

Family organization involves hierarchy and boundaries. For families with children, this optimally includes a family hierarchy in which the adults are in charge, even though the children may have useful roles. McCubbin, McCubbin, Thompson, Han, and Allen (1997) observe that after some disasters, a family organization and a social policy recognizing equality between the adult partners can be important for practical reasons in allowing both to be able to deal with officials.

Patterson (2002a) points out that the need for clear boundaries can include those between the family and outside helpers. This was an important resilience factor in her research on families of children with a disability, in relation to their dealings with medical and educational personnel. One might consider whether similar issues might arise in relation to relief workers after disasters, particularly in situations when a family is displaced (e.g., in a shelter).

Family communication and problem solving

Both Walsh and Patterson stress the importance of family communication during situations of stress. This includes sharing of feelings—both finding ways of expressing positive feelings and appropriate expression of negative feelings. Indeed, Masten and Obradovic (2008) note that parents' modeling appropriate expression of emotions and assistance with children's emotion regulation provide important scaffolding for children in the aftermath of disasters. Regarding ability to express positive feelings at times of stress, Walsh cites the importance of humor, and Garrison and Sasser (2009) describe how this emerged as a positive coping factor in a qualitative study of family coping after Hurricane Katrina.

Adaptive communication also includes sharing information, to the extent that it is available, within a family, with appropriate adjustments for the children's developmental level. As Patterson (2002a) points out, it also can involve skills for communicating with others outside of the family, including those who control needed resources. McCubbin et al. (1997) note the importance of truthful information, not only within the family but also as communicated to the family by those in authority—particularly under circumstances of ambiguity when only incomplete information is available.

Walsh (e.g., 2006, p. 108) combines communication and problem solving, both of which can be considered coping skills in Patterson's model. Part of problem solving in a crisis is the ability to access needed resources, whether within the family, from the extended family or from others in the community—both social resources such as social support and practical resources such as economic ones.

Putting it together: Re-establishing balance

The FAAR model, as depicted in Figure 5.1, provides a guide for integrating the factors discussed above and for considering types of family changes that could bring relief when a family is in crisis—that is, when the situational appraisal indicates a significant mismatch between demands and capabilities. Relief can come from reducing the demands from the current stressor and accompanying secondary adversities, daily hassles or family strains that are residuals of prior family compromises. Balance can be restored by increasing capabilities, recruiting new internal and/or external resources or developing new coping strategies. A third avenue to restoring balance is changing meanings or altering belief systems in a way that decreases the mismatch between the family's beliefs and the situation at hand. This can involve reappraisal of the importance of aspects of the stressor, changes in family expectations about aspects of family functioning (e.g., relaxing some expectations about housekeeping at times of overwhelming stress, redefining family roles) or changes in the more general worldview. Characteristics such as communication and problem-solving skills are both resources and coping skills. Ability to communicate with those beyond the family can also be relevant for the recruitment of resources.

Summary

Based on the work we have reviewed, we view family resilience as the process by which families withstand or overcome adversity. Family resilience is dependent in part on current circumstances, including the nature of the adversity and the developmental status of the family and its members. Belief systems and cognitive appraisals play a central role. Also critical are family organization, communication, coping strategies and the ability to recruit resources from within as well as outside the family. Assessment of resilience must consider cultural variation and the possibility that the factors most central to family resilience may vary over time after events with long-lasting repercussions. Interventions to facilitate resilience can address the stressors, the available resources and coping strategies and/or expectations and beliefs that influence adaptation.

Future directions

In this final section, we first address the complex issue of assessing family-level beliefs and functioning, which is important for both research and clinical practice. Then, we provide recommendations concerning future directions for research on family resilience in the aftermath of disasters and acts of terrorism. We conclude with brief recommendations for interventions to facilitate resilience.

Assessing family beliefs and functioning

The assessment of family beliefs and family functioning needs to be distinguished from ascertaining the views of individual members about these issues. In current disaster research, if family variables are included, they typically are assessed by interviewing or surveying a single family member. We realize that this may be dictated by practical constraints. However, as Patterson (2002b) has emphasized, this measures only one individual's perspective and is not a true measure of family-level functioning. This strategy is additionally problematic when the same individual also reports on outcome measures such as symptoms for him-/herself and for other family members (e.g., a mother's reporting on family functioning, her own symptoms and her child's symptoms), so that the individual's bias affects each of these variables.

We suggest consideration of measurement strategies that provide better approximations of shared family views and functioning, as discussed by Patterson (2002b): joint family interviews; surveying multiple family members and noting areas of concurrence; or, for some areas of functioning, observing the family doing structured tasks. Similar strategies can be used when assessing family variables in clinical settings.

Research recommendations

Research on family resilience requires a combination of methods, as recommended by Patterson (2002b): quantitative research involving rigorous testing of models, complemented by qualitative research to better understand meaning making (a central construct in family resilience) and inductive research to better refine our understanding of the relevant variables. Additionally, research needs to be longitudinal to document processes that occur over time.

Pertinent variables include measures of meaning making, coping strategies and problem solving, as well as the more frequently studied family variables of cohesion, organization and flexibility/adaptability. Although well-established measures of these last three dimensions are likely to be useful, they may not fully capture the ways in which disasters affect family functioning. New measures may be needed to assess some of the disaster-specific perturbations in family functioning. For example, Prinstein, La Greca, Vernberg, and Silverman (1996) developed a measure for use with children affected by Hurricane Andrew that assessed the extent to which parents facilitated the children's coping by reinstituting roles and routines (as well as by facilitating emotional processing and distraction).

Areas to consider in future research and interventions can be derived from a general understanding of family resilience, but need to be tailored to the specifics of the type of stressor, such as disasters or acts of terrorism, just as an existing extensive body of work has explored the factors contributing to family resilience when a child has a chronic illness or developmental disability. In reviewing that work, Patterson (1991) has identified nine factors that emerge as particularly important for resilience in families coping with a child's disability: (a) balancing illness with other family needs, (b) maintaining family flexibility, (c) maintaining commitment to the family unit, (d) engaging in active family coping efforts, (e) developing communication competence, (f) developing collaborative relationships with helping professionals, (g) maintaining clear family boundaries (between family and outside helpers), (h) maintaining social integration and (i) attributing positive meaning to the situation. For families coping with disasters and terrorism, several of these factors are likely to be pertinent and others to have analogues. For example, in relation to complex issues involved in balancing roles and family needs, Dekel and Nuttman-Shwartz (Chapter 14 of this volume) describe the challenges for mental health workers who are also parents and who live and work in an area under constant missile attack.

It is important to consider whether the factors most contributory to resilience change over time. Indeed, exploratory work by Lietz (2006, 2007) suggests that the factors contributing most strongly to resilience may differ at different phases of recovery after a significant stressor has occurred. For a sample of families who had experienced heterogeneous stressors, she used quantitative measures to identify families that had shown resilience, and then performed in-depth interviews with six families about their coping strategies. Lietz identified 10 resilience processes and five phases after the stressor, with different resilience processes more dominant at different phases. These phases were not locked in a linear temporal sequence and not all of the families interviewed went through the phases in the same order. The phases and associated processes are as follows:

- *An initial emphasis on survival.* During this period, the most important resilience processes identified were obtaining internal and external social support, taking charge and relying on morality/spirituality (having a belief system that provides direction and comfort).
- *Adaptation (making significant family changes to adapt to the situation).* During this period, creativity/flexibility and boundary setting (separating from negative influences) were the most important resilience processes.
- *Acceptance of the new reality for family.* During this phase, particularly important were insight, humor, communication (expressing thoughts and feelings about the situation) and morality/spirituality.
- *Growing stronger, find meaning in experience.* As indicated in the label, appraisal (finding meaning in the situation) was most critical in this phase.
- *Helping others.* During this phase, families tended to "give back" by giving social support to others.

It is important to move beyond considering family variables only as predictors of individual members' functioning. A family-resilience perspective includes considering family functioning as an important outcome. As Dekel and

Nuttman-Shwartz's chapter in this volume illustrates, one relevant issue is assessing relationships among domains of family functioning—the ways in which families juggle fulfilling their multiple functions. It is also important to consider the ecosystem factors that influence family functioning.

Interventions

Strategies to support the family as a unit and facilitate family resilience should take into account the range of factors that can be relevant and the corresponding range of possible intervention points. These can include addressing appraisals of the stressors, supporting changes in expectations, taking steps to reduce stressors, facilitating coping strategies or problem solving about resources. This can be done with individual families, but after community-wide events such as major disasters, multi-family groups also can be useful (see Walsh, 2006, Chapter 11). In addition, interventions at other ecosystem levels may be needed at times, for example, facilitating availability of needed resources.

Note

1. This work was funded in part by the Substance Abuse and Mental Health Services Administration (1 U79 SM57278), which established the Terrorism and Disaster Center (TDC) at the University of Oklahoma Health Sciences Center. TDC is a partner in the National Child Traumatic Stress Network.

References

Abramson, D. M., Park, Y. S., Stehling-Ariza, T., & Redlener, I. (2010). Children as bellwethers of recovery: Dysfunctional systems, and the effects of parents, households, and neighborhoods on serious emotional disturbance in children after Katrina. *Disaster Medicine and Public Health Preparedness*, *4*(Suppl. 1), S17–S27.

Anthony, E. J. (1987). Children at high risk for psychosis growing up successfully. In E. J. Anthony & B. J. Cohler (Eds.), *The invulnerable child* (pp.147–184). New York, NY: Guilford Press.

Antonovsky, A. (1979). *Health, stress, and coping*. San Francisco, CA: Jossey-Bass Publishers.

Antonovsky, A. (1988). The sense of coherence: An historical and future perspective. In H. I. McCubbin, E. A. Thompson, A. I. Thompson & J. E. Fromer (Eds.), *Stress, coping and health in families: Sense of coherence and resiliency* (pp. 3–40). Thousand Oaks, CA: Sage Publications.

Antonovsky, A., & Sourani, T. (1988). Family sense of coherence and family adaptation. *Journal of Marriage and the Family*, *50*(1), 79–92.

Becker, C., Sargent, J., & Rolland, J. S. (2000). Human Rights Committee of AFTA sponsors collaboration between Kosova and US mental health professionals: Kosovar Family Professional Education Collaborative (KFPEC). *American Family Therapy Academy Newsletter*, *80*, 26–30.

Becvar, D. S. (Ed.) (2013). *Handbook of family resilience*. New York, NY: Springer.

Bonanno, G. A., Brewin, C. R., Kaniasty, K., & La Greca, A. M. (2010). Weighing the costs of disaster: Consequences, risks, and resilience in individuals, families, and communities. *Psychological Science in the Public Interest, 11*(1), 1–49.

Boss, P. (2002). *Family stress management: A contextual approach.* Thousand Oaks, CA: Sage Publications.

Boss, P. (2004). Ambiguous loss theory, research, and practice: Reflections after 9/11. *Journal of Marriage and the Family, 66*(3), 551–566.

Bromet, E. J., & Litcher-Kelly, L. (2002). Psychological response of mothers of young children to the Three Mile Island and Chernobyl nuclear plant accidents one decade later. In J. M. Havenaar, J. Cwikel & E. J. Bromet (Eds.), *Toxic turmoil: Psychological and societal consequences of ecological disasters* (pp. 69–84). New York, NY: Kluwer Academic.

Elder, G. H. (1974). *Children of the Great Depression.* Chicago: University of Chicago Press.

Garmezy, N. (1987). Stress, competence and development: Continuities in the study of schizophrenic adults, children vulnerable to psychopathology, and the search for stress-resistant children. *American Journal of Orthopsychiatry, 52*(2), 159–174.

Garrison, M. E. B., and Sasser, D. D. (2009). Families and disasters: Making meaning out of adversity. In K. E. Cherry (Ed.), *Lifespan perspectives on natural disasters: Coping with Katrina, Rita, and Other Storms* (pp. 113–130). New York, NY: Springer Verlag.

Hill, R. (1949). *Families under stress.* New York, NY: Harper and Row.

Hill, R. (1958). Generic features of families under stress. *Social Casework, 39*, 139–150.

Knowles, R., Sasser, D. D., & Garrison, M. E. B. (2009). Family resilience and resiliency following Hurricane Katrina. In R. P. Kilmer, V. Gil-Rivas, R. G. Tedeschi & L. G. Calhoun (Eds.), *Helping families and communities recover from disaster: Lessons learned from Hurricane Katrina and its aftermath* (pp. 97–115). Washington, D.C.: American Psychological Association.

Landau, J., & Saul, J. (2004). Facilitating family and community resilience in response to major disaster. In F. Walsh & M. McGoldrick (Eds.), *Living beyond loss* (pp. 285–309). New York, NY: Norton.

Lietz, C. A. (2006). Uncovering stories of family resilience: A mixed methods study of resilient families, Part 1. *Families in Society, 87*(4), 575–582.

Lietz, C. A. (2007). Uncovering stories of family resilience: A mixed methods study of resilient families, Part 2. *Families in Society, 88*(1), 147–155.

Masten, A. S. (2001). Ordinary magic: Resilience processes in development. *American Psychologist, 56*(3), 227–238.

Masten, A. S., & Coatsworth, J. D. (1998). The development of competence in favorable and unfavorable environments: Lessons from research on successful children. *American Psychologist, 53*(2), 205–220.

Masten, A. S., & Obradovic, J. (2008). Disaster preparation and recovery: Lessons from research on resilience in human development. *Ecology and Society, 13*(1), 9 [online]. Retrieved from www.ecologyandsociety.org/vol13/iss1/art9/

McCubbin, H. I., & McCubbin, M. A. (1988). Typologies of resilient families: Emerging roles of social class and ethnicity. *Family Relations, 37*(3), 247–254.

McCubbin, H. I., McCubbin, M. A., Thompson, A. I, Han, S., & Allen, C. T. (1997). *Families under stress: What makes them resilient.* American Association of Family and Consumer Affairs commemorative lecture, Washington, D.C., June 22, 1997. Retrieved from http://www1.cyfernet.org/prog/fam/97-McCubbin-resilient.html

McCubbin, H. I., McCubbin, M. A., Thompson, A. I., & Thompson, E. A. (1998). Resilience in ethnic families: A conceptual model for predicting family adjustment and adaptation. In H. I. McCubbin, M. A. McCubbin, A. I. Thompson & J. E. Fromer (Eds.), *Resiliency in Native and immigrant American families* (pp. 3–48). Thousand Oaks, CA: Sage Publications.

McCubbin, H. I., & Patterson, J. M. (1983a). The family stress process: The double ABCX model of adjustment and adaptation. *Marriage & Family Review, 6*(1–2), 7–37.

McCubbin, H., & Patterson, J. (1983b). Family transitions: Adaptation to stress. In H. I. McCubbin & C. R. Figley (Eds.), *Stress and the family. 1, Coping with normative transitions*. New York, NY: Brunner/Mazel.

McCubbin, L. D., & McCubbin, H. I. (2013). Resilience in ethnic family systems: A relational theory for research and practice. In D. S. Becvar (Ed.), *Handbook of family resilience* (pp 175–195). New York, NY: Springer.

Norris, F. H., Stevens, S. P., Pfefferbaum, B., Wyche, K. F., & Pfefferbaum, R. L. (2008). Community resilience as a metaphor, theory, set of capacities, and strategy for disaster readiness. *American Journal of Community Psychology, 41*(1–2), 127–150.

Osofsky, J. D., Osofsky H. J., & Harris, W. W. (2007). *Katrina's children: Social policy considerations for children in disasters* (Social Policy Report, Vol. 21, No. 1). Ann Arbor, MI: Society for Research in Child Development.

Patterson, J. M. (1988). Families experiencing stress: I. The Family Adjustment and Adaptation Response Model: II. Applying the FAAR Model to health-related issues for intervention and research. *Family Systems Medicine, 6*(2), 202–237.

Patterson, J. M. (1991). Family resilience to the challenge of a child's disability. *Pediatric Annals, 20*(9), 491–499.

Patterson, J. M. (1995). Promoting resilience in families experiencing stress. *Pediatric Clinics of North America, 42*(1), 47–63.

Patterson, J. M. (2002a). Integrating family resilience and family stress theory. *Journal of Marriage* and *Family, 64*(2), 349–360.

Patterson, J. M. (2002b). Understanding family resilience. *Journal of Clinical Psychology, 58*(3), 233–246.

Patterson, J. M. (2005). Weaving gold out of straw: Meaning-making in families who have children with chronic illnesses. In W. M. Pinsof & J. L. Lebow (Eds.), *Family psychology: The art of the science* (Oxford Series in Clinical Psychology) (pp. 521–548). New York, NY: Oxford University Press.

Patterson, J. M., & Garwick, A. W. (1994). Levels of meaning in family stress theory. *Family Process, 33*(3), 287–304.

Pfefferbaum, R. L., & Klomp, R. W. (2013). Community resilience, disasters, and the public's health. In F. G. Murphy (Ed.), *Community engagement, organization, and development for public health practice* (pp. 275–298). New York, NY: Springer.

Prinstein, M. J., La Greca, A. M., Vernberg, E. M., & Silverman, W. K. (1996). Children's coping assistance: How parents, teachers, and friends help children cope after a natural disaster. *Journal of Clinical Child Psychology, 25*(4), 463–475.

Reiss, D., & Oliveri, M. E. (1991). The family's conception of accountability and competence: A new approach to the conceptualization and assessment of family stress. *Family Process, 30*(2), 193–214.

Rutter, M. (1979). Protective factors in children's responses to stress and disadvantage. In M. W. Kent & J. E. Rolf (Eds.), *Primary prevention in psychopathology: Social competence in children* (pp. 49–74). Hanover, NH: Published for the University of Vermont by the University Press of New England.

Rutter, M. (1985). Resilience in the face of adversity: Protective factors and resistance to psychiatric disorders. *British Journal of Psychiatry, 147*(6), 598–611.

Walsh, F. (1996). The concept of family resilience: Crisis and challenge. *Family Process, 35*(3), 261–281.

Walsh, F. (2002). A family resilience framework: Innovative practice applications. *Family Relations, 51*(2), 130–137.

Walsh, F. (2003). Family resilience: A framework for clinical practice. *Family Process, 42*(1), 1–18.

Walsh, F. (2006). *Strengthening family resilience* (2nd ed.). New York, NY: Guilford Press.

Walsh, F. (2013). Community-based practice applications of a family resilience framework. In D. S. Becvar (Ed.), *Handbook of family resilience* (pp. 65–82). New York, NY: Springer.

Werner, E. E. (1984). Research in review: Resilient children. *Young Children, 40*(1), 68–72.

Werner, E. E. (1993). Risk, resilience, and recovery: Perspectives from the Kauai Longitudinal Study. *Development and Psychopathology, 5*(4), 503–515.

Werner, E. E. (2005). What can we learn about resilience from large-scale longitudinal studies? In S. Goldstein, & R. B. Brooks, (Eds.), *Handbook of resilience in children* (pp. 91–105). New York, NY: Kluwer Academic.

Wright, M. O., & Masten, A. (2005). Resilience processes in development. In S. Goldstein, & R. B. Brooks, (Eds.), *Handbook of resilience in children* (pp. 17–35). New York, NY: Kluwer Academic.

Chapter 6

"Playing with fire"

Promoting play and playfulness in toddlers and families exposed to recurrent rocket fire

Esther Cohen

Introduction

It is the afternoon of Sunday, March 11th, 2012. A group of 10 mothers and their preschool children are gathered in a large room in the city of Sderot, in southern Israel, for their seventh meeting of the "Namal" program. Namal is an acronym in Hebrew for "Let's Make Room for Play" (*Naase Makom Lemis'hak*). The word *namal* also means port and has the connotation of a safe haven. This is particularly relevant at the meeting today, as the whole area has been repeatedly shelled by rockets and missiles launched from the Gaza Strip during the previous week.

Following much deliberation about the dangers involved in holding the group meeting, the members and the two moderators have decided not to cancel it. The room is a protective shelter and the participants live within a short walking distance. They figured they could run for safety en route to the meeting, if the early warning radar system was activated and the code "*Tzeva Adom*" ("Color Red") blared all over town. They would have 15 seconds to find shelter before the rocket fell.

The organizing theme for this meeting is imparted by the group leader through a new saying, as is customary in every meeting. Today's saying is "Things that you keep in your belly may give you a bellyache." The objective is to create an atmosphere that encourages the children to express and share their feelings about the recent events, while the parents respond by reflecting and validating their feelings and soothing the children. We know from a previous group meeting with the mothers alone that this is a new parental stance, since parents used to scold their children for expressing fear, encouraging them to act like heroes. They also tended to avoid talking to the children about the anxiety-arousing events and got irritated when the children played out themes of violence and destruction. The change is achieved in the group meeting through multimodal expressive activities. This session highlights the use of an interactive puppet show. The child puppet talks about the confusing events, expresses feelings, asks questions and interacts with the children and their parents. The moderator uses the puppet to help the children to construct a "trauma narrative" that explains the words the children hear (e.g., "Qassam," the name of the rocket) and the sequence of changing events from routine to danger and back to routine. The narrative also includes the protective measures taken by the army, their families and the children themselves. The necessary actions of timely running to a safe place with the caregiver when "Color Red" is sounded are then playfully and symbolically rehearsed through songs and movement. The transitions from a state of routine to a state of urgent protective action and back to relaxation when the danger is over are repeated in various playful games.

An additional objective of the meeting involves helping the parents to better regulate and soothe their child. The group practices breathing and muscle relaxation to music. The mothers then present their children with a surprise: a "soothing box," which they made and decorated at their previous meeting. This box contains the child's transitional objects and favorite toys.

On the following day, the moderators share with me via email their sense of satisfaction and agency and the parents' reported sense of excitement and competence. They feel they have conquered helplessness in the face of trauma, at least temporarily, and can be helpful to the children.

Little has been reported in the literature on families with young children living, like the group described here, in areas suffering from prolonged, recurrent acts of political violence (Feldman & Vengrober, 2011). Research on children exposed to prolonged war situations and acts of terrorism, typically assessing older children or adolescents, has underscored the long-term effects of these experiences on children's well-being, emotional reactivity and mental and physical health (Dybdahl, 2001; Feldman & Vengrober, 2011; Fremont, 2004; Joshi & O'Donnell, 2003; Pine, Costello, & Masten, 2005; Thabet, Karim, & Vostanis, 2006). It appears, however, from recent research that, contrary to popular beliefs about under-fives' imperviousness to traumatic events, exposure to repeated wartime trauma can have particularly profound, lasting effects on children's mental health at this age (Lieberman, 2011).

The need to address the needs of such young children from the perspective of prevention is paramount, as the number of children exposed to ongoing war and terrorism has increased worldwide in recent decades. We set out to meet this challenge of strengthening the resilience of young children exposed to a prolonged war situation in Israel by creating a preventive intervention that would be theoretically grounded and evidence informed. Given the children's developmental stage, play and playfulness seemed to be a natural medium for engaging them and their caregivers. The relevance of both play and playfulness to resilience is discussed in the following sections.

Play and resilience

Play, especially "pretend play" (also referred to as "free play," "imaginative play" and "symbolic play"), has long been considered of central importance to children's cognitive, social and emotional development (Ginsburg, 2007; Singer & Singer, 2006; Vygotsky, 1966). Winnicott (1971) demonstrated that important psychological transformations could take place via the process of play itself, even without psychodynamic interpretations. Similarly, Slade (1999) elaborated on therapists' often-neglected role in helping children "make believe" and develop play, rather than "make meaning" (offering interpretations). In play, children can experience a sense of agency by becoming "masters of their universe" (Alvarez & Phillips, 1998). This can help counteract feelings of depression, anxiety and panic often reported by traumatized children (Schonfeld, 2011), as well as give them the opportunity to create meaning in various ways.

Singer and Singer (2006) emphasized the contribution of play to narrative awareness and expressive linguistic capacities. The ability to construct a coherent trauma narrative has been shown to be associated with better coping with traumatic events and with posttraumatic growth (Cohen, Chazan, Lerner, & Maimon, 2010; Hafstad, Gil-Rivas, Kilmer, & Raeder, 2010; Wigren, 1994).

Play interactions between parent and child are believed to provide the basis for the child's development of reflective functions (Fonagy, Gergely, & Jurist, 2002). The "pretend mode" is supposed to allow the child to learn to use real objects in an imaginary way to express wishes and fantasies. However the play, or fantasy, does not force itself on reality. Holding both perspectives in mind, the imagined and the real, allows the child *self-reflection* and provides the ability to distinguish between subjective experiences and the experiences of others. This contributes to the evolution of the "*interpersonal interpretive function*" (Fonagy et al., 2002) and the development of *self-regulation capacities*. These capacities have been linked to resilience (Fonagy & Target, 2003; Waugh, Fredrickson, & Taylor, 2008).

Posttraumatic play and therapeutic play interventions

The phenomenon of "posttraumatic play" (PTP) has been described in clinical reports as a play pattern observable following traumatic experiences, which is distinctly different from normal play (Wershba-Gershon, 1996). The reports characterize PTP as driven, serious, lacking in joy and frequently morbid. Characteristically, such play consists of compulsively repeated themes that are not resolved (Gil, 1998; Nader & Pynoos, 1991; Varkas, 1998). Additionally, a number of reports point out the defensive reduction in symbolic expression and the concurrent increase in concrete thinking in PTP (Drewes, 2001; Feldman, Vengrober, & Hallaq, 2007). PTP is further described as developmentally regressed, involving simple defenses, such as identification with the aggressor, identification with the victim, displacement, undoing and denial (Cohen et al., 2010; Rafman, Canfield, Barbas, & Kaczorowski, 1996; Terr, 1981).

Play therapy has been used as a major means of helping children process and recover from traumatic experiences, and evidence demonstrating its effectiveness has been accumulating (Ogawa, 2004; Schottelkorb, Doumas, & Garcia, 2012). However, since resources are usually insufficient to provide individual play therapy for the children who need it—those living in situations involving prolonged or repetitive traumatizing events—it is worth considering how natural caregivers (parents and teachers) can support the child's beneficial use of play.

Reports based on clinical observations suggest that engaging in PTP may be adaptive or maladaptive, curative or harmful (Dripchak, 2007; Nader & Pynoos, 1991; Ryan & Needham, 2001; Terr, 1990; Webb & Terr, 2007). Nader & Pynoos (1991) maintain that PTP's ability to alleviate distress depends mainly on the child's perception of control over consequences, his or her ability to cognitively process the trauma and express forbidden feelings. In our own study of children exposed to terrorism (Chazan & Cohen, 2010; Cohen, 2006; Cohen et al., 2010), the children with the lowest levels of posttraumatic stress disorder (PTSD) symptoms (in comparison to those with highest levels) had a greater tendency to engage in play; better ability to plan and play out a coherent, progressive, creative and satisfying imaginary narrative while showing "awareness of oneself as player" (awareness of being the director as well as the actor in one's play); a better capacity for self-soothing; and a greater tendency to engage in relationships with adults. This set of characteristics can be described as the ability to play with a high level of playfulness (Bundy, 2005).

Play and playfulness

Playfulness refers to spontaneous physical, cognitive and social behavior that expresses joy, humor, curiosity, imagination and creativity. From a developmental point of view, it may be regarded as a stable individual characteristic (Lieberman, 1977) that is formed and develops in a relationship. It is displayed in play as well as other verbal and non-verbal interpersonal interactions.

The unique aspects of play that pertain to its level of playfulness were defined by Bundy (2005), who constructed a research tool to measure playfulness in children (the Test of Playfulness). On the basis of previous formulations, she suggests that playfulness is contingent on a combination of four elements: (a) *intrinsic motivation, (b) internal control, (c) the freedom to suspend reality and (d) framing.* According to Bundy (1997), "intrinsic motivation" refers to the self-rewarding aspect of play, as opposed to interest in an external reward. Thus, a child showing intrinsic motivation is drawn to be engaged in play by the interest and enjoyment derived from the activity itself. "Internal control" suggests that the child is largely in control of his or her actions and some aspect of the activity's outcome. This element refers to the child's level of "awareness of him-/herself as a player" (Cohen et al., 2010); namely, that he or she is both the director and the actor in the play. "Freedom to suspend reality" means that the child feels free to decide how close the play transactions will be to objective reality. "Framing" means that the player organizes a frame and rules for the play that are coherent and can be shared with another (a code), thus showing the ability to provide and interpret play cues and reach mutual understandings.

Developmental aspects of playfulness and resilience

Panksepp (2009) argues that the urge for joyous physical engagement with others is built into the instinctual action apparatus of the mammalian brain, and that early playful interactions strengthen interpersonal regulatory circuits in the brain and form the basis for social learning. Similarly, Trevarthen and Aitken (1990) maintain that the baby has a basic need for a joyful dialogic companionship that includes vitality, contingency, rhythmicity and positive affect. They describe how prosodic vocalizations, coordinated visual eye-to-eye messages, and tactile and body gestures serve as channels of communicative signals in the earliest forms of dialogue between infant and mother and induce instant emotional effects.

It is argued that this gradual working out of collaborative strategies for the elaboration of *shared meanings* is a principal function of joint pretend play in early childhood, and this is also one of the critical developmental functions addressed in psychodynamic play therapy. This type of collaboration also helps the child process aspects of traumatic experience and regulate affect (Lyons-Ruth, 1999, 2006). Accordingly, Jung (2010) demonstrated how caregivers' playfulness helped alleviate the emotional distress of infants during the transition to a new childcare setting.

Playfulness, positive affect and resilience

In childhood, the capacity to manage arousal is facilitated by the caregiver's sensitive, attuned responses to both negative and positive affect. This is achieved by repeatedly pairing high arousal states with interpersonal relatedness and playfulness (Ogden, 1985). Schore (2003) underscores the often-overlooked positive mechanism of affect regulation: "Affect regulation is not just the reduction of affective intensity, the dampening of negative emotion. It also involves amplification, an intensification of positive emotion, a condition necessary for more complex self-organization" (p. 78). This intensification of positive emotions is achieved through playful interactions between caregiver and child.

The important adaptational significance of positive emotions in coping with stressful events has been pointed out in a number of reviews (e.g., Folkman & Moskowitz, 2000; Fredrickson, 2000). They show that positive emotions broaden the scope of attention, cognition and action, and help build physical, intellectual and social resources. These become important facilitators of adaptive coping and adjustment to acute and chronic stress. Indeed, a number of post-9/11 studies found positive emotions to be associated with better posttraumatic outcomes in adults (Bonanno, Westphal, & Mancini, 2011).

The present review provides support for the idea that playfulness developed prior to exposure to traumatic events enhances resilience for such events. However, playfulness may be diminished by exposure to overwhelming trauma. We posit that support in regaining playfulness can help children regain the use of "playful play" to successfully process their traumatic experiences.

Caregivers and resilience

Parents are powerful mediators of the effects of traumatic events on their children. The literature shows that parents influence the capacities their children developed prior to the traumatic events, model behavior during the event and shape the healing environment following a traumatic event (Cohen, 2009). Recent investigations of resilience place particular importance on the quality of the attachment relationship and its role in the development of affect regulation in children. It has been shown that children who have experienced sensitive caregiving develop neurological systems that function effectively in regulating emotional arousal (Braungart-Rieker, Garwood, Powers, & Wang, 2001; Fonagy & Target, 2003).

Caregivers also play a central role in the development of playfulness. Children who did not have experiences of playfulness and shared humor in their early relationships may show inhibited patterns of play, as well as difficulties in establishing cooperative relationships with others (Youell, 2008). Winnicott (1971) emphasized that the ability to maintain the illusionary experience needed for the encounter between imagination and reality in play is dependent on the child's caregivers and environment and the way they treat play and play objects. Furthermore, the parent's willingness to directly engage in and support children's play contributes to the level of playfulness, the richness and complexity of play and the child's ability to use play for affective processing (Bronson & Bundy, 2001; Fonagy et al., 2002).

Unfortunately, parents' ability to support the child's play and playfulness, as well as the general quality of parental care giving, is often diminished during stressful periods, when their children need them most. This is due to parental depression, anxiety and posttraumatic distress (Cohen, 2009). Thus, parents often need help themselves if they are to help their children cope successfully with trauma. A few efficacious interventions, such as child–parent psychotherapy (Van Horn & Lieberman, 2009), have been developed for young children exposed to traumatic events, with a focus on the parent–child relationship. However, this intervention is based on an individual child or family format, which limits its widespread use during periods of collective traumatic events.

Preventive interventions

The field of prevention may have been held back by the notion that early interventions are not advisable for those affected by traumatic events. This stance has recently been criticized by Dyregrov and Regel (2012), who argue that "watchful waiting" may even be harmful. We concur with their position that, in the face of the needs of children and parents, especially when they are coping with recurrent stressful, traumatic conditions, a proactive preventive approach is needed. Preventive interventions should be tailored to the needs of the community, rather than focusing on providing conventional individual therapy for particular individuals who have been identified as severely affected.

A small number of interventions have been described that address the needs of large groups of families living under chronic traumatic stress (Kiser, Donohue, Hodgkinson, Medoff, & Black, 2010). Only a few recent reports focus on the needs of families of young children. Dybdahl (2001) describes an intervention based on weekly meetings with refugee mothers of pre-school children, conducted for 5 months. The meetings focused on coping with problems and promoting a good mother–child interaction. The children of the participants showed better weight gain, and both the mothers and the children showed fewer distress symptoms than a control group receiving medical follow-up.

Focusing on families from the general Israeli population rather than specific groups exposed to traumatic events, Kidron and Landreth (2010) reported the effectiveness of intensive child–parent relationship therapy (CPRT) with groups of Israeli parents. Parents are trained to conduct nondirective play therapy with their children. The program significantly increased the parents' level of empathic interactions with their children and their attitude of acceptance toward their children, and significantly reduced the level of stress involved in parenting as compared with parents in the non-treatment comparison group.

The "Namal" program

Unique characteristics

The *Namal* program was created by Esther Cohen specifically for families of young children (initially for toddlers and then adapted for preschoolers as well). It was implemented and adapted by the staff of the Israeli Center for the Treatment of Psychotrauma—Ruth Pat-Horenczyk, Dafna Ba-Gad, Dafna Shamir, Rinat Yalin and Liz Yung.

The program was initially operated in Sderot but is being extended to other areas. Sderot has suffered from recurrent rocket and mortar attacks launched by Hamas and Islamic Jihad since 2001. Although the frequency and intensity of these attacks has varied over the years, they have never stopped for any extended period of time. In 2008, for example, during a period of sharp increase in the shelling, approximately 4,000 rockets and mortars were fired, with an average of 11 incidents per day. All the residents have experienced "Color Red," an early warning radar system that detects a rocket launch and activates a public broadcast alarm that allows residents 15 seconds to rush themselves and their children to protected areas. Unfortunately, many homes and some schools lack adequate protection. The rates of PTSD in mothers and children in this area are the highest in the country, and have reached more than 30% for each group (Pat-Horenczyk et al., 2012).

The *Namal* program uses a group format, simultaneously involving caregivers and young children. This format is economical in its use of professional resources and non-stigmatizing for parents. A group consists of eight to ten mother–child dyads from the general population. Two moderators are responsible for leading ten group meetings: eight meetings with mother–child dyads, one with mothers only and one with the participants and invited members of their extended families. A light supper is served at the end of each meeting; during this time, the moderators make themselves available for individual discussions with caregivers.

The program is aimed at strengthening elements that enhance resilience by focusing on improving everyday positive parent–child interactions, as well as addressing needs associated with the exposure to trauma. These goals are attained by providing opportunities for mutual enjoyment in parent–child multimodal interactions; raising caregivers' awareness of their central role in building the child's sense of security, uniqueness, trust and self-reliance; educating caregivers about the importance of supporting the expression and regulation of emotions, while teaching reflection and soothing skills; and sensitizing parents to their role in supporting their child's curiosity, creativity and imagination through play and playfulness. Additionally, parents are helped to develop the knowledge and skills to help their children process painful feelings and make sense of the traumatic events. This includes creating a coherent, protective trauma narrative and expanding the children's range of self-regulation techniques and soothing and relaxation skills.

Since it is difficult to teach playfulness directly, the learning process in the group is interactive and experiential. It involves engaging the participants in various expressive and artistic modalities, including music, rhymes, movement, art and drama. Furthermore, because traumatic events may decrease the caregivers' level of reflection and symbolization, the program addresses these spheres by organizing each meeting around a theme that is introduced via a saying that carries a developmental or a relational message.

The sayings we use typically have a double meaning—one concrete and one abstract—and this makes their use playful. The saying is introduced and explained briefly at the beginning of each session, and all the activities are connected to the message. At the end of each session, the moderators summarize the meeting by pointing out this connection. The caregivers then take home a printed page with more detailed information about the session's theme, as well as a decorative refrigerator magnet with the saying. The magnets handed out during the meetings, when placed together at the end of the program, form the shape of a house. This is intended both to support reflection upon and internalization of the newly acquired ideas and skills and to increase sharing with other caregivers.

Although the program uses a group format, the activities are aimed mostly at the dyadic interaction of child and caregiver. Large colorful sheer scarves are used in various ways to delineate the intimate dyadic space. Each meeting begins with a welcoming song and ends with some relaxation activities.

Description of the program

Themes, sayings and messages

SESSION 1

Theme: The importance of secure attachment for favorable personality development.

Saying: "If we look at something with love, it becomes beautiful."

Messages: The parent–child relationship is the basis for the child's perceptions of him/herself and others; it is important for parents to spend exclusive time with the child, delight in the child, be emotionally available, soothe and regulate the child and mediate experiences.

Examples of activities: The dyad dances to lyrics, instructing the caregiver to search for her child, who hides behind her back, and then to express delight at find her/him there. The caregiver uses suggested rhymes to invite the child to a "special meeting" under the sheer scarf, which covers them both, and then observes and reflects the child's lovable features. The caregiver oversees the child rocking while lying on a big ball. She encourages the child's independent movement as he or she lies face down and offers greater help and protection when the child lies with his or her back on the ball.

SESSION 2

Theme: The importance of supporting autonomy.

Saying: "All a child needs is one adult who believes in him/her."

Message: Parents can promote the child's strivings for autonomy and self-reliance by focusing on the child's interests and motivations, encouraging and patiently facilitating independent coping, appreciating the process and not only the outcome.

Examples of activities: The dyad is invited to construct leaves out of newspapers. They playfully disperse them to an imaginary wind suggested in the lyrics of a song. The caregiver supports and encourages the child's independent coping. They then neaten each other and the floor. The caregiver facilitates solving the problem of reaching the wastebasket, which is placed too high for the child to reach. A puppet talks to the children about what he or she can do by him/herself and what he or she still finds difficult.

SESSION 3

Theme: The importance of play and playfulness.

Saying: "All you need for playing are a good imagination and a pile of odds and ends."

Message: Playful interactions can be achieved with a variety of play objects (no need for fancy toys), movements, gestures, music, words and ideas. Promote playfulness, creativity, imagination and humor when interacting with your child. These are important for enjoyment, strengthening relationships, reducing stress, and developing cognitive and social flexibility.

Example of activities: Using bodily movements and finger-play to represent animals and objects; completing sentences with funny rhymes; decorating the mother's face with colorful stickers.

SESSION 4

Theme: The advantage of a focus on the positive and accepting the child's uniqueness.

Saying: "Always focus on the doughnut and not on the hole; otherwise, you may remain hungry."

Message: Use observation and reflection to acknowledge and validate your child's plans, choices, effort, achievements and wishes; this will help the child experience and develop self-esteem and self-acceptance.

Examples of activities: The caregiver imitates the child's movements, postures and facial expressions, guided by an appropriate song. The dyads engage in constructing a structure out of scraps, and the caregiver reflects the child's actions, intentions, choices and feelings.

SESSION 5

Theme: The importance of helping children express and share a wide range of feelings.

Saying: "The heart has a mind of its own, which the mind cannot always comprehend."

Messages: Be attentive to your child's various emotions. Label, accept and validate all emotions, even if they appear unjustified or inappropriate. Encourage the child to express them in acceptable ways. Talking with children about unpleasant feelings reduces their loneliness; helps them understand, accept and regulate their feelings; and facilitates correcting misconceptions and problem-solving. Ignoring fears or criticizing emotions does not make them go away.

Example of activities: Songs about various emotions accompanied by movements and facial expressions; the puppet shares her fears at bedtime.

SESSION 6

Theme: Assisting the helpers in providing help.

Saying: "God created parents because He was too busy to do everything Himself."

Message: Processing your own stress and posttraumatic feelings and discussing ways to regulate them is a precondition for you as a parent be able to help your children regulate their feelings and behavior. Transitional objects, rituals and play are important for children's self-regulation.

Example of activities: Mothers alone, group sharing of personal coping resources; preparation of a "surprise box" with soothing objects for the child.

SESSION 7

Theme: Play and playfulness are helpful in coping with life in the shadow of uncontrollable traumatic events.

Saying: "Imagination is one of the best weapons in the struggle against reality."

Messages: Playing with your child offers an enjoyable diversion in stressful times; the mind can transport us to imagined situations and enhance our pleasure and relaxation. It is important to cultivate the ability to imagine a good future. Play advances the child's ability to use symbolic processing of intense experiences, which, in turn, contributes to better coping and resilience.

Examples of activities: Hiding in imaginary, symbolic protective spaces; inviting pleasant memories; jumping from a green hoop to a red hoop (representing the alert code "Color Red") and back; relaxation using guided imagery.

SESSION 8

Theme: The complexity of understanding children's inner experiences and responding to their needs in traumatic situations.

Saying: "Things that you keep to yourself inside your belly may give you a bellyache."

Messages: The child needs the help of the caregiver to understand and create a clear narrative around unusual, confusing and anxiety-arousing experiences, while emphasizing resources and protection. Help your child engage in creative or make-believe play and in playful, soothing interactions; help children introduce coherence and "protection themes" into chaotic play.

Examples of activities: The puppet shares her experience of a recent "Color Red" incident, and the moderator, role-playing her mother, answers her questions and tells her the "story" of the incident. Dyads dance to a song with umbrellas to protect themselves from rain and hail.

SESSION 9

Theme: The importance of adhering to and valuing long-term parenting goals in a supportive human network. Significant others are invited to this meeting by the participants.

Saying: "There are two gifts we can give our children: One is roots, the other is wings."

Message: Parents can achieve seemingly conflicting yet complementary parenting goals through the use of intimate play interactions with their children: a sense of human connectedness, endurance and stability, together with a sense of agency, striving and hope for change.

Example of activities: Various previous activities are shared with the guests.

SESSION 10

Concluding, reviewing, and saying goodbye. Reflecting on the process of change and the achievements gained through the participation in the group.

Conclusion

The program is currently being formally evaluated, but the evaluation is beyond the scope of this chapter. However, it is already clear, as the twentieth group is in progress, that the groups address important needs of caregivers and young children. This is evident from the high level of mothers' interest in joining the groups despite daily pressures, as well as the level of enthusiasm and satisfaction repeatedly expressed by the participants. The fact that many of the toddlers remember the timing of the expected meetings and remind their mothers of them may be seen as evidence for how significant these group experiences are for them. It is our hope that the ideas and the evidence base reviewed here, and our attempt to translate them into an actual preventive intervention, will inspire other professionals to address the needs of families and young children dealing with multiple or recurrent traumatic events.

References

Alvarez, A., & Phillips, A. (1998). The importance of play: A child psychotherapist's view. *Child Psychology & Psychiatry Review, 3*(3), 99–103. doi: 10.1017/s1360641798001579

Bonanno, G. A., Westphal, M., & Mancini, A. D. (2011). Resilience to loss and potential trauma. *Annual Review of Clinical Psychology, 7*(1), 511–535. doi: 10.1146/annurev-clinpsy-032210-104526

Braungart-Rieker, J. M., Garwood, M. M., Powers, B. P., & Wang, X. (2001). Parental sensitivity, infant affect, and affect regulation: Predictors of later attachment. *Child Development, 72*(1), 252–270. doi: 10.1111/1467-8624.00277

Bronson, M. R., & Bundy, A. C. (2001). A correlational study of a test of playfulness and a test of environmental supportiveness for play. *Occupational Therapy Journal of Research, 21*(4), 241–259.

Bundy, A. C. (1997). Play and playfulness: What to look for. In L. D. Parham & L. S. Fazio (Eds.), *Play in occupational therapy for children* (pp. 52–66). St. Louis, MO: Mosby.

Bundy, A. C. (2005). *Test of Playfulness manual.* Sydney, Australia: University of Sydney.

Chazan, S., & Cohen, E. (2010). Adaptive and defensive strategies in post-traumatic play of young children exposed to violent attacks. *Journal of Child Psychotherapy, 36*(2), 133–151.

Cohen, E. (2006). Play and adaptation in traumatized young children and their caregivers in Israel. In L. Barbanel & R. J. Sternberg (Eds.), *Psychological interventions in times of crisis* (pp. 151–180). New York, NY: Springer.

Cohen, E. (2009). Parenting in the throes of traumatic events: Relational risks and protection processes. In J. Ford, R. Pat-Horenczyk & D. Brom (Eds.), *Treating traumatized children: Risk, resilience and recovery* (pp. 72–84). New York, NY: Routledge.

Cohen, E., Chazan, S. E., Lerner, M., & Maimon, E. (2010). Posttraumatic play in young children exposed to terrorism: An empirical study. *Infant Mental Health Journal, 31*(2), 1–23.

Drewes, A. A. (2001). Developmental considerations in play and play therapy with traumatized children. In A. A. Drewes, L. J. Carey, & C. E. Schaefer (Eds.), *School-based play therapy* (pp. 297–314). New York, NY: J. Wiley.

Dripchak, V. L. (2007). Posttraumatic play: Towards acceptance and resolution. *Clinical Social Work Journal, 35*(2), 125–134.

Dybdahl, R. (2001). Children and mothers in war: An outcome study of a psychosocial intervention program. *Child Development, 72*(4), 1214–1230. doi: 10.1111/1467-8624.00343

Dyregrov, A., & Regel, S. (2012). Early interventions following exposure to traumatic events: Implications for practice from recent research. *Journal of Loss and Trauma: International Perspectives on Stress & Coping, 17*(3), 271–291.

Feldman, R., Vengrober, A., & Hallaq, E. (2007, August). *Mother–child relationship, child symptoms, and maternal well-being in Israeli and Palestinian infants and young children exposed to war, terror, and violence.* Paper presented at the 13th International Congress of the European Society for Child and Adolescent Psychiatry, Florence, Italy.

Feldman, R., & Vengrober, A. (2011). Posttraumatic stress disorder in infants and young children exposed to war-related trauma. *Journal of the American Academy of Child & Adolescent Psychiatry, 50*(7), 645–658. doi: 10.1016/j.jaac.2011.03.001

Folkman, S., & Moskowitz, J. T. (2000). Positive affect and the other side of coping. *American Psychologist, 55*(6), 647–654. doi: 10.1037/0003-066x.55.6.647

Fonagy, P., Gergely, G., & Jurist, E. L. (2002). *Affect regulation, mentalization, and the development of the self.* New York, NY: Other Press.

Fonagy, P., & Target, M. (2003). Evolution of the interpersonal interpretive function: Clues for effective preventive intervention in early childhood. In S. Coates, J. Rosenthol & D. Schecliter (Eds.), *September 11: Trauma and human bonds* (pp. 99–113). New York, NY: Analytic Press/Taylor & Francis Group.

Fredrickson, B. L. (2000). Cultivating positive emotions to optimize health and well-being. *Prevention & Treatment, 3*(1). doi: 10.1037/1522-3736.3.1.31a

Fremont, W. P. (2004). Childhood reactions to terrorism-induced trauma: A review of the past 10 years. *Journal of the American Academy of Child & Adolescent Psychiatry, 43*(4), 381–392

Gil, E. (1998). *Essentials of play therapy with abused children* [Manual]. New York, NY: Guilford Press.

Ginsburg, K. R. (2007). The importance of play in promoting healthy child development and maintaining strong parent-child bonds. *Pediatrics, 119*(1), 182–191.

Hafstad, G. S., Gil-Rivas, V., Kilmer, R. P., & Raeder, S. (2010). Parental adjustment, family functioning, and posttraumatic growth among Norwegian children and adolescents following a natural disaster. *American Journal of Orthopsychiatry, 80*(2), 248–257. doi: 10.1111/j.1939-0025.2010.01028.x

Joshi, P. T., & O'Donnell, D. A. (2003). Consequences of child exposure to war and terrorism. *Clinical Child and Family Psychology Review, 6*(4), 275–292. doi: 10.1023/b :ccfp.0000006294.88201.68

Jung, J. (2010) Caregivers' playfulness and infants' emotional stress during transitional times. *Early Child Development and Care, 181*(10), 1397–1407.

Kidron, M., & Landreth, G. (2010). Intensive child parent relationship therapy with Israeli parents in Israel. *International Journal of Play Therapy, 19*(2), 64–78.

Kiser, L. J., Donohue, A., Hodgkinson, S., Medoff, D., & Black, M. M. (2010). Strengthening family coping resources: The feasibility of a multifamily group intervention for families exposed to trauma. *Journal of Traumatic Stress, 23*(6), 802–806. doi: 10.1002/jts.20587

Lieberman, A.F. (2011). Infants remember: War exposure, trauma, and attachment in young children and their mothers. *Journal of the American Academy of Child and Adolescent Psychiatry, 50* (7), 640–641.

Lieberman, J. N. (1977). *Playfulness: Its relationship to imagination and creativity*: New York, NY: Academic Press.

Lyons-Ruth, K. (1999). The two-person unconscious: Intersubjective dialogue, enactive relational representation, and the emergence of new forms of relational organization. *Psychoanalytic Inquiry, 19*(4), 576–617. doi: 10.1080/07351699909534267

Lyons-Ruth, K. (2006). Play, precariousness, and the negotiation of shared meaning: A developmental research perspective on child psychotherapy. *Journal of Infant, Child, and Adolescent Psychotherapy, 5*(2), 142–159.

Nader, K., & Pynoos, R. S. (1991). Play and drawing techniques as tools for interviewing traumatized children. In C. E. Schaffer, K. Gitlin-Weiner & A. Sandgrund (Eds.), *Play diagnosis and assessment* (pp. 375–389). New York, NY: Wiley.

Ogawa, Y. (2004). Childhood trauma and play therapy intervention for traumatized children. *Journal of Professional Counseling: Practice, Theory, and Research, 32*(1), 19–29.

Ogden, T. H. (1985). On potential space. *International Journal of Psychoanalysis, 66*(Pt 2), 129–141.

Panksepp, J. (2009). Brain emotional systems and qualities of mental life: From animal models of affect to implications for psychotherapeutics. In D. Fosha, D. J. Siegel & M. F. Solomon (Eds.), *The healing power of emotion: Affective neuroscience, development & clinical practice* (pp. 1–26). New York, NY: W. W. Norton.

Pat-Horenczyk, R., Achituv, M., Kagan-Rubenstein, A., Khodabakhsh, A., Brom, D., & Chemtob, C.M. (2012). Growing up under fire: Building resilience in toddlers and parents exposed to ongoing missile attacks. *Journal of Child & Adolescent Trauma*, 5(4), pp. 303–314.

Pine, D. S., Costello, J., & Masten, A. (2005). Trauma, proximity, and developmental psychopathology: The effects of war and terrorism on children. *Neuropsychopharmacology*, 30(10), 1781–1792. doi: 10.1038/sj.npp.1300814

Rafman, S., Canfield, J., Barbas, J., & Kaczorowski, J. (1996). Disrupted moral order: A conceptual framework for differentiating reactions to loss and trauma. *International Journal of Behavioral Development*, 19(4), 817–829. doi: 10.1080/016502596385596

Ryan, V., & Needham, C. (2001). Non-directive play therapy with children experiencing psychic trauma. *Clinical Child Psychology and Psychiatry*, 6(3), 437–453. doi: 10.1177/1359104501006003011

Schonfeld, D. J. (2011). Ten years after 9/11: What have we (not yet) learned? *Journal of Developmental & Behavioral Pediatrics*, 32(7), 542–545.

Schore, A. N. (2003). *Affect dysregulation and disorders of the self*. New York, NY: W. W. Norton.

Schottelkorb, A. A., Doumas, D. M., & Garcia, R. (2012). Treatment for childhood refugee trauma: A randomized, controlled trial. *International Journal Play Therapy*, 21(2), 57–73.

Singer, J. L., & Singer, D. G. (2006). Preschoolers' imaginative play as precursor of narrative consciousness. *Imagination, Cognition and Personality*, 25(2), 97–117. doi: 10.2190/0kqu-9a2v-yam2-xd8j

Slade, A. (1999). Making meaning and making believe: Their role in the clinical process. In D. P. Wolf & A. Slade (Eds.), *Children at play: Clinical and developmental approaches to meaning and representation* (pp. 81–107). New York, NY: Oxford University Press.

Terr, L. (1990). *Too scared to cry: Psychic trauma in childhood*. New York, NY: Harper & Row.

Terr, L. C. (1981). Psychic trauma in children: Observations following the Chowchilla school-bus kidnapping. *The American Journal of Psychiatry*, 138(1), 14–19.

Thabet, A. A. M., Karim, K., & Vostanis, P. (2006). Trauma exposure in pre-school children in a war zone. *British Journal of Psychiatry*, 188(2), 154–158. doi: 10.1192/bjp.188.2.154

Trevarthen, C., & Aitken, K. J. (2001). Infant intersubjectivity: Research, theory and clinical applications. *Journal of Child Psychology and Psychiatry*, 42(1), 3–48

Van Horn, P., & Lieberman, A. F. (2009). Using dyadic therapies to treat traumatized young children. In J. Ford, R. Pat-Horenczyk & D. Brom (Eds.), *Treating traumatized children: Risk, resilience and recovery* (pp. 210–224). New York, NY: Routledge/Taylor & Francis Group.

Varkas, T. (1998). Childhood trauma and posttraumatic play: A literature review and case study. *Journal of Analytic Social Work*, 5(3), 29–50.

Vygotsky, L. S. (1966). Play and its role in the mental development of the child. *Voprosy Psikhologii*, 12(6), 62–67.

Waugh, C. E., Fredrickson, B. L., & Taylor, S. F. (2008). Adapting to life's slings and arrows: Individual differences in resilience when recovering from an anticipated threat. *Journal of Research in Personality*, *42*(4), 1031–1046. doi: 10.1016/j.jrp.2008.02.005

Webb, N. B., & Terr, L. C. (2007). *Play therapy with children in crisis: Individual, group, and family treatment* (3rd ed.). New York, NY: Guilford Press.

Wershba-Gershon, P. (1996). Free symbolic play and assessment of the nature of child sexual abuse. *Journal of Child Sexual Abuse: Research, Treatment, & Program Innovations for Victims, Survivors, & Offenders*, *5*(2), 37–58. doi: 10.1300/J070v05n02_03

Wigren, J. (1994). Narrative completion in the treatment of trauma. *Psychotherapy: Theory, Research, Practice, Training*, *31*(3), 415–423. doi: 10.1037/0033-3204.31.3.415

Winnicott, D. W. (1971). *Playing and reality*. Oxford, UK: Penguin.

Youell, B. (2008). The importance of play and playfulness. *European Journal of Psychotherapy & Counselling*, *10*(2), 121–129. doi: 10.1080/13642530802076193

Chapter 7

Haifa dyadic therapy

A mentalization-based treatment for war-traumatized children

Judith Harel and Hanna Kaminer

This chapter describes the Haifa dyadic therapy (HDT) model and its adaptation for treating children traumatized by war. HDT is a psychodynamic relationship-focused model for short-term treatment of emotional difficulties. The major therapeutic factor the model employs is the enhancement of both the parents' and the child's mentalization, making it highly suitable for treating posttraumatic stress disorder (PTSD).

Children in wartime

For five weeks in 2006, day and night, Hezbollah bombarded northern Israel with hundreds of missiles and rockets. Loud sirens preceded most of the attacks, and small children were frightened by the sirens even when they were not followed by missiles. Children and adults were exposed to highly stressful, anxiety-provoking situations, including the recruitment of male family members for defense service. Children and adults who experienced these attacks were at high risk for developing posttraumatic symptoms (PTS)—and many of them did.

Countless children around the world are at high risk for war-related trauma (Betancourt, 2011). Studies suggest that children affected by PTSD are more likely to suffer from various problems in later childhood, adolescence and adulthood. Wartime situations on the home front are particularly risky because of the "dose effect": the closer one is to the traumatic events, the greater the risk of PTS (Yule, Perrin, & Smith, 2000), which, if untreated, could lead to long-lasting PTSD (Cohen, 2010).

To demonstrate the application of the HDT model to war-trauma treatment, we here describe the case of a boy and his parents:

> Eli, four years old at the time of referral, showed posttraumatic symptoms. Until the war, Eli's development had been normal, but, since then, there was significant regression, marked by difficulty in falling asleep, frequent nighttime awakenings, bedwetting and nightmares accompanied by screaming. He frequently said, "I am going to kill Nasrallah" [Hassan Nasrallah was the leader of Hezbollah at that time] and "I have evil eyes,"

showing his preoccupation with the war. The kindergarten teacher complained of his violent behavior toward the other children. Both parents felt helpless to deal with Eli's problems.

Eli's father, a firefighter, was absent during the war due to his work. He was constantly worried about his family. The father told the therapist that he didn't allow Eli to play with toy guns and soldiers at home. The mother said, "During the war, I stayed at home with Eli and my newborn baby. I behaved like a lunatic, and cried all the time. I was alone with two little kids. I used to sit all day in front of the TV, because I felt that I had to be updated. I was looking for my husband on the screen, with Eli near me."

During the first session, the mother was very restless. She wanted the windows opened; she complained of lack of air and left the room to get some water. When she returned, she apologized about Eli's clothes: "He looks as if he just came out of a war." The therapist felt that the mother was very anxious, as if she and Eli were still in the closed space of a shelter, as they had been during the war, with the mother unable to attend to Eli's needs.

As Eli's case shows, the war affected not only Eli but also his parents and the parent–child relationship.

The role of the parent–child relationship in coping with trauma

The skills necessary for coping with traumatic situations include emotional regulation, verbal skills and the cognitive capacity to understand the complexity of the situation. In young children, these skills are still underdeveloped (Salmon & Bryant, 2002), so the child's resilience to trauma depends on that of the parents (Scheeringa & Zeanah, 2001). In war situations, the stress experienced by the caregivers, and conveyed to the child in many verbal and non-verbal ways, limits their protective ability, thus further increasing the child's distress (Scheeringa & Zeanah, 1995).

Eli's parents were unable to protect him. The father was away on a stressful job, and the mother was emotionally unavailable because she had recently given birth to a new baby, and was anxious about the children and her husband. Eli, who was old enough to understand some of the dangers of war, was further traumatized because his fears were not contained and transformed in his relationship with his parents.

The capacity to cope with trauma is linked to the child's interpersonal interpretative function (IIF), which "provides the individual with the crucial capacity for interpretation in psychological terms" (Fonagy & Target, 2003). It includes the functions of stress regulation, selective attention and "mentalization" (defined below) (Fonagy, 2001; Fonagy & Target, 2003). The development of these functions, vital for coping with trauma, depends on a secure parent–child relationship. Accordingly, the attachment system is activated in situations of stress not only to ensure the child's proximity to the caregiver (Bowlby, 1969), but also to enable the child to restore the IIF with the help of the relationship. Thus, the relationship is critical to the child's functioning, particularly in stressful situations. Indeed, several models consider this relationship the focal point of intervention in treating childhood PTSD. Including parents in treatment, thus improving the parent–child relationship, alleviates the trauma-related symptoms and also promotes the child's future development (Cohen, 2010; Pat-Horenczyk, Ford, & Brom, 2009; Scheeringa & Zeanah, 2001; Van Horn & Lieberman, 2009). Similarly, HDT regards "mending the relationship" (Van Horn & Lieberman, 2009) as a prerequisite for the child's return to a healthy developmental path. It differs from previous models by focusing on mentalization as the core concept in the etiology and treatment of PTSD (Fonagy & Target, 2003). HDT is the first parent–child therapy model that has been used in treating war trauma.

Mentalization

"Mentalization" (operationalized as reflective functioning) is a cognitive skill that allows the individual to understand behaviors as motivated by internal states: emotions, intentions, memories, wishes, beliefs, etc. Mentalization enables the child to "read" others' minds and thus predict their behavior (Baron-Cohen, 1995). By helping individuals process interpersonal events, it allows them to distinguish inner from outer reality, pretend modes from real functioning modes and intrapersonal mental and emotional processes from interpersonal communication. It facilitates affect regulation, which is crucial for coping with trauma (Fonagy & Target, 2003).

Mentalization develops in a dyadic process of affect reflection, in which the parent reflects the child's affect. Two features of the process are critical for its development: contingency and markedness. "Contingency" means that the parent reflects the child's exact affect, thus helping the child learn to recognize affects. "Markedness" means that the parent's reflection of the child's affects is modified so as to help the child discriminate its own affect from that of the parent. In the process, the child internalizes a *re-presentation* of its affect, and gradually develops a representational system for mental states (Gergely & Watson, 1996). The development of mentalization may be described as the acquisition of different modes of linking inner and outer reality (Fonagy, 2001):

- the *psychic-equivalence mode*, where the child equates the contents of his or her mind with reality;
- the *pretend mode*, most evident in pretend-play, where fantasy and reality are disconnected;
- the later-developing *mentalizing mode*, which enables the child to link fantasy and reality without equating them—the child understands that the mind is a representation of reality, but not a replica of it.

The restoration of mentalization as the goal of PTSD therapy

The capacity to mentalize is subject to disruption in traumatic situations (Fonagy & Target, 2003), when earlier modes of linking internal and external reality re-emerge and the traumatized individual oscillates between the psychic equivalence and the pretend modes. When the person is in the psychic equivalence mode, the flashbacks occurring in PTSD are experienced as real, while a dissociative reaction to trauma is an expression of the pretend mode. Therefore, the restoration of mentalization should be the goal of therapy for PTSD. This is achievable because the disruption of mentalization in traumatic situations is defensive. During war, it may be too painful and anxiety provoking to imagine the enemy's intentions and emotions. Also, disrupting mentalization helps reduce inner conflicts regarding one's own hostile feelings (Fonagy & Target, 2003). In traumatic situations such as terror and war, there is a risk that both the parent and the child's mentalizing will be affected. Since the child depends on the parents' for the development and application of mentalizing, this becomes a very problematic situation.

Clinical experience with several adult and child pathologies shows that difficulties in mentalizing are effectively addressed in the context of the therapeutic relationship (Allen, Fonagy, & Bateman, 2008; Bateman & Fonagy, 2006; Hurry, 1998; Verheugt-Pleiter, Zevalkink, & Schmeets, 2008). Since HDT regards mentalization as a major therapeutic factor, and parent and child are treated together, it is an optimal model for the restoration of the parent's and the child's mentalizing capacity.

Play and trauma

Play has a central role in the development of mentalization (Fonagy & Target, 1996; Target & Fonagy, 1996) and is the main facilitator of mentalization in HDT (Harel, Kaplan, & Patt, 2006). Play affords the exploration of the internal world as projected onto the external world. Moreover, in our model, the child plays in the presence of the parent and the therapist, both of whom share in the play, thus providing more mature minds to reflect upon and mentalize the play. The adults' mentalizing action, like the alpha function (Bion, 1962), facilitates the child's attempts to play out and process the trauma.

We observed the dominance of pre-mentalizing modes after trauma in both children's and parents' play. Play occurs in a potential space at the interface of reality and fantasy (Winnicott, 1971). Holding the dialectic tension between fantasy and reality is difficult, and one of the poles can collapse into the other. When this happens, the potential space needed for play is lost (Ogden, 1986). In our opinion, a collapse into the fantasy aspect leads to a situation similar to the pretend mode, while a collapse into the reality aspect leads to the psychic equivalence mode. Our experience shows that it is possible to work through a childhood trauma if the child is playing with a more mature person who guards the potential space and employs a mentalizing stance that helps the child and the parent mentalize their experience.

The HDT model

The HDT model of short-term intervention with young children and their parents emphasizes the joint treatment of parent and child and regards mentalization (Harel et al., 2006) as the main therapeutic factor in treating emotional difficulties in childhood. The child's problems are conceptualized as relational difficulties, and not as the child's own problem. Children develop specific types of relationships with each parent as well as with the parenting couple. Thus, the same therapist meets with the mother–child and father–child dyads on a weekly basis, along with regular meetings with the parental dyad. The model is described in a manual (Ben-Aaron, Harel, Kaplan, & Patt, 2001) and sessions are backed by supervision, frequently with videotaped therapy sessions. HDT integrates an intra-psychic, object-relational view with an interpersonal approach to treatment. Accordingly, the therapist attends to the dyad at the level of overt, interpersonal behavior as well as at the covert level of meanings, representations, intentions, affects, memories, etc. The therapist links these two levels, thus facilitating the dyad's mentalizing capacity. Thanks to the participation of the parents in the sessions, the model affords a unique opportunity to observe and intervene in the dyad's implicit relational themes and ways of being together (Lyons-Ruth, 1999; Stern, 1998). The supportive ambience created by the therapist provides a secure base for parents and child, which makes it possible to explore the inner and actual worlds. Compared to comparatively "classic" therapists, the HDT therapist is more open ("I wonder what I should say now"), less neutral ("I think I would feel the same as you did") and more actively cooperative ("Let's try to understand this"), and takes responsibility for failures of empathy ("I am afraid I have confused you").

Adverse life events such as trauma are potentially disruptive factors, by themselves or in interaction with the child's developmental state—in Eli's case, for example, Oedipal concerns complicated by the fears and aggressions aroused by the war. Furthermore, traumatic situations may lead to an increased use of projective identification (Garland, 1998). Parents confronted with trauma are at risk for projecting their "ghosts" onto the child, re-enacting a problem from their own past in the parent–child relationship. This deprives the child of relational experiences appropriate to their developmental needs, and necessary for their potential self (Brazelton & Cramer, 1990; Fraiberg, Adelson, & Shapiro, 1975). The results of the projective process are sometimes observable quite early in parent–child interactions, but freeing the relationship of them takes time.

> Eli's father's difficulties with aggression disturbed his relationship with Eli. The father was projecting his aggression on Eli instead of helping him cope with aggression and the anxiety it aroused. Left to his own devices, Eli

identified with the aggressor, Nasrallah (he felt that they both had "evil eyes"), and he acted aggressively in kindergarten.

Following a war, parents and children referred for therapy need help in freeing or enhancing their mentalizing capacities. In the HDT model, difficulties in mentalizing are addressed in the parent–child sessions and in the sessions with the parental dyad. Each setting affords unique ways of understanding the participants' limitations in mentalizing and facilitating their mentalizing skills.

HDT sessions

Parent–child sessions

In these sessions, the participants express their relational themes in various ways, such as playing, drawing and verbal and non-verbal interactions. The presence of the parent with the child allows the therapist to observe the unconscious projections and implicit relations, which are more difficult to discover in the more usual setting of individual child therapy or parental guidance. The therapist can contain and process the observed interactions in their mind and intervene in the here and now: naming affects, linking behaviors to emotions, and the like.

Sessions with the parental dyad

These help reveal the causes of limitations in parental mentalizing, whether they stem from a current trauma and/or the parent's past. The sessions afford the opportunity to work on the parents' past and forge links with the present, helping to release the child from parental projections.

The specific relevance of HDT to PTSD

This section describes the specific features of the HDT model that are crucial to treating PTSD, namely:

1. the parents' active participation in the therapy process, which helps restore the parent as the child's protector and helper;
2. the enhancement of parental sensitivity to the child, which is decreased by the avoidance that often follows trauma;
3. the central role of play in HDT and trauma therapy.

Restoring the parent as the child's protector and helper

In normal circumstances, the parent is represented as the child's protector, powerful and omnipotent. This representation collapses when parent and child undergo the same traumatic event in which the parent is unable to protect the child and in many cases suffers from PTS as well.

> In his family drawings, Eli painted the mother significantly smaller than other members of the family. The small figure seemed to symbolize Eli's worried mother—her lack of self-confidence and her inability to protect him. The therapist tried to help the mother regain her status in the family. In her sessions with the parents, she explained how important the mother was for Eli, and, during sessions with Eli, she supported the mother's behavior by saying to Eli, "It is amazing how well Mom knows you . . . and understands your intentions". She also spoke directly to the mother, emphasizing her understanding of Eli and her devoted behavior. Gradually, the mother regained her role as a caregiver in the family. Her anxiety, which was very prominent in the early sessions, decreased, and she realized how her emotions and behavior were affecting Eli. She also learned what caused him anxiety and how to calm him down.

We assumed that Eli's mother's representation of his mother was affected by her helplessness during the war and additional potential causes such as the anger Eli felt due to the birth of the baby. The active participation of the mother in the therapy process and the therapist's support for her afforded many opportunities to restore the mother as Eli's protector, both in their interactions and in their minds.

The parents' competence is further enhanced by the role assigned to them by HDT as the main agents helping their child. The parent is "the helper," assisted by the therapist. The therapist takes every opportunity to show the parents how much the child needs them, and remains as much as possible in the background of the parent–child relationship.

With Eli and his parents, the restoration of the caregiving and helper roles was not easy, perhaps because both of them had PTS themselves.

> Eli's parents had only a limited ability to provide the secure context in which he could mentalize his experiences. The mother seemed to need a protector and helper for herself, because she herself had PTS. The father's rejecting attitude and behavior towards Eli contributed to his feelings of being evil. In the sessions with the parents, the therapist empowered them by pointing out the positive aspects of their parenting. She created a parallel process whereby she would empower the parents, and they in turn would strengthen aspects of their child. She pointed out Eli's fragile state after the traumatic events he had experienced and his need to receive support and appreciation from them. But the therapist's support of their parental role was not enough. It was necessary for them to work through their own war experience, so as to release them, especially the mother, from the survival mode, thus helping them become more attuned to Eli and contain and transform his anxieties. Eli's parents seemed to have been

previously limited in their mentalizing capacities, and the stress of the war further decreased their ability. The mother's condition was complicated by the recent birth of the baby and the need to attend to two children while her husband was away in a dangerous job. The father was afraid of his own and Eli's aggression, and it seemed that he dealt with his aggression in part by projecting it onto Eli. His job as a firefighter seemed to be an adaptive sublimation of this aggression. During the war, though, he was exposed to the traumatic results of aggression, blurring the boundaries between reality and his inner fears, which led him to further defend himself by restricting his emotions, thus limiting his empathy for Eli.

Enhancing parental sensitivity to the child

Following trauma, avoidance symptoms and lack of sensitivity in mothers are strongly associated with worse outcomes in young children (Scheeringa & Zeanah, 2001). The secure ambiance created by the therapist in our model, and the presence of the parent, enables the therapist to directly help the parent decrease such avoidance in her interaction with the child.

In a session with the mother, Eli wanted to play with toy soldiers; however, as soon as he spoke about it, even before he touched the toys, the mother moved restlessly and impatiently and Eli panicked and stopped playing. It seemed too early for the mother to face her feelings about the war. Consequently, she couldn't become attuned to Eli's fears and could not help him to use play as a way of mentalizing his experiences. It became clear that, as long as the mother avoided her traumatic experience, she would not be able to support her child. In the following session with the parents, the therapist asked the mother about her feelings in the session with Eli. The mother said that she did not remember anything special about the session. The therapist said she felt it was difficult for the mother when Eli wanted to play with the toy soldiers, perhaps because it made her feel painful emotions. The mother became silent and withdrawn. After a few moments, she said, "True, whenever I encounter something, anything, that reminds me of the war, I feel uneasy and I need to avoid it."

In the therapeutic process, the therapist's interventions are intended to increase the sensitivity of the parent's responsiveness to the child by enhancing mentalization. The therapist takes a mentalizing stance towards both parent and child. The parent identifies with and ultimately internalizes the therapist's stance, later using it for her own and the child's benefit. HDT can be used for children old enough to be developmentally capable of mentalizing, so that their own mentalization can be enhanced by the therapist's and the parent's mentalizing stance (Harel et al., 2006).

The role of play in HDT and trauma therapy

"If one could live a thousand years, one might completely work through a childhood trauma by playing out the terrifying scenario until it is no longer terrified." (Terr, 1991, p. 13) This quote indicates the importance of revealing the trauma and playing it out in the sessions. It also highlights the difficulty of doing so.

Play has a unique status in childhood PTSD; it is both *a symptom* and *a way to heal*. Play as symptom, or repetitive play (traumatic play; Terr, 1991), can take place, expressing themes or aspects of the trauma (Mash & Barkley, 2007, p. 402).

In our experience, "mentalization" is a helpful concept for understanding the effect of trauma on play. When mentalization fails, earlier modes of linking the inner world to reality re-emerge and are expressed in traumatic play, sometimes making it impossible to play at all. Traumatic play looks like the pretend mode because the child is immersed in the fantasy, disconnected from reality. He or she plays the same scene repetitively, attempting to gain control and a sense of relief— but, the more the play continues, the more distressed he becomes. An onlooker may see the play as representing the child's experience, but for the child it is not a representation but a re-experience. They are able to continue playing only as long as they disconnect the played scene from reality. Linking them disrupts the play and causes the child even greater distress. Gradually, the therapist can help the child understand the scene as a *representation* of the experience, thus allowing him or her to continue the play in a less driven way, to change elements in the scenario and gain control over it. Another outcome of failed mentalization is inability to play caused by the dominance of the psychic equivalence mode. In this mode, the traumatized child experiences the toy soldiers as real, terrifying soldiers. Using avoidance as a defense, he or she does not play with the toys at all. In HDT, it often happens that both parent and child avoid playing, when both are traumatized and acting in the psychic equivalence mode. Sometimes, the child is actually able to play, but avoids it to protect the parent.

> Eli's mother was initially in the psychic equivalence mode and Eli noticed her anxiety and stopped playing with the toy soldiers to protect her.

Play as a way to heal

In HDT, since the relationship is the "patient," it is the therapist's task to assist the parent in helping his or her child regain the capacity to play, or help the parent play with the child. The therapist begins by sharing her own mentalizing remarks about the child's and the parent's mental states. The parent is thus encouraged to start mentalizing for the child.

> After several sessions with the parental dyad, working at releasing them from the survival mode, the parents become able to facilitate Eli's play. In the next

mother–child session, Eli once again initiated play with the toy soldiers. This time, the mother followed his lead with her own explanations and the therapist's support. The therapist said, "What do you think Eli is telling us, Mom?" and "How do you feel now?" When Eli played a game of killing Nasrallah, the mother reflected his anger and anxiety. The therapist also tried to help Eli mentalize his mother's inner world, asking Eli, "How do you think Mom is feeling now?" In a later session, the mother told Eli her own story of the war, and this enabled him to begin sharing what he had felt. The therapist encouraged this interaction by saying, "I feel it is important for both of you to understand each other's feelings and thoughts, especially after the war you went through together", "You can talk about these things so as to understand them" and "It feels good to be understood."

The father's attitude changed, too. His didactic, critical, rigid behavior was gradually replaced by patience, and he learned to enjoy the hour shared with his son, although it was still difficult for him to play symbolically. Now, it seemed that the therapist's containment and mentalization diminished his anxiety and aggression and his need to project his feelings onto Eli. The father even praised Eli for his imaginative play, and Eli responded, "I am a smart boy." This was a significant change, in comparison to the remark that Eli made at the beginning of therapy: "I have evil eyes."

Adapting the HDT model to PTSD therapy

To further adapt the HDT model for treating PTSD, two modules were added, as detailed below.

Discussing the traumatic events

Discussing the traumatic events is recommended in PTSD treatment for children (Chemtob & Abramovitz, 2007; Scheeringa & Gaensbauer, 2000). Our goal is to discuss the trauma in the secure setting of dyadic therapy, in the presence of the parent. We have experienced that children are eager to tell their story much sooner than their parents, who try to avoid re-enacting the trauma. Therefore, discussing the trauma is not encouraged unless the therapist senses that the parent is ready to support the child in this difficult task. The therapist has to ensure that the parent's presence adds to the child's feeling of safety, rather than diminishing it. This is the right time for the trauma to be discussed. The parent's participation in the therapy process allows the child to extend his or her feelings of safety in the therapy setting to real-life situations.

When the therapist felt that they were ready, she held a session with both parents and asked them to describe their memories and experiences from the war. The mother began telling about the first time she heard the sirens and how she seized Eli and hid in the closet with him. She went on describing how she and Eli would run to the shelter, and the way Eli grabbed her hand and pulled her towards the door because she was moving very slowly in her ninth month of pregnancy. The father also expressed how worried he was about her and Eli, and how stressed he was in his duties as a firefighter during the missile attacks. Once the parents re-created their experiences during the war with the therapist, they began doing the same in their dyadic sessions with Eli.

Co-constructing the trauma narrative by the dyad with the help of the therapist

Scheeringa and Gaensbauer (2000) state that a major goal in treating children with PTSD is to develop a coherent narrative out of the remembered fragments of the traumatic event and to integrate it into their life story. Others treating PTSD agree that creating a trauma story through reconstruction or cognitive processing helps the individual charge the event with personal meaning and "place it as part of the rest of his life, as opposed to being its focus" (Tuval-Mashiach et al., 2004). As evidenced here, children construct the narrative in play:

> In a mother–child session, Eli arranged the toy soldiers in a combat scene. The soldiers were led by a "very bad commander, Nasrallah." Eli took a mother doll and a child doll from the dollhouse and made them hide in the closet. The mother helped him arrange the scenes, and she and the therapist commented on the protagonists' feelings. Eli felt safe by now to tell their story, because the mother now was able to face and contain her feelings and help him do the same.

Mentalization is sometimes anxiety provoking and painful, especially after traumatic situations. Although discussing the traumatic event and constructing a narrative are essential for therapy, they are also potentially disruptive. The therapist must be sensitive to these problems and anticipate them from their knowledge of the dyad's dynamics and history, as well as from their own counter-transferential feelings. The therapist has to be ready to meet these emotionally charged moments, deal with them in a way that is sensitive to the needs of both participants and transform them from painful, avoided moments to "moments of meeting" (Stern, 1998). In our clinical experience, ongoing supervision for the therapist, preferably supervision with videotaped sessions, is a helpful contribution to the therapeutic process in these complicated situations.

We have noticed that the referred families often had difficulties in parent–child relations even before the trauma, but the families functioned well enough. The added burden of the threat and anxiety caused by the war, and the trauma and its consequences, intensified the problems; their coping mechanisms failed, leading to the child's symptoms. Consequently, understanding the dynamics of the relationship is crucial and also has the potential to ease the PTS.

We consider the HDT model the most suitable framework for the child and the parent to enhance their mentalizing capacity and use it for understanding the links between their representations, and between representations and behavior. In the secure, empathic atmosphere of the sessions, the participants can explore their inner worlds playfully, with the help and support of the therapist. The exploration and clarification of each other's feelings, intents and wishes differentiates the partners' respective mental worlds, leading to understanding and empathy. This process facilitates an enrichment of the ways the dyad's members perceive each other and their own selves, and allows updating and reorganizing of representations, followed by changes in behavior. We regard the mentalizing skills the participants acquire in HDT as a coping skill useful for the ordinary difficulties encountered in everyday life, and not only for resolving trauma consequences.

> Near the end of the therapy, Eli fell and injured his head. The mother panicked upon seeing the blood and screamed, frightening Eli. In the session following this incident, Eli sat with his mother at the table and painted a child with blood on his head. His mother looked at him while he was painting and said, "I know that you were very frightened by my scream, but that was because I was worried you were badly hurt and I got scared. But you have to know that I love you and I will take care of everything that happens to you".

The aim of the therapy is not only to alleviate the trauma symptoms, but also to change the relationship to suit the child's needs. The American Academy of Child and Adolescent Psychiatry (AACAP) survey (Cohen, 2010) recommends therapies that not only treat the PTSD, but also provide the parents and the child with tools for further development. Mentalization is such a tool because it is a skill for processing and responding to new experiences.

Transference and countertransference when HDT is used in war situations

Transference and countertransference issues in trauma are complicated (Dalenberg, 2000) and rarely discussed in reference to situations of terror or war trauma (Chen-Gal & Sroufe, 2006). Here, we will briefly discuss those aspects which we found relevant when applying our model to PTS.

In war situations, it is not only the child and the parents who experience stress, but also the therapist. During the 2006 Lebanon War, for example, therapists were attending to patients while coping with their own painful emotions: fear for themselves and their families, guilt for leaving their family and going to work, uncertainty about what might happen at any moment. Experienced therapists from relatively safe areas volunteered to help. Their help had great practical and emotional importance. The more experienced therapists supervised the younger ones, who generally also had small children and were more stressed. Living through the same experience gave patients and therapists a feeling of sharing and enhanced the positive transference, beyond the "good grandmother transference" (Stern, 1995) that often occurs in the HDT model (Harel, Kaplan, Avimeir-Patt, & Ben-Aaron, 2005).

Countertransference in trauma therapy for children is "painful to consider and difficult to discuss" (Osofsky, 2004) because of the complex feelings the therapists experience. We think that, in domestic and community violence (the situations to which Osofsky is referring), this is very true. In situations of war, the feelings are somewhat different, because the enemy is "outside" the family and some painful feelings e.g. hate, are directed outwards. The therapist and the dyads share negative feelings towards a common enemy, thus decreasing "hate in the countertransference" (Winnicott, 1949) as a disrupting factor in therapy. Nevertheless, in the long run, this situation has its dangers, such as assuming that the enemy is inhuman and mindless (Fonagy & Target, 2003).

In our experience of countertransference in wartime, there have been both concordant and complementary identifications (Racker, 1968). In some dyads, the therapist identified with the frightened child, and, in others, with the depressed and helpless parent, but, most of the time, he or she alternated between the two. For therapists working in the HDT model, these ever-changing countertransferences are well-known. During wartime, they are more exaggerated and difficult to cope with, although they are also more readily detected and understood, since the obvious situation is common to the patient and the therapist. The supervision provided was critical for coping with these reactions and preventing them from impacting negatively on the therapy. The supervisors noted the frustration the therapists felt because the parents seemed more limited in their mentalizing skills than the parents they usually encountered. It was important to understand that, in addition to the trauma of their patients, the therapists were experiencing their own trauma as citizens in wartime. It was also important to accept that most of the parents were still functioning in the survival mode. The therapists had to help the parents in various ways, such as teaching them relaxation techniques, to overcome this mode of functioning and thus be able to help their children. At the same time, the therapists had to help the children express their anxieties, and do so at the right time for the parents to be able to contain and transform them. Thus, it was constantly necessary for the therapist to be sensitive and attuned to the dyad.

Limitations of the model

A potential limitation of the model as applied to war trauma is the possibility that the parents, too, might be affected with PTSD or PTS, which could affect their participation in dyadic treatment. It is important to treat the parents as studies have found a significant association between less adaptive parental functioning and less adaptive child functioning following trauma (Scheeringa & Zeanah, 2001). In our study, we also found that, unless the dyad was treated, more symptoms in the mother (depression and PTSD symptoms) were linked to an increase in the child's symptoms over time (Harel, Eshel, & Levin, 2011). It is therefore important to treat affected parents while carefully considering their vulnerability during the therapy. It is crucial to further explore this association and the potential of dyadic therapy for improving both child and parent functioning.

Conclusions

In the secure context of the therapeutic relationship in the HDT model, the therapist helps restore the parental functions of protecting, containing and mentalizing for the child. The therapist enhances the dyad's mentalization to facilitate the co-construction of a narrative that reveals the child's fears and wishes following the trauma. The process enables the child and the parent to create new meanings for their traumatic experiences and their relationship and use mentalization as a skill for future coping and development. The major difference between this model and other parent–child therapies for PTSD is that the present model emphasizes mentalization in the etiology and treatment of childhood PTSD.

The HDT model seems highly appropriate for the treatment of PTSD in children, as it satisfies the AACAP's recommendations (Cohen, 2010) for empirically proven effective therapies for such children. The model includes the parents in the child's therapy as active participants and agents of change. It directly addresses the traumatic event and it is not merely focused on symptoms, but also highlights the enhancement of mentalization as a therapeutic factor as well as an important adaptive function for the participants' future development .

References

Allen, J. G., Fonagy, P., & Bateman, A. W. (2008). *Mentalizing in clinical practice.* Washington, D.C.: American Psychiatric Publishing.

Baron-Cohen, S. (1995). *Mindblindness: An essay on autism and theory of mind.* Cambridge, MA: MIT Press.

Bateman, A., & Fonagy, P. (2006). *Mentalization-based treatment for borderline personality disorder: A practical guide.* Oxford, England; New York, NY: Oxford University Press.

Ben-Aaron, M., Harel, J., Kaplan, H., & Patt, R. (2001). *Mother–child and father–child psychotherapy: A manual for the treatment of relational disturbances in childhood.* London, England; Philadelphia, PA: Whurr.

Betancourt, T. S., (2011). Attending to the mental health of war-affected children: The need for longitudinal and developmental research perspectives. *Journal of the American Academy of Child and Adolescent Psychiatry, 50*(4), 323–325.

Bion, W. R. (1962). *Learning from experience.* London, England: Tavistock.

Bowlby, J. (1969). *Attachment and loss* (Vol. 1). London, England: Hogarth Press.

Brazelton, T. B., & Cramer, B. G. (1990). *The earliest relationship: Parents, infants, and the drama of early attachment.* Reading, MA: Addison-Wesley Publishing.

Chemtob, C. M., & Abramovitz, R. A. (2007). *Protocol for dyadic treatment in the context of trauma and disaster.* Unpublished manuscript.

Chen-Gal, S., & Sroufe, L. A. (2006). The burden of trauma. *Psichoactualia,* Israeli Psychological Association (in Hebrew).

Cohen, J. A. (2010). Practice parameters for the assessment and treatment of children and adolescents with posttraumatic stress disorder. *Journal of the American Academy of Child and Adolescent Psychiatry*, 49(4), 414–430.

Dalenberg, C. J. (2000). *Countertransference and the treatment of trauma*. Washington, D.C.: American Psychological Association.

Fonagy, P. (2001). The human genome and the representational world: The role of early mother-infant interaction in creating an interpersonal interpretative mechanism. *Bulletin of the Menninger Clinic*, 65(3). 427–448.

Fonagy, P., & Target, M. (1996). Playing with reality: I. Theory of mind and the normal development of psychic reality. *International Journal of Psychoanalysis*, 77(Pt 2), 217–233.

Fonagy, P., & Target, M. (2003). Evolution of the interpersonal interpretative function: Clues for effective preventive intervention in early childhood. In S. W. Coates, J. L. Rosenthal & D. S. Schechter (Eds.), *September 11: Trauma and human bonds*. London, England; Hillsdale, NJ: Analytic Press, pp. 99–113.

Fraiberg, S., Adelson, E., & Shapiro, V. (1975). Ghosts in the nursery. A psychoanalytic approach to the problems of impaired infant-mother relationships. *Journal of the American Academy of Child Psychiatry*, 14(3), 387–421.

Garland, C. (Ed.) (1998). *Understanding trauma: A psychoanalytical approach* (Tavistock Clinic Series). London, England: Duckworth.

Gergely, G., & Watson, J. S. (1996). The social biofeedback theory of parental affect mirroring: The development of self-awareness and self-control in infancy. *International Journal of Psychoanalysis*, 77(Pt 6), 1181–1212.

Harel, J., Eshel, Y., & Levin, M. (2011). *The effectiveness of the Haifa Dyadic Therapy for children suffering from PTSD*. Thesis in preparation, Department of Psychology, Haifa University, Haifa, Israel.

Harel, J., Kaplan, H., Avimeir-Patt, R., & Ben-Aaron, M. (2005). The child's active role in mother–child, father–child psychotherapy: A psychodynamic approach to the treatment of relational disturbances. *Psychology and Psychotherapy: Theory, Research and Practice*, 79(1), 23–36.

Harel, J., Kaplan, H., & Patt, R. (2006). Reflective functioning in mother-child, father-child psychotherapy. In L. Jacobs & C. Wachs (Eds.), *Parent-focused child therapy: attachment, identification, and reflective functions*. Lanham, MD: Jason Aronson.

Hurry, A. (Ed.) (1998). *Psychoanalysis and developmental therapy*. London, England: Karnac Books.

Lyons-Ruth, K. (1999). The two-person unconscious: Intersubjective dialogue, enactive relational representation, and the emergence of new forms of relational organization. *Psychoanalytic Inquiry*, 19(4), 576–617.

Mash, E. J., & Barkley, R. A. (Eds.) (2007). *Assessment of childhood disorders* (4th ed.). New York, NY; London, England: Guilford Press, pp. 405–483.

Ogden, T. (1986). Potential space. In T. H. Ogden, *The matrix of the mind: Object relations and the psychoanalytic dialogue*. Northvale, NJ: Jason Aronson, pp. 203–232.

Osofsky, J. (2004). Perspectives on work with traumatized young children: How to deal with the feelings emerging from trauma work. In J. Osofsky (Ed.), *Young children and trauma: Intervention and treatment*. New York, NY; London, England: Guilford Press, pp. 326–338.

Pat-Horenczyk, R., Ford, D., & Brom, D. (2009). Toward a developing science and practice of childhood traumatic stress: Concluding comments. In D. Brom, R. Pat-Horenczyk &

J. D. Ford (Eds.), *Treating traumatized children: Risk, resilience, and recovery* (pp. 269–276). New York, NY: Routledge.

Racker, H. (1968). *Transference and countertransference*. New York, NY: International Universities Press.

Salmon, K., & Bryant, R. A. (2002). Posttraumatic stress disorder in children: The influence of developmental factors. *Clinical Psychology Review, 22*(2), 163–188.

Scheeringa, M. S., & Gaensbauer, T. J. (2000). Posttraumatic stress disorder. In C. H. Zeanah, Jr. (Ed.), *Handbook of infant mental health* (2nd ed., pp. 360–381). New York, NY: Guilford Press.

Scheeringa, M. S., & Zeanah, C. H. (1995). Symptom expression and trauma variables in children under 48 months of age. *Infant Mental Health Journal, 16*(4), 259–270.

Scheeringa, M. S., & Zeanah, C. H. (2001). A relational perspective on PTSD in early childhood, *Journal of Traumatic Stress, 14*(4), 799–815.

Stern, D. N. (1995). *The motherhood constellation: A unified view of parent-infant psychotherapy*. New York, NY: Basic Books.

Stern, D. N. (1998). The process of therapeutic change involving implicit knowledge: Some implications of developmental observations for adult psychotherapy. *Infant Mental Health Journal, 19*(3), 300–308.

Target, M., & Fonagy, P. (1996). Playing with reality: II. The development of psychic reality from a theoretical perspective. *International Journal of Psychoanalysis, 77*(Pt 3), 459–479.

Terr, L. C. (1991). Childhood trauma: an outline and overview. *American Journal of Psychiatry, 148*(1), 10–20.

Tuval-Mashiach, R., Freedman, S., Bargai, N., Boker, R. Hadar, H., & Shalev, A. Y. (2004). Coping with trauma: Narrative and cognitive perspectives. *Psychiatry: Interpersonal and Biological Processes, 67*(3), 280–293.

Van Horn, P., & Lieberman, A. F. (2009). Using dyadic therapies to treat traumatized young children. In D. Brom, R. Pat-Horenczyk & J. D. Ford (Eds.), *Treating traumatized children: Risk, resilience, and recovery* (pp. 210–224). New York, NY: Routledge.

Verheugt-Pleiter, A. J. E., Zevalkink, D. J., & Schmeets, M. G. J. (2008), *Mentalizing in child therapy: Guidelines for clinical practitioners*. London, England: Karnac.

Winnicott, D. W. (1949). Hate in the counter-transference. *International Journal of Psychoanalysis, 30*, 69–74.

Winnicott, D. W. (1971). *Playing and reality*. Harmondsworth, Middlesex, United Kingdom: Penguin Books.

Yule, W., Perrin, S., & Smith, P. (2000). Traumatic events and post-traumatic stress disorder. In W. K. Silverman & P. D. A. Treffers (Eds.), *Anxiety disorders in children and adolescents* (pp. 212–234). Cambridge, England: Cambridge University Press.

Chapter 8

Home visiting

Benefits and challenges of working with traumatized young children in the home using the child–parent psychotherapy model

Lesley Sternin and Amy Weiss

Home visits have been the foundation of relationship-based dyadic psychotherapy since Selma Fraiberg (1980) developed the infant–parent psychotherapy model in the 1970s. Fraiberg's integration of psychoanalytic theory and social work in the home is partly based on the social work maxim of "meeting people where they are." Fraiberg took this social work value and created a kind of "kitchen table therapy," meeting families in the intimate setting of their home. Home visits became the most accepted practice in infant mental health.

In this chapter, we focus our clinical discussion on child–parent psychotherapy (CPP) (Lieberman & Van Horn, 2005; 2008) with young children exposed to trauma, and describe how home visits can be a vehicle for therapeutic change with this vulnerable, high-risk group.

In the late 1960s, Fraiberg engaged in longitudinal developmental studies of infants blind from birth, which were later expanded into studies of other infants and families with mental health needs. This work is largely carried on through home visits with the baby–parent dyad. Fraiberg saw the importance of understanding the family within their environment:

> The range of observations provided by the home visit cannot be duplicated in any way in an office-centered program for infants. And since infants are frequently constrained in a strange situation (as are their parents very often), we are more likely to get the optimal range of the infant's and his parents' capabilities and the quality of their interactions through the familiar setting of the home and its climate.
>
> (Fraiberg, 1980, p. 7)

CPP is an outgrowth of Fraiberg's infant–parent psychotherapy (IPP), focusing on the impact of trauma on the young child. CPP is an empirically supported, relationship-based treatment for young children (0 to 5 years old) who have experienced trauma. Alicia Lieberman and Patricia Van Horn developed CPP at the University of California, San Francisco/San Francisco General Hospital's

Child Trauma Research Program. Like IPP, CPP is a relationship-based dyadic treatment model. The attachment relationship is the vehicle for addressing the child's trauma-impacted behavioral symptoms and restoring a healthy developmental trajectory.

CPP is multi-theoretical in its approach, viewing attachment, psychoanalytic and trauma theories through a cultural lens, and using them to understand and treat the family. CPP allows for the flexibility necessary to treat children and families facing chronic, complex problems associated with poverty.

CPP can be provided in the office or in the home, with the decision as to where to do so depending on a number of factors. The consistency and calm of an office setting can provide an ideal therapeutic setting, but the clinician cannot witness the normal stressors of the home. If physical safety is a factor, the clinic office may provide the safest environment.

The drama of development and caregiving unfolds within the natural world of the home. Feeding, toileting, bathing, sleeping and other caregiving tasks become the medium through which children interact with their parents, develop speech and learn self-regulation and the social and cultural norms of the family. In the best of circumstances, the foundation for children's social, emotional and cognitive growth is set in place in the home environment during these early years. The home is a reflection of many aspects of a family's identity: the language spoken, the religious artifacts, the picture of the child they had to leave behind in their country of origin due to poverty, the special foods eaten and the family's current economic status. While working in the home, clinicians see families and their complex pleasures and pains in their own context.

History

Concern about outcomes for infants and toddlers facing biological and environmental risks has led to the construction of a variety of early intervention models, two of which are IPP and CPP. As observed by the Administration for Children and Families (Koball et al., 2009), a division of the U.S. Department of Health and Human Services, there is a growing body of evidence that suggests some home visitation programs can be a successful strategy for the prevention of child maltreatment (Bilukha et al., 2005; Gomby, 2005; Olds et al., 2004, 2007; Prinz, Sanders, Shapiro, Witaker & Lutzker, 2009; Sweet & Appelbaum, 2004). Child FIRST, an intensive home-visit program that employs an adaptation of CPP, has been researched and found to have a significant impact on child and family outcomes (Lowell, Carter, Godoy, Paulicin, & Briggs-Gowon, 2011). Home visits for IPP and CPP evolved as effective ways to reach at-risk infants and toddlers without requiring parents to come to the practitioner's location. Although there have been substantial efforts at evaluation, the variability in content, format and outcomes measured by home-visit service models makes it difficult to draw definitive conclusions.

Home visiting programs tend to be complex and multifaceted; practitioners attempt to positively affect multiple domains, be it child socio-emotional development and safety in the house, maternal life enhancement or some other set.

(Sweet & Appelbaum, 2004)

The home and the context of family life

The complications of multidimensional family life take place in the home. The intergenerational transmission of trauma, cultural and religious practices and rituals are all enacted in the theater of the home.

> The ecological context of the family yields important cues about the sources of risk and support for the child's healthy development. Poverty, discrimination, unemployment, lack of education, isolation from social supports and ongoing community violence can be a backdrop of continuing and self-reinforcing adversity.
>
> (Lieberman & Van Horn, 2008, p. 108)

In the home, contextual factors in the family and the community are directly experienced. The clinician can see and feel the influences around them. Are there drug dealers on the corner? Is the house well kept or chaotic? Is there food in the refrigerator? Are there supportive family members around? Is the family a place of comfort or stress? The case vignette below illustrates the added benefit of gathering comprehensive assessment data in the home.

> Becky, a child–parent psychotherapist, arrived at the client's home at the agreed-upon time to meet with Angela, 18-year-old Latina mother of Consuela, 19 months. Angela emigrated from Guatemala at 16, leaving her family behind. Her new life in the United States left Angela isolated, with little support. Consuela was losing weight, refusing to eat and keeping everyone awake with night terrors. Consuela was referred by her pediatrician, who was concerned about her failure to thrive and the problematic attachment between mother and child. The clinician unexpectedly walked into a full-blown domestic violence situation with Consuela's parents physically attacking each other. Angela opened the door for Becky, but, when she entered the apartment, the couple completely ignored her, continuing with their violent fight. Anthony (Consuela's dad) had broken a beer bottle and was threatening Angela with it. Consuela sat on the couch between them and cried uncontrollably.
>
> Becky had met with Angela and Consuela for four sessions in her office. This was the first home visit that had been scheduled. If Angela and Consuela had continued treatment in the office, it is likely that the truth about the domestic violence at home would have taken much longer to be discovered. The home visit allowed for an immediate and vivid assessment that could

address Consuela's failure to thrive and the deleterious effects of domestic violence in the home, with a safety plan and a plan for intervention.

Social, economic and developmental challenges can intervene and disrupt the child's ability to learn and grow. Complex trauma can be one of the challenges for the child and the family. While trauma can occur in any economic class, the poor are particularly at risk due to social problems that often accompany poverty, such as unemployment and lack of housing or access to health care and other services. Providing in-home service allows for direct access to necessary treatment. The case vignette below illustrates an example of trauma in a family in an impoverished neighborhood.

> Tanisha is a 25-year-old, African American single mom raising her 5-year-old son, Kyle, in a violent neighborhood in East Oakland, California. She is part of a large extended family originally from Mississippi. Tanisha and Kyle live in a low-income neighborhood with almost daily gun violence on the streets. Tanisha's brother was murdered in a gang-related shooting a month before. Tanisha's father, whom she adored, was murdered when she was 16. Kyle was playing in the living room with his family when shots rang out. Bullets came through the living room window and hit the couch where Kyle was playing. Tanisha has become very anxious, has difficulty sleeping and eating and has been increasingly unable to care for herself and Kyle. Kyle has become aggressive at school; the kindergarten teacher made the referral to therapy. Through collateral sessions, the therapist was able to address the issue of intergenerational transmission of trauma by supporting Tanisha's exploration of her own feelings of tremendous loss about her beloved father and brother. As Tanisha gained access to her own buried affect, she was able to fully engage in the dyadic treatment with Kyle, providing him with the ability to soothe and begin to self-regulate. Tanisha was able to conclude that she needed to move from the neighborhood that was causing chronic stress for her and her son. The therapist provided case management and psychoeducation about child development and role-modeled prioritizing safety by helping Tanisha develop a safety plan for herself and Kyle.

Meeting families where they are

Acknowledging the obstacles that families face, including the challenges that poverty creates, can be relieving to families. Meeting families on their own turf communicates clinicians' willingness to experience their challenging day-to-day situations, which can foster a deeper therapeutic alliance, as illustrated in the following vignette.

> While I was visiting a mother and her young son in the home, the mother remarked that she was pleasantly surprised that I could be interested in them enough to come to their home. She laughed and said that she appreciated that I came to her family in their home rather than in mine (my office). This

heralded the beginning of treatment for this mother. Forming a therapeutic alliance became psychologically entwined with my interest in and respect for her family. This mother, who struggled with poverty and felt so easily devalued in her life, appreciated the fact that I respected and valued her enough to travel to her home.

When working with poor families who are living on the edge of economic survival, home visits can also mean the difference between getting access to services or receiving none at all. Families with young children can have difficulty with the expense of public transportation, and this can be a primary obstacle to treatment.

Some families may experience home visits as intrusive, which may delay the building of trust—the essential first step in treatment. Feelings of vulnerability can also be triggered for parents when they meet therapists in their home. What will we think of their home? Will we be critical? Mothers often apologize for a messy house with a sense of shame. An attitude of respect and empathy for the difficulties of parenting and managing under stressful circumstances may help alleviate these feelings in the therapeutic relationship. The ability to trust professionals can be affected by previous involvement in the child welfare system and by institutional racism. A therapist who is the home visitor may be seen as a threat, due to the perception that professionals have the authority to remove children from the home. Developing trust takes time and requires sensitivity to culture and class issues as well as the ability to apply "culturally congruent interventions" to the work (Ghosh-Ippen, 2009). Such interventions "incorporate a focus not only on culture but also on the family's history, current situation, and future goals" (Ghosh-Ippen, 2009). When interventions encompass this fuller understanding of the family, they have more felt meaning for them.

Cultural influences

Families are complex systems affected by many factors, including class, race, family and ethnic culture. Culture and its impact on both the family and the therapist is an important lens through which to view the therapy.

> The parents' interpretation of the family's circumstances and of the child's situation needs to be understood in the context of their cultural background. Culture pervades the meanings that individuals ascribe to adversity and to stressful and traumatic events and informs beliefs and traditions about the most effective ways to help children through the recovery process.
>
> (Lieberman & Van Horn, 2008, p. 108)

Families communicate cultural values to their children in the early years through activities of daily living (Martini, 2002), such as mealtimes or discipline. For example, while some cultures value independence, others expect reliance on the family. Variance within a culture may be shaped by the socioeconomic status of the family and other factors. Cultural differences between therapist and family, as well as cultural similarities, can be challenging or supportive to the treatment. Therapists also bring their own cultural values and experiences to bear on the therapeutic session. The home setting can add another dimension to the issue of culture in the therapeutic encounter. Consider the example, below, of a therapist who believed in the therapeutic value of working in the home, yet felt uncomfortable entering families' homes.

> The therapist was Chinese American, and her work with a Chinese American family was particularly challenging. In supervision, the therapist reflected on her discomfort and became aware that her upbringing had been informed by a culturally held belief that you must keep your problems within the family. To seek help outside the family was seen as a breach that compromised the family's privacy.
>
> When this therapist was faced with entering a client's home—and, in particular, a Chinese American home—she was confronted with a dilemma: If the home was the best place for her to observe the life of the family, how could she do so and not feel like she was being intrusive?
>
> Reflective supervision also revealed that there was a parallel process at play. The therapist realized that she was also feeling the family's discomfort. They felt shame due to domestic violence. The therapist was able to untangle the knots of the parallel process and the impact of the culture of the family and her own cultural upbringing. This helped her address the client's cultural belief in privacy and shame at being a victim.
>
> Over time, the therapist resolved her dilemma by choosing to combine her therapeutic beliefs with her cultural identity into a more integrated professional self. As a result, her personal experience gave her special sensitivity to the cultural norms of Chinese families as well as with other families with whom she worked.

Creating a therapeutic frame

While home visits may offer many benefits for treating young children and their caregivers, there are also pitfalls and challenges that the therapist needs to be aware of and navigate. For instance, therapists may find it challenging to maintain professional boundaries without the containment of the treatment office, manage distractions in the home and address safety issues.

The flexible boundaries that the clinician has in the home versus the office require a special container that the therapist needs to hold inside his- or herself. Space and management of the therapeutic frame are normally clearly defined by the therapist in the trappings of their office. Still, it is up to the therapist to help define a safe therapeutic space in the home, particularly when there is stress and trauma in the family. Holding the frame inside means that the therapist makes decisions and judgments in the moment about what is clinically useful in the home. In this setting, sessions may take place in the living room or on the kitchen floor. It is important that the therapist be flexible enough to respect the needs of family practices, norms and cultural values.

There may also be some inherent tension between holding a therapeutic frame and keeping flexible boundaries. As clinicians, it is helpful to be clear with both ourselves and the families we treat that we are entering their home not as a friend but as a supportive professional observer and partner in their family's life.

Creating therapeutic space in the home is an interpersonal process. Family members and friends may wander through the living room where the therapy is being conducted. Other children in the family may need watching while the therapist is working with the parent–child dyad. The notion of private space may be foreign to mothers who have never had their own privacy. Choosing a space where the therapy won't be interrupted or even casually joined by others may mean working with a parent about their right to privacy.

An example of this is the TV, which is a ubiquitous part of family life in the United States. Entering a home-visiting session with the television on may not be unusual. However, it may, for example, make it harder for Danny to focus on and interact with his mother because he is hyperaroused and has difficulty concentrating due to exposure to family violence. In this case, we might say to the mother, "I wonder if it's harder for Danny to pay attention to you when the TV is on?"

Distractions can also be useful in understanding a particular family. Having the TV on, using a cell phone during a session or having people coming in and out of the house can be incorporated into the work and used as material for discussion. Is answering a cell phone during a session a distraction or a need to escape the presence of intense feeling? What does it mean to be close when you've only experienced intimacy as painful? Creating a therapeutic space in such a setting means finding a balance between the challenges and distractions as well as the benefits of working in the client's home.

Safety issues in the home can also affect the therapy. Is the home a safe, healthy place for the child? We should address issues of domestic violence and its impact on the child, along with concerns that the home may be physically unsafe for a young child. While we are a professional "guest" in their home, it is important to always keep the child in mind and think about ways in which we can positively affect the family. We are in a position to help the family understand the need for child safety.

Creating a holding environment for the caregiver and child simultaneously and conducting a dynamic therapy that moves between the past and the present moment are demanding challenges for the therapist's responsiveness and creativity. In this respect, home visits and their malleable boundaries can allow the therapist greater flexibility than the office setting.

Home visits can also lead to unique creative solutions that can further the therapeutic process, as illustrated by the following vignette.

A CPP therapist began working with an African American aunt and her 3-year-old nephew, Todd, in the home. The aunt was referred by her nephew's preschool due to his behavior: hitting other children and staff, throwing tantrums, and not following directions. They lived in a housing project in a large urban area where community violence was common. Todd was exposed to drugs in utero and removed from his mother at birth. He had also recently witnessed a shooting outside their apartment. His energy was difficult to contain in their small apartment. The aunt and the therapist worked together to help Todd learn to regulate his affect. He had difficulty managing his intense feelings. He became angry very easily and lashed out physically, hitting others. His exposure to trauma and his losses contributed to his inability to self-regulate. Progress was slow, and the therapist began to think about other ways to support Todd's development. Todd loved baseball, so the therapist tried to incorporate this play into his therapy, but the apartment was too small for this type of activity. One day, it occurred to the clinician to play outside. Therapist, client and aunt played in a small, sheltered grassy area on the edge of the project just outside their apartment. The next few months, they played ball, adjusting the rules for a 4-year-old. To play, Todd had to comply with the rules. The medium for the therapy now became baseball. When Todd missed hitting or catching the ball, he would sometimes get angry, and his aunt used her skills to help him calm down so that "we can have fun." A few times, other children walked by and became incorporated into the play. Todd's reaction to them became the focal point of the treatment when their presence caused minor conflicts. Todd was learning affect regulation because of his love of the game and his aunt's ability to help him manage his feelings. The therapist served as coach in the process.

This is an example of one of the benefits of working outside the office. Making use of mealtimes, cooking and outside play may be useful alternative means to reaching therapeutic goals.

Assessment

Assessment of the home setting gives us essential information about the child's life and the physical space in which he or she is developing. Are there toys in the home? Is there a space to play? Are activities in the home opportunities for parent and child to interact, such as helping Mom cook or clean? Is the environment safe for a young child? What are mealtimes like? How do family members interact with the child? Observing and assessing the home setting in treatment can offer a clearer picture of the setting in which the child is developing.

The following vignette illustrates how observing mealtimes in the home can help form a fuller diagnostic picture of the child and parent.

A Russian Jewish mother–child dyad, Sarah and 1½- year-old Sonia, were referred with complaints that Sonia refused to eat and "mealtimes were a horror." The parents' relationship was very conflicted, with verbal fighting in the home, and the mother was concerned about the effect on Sonia. The therapist came back during mealtime to see a battle between mother and daughter. Sonia refused most of the food that Sarah offered. She played with the food and threw it on the floor. The mother reacted with anger, and Sonia dug in her heels, refusing all food. They were in a power struggle, each trying to glean some sense of control from what was a very chaotic, conflicted home life. The therapist provided reflective developmental guidance to help Sarah understand her daughter's appropriate need to explore her food, which sometimes was a messy affair. The therapist also demonstrated to Sarah that, when food falls over the side of the highchair, her daughter experiences the magic of objects disappearing. Over time, the mother's feelings of rejection and anger at Sonia eased and mealtimes became less of a battle of wills.

Viewing mealtime in the home allowed direct observation of the dynamics of Sonia's feeding problem. This vignette provides an example of the increased ecological validity of the work that can occur in the home. The therapist can observe key interactions that are an ongoing critical part of the child's development in the context of the parenting relationship. Recognizing that family meals are considered highly important in this culture allowed the therapist to appreciate the heightened conflict between the child and her mother.

Observing the in-the-moment interactions between mother and daughter provided an opportunity to more fully understand and engage with the relational aspects of their struggle. This, in turn, gave the therapist specific behaviors to address.

Safety and danger

Families have many risk factors that are engendered by poverty, such as community and family violence, drug and alcohol abuse and lack of health insurance and care. Clinicians need training and support to assess danger within the family and in the home. While we can't anticipate every dangerous situation, we can stay attuned to our healthy sense of protection and use that as a guide both for ourselves and our clients. Due to the traumas they have experienced, some of the parents we work with have a sense of numbing and an inability to sense danger. Psychotherapists making home visits should be aware of the potential safety risks to themselves and the unconscious pull to collude with a domestic violence victim's denial of the safety risks in the home.

The therapist was working with a young African American mother and her son, Jackson. Both had been traumatized by domestic violence perpetrated by Jackson's father. The father was also a gang member and was currently in jail.

The therapist recounted the session to her supervisor and casually mentioned that the mother had said that "some of the father's gang members are now coming by the house." The supervisor's internal response was one of alarm. This didn't seem safe for anyone, including the therapist. Why was the therapist not showing any concern? After posing some reflective questions about how the therapist felt when the mother had told her about the gang members, the therapist connected to her own healthy sense of danger. The mother, a survivor of domestic violence, had become numbed to danger as a result of repeated exposure to trauma. In a parallel process, the therapist felt the same numbness and, as a result, was colluding with the mother's lack of a sense of danger. When the therapist became aware of the danger to herself and the family, she spoke to the mother about the lack of safety in the home. The mother was surprised, but agreed to meet the therapist at her office and was able make use of the therapist's observation about her numbness to danger and the implications this had for both mother and son.

Therapists and their clinical supervisors/consultants need to be clearly informed about agency policy and attuned to their own healthy sense of danger. Reflective supervision can help to identify when parallel processes might be taking place.

Trauma reminders

Trauma reminders are somatic memories associated with the traumatic experience, which can overwhelm the child (Pynoos, Steinberg, & Piacentini, 1999; Lieberman & Van Horn, 2008). Often, the traumatic experiences have taken place in the home and can become the focus of treatment.

Trauma reminders can come in many forms. The reminder can be triggered by a smell, sound, place, person or behavior. If a child avoids part of the house or seems upset when some activity takes place in the home, this may be the result of a specific trauma reminder. Going to the front door that Daddy kicked in when he was mad may trigger a child's memory of trauma. Parent and child can also be traumatic reminders for each other, escalating overwhelming affect (Lieberman & Van Horn, 2008). A child's developmentally appropriate angry affect may trigger the mother to feel that she is being abused by her child. Mommy's raised voice may cause fear in her child as a reminder of the fight she had with Daddy. The therapist themselves can become a trauma trigger.

The following vignette demonstrates how the therapist, during a home visit, can become a traumatic reminder of a devastating loss for a child.

Joe was a 2-year-old African American boy who was referred for dyadic therapy because his mother had died suddenly in a tragic car accident. He was placed in a foster home with an African American woman who was a part of his mother's extended family of friends. Joe was a somber little boy with large eyes. He had little range of affect and limited interest in playing, and had regressed in his toileting. Joe experienced traumatic grief and did not have the mechanisms to cope and maintain self-regulation. The therapist worked for a few months to help him develop his play and enhance his relationship with his foster mother. She would talk with Joe about his mother and made a special book of pictures of his mother for him. The foster mother commented on his sadness and his missing his mommy. One day, after a few months of seeing them, the therapist entered the home to find that the foster mother was out doing errands. She was told by a family member that the foster mother would return shortly. Joe came into the room where they usually met, and the therapist took out a few of the toys she had brought. Joe began to walk around the room aimlessly. The clinician tried to engage him in play, but he would have none of it. He began to whimper and kick the toys as he walked around the room. Over the next five minutes or so, he became more agitated and would not allow the therapist to soothe him. When the foster mother finally came home and entered the room, he looked at her and turned away. He began to cry harder, but he would not go to her. At one point, he turned to the foster mother, turned away and held his arms out to the therapist. She reached for him, but he let his arms drop and collapsed on the floor, sobbing uncontrollably. The foster mother picked him up and finally, after quite a while, was able to calm him down.

Joe's disorganized behavior and ultimate collapse were the results of his re-experiencing the trauma of losing his mother. The unexpected absence of his foster mother at the home during the session triggered his profound feelings about the loss of his mother. Overwhelmed and unable to cope with these feelings, he re-experienced the original loss.

Conclusion

The theory of developmental contextualism recognizes the importance of family context, since child development is a function of both the environment and genetics (Lerner, 1995). We know that the quality of the home environment and of the parent–child interaction predicts children's social and emotional development and leads to success in transitioning to school. Our knowledge of attachment theory (Bowlby, 1978) predicts that the infant's emotional attachment to the mother gives him or her the capacity to enter into all later interpersonal relationships. Providing supportive relationships for the primary caregivers of young children creates a scaffolding that ultimately supports the primary development of the young child. As Kindermann and Valsiner (1995) concluded that it is the complex interconnectedness and relationships that exist between individuals and their contexts which determine the pathways of the human life course.

Therefore, the opportunity to provide support for young children and their primary caregivers in their home environment offers an important opportunity for therapeutic intervention. Providing treatment in the child's natural environment can also eliminate the primary obstacle to access to services. To hold the complexity of the family system, the home-visiting therapist also needs reflective supervision, which provides quality support and intervention.

Effective training, reflective supervision, self-care and fidelity to the model help support the early childhood mental health therapist working in the child's home. All of these help the therapist become flexible and skillful while navigating the many challenges of therapy, ultimately improving outcomes for children and families. Visiting with families in their homes is an honor that affords a unique intimacy that nurtures the attachment between our youngest children and the adults who care for them.

References

Bilukha, O., Hahn, R. A., Crosby, A., Fullilove, M. T., Liberman, A. Moscicki, E., et al. (2005). The effectiveness of early childhood home visitation in preventing violence: a systematic review. *American Journal of Preventive Medicine*, 28(2) (Suppl. 1), 11–39.

Bowlby, J. (1978). Attachment theory and its therapeutic implications. *Adolescent Psychiatry*, *6*, 5–33. In S. C. Feinstein & P. L. Giovacchini (Eds.), *Adolescent psychiatry: Developmental and clinical studies* (Annals of the American Society for Adolescent Psychiatry). Chicago, IL: University of Chicago Press.

Fraiberg, S. (1980). *Clinical studies in infant mental health: The first year of life* (pp. 5–7). New York, NY: Basic Books.

Ghosh-Ippen, C. (2009). The sociocultural context in infant mental health: toward contextually congruent interventions. In C. Zeanah (Ed.), *Handbook of infant mental health* (pp. 104–119). New York, NY: Guilford Press.

Gomby, D. S. (2005). *Home visitation in 2005: Outcomes for children and parents* (Invest in Kids Working Paper No. 7). Washington, D.C.: Committee for Economic Development, Invest in Kids Working Group.

Kindermann, T. A. & Valsiner, J. (Eds.) (1995). *Development of person-context relations*. Hillsdale, NJ: L. Erlbaum Associates.

Koball, H., Zaveri, H., Boller, K., Daro, D., Knab, J., Paulsell, D., et al. (2009). *Supporting evidence-based home visiting to prevent child maltreatment: Overview of the cross-site evaluation* (p. 1). Children's Bureau, Administration for Children and Families, U.S. Department of Health and Human Services. Princeton, NJ: Mathematica Policy Research.

Lerner, R. M. (1995). Developing individuals within changing contexts: implications of developmental contextualism for human development research, policy and programs. In T. A. Kindermann & J. Valsiner (Eds.) *Development of person-context relations* (pp. 13–37). Hillsdale, NJ: L. Erlbaum Associates.

Lewis, M. L., & Ghosh-Ippen, C. (2004). Rainbows of tears, souls full of hope: cultural issues related to young children and trauma. In J. D. Osofsky (Ed.), *Young children and trauma: Intervention and treatment* (pp. 11–46). New York, NY: Guilford Press.

Lieberman, A. F., & Van Horn, P. (2005). *Don't hit my mommy!: A manual for child-parent psychotherapy with young witnesses of family violence*. Washington, D.C.: ZERO TO THREE.

Lieberman, A. F., & Van Horn, P. (2008). *Psychotherapy with infants and young children: Repairing the effects of stress and trauma on early attachment*. New York, NY: Guilford Press.

Lowell, D. I., Carter, A. S., Godoy, L., Paulicin, B., & Briggs-Gowan, M. J. (2011). A randomized controlled trial of Child FIRST: A comprehensive home-based intervention translating research into early childhood practice. *Child Development, 82*(1), 193–208.

Martini, M. (2002). How mothers in four American cultural groups shape infant learning during mealtimes. *Zero to Three Journal, 22*(4), 14–20.

Olds, D. L., Kitzman, H., Cole, R., Robinson, J., Sidora, K., Luckey, D. W., et al. (2004). Effects of nurse home-visiting on maternal life course and child development: Age 6 follow-up results of a randomized trial. *Pediatrics, 114*(6), 1550–1559.

Olds, D. L., Kitzman, H., Hanks, C., Cole, R., Anson, E., Sidora-Arcoleo, K., et al. (2007). Effects of nurse home visiting on maternal and child functioning: Age 9 follow-up of a randomized trial. *Pediatrics, 120*(4), e832–e845.

Prinz, R. J., Sanders, M. R., Shapiro, C. J., Witaker, D. J., & Lutzker, J. R. (2009). Population-based prevention of child maltreatment: The U.S. Triple P system of population trial. *Prevention Science, 10*(1), 1–12.

Pynoos, R. S., Steinberg, A. M., & Piacentini, J. C. (1999). A developmental psychopathology model of childhood traumatic stress and intersections with anxiety disorders. *Biological Psychiatry, 46*(11), 1542–1554.

Sweet, M. A., & Appelbaum, M. I. (2004). Is home visiting an effective strategy? A meta-analytic review of home visiting programs for families with young children. *Child Development, 75*(5), 1435–1456.

Chapter 9

Broken mirrors

Shattered relationships within refugee families

Elisa van Ee, Trudy Mooren and Rolf J. Kleber

Introduction

People all over the world flee from their homeland and seek refuge in foreign countries because their life is threatened as a consequence of their political or religious convictions or even the simple fact that they belong to an ethnic or social group that is discriminated against. Such dangerous political and social circumstances drive them to forced migration and an application for asylum, through which they may regain hope for new perspectives. Refugees have suffered many hardships and ordeals. For example, they are exposed to a lack of food and water, serious injury, rape, imprisonment, torture, combat situations and murder of close relatives (Nickerson et al., 2011). There is evidence of a strong relation between the multiple and chronic extreme experiences of refugees and the diagnosis of posttraumatic stress disorder (PTSD), which is defined as the consequence of a traumatic event or series of these events characterized by intrusive memories of the trauma and symptoms of avoidance and hyperarousal (American Psychiatric Association, 2000). This disorder often co-occurs with depression and/or anxiety disorders (Fazel, Wheeler, & Danesh, 2005; Lindert, von Ehrenstein, Priebe, Mielck, & Brähler, 2009; Momartin, Silove, Manicavasagar, & Steel, 2004). In addition, exposure to violence, terror and war is thought to change a person's fundamental beliefs, worldview and self-view, such that he or she no longer experiences the world as a secure place and his or her self-efficacy will decrease (Ehlers & Clark, 2000; Hobfoll et al., 2007; Janoff-Bulman & McPherson Frantz, 1997). Thus, the hardships that refugees experience appear to have a significant and long-lasting impact on their functioning.

Furthermore, refugees and asylum seekers experience the profound loss of their home and their homeland as well as the stress and alienation of resettlement in a new country and culture. Papadopoulos (2002) describes home as a safe haven for child development, both literal and figurative. For that reason, the loss of this intimate place could also be recognized as a life event that disturbs important meanings, such as security and belonging to a community. Moro (2003) illustrates the effects of this situation on parents of children born in exile: a mother may feel uncertain about her role and ability to nurture her child in the new environment without the familiar support network, which may interfere with her providing security for her child. Consequently, it is understandable that parenting may be a complicated task for refugees and asylum seekers.

In this chapter, we focus on traumatized refugee parents and their interaction with their children. We will start with providing a theoretical framework for these parent–child interactions by discussing the concept of intergenerational transmission of trauma. Next, we will elaborate on research that specifically addresses the impact of violence, terror and forced migration of refugee parents on their children. We will delineate the concept of emotional availability to enhance our understanding of these interactions. In the following paragraphs, multifamily therapy will be introduced. This systemic family-oriented therapy within a group setting builds on the resilience within families to heal the relationships of a hurt individual with him- or herself, their family members and their future. We close this chapter with conclusions and recommendations.

Intergenerational transmission of trauma?

> An Afghan family applies for psychological assistance. The parents describe as their major concerns the asylum procedure, memories they do not (yet) want to share and the behavioral problems of their teenage son. Their son does not listen to them and is aggressive towards other children. They worry that their son will become a drug addict and a criminal. Their teenage daughter is well adjusted, devoted to school and dreams of becoming a doctor one day. The children describe their parents as anxious and depressed: "All day long, they sit on the coach and often they cry." Both children deny having problems of their own, but do worry about the others in the family.

Whether or not children can be affected by the posttraumatic disturbances of their parents is the topic of a longstanding discussion. Especially in the 1980s and the 1990s, there was a strong debate about the issue of the so-called "second generation of war survivors": do the concentration camp experiences of parents lead to similar or related disturbances in their children born after World War II? The issue has disappeared somewhat from the field of traumatic stress studies, but is nevertheless important these days because of its relevance for refugees and survivors of recent wars (see, for an overview, Danieli, 1998). Case reports provided lively descriptions of clinical cases of children. They described parents who were unavailable to their children because they were occupied with their own suffering. As parents re-experience their traumas, they become frightened or frightening, unable to tolerate emotions, to attune or to respond in any way. As a consequence, their children (even babies) develop a range of behavioral problems, including delayed development and disorganized attachment. Eventually, they are in need of treatment in adulthood.

In contrast to these case reports, most systematic and controlled studies have not found significant differences in health problems and adjustment between (adult) children of war survivors and control groups in countries such as the United States, Israel and the Netherlands. No indications of extreme psychopathology were found, and most subjects have been reported to be within the normal range (e.g., Bar-On et al., 1998; Leon, Butcher, Kleinman, Goldberg, & Almagor, 1981; Sigal & Weinfeld, 1989; Suedfeld, 2000; van der Velden, Eland, & Kleber, 1994). Nevertheless, even systematic research results were not conclusive. Some studies on Holocaust survivors and survivors of recent wars have presented empirical evidence for transmission effects across two generations (e.g., Eland, van der Velden, Kleber, & Steinmetz, 1990; Levav, Levinson, Radomislensky, Shemesh, & Kohn, 2007; Rosenheck & Nathan, 1985; Solomon, Kotler, & Mikulincer, 1998; Yehuda, Schmeidler, Wainberg, Binder-Brynes, & Duvdevani, 1998). These effects include a predisposition to emotional stress, PTSD or other mental disorders. Nevertheless, van IJzendoorn, Bakermans-Kranenburg and Sagi-Schwartz (2003) concluded in a meta-analysis that "no evidence of the influence of parents' traumatic Holocaust experiences on their children could be found in a set of adequately designed nonclinical studies" (p. 459).

However, research results could have been biased. Most analyses were based on the adult children's perceptions of their survivor parents. Children were not screened throughout the developmental span, but as adults looking back on their childhood, which had been troubled by a traumatized parent. Research designs were hence retrospective in nature. Second, convenience or clinical samples were used in the majority of cases, with an emphasis on Holocaust survivors. Finally, it has been found that most victims and survivors recover well after adversity and do not develop serious symptomatology (Kleber & Brom, 2003). Therefore, it is necessary to make a distinction between parents who had experienced extreme events without developing mental disturbances and parents who had experienced these events and who suffered from resulting disorders, such as PTSD. Unfortunately, most of the studies mentioned above did not made this important distinction. We expect that this distinction will be related to quite different transgenerational effects with regard to parenting behavior and child development.

Limitations in parenting

A three-year-old child and his Armenian mother are admitted for therapy. The mother complains about the behavior of the child, and says she cannot handle him any more. He only sleeps for a few hours at night and keeps her awake. He barely speaks, and instead cries or screams to get her attention. He wants attention all day long. During the day, the mother is unable to leave the child alone for a minute. She is afraid that something will happen to him. At night, they sleep in the same room even though the mother's nightmares scare the child.

There is considerable evidence that a parental psychological disorder generally increases the risk of disturbed child development and poor mental health in adulthood. For example, substantial research has been conducted on the impact of maternal depression on child functioning. Maternal depression has been associated with wide-ranging and persistent impairments in child functioning. The adverse outcomes reach into adolescence with elevated rates of affective disorders (Essex, Klein, Cho, & Kalin, 2002; Field, 1995; Halligan, Murray, Martins, & Cooper, 2006; Hay et al., 2001). Interacting with their children, depressed mothers exhibit less positive affect, respond less consistently and positively to their children and engage in fewer vocalizations than non-depressed mothers. They also display more negative affect, are more hostile, irritable and critical, and use more coercive parenting methods when interacting with their children (for reviews, see Downey & Coyne, 1990; Lovejoy, Graczyk, O'Hare, & Neuman, 2000). Thus, several decades of research indicate that there is a strong relationship between maternal depression and parenting behavior.

Our understanding of the intergenerational consequences of traumatization reveals similarities between traumatized mothers and depressed mothers and their children. Research has shown a relation between parental PTSD and the quality of parent–child interaction. Parents with PTSD report significantly poorer parent–child relationships than those without PTSD, especially when the parents experience emotional numbing or avoidance symptoms (Gewirtz, Polusny, DeGarmo, Khaylis, & Erbes, 2010; Lauterbach et al., 2007; Ruscio, Weathers, King, & King, 2002; Samper, Taft, King, & King, 2004). Parent–child relationships of parents with PTSD were also observed to be of lesser quality than of parents without PTSD. Mothers with more symptoms of posttraumatic stress were less emotionally available and responsive (Schechter et al., 2010). Mothers with childhood or cumulative traumatic experiences were more hostile, intrusive, punitive, aggressive and neglectful of the child (Banyard, Williams, & Siegel, 2003; Cohen, Hien, & Batchelder, 2008; Lyons-Ruth & Block, 1996). Parental PTSD has been associated with child outcome as well. More psychopathological and abnormal behaviors such as anxiety, depression, aggression and deviant behavior have been reported for children of parents with PTSD (Ahmadzadeh & Malekian 2004; Al-Turkait & Ohaeri, 2008; Gold et al. 2007; Jordan et al., 1992). Although general parenting ability may remain intact after a history of traumatic experiences, traumatized parents can be affected in their parenting.

However, the links that have been found between parental disorders and the presence of similar disorders in the child have mostly been weak. The main threat to child development does not lie in temporary, situation-specific stress reactions, but in disturbances that are pervasive across various situations and persistent over time (Rutter & Quinton, 1984). This evokes doubts about the term "intergenerational transmission of trauma." It is *not* trauma that is transmitted over generations. Traumatization can cause parenting limitations, and these limitations disrupt the development of the young child. Although we must not forget the remarkable resilience of many of these parents and children, parental traumatization may alter parent–child interaction and therefore constitute a risk to the development of the child.

Refugee parents and the interaction with their children

> An Iraqi father sits on the couch remembering his friends who died fighting next to him during the war. He has a blank expression and sits there silently all day long. In the corner plays a five-year-old girl. She plays quietly so as not to disturb father or he will get angry. Sometimes, suddenly, her father gets up and screams something she does not understand. It scares her and she presses herself into the corner. After a few minutes it stops and her father will sit down again, barely noticing the reaction of his little daughter.

Refugee parents face major challenges in rearing their children. These families are confronted with terror, forced migration and asylum procedures. Their members often suffer from various symptoms such as sleep problems, flashbacks, aggression, concentration problems and somatic complaints. It is not surprising that these disturbances are often referred to by the term "complex PTSD" (Mooren & Stöfsel, 2014). The parents that apply for help at Centrum '45, the Dutch national institute for research on and treatment of psychotrauma, are less able to react sensitively to the needs of their children and are preoccupied with their own problems. They are emotionally and functionally unavailable to their children.

Despite increased attention on parental posttraumatic disturbances and the impact on children, there is still a dearth of studies on refugee families. Vaage et al. (2011) conducted a longitudinal prospective cohort study of the long-term effects of PTSD on Vietnamese refugee parents and their children 23 years after resettlement. Although 30% of the families had one parent with a high psychological distress score, only 4% of the children (10–23 years old) reported probable mental health problems. However, PTSD in fathers did predict the risk of mental health problems among their offspring. In order to explore resilience, Daud, Klinteberg and Rydelius (2008) assessed 80 refugee children (aged 6–17) who had not developed posttraumatic stress symptoms despite a history of parental PTSD. Non-exposed children without posttraumatic stress symptoms but with traumatized parents had more favorable outcomes on emotionality, family relations, peer relations and prosocial behavior than non-exposed children with PTSD.

Resilience

> A teenage boy, whose father died in the concentration camps of former Yugoslavia, finds his escape in music. In his lyrics, he expresses his sadness and his anger because of the losses, his regrets of the past, but also his love for his mother and his dreams for the future. When asked about his music, he answers: "I was so confused, but I survived because I started writing."

Despite a troubled childhood, many children of traumatized parents have the potential to function well. Resilience is a key concept for understanding positive adaptation within the context of significant adversity. Resilience has been operationalized in various ways, but, in general, it is regarded as an individual's capacity to withstand, adapt to and rebound from challenging or threatening circumstances. It is a dynamic process involving the interplay of multiple risk and protective processes over time, incorporating individual, family and larger sociocultural influences (Brom & Kleber, 2009; Walsh, 2003). The same adversity can result in different outcomes for different individuals.

In studies on children of traumatized parents, the concept of resilience only received explicit attention within the study of Daud et al. (2008). Their results show the importance of family and peer relationships. The study of Al-Turkait and Ohaeri (2008) addresses the independent contribution of traumatized fathers and mothers in relation to child outcome variables. The results suggested the importance of a non-affected parent. Children with one affected and one non-affected parent were more resilient than children with two affected parents. The non-affected parent has the potential to build resilience in the child. The role of the mother was especially significant for the psychosocial functioning of the child. Although PTSD of both parents affected the children, the mother's anxiety was the most frequent and important predictor of children's anxiety, depression or abnormal behavior. These results are in line with the results of studies of at-risk children. The studies noted the crucial influence of significant relationships with caring adults and mentors who supported, encouraged and believed in the potential of these children (Walsh, 1996). This underlines the importance of research that focuses not only on parental pathology, but also on family relational networks and child resilience. In addition, it alludes to the clinical importance of establishing compensating relationships within the child's environment.

Parent–child interaction among refugees and asylum seekers: empirical findings

> A Sudanese mother, suffering from severe PTSD and depression, ordered her three-year-old daughter to stay near her bed when she was very sad. If the little girl went off to play, she told her, the mother would die. The father taught his daughter to bring her mother tissues. He thought that it was cute to see the three-year-old take care of her mother.

Healthy parent–child interaction is recognized as an essential focus for the development of children, as, through the behavior of the primary caregivers, both protective factors and risk factors for a healthy physical and psychological development can be transmitted to the child (Scheeringa & Zeanah 2001; Zeanah, Boris, & Larrieu, 1997). Therefore, we will elaborate on our study on parent–child interaction in a refugee and asylum seeker population. Earlier in this chapter, we referred to the longstanding debate on the intergenerational transmission of trauma. In the past, this research focused on the psychosocial functioning of adult children and no distinction was made between parents who had experienced extreme events and those who suffered from long-term consequences of these events. In order to understand the mechanisms underpinning the interplay between traumatized parents and their children, research investigating these parents and their (young) children is crucial. This impact needs to be "caught" within the research room and throughout the developmental span. To contribute to an understanding of the influence of war trauma of parents on the interaction with their children, we designed a study in which the impact of posttraumatic stress of refugee parents with young children, not exposed to traumatic events themselves, on the parent–child interaction was studied.

Refugee and asylum seeker parents and their children were recruited from Dutch asylum seeker centers and from client groups at Centrum '45. Participants included in this study met the following criteria: (a) they were asylum seekers or refugees that had been exposed to traumatic events; (b) they had at least one child in the age range of 18–42 months, who had been born in the Netherlands and had not been exposed to a traumatic event; and (c) the parents did not suffer from addiction, mental retardation or psychosis. The final sample consisted of 80 parents and their children: 29 fathers, 51 mothers, 45 sons and 35 daughters. Parents had fled from various geographical regions: Middle East (43.8%), Africa (32.5%), Eastern Europe (12.5%), Asia (8.8%) and South America (2.6%). Of the sample, 55% were refugees and 45% were asylum seekers. Furthermore, 49% of the participant population was living in an asylum seeker center. The measurements consisted of trauma experiences and symptoms of PTSD (Harvard trauma questionnaire), symptoms of anxiety and depression (Hopkins symptom checklist), quality of parent–child interaction (emotional availability scale) and psychosocial functioning of the child (child behavior checklist).

As a good understanding of the measurement of the emotional availability scale (EAS) (Biringen, 2008) is of importance to the interpretation of the results, the issue of emotional availability will here be delineated in some detail. Parents establish expectable interactions with their young child through their voices, facial expressions and gestures (Bornstein et al., 2006). When the caregiver is emotionally available and interacts in a sensitive and responsive manner, secure attachment is fostered (Bowlby, 1969/1982; Rothbaum, Rosen Schneider, Pott, & Beatty, 1995). Emotional availability can be described as the quality of emotional transactions between parent and child, specifically focusing on parents' accessibility and ability to read and respond properly to the child (Biringen & Robinson, 1991). The EAS (Biringen, 2008) was designed to measure dyadic interactions between an adult and a child. The EAS consists of six dimensions, of which four dimensions concern the emotional availability of the adult toward the child (sensitivity, structuring, non-intrusiveness and non-hostility) and two dimensions concern the emotional availability of the child toward the adult (responsiveness and involvement). An emotionally available parent is able to be warm and emotionally connected with the child, and to provide appropriate structure for the child in the right amount. The parent is able to be available to the child when needed, without being intrusive, hostile or undermining of the child's autonomy. An emotionally available child exhibits positive affect and behavior regulation. The child is likely to respond to the adult and shows initiative in bringing the adult into interaction.

In our sample of 80 refugee parents and their young children, 72% of all mothers and 86% of all fathers were classified as having PTSD. Between refugee mothers and fathers, no significant differences were found on posttraumatic stress and emotional availability. Fathers were as traumatized, but also as emotionally available to their children, as mothers. Posttraumatic stress was found to predict sensitivity, structuring and non-hostility within the parent–child interaction. Parents with symptoms of PTSD were less sensitive, less structuring and more hostile. Posttraumatic stress was marginally significant ($p < .10$) on the non-intrusiveness scale (van Ee, Sleijpen, Kleber, & Jongmans, 2013). This indicates that parents with symptoms of PTSD are more intrusive. It is possible that our small sample size prevented significant results on the non-intrusiveness scale.

We took a closer look at the severity of maternal posttraumatic stress symptoms of 45 refugee mothers, the emotional availability within the mother–child interaction and the children's psychosocial functioning. Severity of maternal posttraumatic stress symptoms was significantly correlated with children's internalizing behavior and total problems (a composite of internalizing and externalizing problems). Mothers experiencing posttraumatic stress symptoms scored lower on all single scales of the EAS. This means that mothers with symptoms of PTSD were less sensitive, less structuring, more intrusive and more hostile. Both child scores on the EAS were lower for mothers experiencing posttraumatic stress. Children of mothers with symptoms of PTSD were less responsive to and less involved with their mothers. We tested whether the association between maternal trauma and child's psychosocial functioning is mediated via the quality of dyadic emotional availability. Although mother's posttraumatic stress symptoms correlated significantly with the occurrence and severity of children's psychosocial symptoms, as well as with the emotional availability within the parent–child interaction, only non-hostility within the parent–child interaction correlated significantly with child's internalizing behavior and total problems. A mediation model with emotional availability as a mediator between maternal posttraumatic stress and children's psychosocial functioning did not hold (van Ee, Kleber, & Mooren, 2012). Even though maternal emotional availability encompasses key markers of the parent–child interaction, it does not explain the relation between maternal posttraumatic stress and child functioning. Still, it is possible that posttraumatic stress hinders a parent interacting with or attuning to the child. Maybe more extreme alterations within the parent–child interaction, such as parental dissociation and extreme insensitivity, could then lead to the child's symptoms.

What is striking is the combination of a negative association between maternal posttraumatic stress symptoms and sensitivity of the mother, as well as a negative association with responsiveness of the child. A child's responsiveness to the mother is reflected in a positive affect and the regulation of emotions in response to the mother. A mother's sensitivity to the child is reflected in a warm affect and an emotional connectedness. It is precisely this capacity that might be hindered by posttraumatic stress symptoms, as it includes impairment of the ability to regulate affect and arousal. Lack of caregivers' regulation impairs the development of the child's self-regulation, and, as a consequence, behavioral adaptations may result.

Considering these results, it makes sense for clinicians counseling refugee parents, and perhaps even traumatized parents in general, to inquire about parenthood and the well-being of children. In addition, the results indicate a need to re-establish "attunement" between traumatized parents and their children. However, most parent–child interventions are aimed at the mothers, while the quality of involvement of both fathers and mothers is equally affected by posttraumatic stress symptoms. As the quality of father involvement is of importance to the development of the child, traumatized fathers are as much in need of clinical intervention as mothers.

Multifamily therapy groups with refugee families

How to facilitate bonding and improve emotional availability of parents towards their children? How to apply interventions to refugee families with various cultural backgrounds? The remainder of this chapter will describe the efforts at our institute to strengthen resilience and parenting competencies in a high-risk population of families, as has been described earlier. We have adopted a specific psychosocial treatment format that has been used in the treatment of various mental disorders: multifamily group therapy (MFGT). Although alternative approaches are possible as well (such as parent–child interaction therapy and video-feedback intervention to promote positive parenting) and have also been applied by us, we elaborate on MFGT because we consider it particularly useful for improving parent–child interaction in refugees.

Multiple family therapy (MFT), or multifamily therapy, is a form of systemic therapy that uses principles derived from family therapy as well as group therapy. Laqueur and his colleagues developed MFGT in the 1960s (Asen, 2002; Kiser, Donahue, Hodgkinson, Medoff, & Black, 2010; Lemmens, 2007; McFarlane, 2002). At that time, it was decided to involve the patients' relatives as an attempt to better help people with schizophrenia. The consequence of involving family members was that patients, family members and professional staff altered their manner of communicating about and with schizophrenic patients. Since that beginning, multifamily groups have been developed with different foci (e.g., psychoeducation (Anderson, 1983), for different target groups (adolescents with eating disorders, mother–infant troubled attachment relationships) and in various settings (e.g., schools) (Asen, 2002; Lemmens, 2007). In general, it has been found that MFT groups are accepted well by the participants and lead to an increase of knowledge about the problem at stake, a better collaboration with the mental health professionals and a decrease of stigmatization. MFGT has resulted in a decrease of drop-outs of therapy, of patients' relapse and to symptom improvement (Asen, 2002; Lemmens, 2007; McFarlane, 2002).

It is our opinion that MFT works well for refugee families coping with traumatic stress and parenting difficulties because of the following elements: (a) a multifamily format, (b) the facilitation of mentalizing, and (c) bringing in the context. We will discuss these three elements below.

Multifamily format

The central idea behind MFT is bringing together different families suffering with traumatic stress, creating connections among them and thereby using their strengths and resources (empowerment). Creating solidarity as well as counteracting or overcoming stigmatization and social isolation stem from this group work and will lead to a mutual understanding and acknowledgement of the problem and of the efforts of dealing with it. As a result of sharing commonalities, the self-confidence of both parents and children can grow within a group because of the feeling of hope ("others have problems as bad or even worse") and competencies can be discovered and practiced. Mutual recognition and feedback generate social support and sharing. Group members learn from one another and provide one another with new perspectives.

The presence of several families sharing similar difficulties provides the opportunity for both family and individual work. The group creates a kind of micro-society with certain rules and values, and this elicits different aspects of the roles of the members (e.g., being a mother, daughter, sister, professional, etc.). These different roles evoke various narratives that are needed to change disruptive family patterns. A group setting in which parents and children feel comfortable and are curious to learn about themselves and others is the basis for the exchange of beliefs. Further, family narratives reveal how certain parental beliefs have prevailed throughout different generations or in different communities. In general: telling stories helps to generate meaning to the experiences of the families and gives a sense of control.

Facilitating mentalizing

The type of MFT that has been developed in London (Asen, 2002; Asen & Scholz, 2010) underlines the importance of "mentalization." This can be defined as the ability to distinguish and to see one's own and another person's mind as separate perspectives (having one's mind in mind). The concept is grounded in object relations theory. Being capable of mentalizing contributes to the development of sensitivity and a good attachment relationship between parents and children, and will eventually lead to a healthy increase of autonomy. Viewing different perspectives and being curious about differences rather than similarities offers freedom of thinking. Psychological disturbances are frequently chained to more or less rigid cognitions ("nobody is to be trusted"). Reduction of symptoms is achieved by allowing oneself to think differently, to see more alternatives than just the dominant idea (Allen, Fonagy, & Bateman, 2008; Asen, Dawson, & McHugh, 2001; Fonagy & Bateman, 2006; Schore, 2003). To increase mentalizing capacities and parental emotional availability, the group can be used for "mirroring" purposes and encouraged to offer feedback. Parents may be, for instance, encouraged in coaching each other (using walkie-talkies) when interacting with their child. In some activities, parents are invited to play with other children than their own—thereby increasing their critical observation and curiosity.

Bringing in the context

By inviting family members to therapy, it means bringing in the outside world, while, at the same time, it makes the therapy setting more representative of daily reality. The functioning of the patient within his or her own naturalistic context is crucial. MFT is therefore a context-based method. In therapy sessions, contexts for interaction are created that elicit representative family interactions. Through explicit attention on the behavior of families during the session, experiences are intensified and feedback of group members is used. New target parenting behavior may be experimented with in a safe environment.

> A group of refugee families gathered for their multifamily therapy. One mother, worried about the delayed development of her baby of 6 months old, tended not to accept feedback about her interactions with the child. She attributed the delay to some unrevealed disorder of the child. The therapist kindly and respectfully responded that it is difficult for any parent to receive feedback on their parenting style. She had also been worried about her own babies, but had discovered that paying proper attention was very helpful. Mrs. C. found these comments supportive.
>
> Within the session, families were mixed and asked to work together in creating houses made of board. They were organized by working at three different tables. At one table, difficulties arose when a fantasy house was created. For one girl, aged 12, it caused trouble that the house was not like a "real house." A younger girl enjoyed building a funny, mushroom-like house with strange sculptures. During reflection, there was an exchange, first of all, on the significance of having a house, being refugees and asylum seekers. Next, the importance of playfulness and fantasy was underlined for parents and children.

MFT as a method can be well combined with other forms of therapy; at the same time, within a MFT group, different techniques derived from other methods such as cognitive behavior therapy and eye movement desensitization and reprocessing may be applied. MFT may also be used with open or closed groups. An open group has the advantage of having senior members or families who serve as seniors and models to newcomers. Closed groups may be preferred when trust is a significant issue to members and the opportunity to create strong bonding is aimed at. The number and duration of sessions differ. In general, several subsequent phases may be distinguished: gathering and introduction, problem-focused work, relation-focused work and relapse prevention (Asen & Bianchi, 2011). Sessions are manually based and have a defined structure. First, there is an ice-breaking activity: an energizing, pleasant and interactive game (such as playing a ball or jumping a rope). The main activity usually develops around a theme that is of significance to the group. The therapist facilitates interactions between families and individuals. Where needed, the therapist zooms in and focuses on certain interactions. Other than that, he or she refrains from interventions in the group activity as much as possible, but is, however, responsible for facilitating interactions. The last part of the session is spent on reflection and exchange. Because MFT involves adults and children, it is important to create fun in the session; for instance, by physical exercise or music making. Consequently, interactions are more frequent and learning is more likely to occur.

Originally, multifamily therapy was introduced to change the manner of working in a group of difficult-to-treat patients: family members of schizophrenic patients were invited into the hospital wards. The work with multi-problem and traumatized refugee families appears to benefit from this contextual approach. The combination of family work with group dynamics creates a setting in which the relationships of a hurt individual with himself or herself, significant others and their future can be healed. Nonetheless, there is a necessity to examine the prerequisites (e.g., using competent interpreters) and the outcomes of this therapy in a scientifically thorough way. Unfortunately, controlled studies of the results of system therapy with regard to traumatic stress are still extremely rare.

Epilogue

Refugees have faced many major events. They struggle with the serious consequences of the various horrors and hardships they have experienced. Consequently, their difficulties are complicated. Understanding and addressing these difficulties requires special attention, especially when it comes to families. The children, however young, sometimes can suffer from the aftermath of the experiences and the current problems of the parents. In this chapter, we sought to make this issue comprehensible. The concept of intergenerational traumatization has been discussed and attention has been paid to developmental interferences, as manifested in the difficulties with regard to emotional availability. Sensitivity, in particular, is of importance to the development of the child. A warm affect, an emotional connectedness and an ability to read and respond to the cues of the child is precisely the capacity that might be hindered by parental posttraumatic stress symptoms. It is clear that the area of the impact of traumatic stress on families and children is still quite unexplored, clinically as well as empirically. There is undoubtedly a need for more research and more fine-tuned interventions. Nevertheless, it is clear that reestablishing attunement is an important starting point for treatment. To see one another with genuine interest and curiosity is a welcome experience for both parents and children. Patients frequently mention the experience of hope as a major outcome of family-focused treatment. This experience fosters intimacy and growth, at the individual as well as relational level.

References

Ahmadzadeh, Gh., & Malekian, A. (2004). Aggression, anxiety, and social development in adolescent children of war veterans with PTSD versus those of non-veterans. *Journal of Research in Medical Sciences*, *9*(5), 231–234.

Allen, J. G., Fonagy, P., & Bateman, A. W. (2008). *Mentalizing in clinical practice*. Washington, D.C.: American Psychiatric Publishing.

Al-Turkait, F. A., & Ohaeri, J. U. (2008). Psychopathological status, behavior problems, and family adjustment of Kuwaiti children whose fathers were involved in the first Gulf War. *Child and Adolescent Psychiatry and Mental Health*, *2*(1), 2–12.

American Psychiatric Association. (2000). *Diagnostic and statistical manual of mental disorders* (4th ed.). Washington, D.C.: Author.

Anderson, C. M. (1983). A psychoeducational program for families of patients with schizophrenia. In W. R. McFarlane (Ed.), *Family therapy in schizophrenia*. New York, NY: Guilford Press.

Asen, E. (2002) Multiple family therapy: An overview. *Journal of Family Therapy*, *24*(1), 3–16.

Asen, E., & Bianchi, S. (2011). *Multi-family approach training package for professionals working with abusive and violent high risk families* (E-Manual). London, England: Marlborough Centre.

Asen, E., Dawson, N., & McHugh, B. (2001). *Multiple family therapy. The Marlborough model and its wider applications*. London, England; New York, NY: Karnac.

Asen, E., & Scholz, M. (2010). *Multi-family therapy: Concepts and techniques*. Hove, East Sussex, England: Routledge.

Banyard, V. L., Williams, L. M., & Siegel, J. A. (2003). The impact of complex trauma and depression on parenting: An exploration of mediating risk and protective factors. *Child Maltreatment*, *8*(4), 334–349.

Bar-On, D., Eland, J., Kleber, R. J., Krell, R., Moore, Y., Sagi, A., et al. (1998). Multigenerational perspectives on coping with the Holocaust experience: An attachment perspective for understanding the developmental sequelae of trauma across generations. *International Journal of Behavioral Development*, *22*(2), 315–338.

Biringen, Z. (2008). *The emotional availability scales* (4th ed.). Fort Collins, CO: Colorado State University. Retrieved from http://www.emotionalavailability.com

Biringen, Z., & Robinson, J. (1991). Emotional availability in mother-child interactions: A reconceptualization for research. *American Journal of Orthopsychiatry*, *61*(2), 258–271.

Bornstein, M. H., Gini, M., Putnick, D. L., Haynes, O. M., Painter, K. M., & Suwalsky, J. T. D. (2006). Short-term reliability and continuity of emotional availability in mother-child dyads across contexts of observation. *Infancy*, *10*(1), 1–16.

Bowlby, J. (1969/1982). *Attachment and loss. Vol. 1, Attachment*. New York, NY: Basic Books.

Brom, D., & Kleber, R. J. (2009). Resilience as the capacity for processing traumatic experiences. In D. Brom, R. Pat-Horenczyk & J. D. Ford (Eds.), *Treating traumatized children: Risk, resilience and recovery* (pp.133–149). New York, NY: Routledge.

Cohen, L. R., Hien, D. A., & Batchelder, S. (2008). The impact of cumulative maternal trauma and diagnosis on parenting behavior. *Child Maltreatment, 13*(1), 27–38.

Danieli, Y. (Ed.) (1998). *International handbook of multigenerational legacies of trauma.* New York, NY: Plenum Press.

Daud, A., af Klinteberg, B., & Rydelius, P.-A. (2008). Resilience and vulnerability among refugee children of traumatized and non-traumatized parents. *Child and Adolescent Psychiatry and Mental Health, 2*(1), 7 (1–11). doi:10.1186/1753-2000-2-7.

Downey, G., & Coyne, J. C. (1990). Children of depressed parents: an integrative review. *Psychological Bulletin, 108*(1), 50–76.

Ehlers, A., & Clark, D. M. (2000). A cognitive model of posttraumatic stress disorder. *Behaviour Research and Therapy, 38*(4), 319–345.

Eland, J., van der Velden, P. G., Kleber, R. J., & Steinmetz, C. H. D. (1990). *Tweede generatie Joodse Nederlanders: Een onderzoek naar gezinsachtergronden en psychisch functioneren* (in Dutch). Deventer, Netherlands: Van Loghum Slaterus.

Essex, M. J., Klein, M. H., Cho, E., & Kalin, N. H. (2002). Maternal stress beginning in infancy may sensitize children to later stress exposure: Effects on cortisol and behavior. *Biological Psychiatry, 52*(8), 776–784.

Fazel, M., Wheeler, J., & Danesh, J. (2005). Prevalence of serious mental disorder in 7000 refugees resettled in western countries: A systematic review. *The Lancet, 365*(9467), 1309–1314.

Field, T. (1995). Infants of depressed mothers. *Infant Behavior and Development, 18*(1), 1–13.

Fonagy, P., & Bateman, A. W. (2006). Mechanism of change in mentalization-based treatment of BPD. *Journal of Clinical Psychiatry, 62*(4), 411–430.

Gewirtz, A. H., Polusny, M. A., DeGarmo, D. S., Khaylis, A., & Erbes, C. R. (2010). Posttraumatic stress symptoms among national guard soldiers deployed to Iraq: Associations with parenting behaviors and couple adjustment. *Journal of Consulting and Clinical Psychology, 78*(5), 599–610.

Gold, J. I., Taft, C. T., Keehn, M. G., King, D. W., King, L. A., & Samper, R. E. (2007). PTSD symptom severity and family adjustment among female Vietnam veterans. *Military Psychology, 19*(2), 71–81.

Halligan, S. L., Murray, L., Martins, C., & Cooper, P. J. (2006). Maternal depression and psychiatric outcomes in adolescent offspring: A 13-year longitudinal study. *Journal of Affective Disorders, 97*(1–3), 145–154.

Hay, D. F., Pawlby, P., Sharp, D., Asten, P., Mills, A., & Kumar, R. (2001). Intellectual problems shown by 11-year-old children whose mothers had postnatal depression. *Journal of Child Psychology and Psychiatry, 42*(7), 871–889.

Hobfoll, S. E., Watson, P., Bell, C. C., Bryant, R. A., Brymer, M. J., Friedman, M. J., et al. (2007). Five essential elements of immediate and mid-term mass trauma intervention: Empirical evidence. *Psychiatry: Interpersonal and Biological Processes, 70*(4), 283–315.

Janoff-Bulman, R., & McPherson Frantz, C. (1997). The impact of trauma on meaning: From meaningless world to meaningful life. In M. Power & C. R. Brewin (Eds.), *The transformation of meaning in psychological therapies* (pp. 91–106). Hoboken, NJ: John Wiley & Sons Ltd.

Jordan, K. B., Marmar, C. R., Fairbank, J. A., Schlenger, W. E., Kulka, R. A., Hough, R. L., et al. (1992). Problems in families of male Vietnam veterans with posttraumatic stress disorder. *Journal of Consulting and Clinical Psychology*, *60*(6), 916–926.

Kiser, L. J., Donohue, A., Hodgkinson, S., Medoff, D., & Black, M. M. (2010). Strengthening family coping resources: The feasibility of a multifamily group intervention for families exposed to trauma. *Journal of Traumatic Stress*, *23*(6), 802–806.

Kleber, R. J., & Brom, D. in collaboration with Defares, P. B. (2003). *Coping with trauma: Theory, prevention and treatment*. Amsterdam, Netherlands: Swets & Zeitlinger.

Lauterbach, D., Bak, C., Reiland, S., Mason, S., Lute, M. R., & Earls, L. (2007). Quality of parental relationships among persons with a lifetime history of posttraumatic stress disorder. *Journal of Traumatic Stress*, *20*(2), 161–172.

Lemmens, G. (2007). *Multi-family group therapy in the treatment of major depression.* Doctoral dissertation, Catholic University of Leuven, Leuven, Belgium.

Leon, G. R., Butcher, J. N., Kleinman, M., Goldberg, A., & Almagor, M. (1981). Survivors of the Holocaust and their children: Current status and adjustment. *Journal of Personality and Social Psychology*, *41*(3), 503–516.

Levav, I., Levinson, D., Radomislensky, I., Shemesh, A., & Kohn, R. (2007). Psychopathology and other health dimensions among the offspring of Holocaust survivors: Results from the Israel national health survey. *Israel Journal of Psychiatry*, *44*(2), 144–151.

Lindert, J., von Ehrenstein, O. S., Priebe, S., Mielck, A., & Brähler, E. (2009). Depression and anxiety in labor migrants and refugees: A systematic review and meta-analysis. *Social Science & Medicine*, *69*(2), 246–257.

Lovejoy, M. C., Graczyk, P. A., O'Hare, E., & Neuman, G. (2000). Maternal depression and parenting behavior: A meta-analytic review. *Clinical Psychology Review*, *20*(5), 561–592.

Lyons-Ruth, K., & Block, D. (1996) The disturbed caregiving system: Relations among childhood trauma, maternal care giving, and infant affect and attachment. *Infant Mental Health Journal*, *17*(3), 257–275.

McFarlane, W. R. (2002). *Multifamily groups in the treatment of severe psychiatric disorders*. New York, NY: Guilford Press.

Momartin, S., Silove, D., Manicavasagar, V., & Steel, Z. (2004). Comorbidity of PTSD and depression: Associations with trauma exposure, symptom severity and functional impairment in Bosnian refugees resettled in Australia. *Journal of Affective Disorders*, *80*(2–3), 231–238.

Mooren, T., & Stöfsel, M. (2014). *Diagnosing and treating complex trauma*. London, England: Routledge, forthcoming.

Moro, M. R. (2003). Parents and infants in changing cultural context: Immigration, trauma and risk. *Infant Mental Health Journal*, *24*(3), 240–264.

Nickerson, A., Bryant, R. A., Brooks, R., Steel, Z., Silove, D., & Chen, J. (2011). The familial influence of loss and trauma on refugee mental health: A multilevel path analysis. *Journal of Traumatic Stress*, *24*(1), 25–33.

Papadopoulos, R. K. (Ed.). (2002). *Therapeutic care for refugees: No place like home.* London, England: Karnac.

Rosenheck R., & Nathan, P. (1985). Secondary traumatization in children of Vietnam veterans. *Hospital and Community Psychiatry*, *36*(5), 538–539.

Rothbaum, F., Rosen Schneider, K., Pott, M., & Beatty, M. (1995). Early parent-child relationships and later problem behavior: A longitudinal study. *Merrill-Palmer Quarterly: Journal of Developmental Psychology, 41*(2), 133–151.

Ruscio, A. M., Weathers, F. W., King, L. A., & King, D. W. (2002). Male war-zone veterans' perceived relationships with their children: The importance of emotional numbing. *Journal of Traumatic Stress, 15*(5), 351–357.

Rutter, M., & Quinton, D. (1984). Parental psychiatric disorder: Effects on children. *Psychological Medicine, 14*(4), 853–880.

Samper, R. E., Taft, C. T., King, D. W., & King, L. A. (2004). Posttraumatic stress disorder symptoms and parenting satisfaction among a national sample of male Vietnam veterans. *Journal of Traumatic Stress, 17*(4), 311–315.

Schechter, D. S., Willheim, E., Hinojosa, C., Scholfield-Kleinman, K., Turner, J. B., McCaw, J., et al. (2010). Subjective and objective measures of parent-child relationship dysfunction, child separation distress, and joint attention. *Psychiatry: Interpersonal and Biological Processes, 37*(2), 130–144.

Scheeringa, M. S., & Zeanah, C. H. (2001). A relational perspective on PTSD in early childhood, *Journal of Traumatic Stress, 14*(4), 799–815.

Schore, A. N. (2003). *Affect regulation and repair of the self.* New York, NY: W.W. Norton & Company.

Sigal, J. J., & Weinfeld, M. (1989). *Trauma and rebirth: Intergenerational effects of the Holocaust.* New York, NY: Praeger.

Solomon, Z., Kotler, M., & Mikulincer, M. (1998). Combat-related posttraumatic stress disorder among second-generation Holocaust survivors: Preliminary findings. *American Journal of Psychiatry, 145*(7), 865–868.

Suedfeld, P. (2000). Reverberations of the Holocaust fifty years later: Psychology's contributions to understanding persecution and genocide. *Canadian Psychology (Psychologie Canadienne), 41*(1), 1–9.

Vaage, A. B., Thomsen, P. H., Rousseau, C., Wentzel-Larsen, T., Ta, T. V., & Hauff, E. (2011). Paternal predictors of the mental health of children of Vietnamese refugees. *Child and Adolescent Psychiatry and Mental Health, 5*(2), doi: 10.1186/1753-2000-5-2

van Ee, E., Sleijpen, M., Kleber, R. J., & Jongmans, M. J. (2013). Father-involvement in a refugee sample: Relations between posttraumatic stress and caregiving. *Family Process.* doi: 10.1111/famp.12045

van Ee, E., van Kleber, R .J., & Mooren, T. T. M. (2012). War trauma lingers on: Associations between maternal posttraumatic stress disorder, parent-child interaction, and child development. *Infant Mental Health Journal, 33*(5), 459–468.

van IJzendoorn, M. H., Bakermans-Kranenburg, M. J., & Sagi-Schwartz, A. (2003). Are children of Holocaust survivors less well-adapted? A meta-analytic investigation of secondary traumatization. *Journal of Traumatic Stress, 16*(5), 459–469.

van der Velden, P. G., Eland, J., & Kleber, R. J. (1994). *De Indische na-oorlogse generatie: Een psychologisch onderzoek naar gezinsachtergronden en gezondheid.* Houten, Netherlands: Bohn Stafleu Van Loghum.

Walsh, F. (1996). The concept of family resilience: Crisis and challenge. *Family Process, 35*(3), 261–281.

Walsh, F. (2003). Family resilience: A framework for clinical practice. *Family Process, 42*(1), 1–18.

Yehuda, R., Schmeidler, J., Wainberg, M., Binder-Brynes, K., & Duvdevani, T. (1998). Vulnerability to posttraumatic stress disorder in adult offspring of Holocaust survivors. *American Journal of Psychiatry, 155*(9), 1163–1171.

Zeanah, C. H., Boris, N. W., & Larrieu J. A. (1997). Infant development and developmental risk: A review of the past 10 years. *Journal of the American Academy of Child and Adolescent Psychiatry, 36*(2), 165–178.

Section III

Community

Chapter 10

A child-oriented perspective on community resilience

Nathaniel Laor, Leo Wolmer, Smadar Spirman, Daniel Hamiel and Zeev Wiener

Introduction

The concept of "community resilience" in the face of disaster has received increased attention over the past years (Norris, Stevens, Pfefferbaum, Wyche, & Pfefferbaum, 2008; Sherrieb, Norris, & Galea, 2010; Tierney, 2003). Children, adults and whole communities are significantly challenged when required to confront mass emergencies. This chapter deals with how urban resilience can be enhanced from a child's perspective.

First, we briefly summarize how disaster affects children and their protective matrix. We further discuss the concept of personal and community resilience, its definitions and components. We then describe what makes a community a resilient one, and the role played by preparedness. Finally, we describe the Cohen-Harris model of urban resilience, its rationale and its four resilience programs.

Children and mass disaster

As defined by the United Nations International Strategy for Disaster Reduction (UNISDR), a disaster is "a serious disruption of the functioning of society, causing widespread human, material, or environmental losses which exceed the capacity of the affected society to cope using only its own resources" (UNISDR, 2009). Laor and Wolmer (2002) define it as a "relatively sudden, more or less time-limited, and public event that extensively damages properties and lives, engendering a systemic continuously disruptive impact on the social network and basic daily routines of children and families."

Models of disaster response distinguish among four stages of a disaster. The pre-disaster stage involves the identification and warning of an imminent threat. Then, there is the event itself and the efforts to minimize its damage by protecting human lives and addressing the population's basic needs. In the second stage, the society undergoes massive structural and functional changes, thus experiencing a regression and loss of norms. The third stage consists of threats to the collective ideology and identity (Laor & Wolmer, 2002).

Disasters have serious consequences for both individuals and communities. People experience grief, dissociation and posttraumatic symptoms in response to physical, material, social and functional losses (Wolmer, Laor, & Yazgan, 2003). As disasters often involve damage to infrastructure, communities face economic impact, displacement of populations and a decrease in the community's morale and well-being (Norris et al., 2008).

Children are a particularly vulnerable group (Fitzgerald & Fitzgerald, 2005). Young children have to cope with developmental challenges, such as formation of the self and their sense of identity, regulation of impulses, sense of security and attachment to others. A disaster may disrupt some of these processes, since experiencing disasters may lead to the loss of assumptions about the world as a safe place (Laor & Wolmer, 2002).

Children's reactions to disasters vary according to the character of the disaster itself, their proximity to the area and the reactions of adult caregivers. Increased vulnerability is associated with younger age, prior traumatic events or psychological pathology, viewing explicit images of death and mutilations on television and continual displacement (Kar, 2009).

Most children are able to recover after a disaster, but they need to achieve renewed attachments and sense of safety to accomplish this task (Chemtob, Nakashima, & Hamada, 2002). Strong evidence suggests that developing such abilities involves social support, especially from parents and teachers (La Greca Silverman, Vernberg, & Prinstein, 1996; Prinstein, La Greca, Vernberg, & Silverman, 1996), to help them with specific coping skills, emotional processing, reinstitution of roles and routines and distractions.

Community resilience

The word "resilience" stems from the Latin verb "*resilier*," which means "jump back" (Manyena, 2006; Mayunga, 2007). Although the term has become increasingly common in the literature of trauma and disaster, there is some obscurity regarding its definition. It has been presented as an outcome, a strategy, a set of capacities or a quality (Fitzgerald & Fitzgerald, 2005; Longstaff, Armstrong, Perrin, Parker, & Hidek, 2010). Butler, Morland and Leskin (2007) define it as "good adaptation under extenuating circumstances; a recovery trajectory that returns to baseline functioning following a challenge." According to Walsh (2003), it is "the capacity to rebound from adversity, strengthened and more resourceful. It is an active process of endurance, self-righting, and growth in response to crisis and challenge . . . the ability to withstand and rebound from disruptive life challenges."

Researchers have pointed out that, on the community level, resilience is substantially different from the sum of each individual's capacity (Sherrieb et al., 2010). Community resilience can be described as "a community's capacity, hope and faith to withstand major trauma or loss, overcome adversity, and to prevail, usually with increased resources, competence and connectedness" (Landau & Saul, 2004).

Characteristics of a resilient community in the face of disaster

Social capital is the function of mutual trust and social networking of both individuals and groups as they are obligated and willing to partake in mutually beneficial collective action (Putnam, 2000). Community resilience as expressed in post-disaster recovery is positively affected by social capital (Nakagawa & Shaw, 2004).

In accordance with data that show the significance of the child's protective matrix to his or her well-being, social capital is associated with improved child mental health (McKenzie, Whitley & Weich, 2002). Unlike most child-specialized programs, which aim at the individual and the family levels, the model described in this chapter addresses the multiple layers of the child's protective matrix, adding the communal and the institutional.

A resilient community is measured not only by its logistic preparedness, but also by its "culture of safety" (Aguirre, 2006). One of the most important qualities of a resilient society is creativity. Communities that acknowledge that disasters are unpredictable and equilibrium-disturbing respond to them in adaptive and creative ways (Bahadur, Ibrahim, & Tanner, 2010; Tierney, 2003). Consequently, preparedness is a central element of community resilience. A prepared community reacts to disaster in a more rapid, coordinated, cost-effective and effective manner, thereby having a chance of "bouncing forward," rather than just "bouncing back" (Austin, 2012; Sherrieb et al., 2010; Venton, 2007).

The systemic/ecological approach

Since the 1991 Gulf War, the civilian population of Israel has been aware that it is vulnerable to missile attacks. These circumstances, which worsened during the 2006 Lebanon War and the attacks from Gaza, have transformed the home front into a battlefront, creating a new challenge that local authorities must face: providing a direct, immediate, ongoing response to complex array of problems, including displacement and the need to spend prolonged periods of time in shelters.

The comprehensive report submitted by the State Comptroller and Ombudsman in Israel (2007) concerning the preparation and functioning of the home front revealed serious failings. For example, most governmental institutions had not held an evaluation of the home front for many years. The level of preparedness was poor, with no central institution in charge of national preparation. Authorities were not clearly divided among institutions. In the absence of contingency plans and drills, there was much uncertainty about what to do in the case of an actual emergency. Treatment of problems was mostly responsive, partial or inappropriate. Similar conclusions appear in the U.S. Congress House Select Bipartisan Committee report (2006) that investigated the preparations for and responses to Hurricane Katrina, suggesting that insufficient preparation is a worldwide problem.

Most available position papers and guidelines for the organization of emergency services are partial. For example, in regard to children's mental health services, they deal primarily with the large-scale considerations and guidelines for interventions in the aftermath of a disaster (DeWolfe & Nordboe, 2000; Young, Ford, Ruzek, Friedman, & Gusman, 1998). Further, they are specific to biological and psychological interventions to alleviate children's suffering. However, they remain almost oblivious to disaster preparedness and the municipal systemic context within which child mental health services ought to be implemented.

Working under disasters has taught us that responsible disaster intervention calls for proper preparation worked out both from the top down (from the state level to the local ones) and from the bottom up (Austin, 2012). Individuals, families, neighborhoods and communities need to be considered. Families may have suffered the death or injury of loved ones, the loss of their home and disruptions in their daily routine. Others have to cope with unemployment, loss of esteem or relocation. Neighborhoods may have undergone physical destruction. Families feel the disintegration of social networks, whereas communities may be beset by insufficient resources, poor leadership and the destruction of social and cultural institutions.

Employing a systemic perspective, preventive and post-disaster interventions with children should be integrated by collaboration with community leadership, local schools, welfare units, social institutions and medical centers. By integrating screening, assessment and interventions, child professionals facilitate the normal recovery processes and alleviate the sequelae of the disaster. In addition, community programs stressing the enhancement of initiative, empowerment, resilience and responsibility can be modified for disaster situations.

The urban resilience model

The key to decreasing the impact of mass disasters is to prepare the population to cope with their consequences. Recognizing that national emergencies are likely to occur, the Cohen-Harris Center developed the "Urban Resilience Program," a comprehensive model for reinforcing civilian resilience and preparing the population to cope with the consequences of disasters. The model operates in areas at risk by forming multidisciplinary and multi-systemic coordinated networks with clear command and control. This model of preparedness, intervention and rehabilitation was developed and has been implemented in Tel Aviv since 1991. Following the second Lebanon war (2006) and the Gaza War (or Operation Cast Lead, 2008–2009), it has been successfully implemented in 18 cities as a national pilot program (2010-2012) under the aegis of the Ministry of Home Front Defense.

The program's worldview is system oriented, integrating perceptions of public health and administration, community capital and resilience and preventive education. Within the program, communities under threat of hostilities are helped to develop functional flexibility and social development without disregarding the need to cope with distress and trauma. The model is based on the following principles:

- The local authority is the major element in emergency preparedness.
- Resilience is built during routine times, in daily activities integrated into the activity of the urban system.
- The process of empowerment during routine times includes locating sources of influence and resources of individuals, communities and organizations.
- The community and its institutions have the ability to retain and develop social capital and create inter-institutional and inter-organizational bridges.
- These social bridges can be used to create a meta-community of institutions, organizations and communities, under a unified hierarchical management. This is a "resilience network" that can arise between cities throughout the country.
- The emergency system is based on existing human resources as well as community, organizational and physical infrastructure, creating a force multiplier that increases the emergency intervention resources many times over.
- The conception is multi-professional and multi-organizational.

The common approach to the organizational aspects of urban disaster preparedness is that specific expertise is concentrated in a sub-unit (e.g., the municipal security department). This usually leads to a situation in which other elements of the disaster preparedness and response effort lack the required knowledge, skills, guidelines and language. In addition, the available staff for disaster preparedness and response is limited. The approach described in this chapter represents a conceptual change in perspective to a model of *systemic* expertise developed and implemented ecologically during routine times.

In such a perspective, interest in children's welfare serves as the best prod for enlisting leaders, institutions and communities for action, as well as a way to reach the whole community and implement far-reaching systemic changes. The interest in the various aspects of children's lives becomes an integrator on the familial, organizational and communal levels. Such integration is also important for community institutions, such as public health ("well baby" clinics), mental health (clinics, school psychologists) and welfare (social services), as well as formal and informal education (schools, youth movements). Also, information needs to be disseminated and carefully formulated to allow children of all ages and their parents to make effective use of it. Our Urban Resilience Program covers all these needs.

Urban resilience model: Four programs

Each component of the program is put into practice once it has been specifically adapted to serve individual local authorities. Implementation follows an annual operational chart, structured on the basis of weekly milestones. A comprehensive system analysis and continual assessment of the effectiveness of implementation allows for an assessment of each city's level of preparedness (see also Cutter, Burton, & Emrich, 2010). The four programs described below are hierarchically and horizontally integrated locally under the mayor and nationally under the Ministry of Home Front Defense in collaboration with other ministries. First, we briefly describe the health/mental health and the public information resilience programs. Then, we describe in more detail the other two programs: population and school resilience.

Health and mental health resilience

Since the statutory responsibility for health and mental health in Israel in times of disaster lies with the Ministry of Health, the objective of this program is to bring this responsibility under the urban unified command. To this end, health headquarters are established in each city to coordinate medical emergency operation and facilitate the integration of community and public health institutions, general and mental health hospitals, as well as private health and mental health agents. Health and mental health professionals are trained according to specific guidelines (Raphael & Ma, 2011).

To build up the capacity for treating masses of traumatized individuals and providing assessment and preventive interventions within the community, emergency stress sites are established in collaboration with the Ministry of Health. Teams of school psychologists and child social workers are trained and assigned to these sites (see also National Commission on Children and Disasters, 2010).

Information resilience

One of people's major needs during an emergency is obtaining timely, reliable information, not only from national bodies but also from local authorities (Eyre, 2008). This can significantly help in reducing uncertainty and directing preparedness and coping of children, parents, families and communities. This program prepares the city's emergency system for the effective flow of information from the municipal command to the general public (top down) and from civilians, including children and parents, to the leaders (bottom up). Top-down flow of information is critical to help the public prepare responsibly according to the expected scenarios (e.g., preparation of the house) and make proper decisions (e.g., enter bomb shelters, leave the city). Bottom-up information is required for leaders to evaluate situations accurately, assess needs and correct plans.

Innovative unified guidelines and protocols are being developed to gather sensitive emergency information about parents and children from the community and disseminate it in coordination with the Home Front Command (an Israel Defense Forces regional command) and the Ministry of Home Front Defense.

Population resilience

The population resilience component of the program addresses (a) the urban municipality's emergency preparedness, (b) the local authority's emergency psychosocial intervention system, (c) the city's institutional infrastructure and (d) the urban communities' and inhabitants' preparedness for disaster. Leadership, organizational guidelines, training protocols, emergency simulations and disaster drills are being developed for all urban aspects, with specific attention to the needs of children and parents in the community.

In each city, multidisciplinary units are being developed and trained to deal with on-site crises (triage and evacuation), family notification (of losses), hospital liaison, population behavior (information center), psychological support over the phone, emergency shelters, community resources (volunteers and donations) and the delivery of basic needs.

For example, emergency rescue teams are the first to arrive on the scene in response to a crisis, followed by multidisciplinary interventions teams (psychologists, social workers, educators and nurses). The latter screen the vicinity, refer identified victims to specialized interventions and provide immediate assistance (physical and mental) at the disaster area. Clinical teams (child and adult psychologists, psychiatrists and social workers) at the regional trauma centers or stress sites provide assessment and treatment, while the information unit gathers and transmits information from and to the public. The liaison unit follows up hospitalized victims by visiting them at their homes upon discharge and referring them for professional support when appropriate.

The family notification unit receives information about casualties from hospitals and the victim identification center, and then transfers it sensitively to children and families. This unit also assists in every detail of the funeral arrangements. At the victim identification center, a liaison team supports families, whereas mental health teams assist pathologists and families during and after the identification process.

The Urban Resilience Program considers the empowerment of communal resources as paramount. Empowerment is the process by which individuals and communities avoid helplessness by recovering their dignity and self-esteem, enhancing their critical self-awareness, control over resources and objectives and sense of personal and collective responsibility (Rappaport, 1987). Individuals identify specific needs and discover hidden leadership qualities, while communities gain a greater sense of interdependence, cohesion and cooperation. These interventions address the long-term effects of the disaster, the sociocultural losses that threaten the existing collective ideology and identity.

Another element focuses on community resilience, in which local informal and formal leadership is empowered and citizens in neighborhoods and institutions, including schools, are trained in home and institutional preparation, medical and psychological first aid and community and family resilience. Emphasis is also put on taking care of the emergency personnel. Professional role containment and enhancement before, during and after disaster is essential to a good outcome. This may be achieved by defining a professional vision, creating an atmosphere of intellectual stimulation (supporting initiatives, delegating authority) and transmitting positive expectations concerning capacities and end results. Team members need to feel cared for and develop a sense of belonging and purpose.

Within this program, each local authority goes through a process that includes a comprehensive assessment, a systematic review and adaptation of the organizational chart, pooling of human resources to increase the number of emergency workers available and staffed by 200–500%, in-depth training of multidisciplinary units with specific guidelines and protocols, as well as partial and general drills to practice skills and learn lessons.

School resilience

The education system is responsible for the physical and mental well-being of the students. The school resilience component of the program includes (a) establishing school emergency teams to manage emergencies in collaboration with municipal and emergency bodies; (b) implementing trauma- and resilience-focused, preventive, teacher-delivered interventions from preschool to high school; (c) training school psychologists to become experts in trauma interventions; and (d) establishing a municipal educational headquarters to interface between educational programs and security issues.

We now describe the teacher-delivered resilience element of the program. As part of this component, hundreds of teachers, school counselors and school psychologists receive intensive training in collaboration with the Israeli Ministry of Education, and ongoing supervision to identify children at risk for trauma effects. About 250,000 students have participated in the program. The Ministry of Education endorsed the program as an integral part of the school curriculum in the 18 cities where the Urban Resilience Program has been implemented.

There are several reasons why schools are ideal sites for implementing interventions before and after exposure to trauma. First, school-based programs can deal with survivors' reluctance to seek help. Because children are already in attendance at school, compliance rates are higher (Schwartz & Kowalski, 1992). In addition, certain symptoms (e.g., difficulty concentrating, behavioral problems) tend to appear specifically in the school setting (Wolmer, Laor, Dedeoglu, Siev, & Yazgan, 2005; Yule & Williams, 1990). The familiar teacher–student relationship allows for immediate feedback and follow-up, avoiding the undesirable stigma of being singled out for special treatment (Klingman, 1993).

School-based programs have been shown to increase resilience and hope, improve daily function and decrease symptoms more than is usual (Chemtob, Nakashima & Hamada, 2002). Schools have the capacity and the human resources to strengthen children's protective factors, such as their social network and self-efficacy (Doll & Lyon, 1998). Traumatized children benefit from talking to other child survivors with similar experiences and discovering that they have responded similarly to the event (Vernberg & Vogel, 1993; Yule & Williams, 1990). Meeting the children within the classroom environment with a well-known set of rules and routines, in a normative context and at a developmentally appropriate level, also conveys a message of normalcy (Klingman, 1993; Wolmer et al., 2003). The school setting allows a developmentally appropriate program to be integrated into the children's routine, continuing a sense of normalcy within a familiar setting.

TEACHER-DELIVERED INTERVENTIONS

School-based interventions, with either an individual (Chemtob, Nakashima, & Carlson, 2002) or a group (Saltzman, Layne, Sternberg, Arslanagic, & Pynoos, 2003) format, have traditionally been conducted by mental health professionals. These approaches are cost-ineffective and unsuitable for reaching masses of affected children. A creative professional shift is thus required for implementing clinically informed interventions for masses of children with the available human resources. A set of studies that developed a professional shift in the role of teacher/educator tested whether trained educators can serve as clinical mediators in preparation for and following mass emergencies.

Mass events call for whole-school revitalization, which includes mental health professionals training teachers to provide efficient clinical mediation. Although teachers and children may be traumatized by the same event, there are several justifications for this systemic/ecological approach (Laor, Wolmer, Spirman, & Wiener, 2003; Wolmer et al., 2003). First, most teachers are willing to join the training process and accept a leadership position once they understand their role as educators and provided that they are properly supported. Teachers are familiar and trusted figures in the child's life (Wolmer et al., 2003) who provide a sense of physical security and offer factual information about disasters and their consequences (Vernberg, La Greca, Silverman, & Prinstein, 1996).

Enhancing the teachers' role as educators able to significantly support children in preparation for and in response to traumatic events includes both the translation of clinical knowledge into didactic material as well as helping the teachers understand their new role vis-à-vis the children in the face of human-made or natural traumatic events.

This approach was tested for the first time after a major earthquake that resulted in more than 30,000 deaths (Wolmer et al., 2003). In that study, teachers were trained to employ a supervised, 8-session, trauma-focused intervention. This structured protocol of twice-weekly, 2-hour classroom sessions was provided to all the children in the school during the course of a month. In a follow-up study, we found a significant immediate decrease in symptoms in the exposed children that continued over the next three years in the three domains assessed: post-trauma, grief and dissociation (Wolmer et al., 2005). Most importantly, compared to a matched control group, the study children displayed better academic, social and behavioral adaptation three years after the earthquake.

Similarly, Berger, Pat-Horenczyk and Gelkopf (2007) documented a significant reduction in symptoms in a controlled study of a different model of teacher-delivered school intervention. In a study of a classroom-based intervention of this sort in Sri Lanka, Berger and Gelkopf (2009) found a significant reduction in posttraumatic stress disorder severity, functional problems, somatic complaints and depression, as well as increased hope in comparison to a waiting-list group, especially in those with prior life stressors.

The original teacher-delivered intervention (Wolmer et al., 2003) combined clinically accepted psychoeducational modules and cognitive-behavioral techniques focusing on the different aspects of posttraumatic states. Following continuous bomb attacks in Israel since September 2000, the contents of the intervention were modified and implemented to focus on resilience enhancement.

The program's implementation started with meetings with the school principal and the school staff to construct a working alliance and ensure the necessary resources. The supervisors received a 20-hour training course and bi-weekly supervision by clinical psychologists. All the teachers received a 4-hour basic training course followed by weekly meetings with the supervisors dedicated to preparation, guidance and qualitative check of protocol fidelity.

The manualized protocol consists of fourteen 45-minute educational modules delivered weekly, promoting a salutogenic setting to strengthen adaptive coping mechanisms (Antonovsky, 1979). The children are encouraged to share the coping skills learned with their families. The program promotes a stress-inoculation training framework, focusing on cognitive control or restructuring techniques to regulate negative emotions and distracting thoughts, as well as relaxation training to enhance physiological control (awareness, muscle tension, breathing), rehearsed through the use of mental imagery (Saunders, Driskell, Johnston, & Salas, 1996). These are in accordance with the work of Zohar, Sonnino, Juven-Wetzler and Cohen (2009), who claim that acute distress management should help traumatized individuals contain and attenuate emotional reaction, regain emotional control, restore interpersonal communications and encourage their return to full function and activity.

In the professional shift created by the interface between the clinical and the educational disciplines, teachers go beyond transferring knowledge and values by employing clinical principles and practices as part of their professional repertoire, whereas the role of clinicians focuses on (a) collaborating in the development of clinically informed educational procedures to be implemented by the empowered educators and (b) leading the process of supervision.

From such an empowered role, the educators in a number of studies were able to enhance the preparedness of communities and children to confront mass trauma and reduce the level of posttrauma distress in the exposed students by 50% (Wolmer, Hamiel, & Laor, 2011). They also significantly decreased posttraumatic distress in preschool and school-age children (Wolmer, Hamiel, Barchas, Slone, & Laor, 2011; Wolmer et al., submitted b), among Jewish and Arab students alike (Wolmer et al., submitted a).

Finally, these important effects were accompanied by an impact on the educators themselves and the classroom climate. Among the empowered teachers, the enhancement of their professional role to include leading resilience-based interventions helped them develop higher levels of self-efficacy and perceived role identity, compared to a control group (Hamiel et al., submitted). In this way, another aspect supporting children's resilience—the teachers' functioning—was heightened.

The preventive impact of such role empowerment was also noticeable during ordinary times, as demonstrated by the increase in the level of classes' preparedness to cope with national emergency drills, with better anxiety management, higher drill success and better control effectiveness than a comparison group (Wolmer, 2012).

The empowered teachers' success in their role as clinical mediators seems pioneering. Indeed, Weisz, Donenberg, Han and Weiss (1995) observed that psychological interventions that yield substantial effects in research settings often produce small or no effects when delivered by community providers (e.g., teachers). Our studies showed that teachers can be very powerful clinical mediators. However, this demands a reorientation in the role of the educator as well as the training and supervision of the teachers.

Conclusion

This chapter described the child-oriented Urban Resilience Program developed by the Cohen-Harris Center and implemented in 18 Israeli cities. It incorporates 20 years of experience in urban disaster preparedness and response, and covers four main areas: population, education, health/mental health and information.

Most models of urban disaster preparedness build on the expertise concentrated in municipal subunits responsible for the organizational aspects of that task. We described a conceptual change. Rather than focusing expertise in one subunit, systemic expertise ought to be developed and implemented during routine times in the city as a whole.

Moreover, concern for children helps muster the services of the whole urban community and its institutions to implement the resilience programs (e.g., school resilience programs that enhance children's coping, family resilience community programs, health resilience with its component of child trauma relief protocols, and the like). This way, the community's interest in the various aspects of children's lives serves as an integrator for the community institutions to work together.

Implementing such a complex endeavor, which includes hundreds of emergency personnel per city, requires steadfast commitment by the administrative and professional leadership. The endorsement of the model by national authorities could facilitate the comprehensive implementation of a nationwide network of child-oriented disaster preparedness and resilience programs.

References

Aguirre, B. E. (2006). *On the concept of resilience* (preliminary paper no. 356). Newark, DE: Disaster Research Center, University of Delaware.

Antonovsky, A. (1979). *Health, stress and coping*. San Francisco, CA: Jossey-Bass Publishers.

Austin, D. W. (2012). Preparedness clusters: A research note on the disaster readiness of community-based organizations. *Sociological Perspectives*, *55*(2), 383–393.

Bahadur, A. V., Ibrahim, M., & Tanner, T. (2010). *The resilience renaissance? Unpacking of resilience for tackling climate change and disasters* (Strengthening Climate Resilience working paper). Brighton, Sussex, England: Institute of Development Studies.

Berger, R., & Gelkopf, M. (2009). School-based intervention for the treatment of tsunami-related distress in children: A quasi-randomized controlled trial. *Psychotherapy and Psychosomatics*, *78*(6), 364–371.

Berger, R., Pat-Horenczyk, R., & Gelkopf, M. (2007). School-based intervention for prevention and treatment of elementary-students' terror-related distress in Israel: A quasi-randomized controlled trial. *Journal of Traumatic Stress*, *20*(4), 541–551.

Butler, L. D., Morland, L. A., & Leskin, G. A. (2007). Psychological resilience in the face of terrorism. In B. Bongar, L. Brown, L. E. Beutler, J. Breckenridge, & P. G. Zimbardo (Eds.), *Psychology of terrorism* (pp. 400–417). New York, NY: Oxford University Press.

Chemtob, C. M., Nakashima, J., & Carlson, J. G. (2002). Brief treatment for elementary school children with disaster-related posttraumatic stress disorder: A field study. *Journal of Clinical Psychology*, *58*(1), 99–112.

Chemtob, C. M., Nakashima, J. P., & Hamada, R. S. (2002). Psychosocial intervention for postdisaster trauma symptoms in elementary school children: A controlled community field study. *Archives of Pediatrics & Adolescent Medicine*, *156*(3), 211–216.

Cutter S. L., Burton C. G., & Emrich C. T. (2010). Disaster resilience indicators for benchmarking baseline conditions. *Journal of Homeland Security and Emergency Management*, *7*(1), 1–22.

DeWolfe, D. J., & Nordboe, D. (2000). *Field manual for mental health and human services workers in major disasters*. Washington, D.C.: Center for Mental Health Services, Substance Abuse and Mental Health Services Administration, U.S. Department of Health and Human Services.

Doll, B., & Lyon, M. A. (1998). Risk and resilience: Implications for the delivery of educational and mental health services in schools. *School Psychology Review*, *27*(3), 348–363.

Eyre, A. (2008). Public information and support after disasters: A research project. *Journal of Public Mental Health*, *7*(2), 25–28.

Fitzgerald, G., & Fitzgerald, N. (2005). *Assessing community resilience to wildfires: Concepts and approach* (Fitzgerald Applied Sociology paper prepared for Scion). Christchurch, New Zealand: Scion.

Hamiel, D., Wolmer, L., Versano-Eisman, T., Slone, M., Findler, Y., & Laor, N. (submitted). Empowerment of teachers to lead resilience-enhancement interventions: The impact on self-efficacy and role identity.

Kar, N. (2009). Psychological impact of disasters on children: Review of assessment and interventions. *World Journal of Pediatrics*, *5*(1), 5–11.

Klingman, A. (1993). School-based intervention following a disaster. In C. F. Saylor (Ed.), *Children and disasters* (pp. 187–210). New York, NY: Plenum Press.

La Greca, A. M., Silverman, W. K., Vernberg, E. V., & Prinstein, M. J. (1996). Symptoms of posttraumatic stress in children after Hurricane Andrew: A prospective study. *Journal of Consulting and Clinical Psychology, 64*(4), 712–723.

Landau, J., & Saul, J. (2004). Facilitating family and community resilience in response to major disasters. In F. Walsh & M. McGoldrick (Eds.), *Living beyond loss: Death in the family* (pp. 285–309). New York, NY: W. W. Norton.

Laor, N., & Wolmer, L., (2002). Children exposed to disaster: The role of the mental health professional. In M. Lewis (Ed.), *Textbook of child and adolescent psychiatry: A comprehensive textbook* (3rd ed.) (pp. 925–937). Baltimore, MD: Williams & Wilkins.

Laor, N., Wolmer, L., Spirman, S., & Wiener, Z. (2003). Facing war, terrorism, and disaster: Toward a child-oriented comprehensive emergency care system. *Child and Adolescent Psychiatric Clinics of North America, 12*(2), 343–361.

Longstaff, P. H., Armstrong, N. J., Perrin, K., Parker, W. M., & Hidek, M. (2010). Building resilient communities: A preliminary framework for assessment. *Homeland Security Affairs, 6*(3). Retrieved from http://www.hsaj.org/?fullarticle=6.3.6

Manyena, S. B. (2006). The concept of resilience revisited. *Disasters, 30*(4), 433–450.

Mayunga, J. S. (2007). *Understanding and applying the concept of community disaster resilience: A capital-based approach*. Draft working paper prepared for the Munich Re Foundation (MRF) and United Nations University Institute for Environment and Human (UNU–EHS) Security Second Annual Summer Academy on Social Vulnerability: "Megacities as Hotspots of Risk: Social Vulnerability and Resilience Building," Munich, Germany, July 22–28, 2007.

McKenzie, K., Whitley, R., & Weich, S. (2002). Social capital and mental health. *British Journal of Psychiatry, 181*, 280–283.

Nakagawa, Y., & Shaw, R. K. (2004). Social capital: a missing link to disaster recovery. *International Journal of Mass Emergencies and Disasters, 22*(1), 5–34.

National Commission on Children and Disasters. (2010). *Report to the President and Congress* (AHRQ publication no. 10-M037). Rockville, MD: Agency for Healthcare Research and Quality.

Norris, F. H., Stevens, S. P., Pfefferbaum, B., Wyche, K. F., & Pfefferbaum, R. L. (2008). Community resilience as a metaphor, theory, set of capacities, and strategy for disaster readiness. *American Journal of Community Psychology, 41*(1–2), 127–150.

Prinstein, M. J., La Greca, A. M., Vernberg, E. M., & Silverman, W. K. (1996). Children's coping assistance: How parents, teachers, and friends help children cope after a disaster. *Journal of Clinical Child Psychology, 25*(4), 463–475.

Putnam, R. (2000). *Bowling alone: The collapse and revival of American community*. New York, NY: Simon and Schuster.

Raphael, B., & Ma, H. (2011). Mass catastrophe and disaster psychiatry. *Molecular Psychiatry, 16*(3), 247–251.

Rappaport, J. (1987). Terms of empowerment/exemplars of prevention: Toward a theory for community psychology. *American Journal of Community Psychology, 15*(2), 121–145.

Saltzman, W. R., Layne, C. M., Sternberg, A. M., Arslanagic, B., & Pynoos, R. S. (2003). Developing a culturally and ecologically sound intervention program for youth exposed to war and terrorism. *Child and Adolescent Psychiatric Clinics of North America, 12*(2), 319–342.

Saunders, T., Driskell, J. E., Johnston, J. H., & Salas, E. (1996). The effect of stress inoculation training on anxiety and performance. *Journal of Occupational Health Psychology, 1*(2), 170–186.

Schwartz, E. D., & Kowalski, J. M. (1992). Malignant memories: Reluctance to utilize mental health services after a disaster. *Journal of Nervous and Mental Disease, 180*(12), 767–772.

Sherrieb, K., Norris, F. H., & Galea, S. (2010). Measuring capacities for community resilience. *Social Indicators Research, 99*(2), 227–247.

State Comptroller and Ombudsman in Israel. (2007). Preparedness of the home front and its functioning during the second Lebanon war. Retrieved from www.mevaker.gov.il

Tierney, K. J. (2003). *Conceptualizing and measuring organizational and community resilience: Lessons from the emergency response following the September 11, 2001 attack on the World Trade Center.* Newark, DE: University of Delaware Disaster Research Center.

UNISDR (2009). *2009 UNISDR terminology on disaster risk reduction.* Geneva, Switzerland: United Nations Office for Disaster Risk Reduction. Retrieved from www.unisdr.org/eng/terminology/UNISDR-terminology-2009-eng.pdf

U.S. Congress House Select Bipartisan Committee to Investigate the Preparation for and Response to Hurricane Katrina. (2006). *A failure of initiative: Final report of the Select Bipartisan Committee to Investigate the Preparation for and Response to Hurricane Katrina.* Washington, D.C: U.S. Government Printing Office.

Venton, C. C. (2007). Justifying the cost of disaster risk reduction: A summary of cost–benefit analysis. *Humanitarian Exchange Magazine, 38*, 22–24.

Vernberg, E. M., La Greca, A. M., Silverman, W. K., & Prinstein, M. J. (1996). Prediction of posttraumatic stress symptoms in children after Hurricane Andrew. *Journal of Abnormal Psychology, 105*(2), 237–248.

Vernberg, E. M., & Vogel, J. M. (1993). Part 2: Interventions with children after disasters. *Journal of Clinical Child Psychology, 22*(4), 485–498.

Walsh, F. (2003). Family resilience: A framework for clinical practice. *Family Process, 42*(1), 1–18.

Weisz, J. R., Donenberg, G. R., Han, S. S., & Weiss, B. (1995). Bridging the gap between laboratory and clinic in child and adolescent psychotherapy. *Journal of Consulting and Clinical Psychology, 63*(5), 688–701.

Wolmer, L. (2012). *Crossing discipline borders to establish a professional shift: Teacher-delivered resilience-focused intervention in schools as clinical mediation before and after traumatic exposure.* Doctoral thesis, Tel Aviv University, Tel Aviv, Israel.

Wolmer, L., Hamiel, D., Barchas, J. D., Slone, M., & Laor, N. (2011). Teacher-delivered resilience-focused intervention in schools with traumatized children following the second Lebanon war. *Journal of Traumatic Stress, 24*(3), 309–316.

Wolmer, L., Hamiel, D., & Laor, N. (2011). Preventing children's posttraumatic stress after disaster with teacher-based intervention: A controlled study. *Journal of the American Academy of Child and Adolescent Psychiatry, 50*(4), 340–348.

Wolmer, L., Hamiel, D., Slone, M., Faians, M., Picker, M., & Laor, N. (submitted, a). *Posttraumatic reaction of Israeli Jewish and Arab children exposed to rocket attacks before and after teacher-delivered intervention.* Paper submitted for publication.

Wolmer, L., Hamiel, D., Versano-Eisman, T., Slone, M., Faians, M., & Laor, N. (submitted, b). *Preschool Israeli children exposed to rocket attacks before and after teacher-delivered intervention.* Paper submitted for publication.

Wolmer, L., Laor, N., Dedeoglu, C., Siev, J., & Yazgan, Y. (2005). Teacher-mediated intervention after disaster: A controlled three-year follow-up of children's functioning. *Journal of Child Psychology and Psychiatry, 46*(11), 1161–1168.

Wolmer, L., Laor, N., & Yazgan, Y. (2003). School reactivation programs after disaster: Could teachers serve as clinical mediators? *Child and Adolescent Psychiatric Clinics of North America, 12*(2), 363–381.

Young, B. H., Ford, J. D., Ruzek, J. I., Friedman, M. J., & Gusman, F. D. (1998). *Disaster mental health services: A guidebook for clinicians and administrators.* Menlo Park, CA; Vermont, Washington, D.C.: National Center for Post-Traumatic Stress Disorder; United States Department of Veterans Affairs.

Yule, W., & Williams, R. M. (1990). Post-traumatic stress reactions in children. *Journal of Traumatic Stress, 3*(2), 279–295.

Zohar, J., Sonnino, R., Juven-Wetzler, A., & Cohen, H. (2009). Can posttraumatic stress disorder be prevented? *CNS Spectrums, 14*(1), 44–51.

Chapter 11

The centrality of the school in a community during war and conflict[1]

Michelle Slone and Anat Shoshani

Disintegration of community life in wartime

Despite ever-increasing calls for peace and the proliferation of peacekeeping initiatives, many areas in the world continue to be besieged by war and conflict, producing unstable and dangerous environments in which children develop and grow up amid frightening conditions. Perhaps one of the most tragic consequences of modern warfare is that present global conflicts are mostly a prolonged series of violent events instigated by irregular forces and occurring within cities and communities. Like weeds that spread rapidly and uncontrollably, the impact of war and conflict extends beyond the immediate victims to produce fear and insecurity at all levels of the community and the society. The horrors of war extend beyond traditional battlefields to communities where life is played out and where families and children live, study and work.

The sights and sounds of war are inseparable parts of Israeli life. From the very establishment of the state and until today, conflict and hostilities have been interwoven in everyday reality. These events include frontline wars, terrorism and missile attacks in the heart of the population. Disruption of everyday life hinders smooth societal functioning at every level.

Galia, who lives in Sderot, an Israeli town bordering on Gaza that suffered a continual bombardment of missile and rocket attacks for eight years, tells the following story:

> I was walking with my child to the library when the Code Red siren sounded. I took Or's hand and told him to run. Or screamed, "Mommy, I am scared." I said, "I am looking after you. Run, run." That helped him run as fast as his little legs could. No sooner had we reached the shelter than the Qassam rocket fell with a deafening explosion. I was shaking and I hugged Or. When I raised my eyes, I saw that we were huddled together in the shelter with mothers and babies, children who had been playing in the nearby park and an old man. A few minutes later, Or was already playing with the children in the park. I sat on the bench in the park trembling and panting for a long time.

It appeared that the incident had passed uneventfully for Or. However, occurrences such as these, as part of a chronic environment of conflict, do not pass uneventfully. They reverberate through different dimensions of the community and affect the basic processes of community life at the societal, educational, family, individual and developmental levels. The children are frequently the most at risk, forced to negotiate their normal developmental tasks against a backdrop of violence and conflict.

The normal developmental tasks that confront children are considerably more difficult when they grow up in an environment of political violence (Barber, Schluterman, Denny, & McCouch, 2006; Gurwitch, Sitterle, Young, & Pfefferbaum, 2002). Findings have indicated that exposure to war and conflict can result in developmental impairment and psychiatric disturbance, ranging from isolated symptoms to more pervasive disorders (Allwood, Bell-Dolan, & Husain 2002; Thabet, Abed, & Vostanis, 2002). The symptoms can include anger and other externalizing behaviors (Barber, 2001; Muldoon, 2004), while the more pervasive disorders are anxiety and depression (Barber, 2001), posttraumatic stress and full-blown posttraumatic stress disorder (PTSD) (Masinda & Muhesi, 2004).

The child's adjustment can be enhanced if the exposure to violence occurs when the child is part of a well-functioning family (Garbarino & Kostelny, 1996; Qouta, El-Sarraj, & Punamäki, 2001). However, in prolonged and chronic exposure to war, family resources are impeded by dramatic changes in family status, routine and support, as well as uncertainty about the future. There is the constant danger that this major protective factor for children cannot function adequately during war. Thus, there is a need to find appropriate ways of effectively satisfying the needs of large numbers of children in the community. The present chapter advocates empowering the school as a potentially optimal setting for rehabilitating and strengthening such large numbers of children.

Reconceptualization of the school as a center for integration and stability

The community allocates different functions to its institutions, separating mental health services from educational services, congruent with the traditional conceptualization of the school as responsible for educational and developmental functions. In routine conditions, this division of resources allows specialization in the various domains. However, in circumstances of war, the needs of children may be best met by integrating previously separated functions. In this sense, the school is the ideal institution in which educational and clinical functions can be combined. However, this necessitates a change in the traditional conceptualization of the role of the school.

Schools are particularly well positioned for implementation of interventions during conflict for several reasons. The school is located at the center of the community and represents the focal point of children's daily lives. School attendance entails a return to routine and structure during disorganized and confusing circumstances. The teachers' and school staff's acquaintance with the children allows them to recognize and attend to children's needs during crisis periods (Wolmer, Laor, & Yazgan, 2003). The school supplies a safe, familiar base within which the child can access and mobilize networks of support. Schools represent routine and normalcy by providing a classroom environment with a familiar set of rules at a developmentally appropriate level (Klingman, 1993; Vernberg & Vogel, 1993; Wolmer et al., 2003). In addition, programs and interventions implemented in this setting avoid the stigma of seeking professional help that is frequently encountered among adolescents, thus increasing compliance with the treatment.

Most school-based interventions have been conducted by mental health professionals who supply individual counseling (Chemtob, Nakashima, & Carlson, 2002) or group sessions (Saltzman, Layne, Sternberg, Arslanagic, & Pynoos, 2003). In both these formats, introduction of foreign mental health professionals into the school environment is not cost effective for reaching large numbers of children. On the other hand, working within the school strengthens the existing resources with which the child is familiar and allows for reaching large amounts of children cost-effectively in the classroom environment.

In line with the rationale of utilizing the existing school setting and educational staff following mass trauma, several school-based interventions have been constructed and evaluated and have proven effective (Udwin, Boyle, Yule, Bolton, & O'Ryan, 2000). In one of the first reports of post-disaster, school-based psychotherapy interventions, Galante and Foa (1986) found that seven monthly sessions were effective in reducing the posttraumatic symptoms of children exposed to an earthquake. A similar approach following a major earthquake in Armenia resulted in a significant decrease in PTSD symptoms (Goenjian, 1993), which prevented deterioration in depressive symptoms (Goenjian et al., 1997).

More recently, as the value of school-based interventions has been recognized, there has been a surge of posttrauma school programs in different contexts, using various formats and methodologies. For example, an intervention implemented in postwar Bosnia—consisting of distributing psychoeducational material, training children in coping strategies and providing specialized consultation for high-risk children—was successful in decreasing posttrauma symptoms (Layne et al., 2008). Working with traumatized refugees and asylum seekers from war-affected countries, Ehntholt, Smith and Yule (2005) implemented a manualized cognitive behavioral therapy, classroom-based intervention that produced significant improvement in overall behavioral difficulties and emotional symptoms.

Following the continual bomb attacks in Israel, beginning in September 2000, several programs have been successfully implemented in schools. Gelkopf and Berger (2009) administered a program to adolescent students based on homeroom-teacher delivery of psychoeducational material, skill training and resilience-enhancing strategies. Three-month post-intervention evaluations showed significantly fewer posttraumatic, depressive and somatic symptoms as compared to a waiting-list control group.

A similar program, developed by NATAL (the Israel Trauma Center for the Victims of Terror and War) and delivered to all elementary schoolchildren in Israel, was effective in producing a significant improvement in mental health and adjustment measures (Berger, Pat-Horenczyk, & Gelkopf, 2007). This program was based on guidance with psychoeducational material and skill training for stress reduction, including meditation, bio-energy exercises, art therapy and narrative techniques.

A teacher-delivered protocol focusing on enhancing personal resilience proved successful in enhancing the resilience of children in northern Israel after the 2006 Lebanon War, during which they had been exposed to substantial daily rocket attacks (Wolmer, Hamiel, Barchas, Slone, & Laor, 2011). The children were assessed for risk factors, symptoms and adaptation before the 16-week program (Time 1; $n = 983$) and after its completion (Time 2; $n = 563$). At a 3-month follow-up (Time 3; $n = 754$), the children were assessed along with a waiting-list comparison group ($n = 1,152$). The participating children showed significantly fewer symptoms and better adaptation at the post-intervention evaluations, and these were maintained at the 3-month post-test.

The common denominator of most programs is that they are teacher delivered and based on psychoeducation or emotional, cognitive and behavioral stress-reduction techniques. A different approach was used by Slone and Shoshani (2008) in a study evaluating the effectiveness of a resilience-promoting school intervention for adolescents during a peak of national terrorism at the time of the second Palestinian uprising (*intifada*). The program was constructed to target three factors found to function as resilience variables in a study aimed at detecting variables moderating between exposure and psychological distress. These factors were (a) the mobilization of social support, (b) self-efficacy and problem solving and (c) the attribution of meaning. The results confirmed the program's efficacy in moderating psychological distress.

Maximizing resilience and coping within the school

During crisis periods, the community needs an island of security in an insecure environment. This can be provided by settings that function to enhance resilience factors, thus weakening the association between traumatic exposure and adverse outcomes. Just as a stone thrown into a pond creates widening circles of ripples, a school can become a center of circles of change that are transmitted through the teachers, children and families.

In line with this rationale, we present a model for an intervention program administered in the schools for strengthening community coping during war, conflict and other crisis periods. This intervention program was implemented and evaluated in Beersheba immediately after Operation Cast Lead (the Gaza War), when the city was bombarded by missiles and rockets fired from Gaza.

Operation Cast Lead was a three-week armed conflict that occurred in the Gaza Strip and southern Israel between December 2008 and January 2009. The operation began as a military offensive by Israel following Palestinian militants' rocket attacks on southern Israel, and included a heavy air and ground offensive in the Gaza Strip. Meanwhile, Hamas intensified its rocket and mortar attacks against southern Israel, reaching Ashkelon and Sderot, as well as hitting the major cities of Beersheba and Ashdod for the first time. These rocket attacks caused deaths and injuries as well as significant damage to homes and property and major community psychological distress. During this time, schools in Beersheba were closed and children were forced to spend long periods indoors in bomb shelters. Everyday activities in the city ground to a halt. Operation Cast Lead ended on January 18, 2008, in a unilateral ceasefire. Almost immediately, the children returned to routine life, with the opening of schools and the resumption of everyday activities.

The intervention program presented here was based on workshops for training teachers to administer activities designed to promote the resilience factors that alleviate the impact of exposure to violence. The program was constructed to target three factors previously found to function as resilience variables for children (Slone, 2006). As previously noted, mobilization of social support, self-efficacy and attribution of meaning were the resilience factors, in accordance with the conceptualization of resilience as a protective process that mitigates the effects of risk exposure (Werner, 2000).

Social support

"Social support"—the perception that one is cared for and part of a social network of mutual assistance and obligations—is known to relieve the experience of stress, enhance well-being and speed mental and physical recovery (Seeman, 1996). The decision to solicit and receive support depends on both individual tendencies and the availability of support resources. Strong social networks are key predictors of psychiatric resilience because they facilitate processing and coping with traumatic events, thereby acting as a safeguard against the development of psychopathology (Pina et al., 2008). In disaster situations, peer support can provide significant comfort on the basis of shared experiences (Moore & Varela, 2010).

Promoting the utilization of social support is one of the main objectives in teaching children effective coping skills. The presence of a significant adult who acts as a role model, providing emotional support and promoting self-esteem and effective coping mechanisms, can reduce the potential short- and long-term negative effects of terrorism-induced stress (Fremont, 2004; Lynch, Geller, & Schmidt, 2004). The absence of a competent, caring adult in the life of a child exposed to highly adverse conditions creates a great risk for maladjustment (Masten & Coatsworth, 1998).

Self-efficacy

In addition, there are personal characteristics known to improve prognosis after traumatic exposure, central among which is a strong sense of self-efficacy

(Benight & Bandura, 2004; Luszczynska, Benight, & Cieslak, 2009). The second factor promoted in the presently described intervention is self-efficacy, which has been defined as the belief in one's own competence and personal ability to solve problems and execute actions required to manage life situations (Bandura, 2001). Research has shown that children with below-average problem-solving skills and a low sense of their own competence have more difficulty managing threatening circumstances (Masten & Coatsworth, 1998). This is congruent with findings showing that life satisfaction in adolescence is associated with high levels of self-efficacy (Fogle, Huebner, & Laughlin, 2002).

Attribution of meaning

The third factor is attribution of meaning, which reinforces the use of ideology, positive thinking and reality assessment. Placing the meaning of an event within a broad social and political context has been found to be of assistance in coping with stressors (Garbarino, Kostelny & Dubrow, 1991). Among inner-city African Americans contending with a sense of discrimination, fundamentalist religious groups that offer a political ideology have been found to serve a stress-moderating function (Garbarino et al., 1991). Research in Israel has shown that ultra-Orthodox Jews manifest fewer distress reactions to political conflict (Pines, 1989), and ideological commitment has been shown to serve as a protective factor for Palestinian children (Punamäki, Qouta, & El-Sarraj, 2001). Recent research indicates that children who attempted to understand the September 11 attacks on the United States through cognitive appraisal of the situation were able to significantly reduce their sense of anxiety (Hock, Hart, Kang, & Lutz, 2004).

The school-based intervention program

For each resilience factor—mobilization of support, self-efficacy and attribution of meaning—a handbook was developed containing theoretical explanations of the concepts, a series of experiential activities aimed at strengthening the factor, and all the complementary materials necessary for implementing the activities in the classroom.[2] The program functioned as a training workshop, in which school counselors and class teachers participated in a series of three group seminars aimed at imparting information and strategies for implementing the activities in the handbooks. The workshops adopted an experiential focus in which the educational staff both received instruction about theoretical aspects of the three resilience factors and participated in some of the actual activities themselves. The school staff seminars were co-facilitated by two clinical psychologists trained in group dynamics. Thereafter, it was the teachers' task to implement the activities presented in the handbook in the classroom at least twice weekly over a nine-week period.

The classroom program included activities, discussions, reading poems and stories, listening to songs and viewing movie clips. An example of an activity for mobilizing support was the "support map," in which schoolchildren produced a class map of support agents available to the group and the frequency with which they were utilized by individual students. Other activities in this category included games in which the child selected objects or images to take along in different situations, such as embarrassing, frightening or new situations; listening to songs dealing with loneliness and discussing associated feelings and ways of dealing with being alone; games aimed at strengthening group cohesiveness; and activities involving supporting others. An example of an activity for self-efficacy was giving the children a set of picture cards and asking each child to select those that illustrated their strategies for coping under stress. In this way, each child produced a personal repertoire of coping strategies. The class teacher then encouraged discussion of both one's own and others' coping repertoires. Other activities in this category included "Fear and protection against fear," a set of poems and paintings depicting ways of dealing with fear and anxiety; positive modes of releasing aggression, such as artwork and sport; and activities allowing children to discover and explore their own personal ways of dealing with stress and anxiety. An example of an activity for meaning attribution was "Dark glasses and rose-colored glasses," in which groups of children looked at the same situation from a pessimistic or optimistic perspective and then compared meaning frameworks and conclusions. Other activities in this category included a multiple-choice questionnaire with personal interpretations of everyday events, games for exploring age-appropriate moral dilemmas and analyses of possible solutions, and creating a journal of personal aims, beliefs and wishes.

Most of the activities stimulated lively discussion and frequently generated emotional responses, novel group interactions, new channels for communication among students and new interactions between educators and students. Most of the activities in the program took place within individual classrooms. However, there were several activities initiated by the children themselves that extended to the entire school. In a session on self-efficacy for dealing with uncontrollable anxiety during the trauma period, a class discussion led to the strategy of engaging in sport activities as a means of releasing emotional stress. In accordance with this conclusion, the educational staff arranged the school schedule to increase sporting activities and teachers organized tournaments in different types of sports. These activities exemplify the multichannel communication and networks of dialogue and support that developed in the school as a result of the participants' willingness to embrace a new role for the school.

The program ended with seminars including feedback from implementing classroom activities and a summary of the process that the school staff and the children had experienced. The combined program acknowledged the school's place at the center of children's lives, and its circles of influence extended to individual teachers, the educational staff as a group, individual children and the classroom as a group.

Empirical evidence

In the study described here, the participants in the school-based program were 158 children, mean age 10.7, approximately half girls and half boys, in the fifth grade at a public elementary school in Beersheba, where the intervention began as soon as the children returned to school at the conclusion of Operation Cast Lead. Children in four classes were allocated randomly to an intervention ($N = 80$) or control condition ($N = 78$). The control groups were the waiting-list groups that received the intervention at the termination of the study. Unfortunately, the control group was not available for evaluation at the termination of their own intervention, thus preventing assessment of the success of delayed intervention. The entire intervention program was administered over a period of nine weeks. Before and after the implementation of the program, a test battery was administered to participants in the classroom in both the intervention and the control groups.

All the participants completed several measures: (a) a demographic question-naire; (b) the "social support matrix" (Slone, Shoshani, & Paltieli, 2009), for assessing ability to mobilize support from various support providers; (c) the "self-efficacy questionnaire for children" (Muris, 2001), to measure children's beliefs about their social, academic and emotional competence; (d) the "purpose of life test" (Crumbaugh & Maholick, 1964), which measures children's attribu-tion of meaning; and (e) the "brief symptom inventory" (Derogatis & Spencer, 1982), for assessing mental health symptoms. There were no significant pre-test differences between the intervention and the control groups in psychological dis-tress and resilience factors. Difference scores between pre- and post-test levels for social support, self-efficacy, attribution of meaning and psychological distress were used to assess changes as a result of the intervention. A significant effect emerged for type of intervention on the variables' modifications, Wilks's lambda $= 0.66$, $F(4,153) = 17.64$, $p = .000$, $\eta^2 = .33$. Specifically, significant effects emerged for type of intervention for the ability to mobilize support, $F(1,156) = 44.37$, $p = .000$, $\eta^2 = .20$; self-efficacy, $F(1,156) = 4.84$, $p = .02$, $\eta^2 = .03$; and psychological distress, $F(1,156) = 19.45$, $p = .000$, $\eta^2 = .06$. Pre-test and post-test scores for the dependent variables in the intervention and the control groups are presented in Table 11.1.

The participants in the intervention group reported significant increases in their ability to mobilize support ($M = 4.96$, $SD = 0.94$), whereas there were significant decreases in the control group ($M = -2.05$, $SD = 0.68$). A significant effect also emerged for self-efficacy, with the intervention group participants reporting significantly greater increases in self-efficacy ($M = 12.51$, $SD = 3.11$) than those in the control group ($M = 2.96$, $SD = 3.38$). In addition, the intervention group participants reported decreases in psychological distress ($M = -0.41$, $SD = 0.03$), while those in the control group reported increases ($M = 0.24$, $SD = 0.02$). Finally, there was no significant difference between the intervention and the control groups in changes in attribution of meaning, $F(1,156) = 0.20$, $p = .15$, $\eta^2 = .00$. There were no gender differences in pre-test levels of the resilience factors or

Table 11.1 Pre- and post-test data for comparison of intervention and control groups

| | Control group | | | | Intervention group | | | |
| | Pre-test | | Post-test | | Pre-test | | Post-test | |
	M	SD	M	SD	M	SD	M	SD
Mobilization of support	19.67	3.49	17.62	3.56	18.95	3.04	23.91	2.94
Self-efficacy	74.70	11.22	77.66	12.34	76.71	9.86	89.22	9.38
Psychological distress	1.09	0.81	1.33	0.73	1.15	0.77	0.74	0.65
Attribution of meaning	104.26	16.64	104.81	16.52	103.86	16.82	104.27	16.63

psychological distress. In addition, there was no significant interaction between gender and type of intervention for changes in the resilience factors.

Effectiveness of the intervention

War and other disasters demand an immediate response from professionals to extend aid to all sectors of the affected community. The workload entailed for rapid response and administration of programs in crisis periods may not leave time for the empirical evaluation of the efficacy of the aid programs. There is an obvious need for evidence-based post-disaster programs.

The strategy underlying the program presented here was to enhance resilience factors and improve coping, rather than focus directly on posttraumatic stress symptoms. The evaluation study underlined the program's success in achieving its goals. The reduction in the children's general psychological distress and symptomatology in the group receiving the intervention was significantly greater than that in the control group. One limitation of this study is the lack of an active placebo control group that might have made it possible to attribute the effects found to the specific elements of this school-based intervention.

The program was effective in increasing self-efficacy and the ability to mobilize support, but it did not change meaning attribution. A possible explanation for this may be that mobilization of social support was inherently built into the program by its very format. The program was based on teacher workshops that imparted skills for administering the activities in the classroom, and also encouraged teacher–student dialogue and mutual experience during activities. It was thus based on opening avenues of dialogue between teachers and students and among peers. Group experiential exercises for teachers may have released their potential for easier communication and enhanced their ability to support the students.

In addition, the group format of the classroom activities, in which emotions and anxieties were discussed in a controlled environment, may have legitimized the development of new friendships and more openness in peer communications. Studies have established the central function of peer relations as a protective factor and in enhancing life satisfaction (Dew & Huebner, 1994). This focus on peer relations should be developed further in future programs.

The increase in self-efficacy showed that children can learn to be proactive in problem-solving, thereby boosting their perceptions of their own efficacy and coping abilities. There is evidence showing that active coping is associated with lower levels of psychological distress and increased well-being during crisis periods (Roth & Cohen, 1986).

The intervention program was not effective in promoting meaning attribution. Fostering attribution of meaning among non-religious schoolchildren living in a violent environment may be difficult to achieve in a brief intervention program. However, although the program was effective in modifying only two of the three resilience factors, the results showed a greater decrease in psychological distress among intervention group than control group participants.

Rethinking the potential of the school

The type of school intervention program described in this chapter represents a public health perspective during times of war and conflict, and exemplifies ways in which school-based intervention can put the school at the center of the community. The school staff holds a pivotal position in introducing and implementing extracurricular clinical programs during crises. Teachers' availability to schoolchildren and their central position in the community locate them as accessible professionals to mediate the needs of the schoolchildren, especially in times of war.

Perceiving the school as a potential source of support and therapy, together with a flexible approach to the role and function of school facilities during crisis periods, can transform the school into a community center. In this program, the new role of the school was readily mobilized. This new conceptualization of the school in times of trauma provides a suitable setting that allows outreach access to children in need, with a salutogenic rather than a pathology-based approach. These views, and the encouraging effectiveness studies of school-based interventions thus far, warrant rethinking the use of the unrealized potential embodied in the school not only during times of war.

Notes

1 The use of the intervention program in schools after Operation Cast Lead and the effectiveness study reported here were supported by a generous grant from the French Friends of Tel Aviv University.
2 The manuals described here are available from the first author, Michelle Slone (email: mich@post.tau.ac.il).

References

Allwood, M. A., Bell-Dolan, D., & Husain, S. A. (2002). Children's trauma and adjustment reactions to violent and non-violent war experiences. *Journal of the American Academy of Child and Adolescent Psychiatry, 41*(4), 450–457.

Bandura, A. (2001). Social cognitive theory: An agentic perspective. *Annual Review of Psychology, 52*, 1–26.

Barber, B. K. (2001). Political violence, social integration, and youth functioning: Palestinian youth from the Intifada. *Journal of Community Psychology, 29*(3), 259–280.

Barber, B. K., Schluterman, J. M., Denny, E. S., & McCouch, R. J. (2006). Adolescents and political violence. In M. Fitzduff & C. E. Stout (Eds.), *The psychology of resolving global conflicts: From war to peace* (Vol. 2, pp. 171–190). Westport, CT: Praeger Security International.

Benight, C. C., & Bandura, A. (2004). Social cognitive theory of posttraumatic recovery: the role of perceived self-efficacy. *Behavior Research and Therapy, 42*, 1129–1148.

Berger, R., Pat-Horenczyk, R., & Gelkopf, M. (2007). School-based intervention for prevention and treatment of elementary-student's terror related distress in Israel: A quasi-randomized controlled trial. *Journal of Traumatic Stress, 20*(4), 541–551.

Chemtob, C. M., Nakashima, J., & Carlson, J. G. (2002). Brief treatment for elementary school children with disaster-related posttraumatic stress disorder: A field study. *Journal of Clinical Psychology, 58*(1), 99–112.

Crumbaugh, J. C., & Maholick, L. T. (1964). An experimental study in existentialism: The psychometric approach to Frankl's concept of neogenic neurosis. *Journal of Clinical Psychology, 20*(2), 200–207.

Derogatis, L. R., & Spencer, P. M. (1982). *The Brief Symptom Inventory (BSI): administration, scoring and procedures manual, I.* Baltimore, MD: Clinical Psychometric Research.

Dew, T., & Huebner, E. S. (1994). Adolescent perceived quality of life: An exploratory investigation. *Journal of School Psychology, 32*(2), 185–199.

Ehntholt, K. A., Smith, P. A., & Yule, W. (2005). School-based cognitive-behavioral therapy group intervention for refugee children who have experienced war-related trauma. *Clinical Child Psychology and Psychiatry, 10*(2), 235–250.

Fogle, L. M., Huebner, E. S., & Laughlin, J. E. (2002). The relation between temperament and life satisfaction in early adolescence: Cognitive and behavioral mediation models. *Journal of Happiness Studies, 3*(4), 373–392.

Fremont, W. P. (2004). Childhood reactions to terrorism-induced trauma: A review of the past 10 years. *Journal of the American Academy of Child and Adolescent Psychiatry, 43*(4), 381–392.

Galante, R., & Foa, D. (1986). An epidemiological study of psychic trauma and treatment effectiveness for children after a natural disaster. *Journal of the American Academy of Child and Adolescent Psychiatry, 25*(3), 357–363.

Garbarino, J., & Kostelny, K. (1996). The effects of political violence on Palestinian children's behavioral problems: A risk accumulation model. *Child Development, 67*(1), 33–45.

Garbarino, J., Kostelny, K., & Dubrow, N. (1991). What children can tell us about living in danger. *American Psychologist, 46*(4), 376–383.

Gelkopf, M., & Berger, R. (2009). A school-based, teacher-mediated prevention program (ERASE-Stress) for reducing terror-related traumatic reactions in Israeli youth:

A quasi-randomized controlled trial. *Journal of Child Psychology and Psychiatry*, *50*(8), 962–971.

Goenjian, A. K. (1993). A mental health relief program in Armenia after the 1988 earthquake: Implementation and clinical observations. *British Journal of Psychiatry*, *163*, 230–239.

Goenjian, A. K., Karayan, I., Pynoos, R. S., Minassian, D., Najarian, L. M., Steinberg, A. M., et al. (1997). Outcome of psychotherapy among early adolescents after trauma. *American Journal of Psychiatry*, *154*(4), 536–542.

Gurwitch, R. H., Sitterle, K. A., Young, P. H., & Pfefferbaum, B. (2002). The aftermath of terrorism. In A. M. La Greca, W. K. Silverman, E. M. Vernberg & M. C. Roberts (Eds.), *Helping children cope with disasters and terrorism* (pp. 327–357). Washington, D.C.: American Psychological Association.

Hock, E. H., Hart, M., Kang, M. J., & Lutz, W. J. (2004). Predicting children's reactions to terrorist attacks: The importance of self-reports and preexisting characteristics. *American Journal of Orthopsychiatry*, *74*(3), 253–262.

Klingman, A. (1993). School-based intervention following a disaster. In C. F. Saylor (Ed.), *Children and disasters* (pp. 187–210). New York, NY: Plenum Press.

Layne, C. M., Saltzman, W. R., Poppleton, L., Burlingame, G. M., Pasǎlić, A., Duraković, E., et al. (2008). Effectiveness of a school-based group psychotherapy program for war-exposed adolescents: A randomized controlled trial. *Journal of the American Academy of Child and Adolescent Psychiatry*, *47*(9), 1048–1062.

Luszczynska, A., Benight, C. C., & Cieslak, R. (2009). Self-efficacy and health-related outcomes of collective trauma: A systematic review. *European Psychologist*, *14*(1), 51–62.

Lynch, K. B., Geller, S. R., & Schmidt, M. G. (2004). Multi-year evaluation of the effectiveness of a resilience-based intervention program for young children. *Journal of Primary Intervention*, *24*(3), 335–353.

Masinda, M. T., & Muhesi, M. (2004). Trauma in children/adolescents: A special focus on third-world countries. *Journal of Child and Adolescent Mental Health*, *16*(2), 69–76.

Masten, A. S., & Coatsworth, J. D. (1998). The development of competence in favorable and unfavorable environments. *American Psychologist*, *53*(2), 205–220.

Moore, K. W., & Varela, R. E. (2010). Correlates of long-term posttraumatic stress symptoms in children following Hurricane Katrina. *Child Psychiatry and Human Development*, *41*(2), 239–250.

Muldoon, O. T. (2004). Children of the troubles: The impact of political violence in Northern Ireland. *Journal of Social Issues*, *60*(3), 453–468.

Muris, P. (2001). A brief questionnaire for measuring self-efficacy in youth. *Journal of Psychopathology and Behavior Assessment*, *23*(3), 145–149.

Pina, A. A., Villalta, I. K., Ortiz, C. D., Gottschall, A. C., Costa, N. M., & Weems, C. F. (2008). Social support, discrimination, and coping as predictors of posttraumatic stress reactions in youth survivors of Hurricane Katrina. *Journal of Clinical Child and Adolescent Psychology*, *37*(3), 564–574.

Pines, R. (1989, January). *Why do Israelis burn out? The role of the Intifada*. Paper presented at the Fourth International Conference on Psychological Stress and Adjustment in Time of War and Peace, Tel Aviv, Israel.

Punamäki, R.-L., Qouta, S., & El-Sarraj, E. (2001). Resiliency factors predicting psychological adjustment after political violence among Palestinian children. *International Journal of Behavioral Development*, *25*(3), 256–267.

Qouta, S., El-Sarraj, E., & Punamäki, R.-L. (2001). Mental flexibility as resiliency factor among children exposed to political violence. *International Journal of Psychology*, *36*(1), 1–7.

Roth, S., & Cohen, L. J. (1986). Approach, avoidance, and coping with stress. *American Psychologist*, *41*(7), 813–819.

Saltzman, W. R., Layne, C. M., Steinberg, A. M., Arslanagic, B., & Pynoos, R. S. (2003). Developing a culturally and ecologically sound intervention program for youth exposed to war and terrorism. *Child and Adolescent Psychiatric Clinics of North America*, *12*(2), 319–342.

Seeman, T. E. (1996). Social ties and health: The benefits of social integration. *Annals of Epidemiology*, *6*(5), 442–451.

Slone, M. (2006). Promoting children's coping in politically violent environments: Suggestions for intervention in educational contexts. In C. W. Greenbaum, P. E. Veerman & N. Bacon-Shnoor (Eds.), *Protection of children during armed political conflict: A multidisciplinary perspective* (pp. 169–195). Antwerp, Belgium: Intersentia.

Slone, M. & Shoshani, A. (2008). Efficacy of a school-based primary prevention program for coping with exposure to political violence. *International Journal of Behavioral Development*, *32*, 348–358.

Slone, M., Shoshani, A., & Paltieli, T. (2009). Psychological consequences of forced evacuation on children: Risk and protective factors. *Journal of Traumatic Stress*, *22*(4), 340–343.

Thabet, A. A. M., Abed, Y., & Vostanis, P. (2002). Emotional problems in Palestinian children living in war zone: A cross-sectional study. *The Lancet*, *359*(9320), 1801–1804.

Udwin, O., Boyle, S., Yule, W., Bolton, D., & O'Ryan, D. (2000). Risk factors for long-term psychological effects of a disaster experienced in adolescence: predictors of post traumatic stress disorder. *Journal of Child Psychology and Psychiatry*, *41*(8), 969–979.

Vernberg, E. M., & Vogel, J. M. (1993). Part 2: Interventions with children after disasters. *Journal of Clinical Child Psychology*, *22*(4), 485–498.

Werner, E. E. (2000). Protective factors and individual resilience. In J. P. Shonkoff & S. J. Meisels (Eds.). *Handbook of early childhood intervention* (pp. 115–132). Cambridge, England: Cambridge University Press.

Wolmer, L., Hamiel, D., Barchas, J. D., Slone, M., & Laor, N. (2011). Teacher-delivered resilience-focused intervention in schools with traumatized children following the second Lebanon war. *Journal of Traumatic Stress*, *24*(3), 309–316.

Wolmer, L., Laor, N., & Yazgan, Y. (2003). School reactivation programs after disaster: Could teachers serve as clinical mediators? *Child and Adolescent Psychiatric Clinics of North America*, *12*(2), 363–381.

Chapter 12

Ecological perspectives on trauma and resilience in children affected by armed conflict

Bridging evidence and practice

Wietse A. Tol, Emily E. Haroz, Rebecca S. Hock, Jeremy C. Kane and Mark J. D. Jordans

When armed conflicts occur, the social fabric that fosters healthy child development is often torn apart. Nurturing systems such as family and neighborhood supports, schools and religious associations may be negatively impacted. Although strengthening family- and community-based supports are among the most widely-used types of mental health interventions in armed conflicts, most research in these settings remains focused on psychiatric epidemiology and the treatment of individual symptomatology (Tol, Barbui, et al., 2011; Tol, Patel, et al., 2011).

This chapter describes a framework for intervention approaches in which sociocultural and protective factors are central considerations, and discusses recent research findings in this area. The chapter starts with an overview of how ecological and resilience perspectives are currently integrated in consensus guidelines for mental health and psychosocial support (MHPSS) interventions in armed conflicts. Subsequently, we summarize research findings on resilience and effectiveness of interventions in low- and middle-income countries (LMICs) affected by armed conflicts. We end the chapter with examples of intervention approaches that highlight some of these principles. Our focus is on LMICs as the large majority of armed conflicts take place there (Themnér & Wallensteen, 2011).

Resilience and consensus on best practices

Despite the recognized need for a concerted approach to addressing trauma and resilience in children in LMICs, both researchers and practitioners working on this issue have experienced ideological divisions among themselves. These divisions have contributed to fragmented and inconsistent services for populations in need. In response, three recent initiatives have focused on building consensus around best practices. First, an Inter-Agency Standing Committee (IASC) task force, consisting of staff of 27 agencies, developed and issued *Guidelines on Mental Health and Psychosocial Support in Emergencies* (Inter-Agency Standing

Committee, 2007). In these guidelines, MHPSS is defined as "any type of local or outside support that aims to protect or promote psychosocial wellbeing and/or prevent or treat mental disorder" (p. 1). Second, the revised Sphere Project handbook (2011) includes guidance on MHPSS. The Sphere Project was established in 1997 by non-governmental organizations and the Red Cross and Red Crescent Movement. The project's objective was to create a humanitarian charter and an accompanying set of standards that could be used by the international humanitarian system to ensure a universal minimum standard of care and accountability for affected populations. Finally, Ager, Boothby and Wessells (2006) used the Delphi method to achieve a similar set of consensus-based best practices for the care and protection of children associated with fighting forces.

Some themes are common to these documents. First, the guidelines highlight the notion that child health and development are closely tied to sociocultural factors (e.g., cultural notions on child development and the expression of distress, existing social support systems, parenting practices, education and religious institutions) and health system factors (e.g., help-seeking strategies, types and accessibility of health care). Second, the IASC and Sphere guidelines envision an intervention "pyramid" in which the most intensive interventions are reserved for the most severe cases, occurring in the smallest section of a population (e.g., people in need of specialized mental health care), while the base of the pyramid represents the most broad-based interventions for the largest proportion of a population (e.g., providing a chance for people to perform appropriate mourning rituals; having separate, well-lit toilets for men and women in order to help prevent sexual- and gender-based violence in camps; strengthening existing supports at the family and community levels). Interventions at the base of the pyramid are aimed at preventing mental health problems and promoting mental health in the larger population. The intervention pyramid suggests an integrated multilayered system of interventions that focuses on providing different types of services for varying needs and mental health concerns in emergency settings. Finally, and importantly, there is a common message that the process of developing an intervention is just as important as its content, in the sense that affected populations must be active participants in this process at all stages of design and implementation.

These common themes overlap with basic tenets in child development research on the notion of "resilience"; that is, "a dynamic process encompassing positive adaptation within the context of significant adversity" (Luthar, Cicchetti, & Becker, 2000, p. 543). There has been growing recognition in the child development literature that resilience is not a unique quality of certain children who are invulnerable to harm, but, rather, is a collection of protective processes that include and extend beyond the individual child (Masten, 2011). These processes include attitudes and behaviors at the individual level and attachment relationships, caregiver functionality, neighborhood social cohesion and other resources at the family, neighborhood, school and wider community levels. The themes of the guidelines and standards fit well with the current understanding of resilience, since they emphasize the active involvement of the affected population at every stage of the intervention process and focus on the community's internal resources and strengths. For example, a sense of self- and community efficacy, as well as connectedness and hope, were three of the five essential elements for mass trauma interventions identified in a systematic review by Hobfoll and colleagues (2007).

In short, growing consensus in the humanitarian aid field highlights the importance of dedicating attention to protective resources at diverse socio-ecological levels, which is a common notion in the literature on resilience. Resilience lends itself well to guiding humanitarian interventions, since the focus is on factors and processes that can be modified, as opposed to fixed, innate qualities of individuals. The impact of trauma extends beyond the event or series of events and can negatively impact the social world in which a child is growing up. In this sense, the impact of trauma can be enduring and far-reaching. However, by this same token, strengthening and repairing components of the social fabric can lead to resilient outcomes for individuals and communities (Tol, Jordans, Kohrt, Betancourt, & Komproe, 2013 a, b).

Resilience from an ecological perspective

A focus on contextual processes has been part of resilience research from its conception. An early definition of "resilience" by Rutter (1987) described the phenomenon as an ever-changing interactive process rather than a fixed characteristic of specific individuals. More recently, researchers have started studying these interactive processes at multiple socio-ecological levels (e.g., individual, family, community, society), taking advantage of advances in multilevel statistical computing (Ungar, 2012). For example, in discussing an ecological approach to children affected by armed conflict, Boothby (2008) advises focusing on a combination of factors from both the micro-system (consisting of the direct activities, roles and interpersonal relations in a certain setting; e.g., the home setting or the school setting) and the macro-system (consistencies in the form of culture or sub-culture in the different systems a child grows up in) that "can be seen to form a protective shield around children, not eliminating risks and vulnerabilities but protecting children from their full impact" (Boothby, 2008). Of particular importance, he notes, are the community factors that could be protective and promote resilience, since these may be beneficial to larger groups of children. Similarly, other authors have highlighted the importance of teasing apart the risk and protective processes taking place across a child's social world in understanding how best to support healthy development in children affected by armed conflict (Kohrt et al., 2010; Tol, Jordans, Reis, & de Jong, 2009).

It would stand to reason that resilience as a concept might best be measured among children who have faced a significant amount of adversity, including armed conflicts. Armed conflicts currently take place mainly in LMICs. Unfortunately, as many researchers have pointed out, comparatively few studies looking at resilience have been conducted in LMICs, leading to a significant gap in the literature and limiting our understanding of the resilience of the majority of the world's children (Reed, Fazel, Jones, Panter-Brick, & Stein, 2012; Tol, Song, & Jordans, 2013).

In the following sections, we discuss current knowledge about resilience in children affected by armed conflicts in LMICs, based on recently conducted systematic reviews. As a basis for discussion, we follow an ecological model, involving risk and protective factors at individual, family, community and society levels. Before discussing what is known about ecological resilience from research with children and adolescents living in settings of armed conflicts in LMICs, we note some limitations of our current knowledge. First, a major limitation of the literature in this field is the lack of longitudinal data (Fazel, Reed, Panter-Brick, & Stein, 2012; Reed, et al., 2012; Tol et al., 2013). Without longitudinal data, it is difficult to make causal inferences or study possible transactional processes (e.g., poverty negatively impacts child development, which, in turn, puts children at risk for worse economic outcomes). Other limitations include the narrow use of indicators to measure resilience and a lack of controlled designs when intervening to promote resilience. A lack of attention to teasing out mediators and moderators in these complex relationships, as opposed to simple correlational studies, has also been mentioned as a concern (Reed et al., 2012; Tol et al., 2010).

Individual factors

The review by Reed and colleagues (2012) of refugee and displaced children resettled in LMICs found mixed results for age, whereas some studies reported older children having more symptoms (Goldstein, Wampler, & Wise, 1997; Hasanović, Sinanović, & Pavlović, 2005), while others found younger children having more symptoms (Mels, Derluyn, Broekaert, & Rosseel, 2010) and yet others found no difference by age (Morgos, Worden, & Gupta, 2007; Servan-Schreiber, Le Lin, & Birmaher, 1998; Yurtbay, Alyanak, Abali, Kaynak, & Durukan, 2003).

With regard to gender, studies in the review found boys to be at greater risk for behavioral disorders (Karacic & Zvizdic, 2000) and other externalizing symptoms (Đapo & Kolenović-Đapo, 2000; Mels et al., 2010), while girls had a higher risk of depression and anxiety (Mels et al., 2010; Sujoldzić, Peternel, Kulenović, & Terzić, 2006; Van Ommeren et al., 2001). Individual exposure to potentially traumatic events was almost universally associated with greater risk for mental health symptoms, as compared to individuals who had not experienced such events (Allwood, Bell-Dolan, & Husain, 2002; Giacaman, Abu-Rmeileh, Husseini, Saab, & Boyce, 2007; Mels et al., 2010; Sujoldzić et al., 2006; Thabet, Abed, & Vostanis, 2004; Van Ommeren et al., 2001).

Individual protective factors identified in a review of both qualitative and quantitative studies of resilience in children affected by armed conflicts in LMICs (Tol et al., 2013) included individual coping mechanisms (Fernando & Ferrari, 2011), a positive self-perception (Kryger & Lindgren, 2011) and perseverance and self-esteem (Betancourt et al., 2011).

Family factors

Together with individual-level factors, family factors are some of the best-studied issues among children in areas of armed conflict. In a study of Bosnian adolescents, Sujoldzić et al., (2006) found that family connectedness was associated with reduced risk for depression. Family cohesion was also found to be a key protective factor among refugee children resettled in high-income countries, according to a review by Fazel and colleagues (2012) (Berthold, 1999; Grgić et al., 2005; Kovacev & Shute, 2004; Rousseau, Drapeau, & Platt, 2004; Sujoldzić et al., 2006). Similarly, a review by Tol and colleagues (2013) identified family unity (Betancourt et al., 2011), improved family life (Panter-Brick, Goodman, Tol, & Eggerman, 2011) and family relations (Qouta, Punamäki, Montgomery, & El Sarraj, 2007) as significant protective factors.

Community factors

Social support and school connectedness were associated with fewer internalizing symptoms in two studies included in the review by Reed and coworkers (2012) (Hasanović et al., 2005; Sujoldzić et al., 2006); however, the authors noted that social support might act as a moderator in many relationships (e.g., between other protective variables and mental health) and it might be challenging to assess social relations, especially in cross-sectional studies.

Fazel et al. (2012) described studies which found that perceptions of safety and connectedness at school were protective for symptoms of anxiety and depression (Geltman et al., 2005; Kia-Keating & Ellis, 2007; Rousseau et al., 2004; Sujoldzić et al., 2006). Social support was also found to be important in several studies in the review by Tol et al. (2013) as protecting against mental health problems (Betancourt et al., 2011; Harel-Fisch et al., 2010; Kryger & Lindgren, 2011) and promoting prosocial behavior (Betancourt et al., 2010).

Societal factors

A review by Reed et al. (2012) found that the most important societal risk for mental health symptoms was prolonged settlement in a refugee camp (Giacaman et al., 2007; Khamis, 2005; Thabet & Vostanis, 1998). The Fazel et al. (2012) review identified immigration processes as one of the key societal risk factors, including detention (Rothe et al., 2002) and unsure asylum status (Bean, Eurelings-Bontekoe, & Spinhoven, 2007; Bodegård, 2005; Nielsen et al., 2008). Political developments (e.g., phase of conflict) (Punamäki, 1988) were associated with the types of coping strategies employed by children that were found in a study by Tol and colleagues (2013).

Despite a growing body of literature on resilience from an ecological perspective, the paucity of knowledge about protective factors at the community and societal levels is striking. Reed et al. (2012) reasoned that this is so primarily because individual level factors are easier to measure. This is particularly concerning because, as Fazel et al. (2012) pointed out, interventions focused on protective factors in larger systems can be implemented on a larger scale, such as improving connectedness at schools. All the reviews mentioned above have emphasized the need for future work to focus on macro-system (i.e., community and societal) level interventions. The next section of this chapter will summarize the evidence base for designing, implementing and measuring the effectiveness of such clinical and community interventions.

Effectiveness of clinical and community interventions

There is growing consensus that interventions promoting the mental health and resilience of children affected by armed conflict should include an ecological approach that incorporates knowledge of risk and protective factors at each level of a child's environment (Boothby, Strang, & Wessells, 2006). While many MHPSS programs are designed to influence familial, community and environmental factors, there are only a few studies that have actually evaluated the effectiveness of such interventions. As MHPSS programs are increasingly incorporated into humanitarian assistance programs, it is important to consider the evidence that does exist when designing and implementing programs to promote mental health, well-being and resilience for children affected by armed conflict.

In their review of MHPSS programs in humanitarian settings, Tol, Barbui, et al. (2011) investigated the links between practice, funding and evidence for MHPSS interventions in humanitarian settings in LMICs. By systematically reviewing the "grey literature" of reports found through organizational websites or dissemination to funders, the authors found that the majority of MHPSS interventions in these settings consist of psychoeducation and awareness building, structured recreational and creative activities, basic counseling for groups and families and the creation of child-friendly spaces (Tol, Barbui, et al., 2011).

Despite the proliferation of this type of programming and an increase in the numbers of studies evaluating MHPSS interventions, the evidence base remains small in proportion to the scale of the problem. Moreover, there is a disconnect between the types of interventions that are currently most widely-used and those that have been evaluated in controlled studies. The most rigorous evidence exists for more specialized services with posttraumatic stress disorder (PTSD) as the outcome variable, whereas these were not among the most widely implemented interventions.

The largest gap between research and practice exists in the lower half of the intervention pyramid, especially the programs aimed at preventing mental disorders and promoting psychosocial well-being. To bridge this gap, the authors recommend more systematic integration of monitoring and evaluation in all MHPSS programming to help determine if and how psychosocial interventions are effective for people located in these settings (Tol, Barbui, et al., 2011).

Jordans, Tol, Komproe and de Jong (2009) conducted a systematic review of intervention approaches and evidence for psychosocial and mental health care,

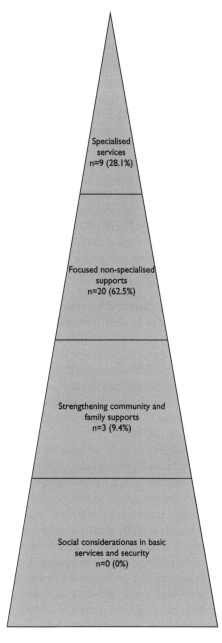

Specialised services
Eg, mental health care by mental health specialists
(psychiatric nurses, psychologists, psychiatrists, etc)
Children and adolescents:
  • Group IPT and KIDNET (one RCT)[47]
  • KIDNET and meditation-relaxation
    (two RCTs)[48,49]
Adults:
  • Control-focused behavioural treatment
    (two RCTs)[50-52]
  • NET, psychoeducation, and counselling
    (four RCTs; Frank Neuner, Bielefeld
    University, personal communication)[53-55]

Focused non-specialised supports
Eg, basic mental health care by primary
health-care doctors, basic emotional support by
community workers.
Children and adolescents:
  • Basic psychosocial support or medical care
    (one RCT)[54]
  • Classroom-based interventions (four RCTs,
    one CCT)[57-61]
  • ERASE Stress Sri Lanka (one RCT)[42]
  • Group CBT (one CCT)[43]
  • Group crisis intervention (one CCT)[64]
  • Group IPT and creative play (one RCT)[65]
  • Reconciliation in education (one CCT)[66]
  • Psychodynamic and contextual programme
    (one RCT)[67]
  • Trauma or grief component therapy
    (one RCT, one CCT)[68,69]
Adults:
  • Basic psychosocial support or medical care
    (one RCT)[54]
  • Individual counselling (one RCT; Frank
    Neuner, Bielefeld University, personal
    communication)[59]
  • Multidisciplinary rehabilitation torture
    survivors (one CCT)[63]
  • Problem-solving group counselling (one CCT)[60]
  • Testimony therapy (one RCT)[45]
  • Trauma healing and reconciliation (one RCT,
    one CCT)[57,59]

**Strengthening community and
family supports**
Eg, activating social networks, communal traditional
supports, supportive child-friendly spaces
Children and adolescents:
  • Creative play (one RCT)[45]
  • Recreational cultural, and other non-formal
    activities (one RCT, one CCT)[70-71]
Adults:
  • Befriending for bereaved (one CCT)[72]

Figure 12.1 Studies included in systematic review displayed in IASC intervention
pyramid for mental health and psychosocial support in humanitarian
settings format (Tol, Barbui, et al., 2011)

specifically for children affected by armed conflict. Sixty-six publications were included in the review, covering studies that included children as primary or secondary benefactors of programs. The studies took place in LMIC settings, and focused on interventions implemented during or after armed conflict. Of the 66 studies that were reviewed, only 12 were classified as outcome studies; that is, as studies in which the evaluation methodology was specifically reported. These 12 studies focused mostly on symptoms of PTSD. Among the studies reporting intervention approaches, 13 involved targeting general well-being, 22 targeted psychosocial distress, 13 focused on psychopathology and 13 involved multiple foci, including psychosocial distress, differing levels of distress and/or other environmental and social outcomes (the remaining studies included in the review were not classified; Jordans, Tol, et al., 2009). The studies encompassed a wide range of intervention modalities, but the most frequently mentioned ones involve creative, recreational and psychoeducational activities (Jordans, Tol, et al., 2009). Overall, the authors concluded that, although the interventions cover a broad range of risk and protective factors for a variety of mental health problems, more rigorous research remains focused more narrowly on PTSD symptoms.

Concerning the evidence for treatment of children affected by armed conflict, the few outcome studies that have been conducted have produced encouraging but limited results. Of the 12 outcome studies, 11 indicated positive treatment effects such as symptom reduction and an increase in protective factors. While the effect sizes were fairly large for the non-controlled studies (indicating positive change, but not efficacy of treatment), the effect sizes for the controlled studies were only moderate. In general, most of the studies were not designed to determine the causality or the strength of the reported changes, and the intervention efficacy can only be classified as moderate (Jordans, Tol, et al., 2009).

The literature on treatment approaches for children adversely affected by armed conflict advocates a paradigm shift. Researchers and program designers have been calling for a public mental health framework, including a preventative and/ or ecological approach, for psychosocial interventions aimed at this population. However, because of the paucity of research that measures the effectiveness of this approach, it is not yet clear what this approach actually entails and how it is to be implemented (Jordans, Tol, et al., 2009). The public mental health framework calls for the development of intervention programs that incorporate joint partnerships with local and ministerial stakeholders, comprehensive assessment of the range and severity of trauma and loss, consideration of current stressors among the affected population, training programs aimed at building capacity among in-country service providers and local support for the infrastructure used to carry out such programs (Pynoos, Goenjian & Steinberg, 1998; de Jong, 2002). Ecological approaches to psychosocial and mental health care fit into this framework by removing the individual as the sole focus of treating symptoms, and expanding programmatic goals to include the child's well-being from an individual, familial, social, cultural and political perspective.

Thus, while most of the rigorous studies have focused on treatment or tertiary prevention, many programmatic interventions are aimed at primary or secondary prevention. Peltonen and Punamäki (2010) conducted a comprehensive review of primary and secondary prevention interventions for children exposed to political violence. They found only 16 relevant published studies, 4 of which had research designs that were experimental or quasi-experimental. While the remainder reported researcher-subjective positive outcomes, the outcomes of the 4 studies that had reasonably strong designs were mixed. Moreover, while the studies reviewed claimed to be preventive, most of them only aimed to change children's cognitive processes and negative emotions and only a few targeted multiple domains of child development and functioning in multiple ecological systems. Thus, while advocates and program devisers emphasize enhancing strengths and protective mechanisms, there are, as yet, very few studies that generate the kind of rigorous evidence needed to support this focus on the prevention of disorder in the face of trauma resulting from violence or armed conflict.

Examples of interventions utilizing a primary/ secondary prevention and ecological approach

Case description 1

Despite the lack of soundly designed studies in general, there are several programs and evaluations of those programs that provide a model of how to approach intervention with conflict-affected children from a broader ecological standpoint in a systematic manner. Loughry et al. (2006) investigated the impact of an intervention comprised of structured activities on the well-being of conflict-affected youths in the Palestinian territories. The intervention centered on participation in recreational and cultural activities to develop resilience and promote well-being. Outcomes included social/emotional well-being, improved quality of parent–child relationships and enhanced thinking/planning for the future. They were measured using adapted versions of Western measures of children's behavior, hopefulness and parental support. The sample consisted of 300 children recruited from the West Bank and Gaza in the intervention group and 50 children from each area in the comparison group. The children were measured at baseline and followed up for 12 months. The results indicated that children in both intervention groups had fewer internalizing and externalizing symptoms than the children in the comparison groups, and parental support was greater in the intervention group in the West Bank than in the control group. Children's hopefulness was not impacted by the intervention.

The results of this study are limited for several reasons. First, although the intervention made provisions for structured activities, the level of participation in the program and whether the child participated in other psychosocial programming concurrently is unknown. Second, since the selection of study and control participants was not random, it is hard to make direct inferences about the efficacy of the intervention. However, in general, the program that was implemented was economical and feasible, and the results indicated positive gains for children who participated in the program. This study is an example of an intervention that targeted children exposed to war and violence, but who did not necessarily meet the criteria for a psychological disorder, thus providing an illustration of how an ecological and preventive intervention for children affected by armed conflict can be implemented and evaluated.

Case description 2

More recently, Ager and colleagues (2011) evaluated the impact of a school-based psychosocial structured activities (PSSA) program on war-affected youths in northern Uganda. The PSSA program was implemented in 21 schools that had been identified as being in areas that were most affected by displacement of people as a result of the violence. The intervention involved 15 class sessions and was designed to increase children's resilience through structured activities, such as drama, movement, music and art, as well as parental support and community involvement. These class sessions involved all students in the school. To study the efficacy of this program, the researchers, using random quota sampling, selected 8 schools as target schools that would receive PSSA and 8 geographically matched schools that would serve as controls. The teachers recommended certain students to be followed, based on whether they thought the child was struggling with self-isolation or low self-esteem, or had a violent family background. The children in the comparison schools were selected in the same way. The resulting study consisted of $n = 403$ children, 203 of whom were given the intervention. The outcome measures were developed through a brief ethnographic interviewing technique—students, teachers and parents at each of the intervention schools were interviewed about the characteristics of the children who demonstrated well-being, and these characteristics made up the indicators for the study. The children were evaluated 12 months after the initiation of the program. The results indicated that all the children were rated higher on well-being at the end than at the beginning of the program, regardless of the treatment group, but the well-being of the children who had received PSSA increased to a greater extent, according to parent and child reports (Ager et al. 2011).

While this study yielded positive results, there are several limitations that should be considered when interpreting the findings. There was a very long follow-up time, resulting in heavy attrition that may have biased the results. The researchers tried to address this both in the study design phase and during analysis, but their resources ran out and they were unable to track down participants who had moved. Moreover, the study design was not fully randomized, and, while the intervention and non-intervention groups were comparable in gender and age balance, more could have been done during the analysis phase to adjust for potential bias with a non-randomized design (such as propensity score weighting). However, despite these limitations, this intervention is a good example of a program that sought to incorporate a preventive model and utilize children's ecological environment to promote resilience and well-being. Incorporation of multiple aspects of the social environment, culturally relevant and appropriate outcome measures and structured evaluation procedures should all be considered for future programs.

Case description 3

This chapter started with an account of the current consensus for applying an integrated multilayered system of interventions focusing on providing different types of services for a variety of needs and mental health concerns in emergency settings. One example of such a multilayered system is the "child thematic program" (CTP), a mental health and psychosocial care package developed for children in areas of armed conflict (Jordans, Komproe, Tol, Susanty, et al., 2010). This system ensures the flow of clients between a set of interventions at different levels, thereby integrating services promoting community resilience, with focused care for distressed children and treatment for those with persistent, severe problems.

An essential element of this or any other care system is that the different interventions are appropriately matched with the target population. To facilitate this allocation process, the CTP developed an instrument to identify children with elevated psychosocial distress. The "child psychosocial distress screener" (CPDS) is a multidimensional tool that combines assessment of children's problems (e.g., distress, absence from school) and protective factors (e.g., coping, social support). Validation studies have demonstrated that the core template of the CPDS, which is custom designed for each sociocultural setting, works well across different settings (Jordans, Komproe, Tol, & de Jong, 2009).

As a result of the outcomes of this screening procedure, children scoring above a cut-off point are offered the opportunity to participate in the "classroom-based intervention" (CBI). The other children can join a "child resilience group," which combines group recreational and traditional activities (e.g., songs and dances, drumming, sports games) with psychoeducation. The aim of this intervention is to strengthen existing resilience by enhancing social support systems and normalization through peer-group discussion and activities.

Children participating in CBI follow a 15-session intervention that combines expressive and creative techniques with elements of cognitive behavioral therapy (Macy, Macy, Gross, & Brighton, 2003). Different efficacy studies have demonstrated that CBI is efficacious for a number of outcome indicators and a variety of subgroups in Indonesia, Nepal and Sri Lanka (Jordans, Komproe, Tol, Kohrt, et al., 2010; Tol et al., 2012; Tol et al., 2008). However, its efficacy is not unequivocal, with results in Burundi indicating the positive and negative findings. Consequently, the CTP developed a new intervention to replace CBI in Burundi. An intervention that aims to support families is more useful in a country where the natural social structures have been severely undermined through years of violence.

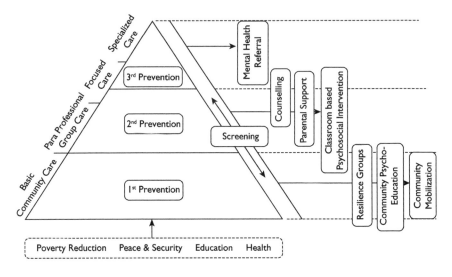

Figure 12.2 Multilayered care system for children (Jordans et al., 2010)

This family-focused intervention brings together primary prevention strategies, such as promoting the social connectedness of families through parental training to deal with children's behavioral problems. The intervention has been developed following a new four-step research procedure, allowing countries with limited resources to assemble intervention strategies based on effectiveness and feasibility (Jordans, Komproe, & Tol, 2011).

Conclusion

Practitioners and researchers largely agree on the importance of focusing on protective factors and processes across the socio-ecological context. An interest in resilience is evident in policy documents relevant to humanitarian mental health and psychosocial interventions, as well as in an increasing academic interest in research on protective factors. As of yet, however, knowledge about resilience in children affected by armed conflicts in LMICs remains limited by a lack of longitudinal studies, a narrow range of indicators from which resilience is inferred, a lack of controlled designs and a lack of attention to mediators and moderators of change over time. There is evidence that supports the importance of protective factors at the family level, but very little research has focused on protective factors and processes at school, neighborhood, community and societal levels, despite the observation that humanitarian organizations often work at these levels. Similarly, the popularity of mental health and psychosocial interventions at the family and community levels has not been matched by rigorous studies investigating the effectiveness of resilience-focused interventions.

If resilience-focused interventions are not grounded in empirical evidence, there is a risk that such interventions may not build optimally on the processes that support resilience in different populations and contexts, and could even do harm. The empirical evidence needed includes qualitative and quantitative research aimed at teasing apart resilience processes as well as evaluation studies documenting the impact of interventions. The notion of resilience is currently gaining ground with humanitarian agencies. We argue for a better alignment between the interests of researchers and interventionists in this field to address the major gaps in knowledge described in this chapter. This will enable the current popularity of the concept of resilience to be ultimately translated into a larger set of mental health and psychosocial interventions with known effectiveness that can be applied flexibly and adapted across contexts.

References

Ager, A., Akesson, B., Stark, L., Flouri, E., Okot, B., McCollister, F., et al. (2011). The impact of the school-based psychosocial structured activities (PSSA) program on conflict-affected children in northern Uganda. *Journal of Child Psychology and Psychiatry*, *52*(11), 1124–1133.

Ager, A., Boothby, N., & Wessells, M. (2006). The use of consensus methodology in determining key research and practice: Development questions in the field of intervention with children associated with fighting forces. *Intervention: International Journal of Mental Health, Psychosocial Work & Counselling in Areas of Armed Conflict*, *5*(2), 124–129.

Allwood, M. A., Bell-Dolan, D., & Husain, S. A. (2002). Children's trauma and adjustment reactions to violent and nonviolent war experiences. *Journal of the American Academy of Child and Adolescent Psychiatry*, *41*(4), 450–457.

Bean, T. M., Eurelings-Bontekoe, E., & Spinhoven, P. (2007). Course and predictors of mental health of unaccompanied refugee minors in the Netherlands: One year follow-up. *Social Science & Medicine (1982)*, *64*(6), 1204–1215.

Berthold, S. M. (1999). The effects of exposure to community violence on Khmer refugee adolescents. *Journal of Traumatic Stress*, *12*(3), 455–471.

Betancourt, T. S., Borisova, I. I., Williams, T. P., Brennan, R. T., Whitfield, T. H., de la Soudière, M., et al. (2010). Sierra Leone's former child soldiers: A follow-up study of psychosocial adjustment and community reintegration. *Child Development*, *81*(4), 1077–1095.

Betancourt, T. S., Meyers-Ohki, S., Stulac, S. N., Barrera, A. E., Mushashi, C., & Beardslee, W. R. (2011). Nothing can defeat combined hands (Abashize hamwe ntakibananira): Protective processes and resilience in Rwandan children and families affected by HIV/AIDS. *Social Science & Medicine (1982)*, *73*(5), 693–701.

Bodegård, G. (2005). Pervasive loss of function in asylum-seeking children in Sweden. *Acta Paediatrica*, *94*(12), 1706–1707.

Boothby, N. (2008). Political violence and development: An ecologic approach to children in war zones. *Child and Adolescent Psychiatric Clinics of North America*, *17*(3), 497–514, vii.

Boothby, N., Strang, A., & Wessells, M. G. (2006). *A world turned upside down: Social ecological approaches to children in war zones*. Bloomfield, CT: Kumarian Press.

Đapo, N., & Kolenović-Đapo, J. (2000). Evaluation of the psychosocial adjustment of displaced children from Srebrenica. In S. Powell & E. Duraković-Belko (Eds.), *Sarajevo 2000: The psychosocial consequences of war. Results of empirical research from the territory of former Yugoslavia* (pp. 150–54). Presentations from a symposium held at the Faculty of Philosophy, University of Sarajevo, July 7 and 8, 2000. Sarajevo, Bosnia and Herzegovina: UNICEF B&H.

Fazel, M., Reed, R. V., Panter-Brick, C., & Stein, A. (2012). Mental health of displaced and refugee children resettled in high-income countries: Risk and protective factors. *Lancet, 379*(9812), 266–282.

Fernando, C., & Ferrari, M. (2011). Spirituality and resilience in children of war in Sri Lanka. *Journal of Spirituality in Mental Health, 13*(1), 52–77.

Geltman, P. L., Grant-Knight, W., Mehta, S. D., Lloyd-Travaglini, C., Lustig, S., Landgraf, J. M. et al. (2005). The "lost boys of Sudan": Functional and behavioral health of unaccompanied refugee minors re-settled in the United States. *Archives of Pediatrics & Adolescent Medicine, 159*(6), 585–591.

Giacaman, R., Abu-Rmeileh, N. M. E., Husseini, A., Saab, H., & Boyce, W. (2007). Humiliation: The invisible trauma of war for Palestinian youth. *Public Health, 121*(8), 563–571; discussion 572–577.

Goldstein, R. D., Wampler, N. S., & Wise, P. H. (1997). War experiences and distress symptoms of Bosnian children. *Pediatrics, 100*(5), 873–878.

Grgić, M., Vidović, V., Butković-Soldo, S., Vukšić-Mihaljević, Z., Degmečić, D., & Laufer, D. (2005). The mental health of children upon their return home after a long displacement period. *Collegium Antropologicum, 29*(2), 537–542.

Harel-Fisch, Y., Radwan, Q., Walsh, S. D., Laufer, A., Amitai, G., Fogel-Grinvald, H. et al. (2010). Psychosocial outcomes related to subjective threat from armed conflict events (STACE): Findings from the Israeli-Palestinian cross-cultural HBSC study. *Child Abuse & Neglect, 34*(9), 623–638.

Hasanović, M., Sinanović, O., & Pavlović, S. (2005). Acculturation and psychological problems of adolescents from Bosnia and Herzegovina during exile and repatriation. *Croatian Medical Journal, 46*(1), 105–115.

Hobfoll, S. E., Watson, P., Bell, C. C., Bryant, R. A., Brymer, M. J., Friedman, M. J. et al. (2007). Five elements of immediate and mid-term mass trauma intervention: Empirical evidence. *Psychiatry: Interpersonal and Biological Processes, 70*(4), 283–315.

Inter-Agency Standing Committee. (2007). *IASC guidelines on mental health and psychosocial support in emergency settings.* Geneva: Author.

de Jong, J. T. V. M. (2002). *Trauma, war, and violence: Public mental health in socio-cultural context.* New York, NY: Kluwer Academic/Plenum Publishers.

Jordans, M. J. D., Komproe, I. H., & Tol, W. A. (2011). Mental health interventions for children in adversity: Pilot-testing a research strategy for treatment selection in low-income settings. *Social Science and Medicine, 73*(3), 456–466.

Jordans, M. J. D., Komproe, I. H., Tol, W. A., & de Jong, J. T. V. M. (2009). Screening for psychosocial distress amongst war-affected children: Cross-cultural construct validity of the CPDS. *Journal of Child Psychology and Psychiatry, 50*(4), 514–523.

Jordans, M. J. D., Komproe, I. H., Tol, W. A., Kohrt, B., Luitel, N. P., Macy, R. D. M. et al. (2010). Evaluation of a classroom-based psychosocial intervention in conflict-affected Nepal: A cluster randomized controlled trial. *Journal of Child Psychology and Psychiatry, 51*(7), 818–826.

Jordans, M. J. D., Komproe, I. H., Tol, W. A., Susanty, D., Vallipuram, A., Ntamatumba, P. et al. (2010). Practice-driven evaluation of a multi-layered psychosocial care package for children in areas of armed conflict. *Community Mental Health Journal, 47*(3), 267–277.

Jordans, M. J. D., Tol, W. A., Komproe, I. H., & de Jong, J. T. V. M. (2009). Systematic review of evidence and treatment approaches: Psychosocial and mental health care for children in war. *Child and Adolescent Mental Health, 14*(1), 2–14.

Jordans, M. J. D., Tol, W. A., Komproe, I. H., Susanty, D., Vallipuram, A., Ntamatumba, P. et al. (2010). Development of a multi-layered psychosocial care system for children in areas of political violence. *International Journal of Mental Health Systems, 4*(1), 15.

Karacic, S., & Zvizdic, S. (2000). The effect of war-related trauma on the behaviour of adolescents. In S. Powell, & E. Durakovic-Belko (Eds.), *Sarajevo 2000: The psychosocial consequences of war. Results of empirical research from the territory of former Yugoslavia* (pp. 192–195). Presentations from a symposium held at the Faculty of Philosophy, University of Sarajevo, July 7 and 8, 2000. Sarajevo, Bosnia and Herzegovina: UNICEF B&H.

Khamis, V. (2005). Post-traumatic stress disorder among school age Palestinian children. *Child Abuse & Neglect, 29*(1), 81–95.

Kia-Keating, M., & Ellis, B. H. (2007). Belonging and connection to school in resettlement: young refugees, school belonging, and psychosocial adjustment. *Clinical Child Psychology and Psychiatry, 12*(1), 29–43.

Kohrt, B. A., Jordans, M. J. D., Tol, W. A., Perera, E., Karki, R., Koirala, S. et al. (2010). Social ecology of child soldiers: Child, family, and community determinants of mental health, psychosocial well-being, and reintegration in Nepal. *Transcultural Psychiatry, 47*(5), 727–753.

Kovacev, L., & Shute, R. H. (2004). Acculturation and social support in relation to psychosocial adjustment of adolescent refugees resettled in Australia. *International Journal of Behavioral Development, 28*(3), 259–267.

Kryger, L. S., & Lindgren, C. L. (2011). Fighting for a future: The potential for posttraumatic growth among youths formerly associated with armed forces in Northern Uganda. *Intervention: International Journal of Mental Health, Psychosocial Work & Counselling in Areas of Armed Conflict, 9*(1), 6–20.

Loughry, M., Ager, A., Flouri, E., Khamis, V., Afana, A. H., & Qouta, S. (2006). The impact of structured activities among Palestinian children in a time of conflict. *Journal of Child Psychology and Psychiatry, 47*(12), 1211–1218.

Luthar, S. S., Cicchetti, D., & Becker, B. (2000). The construct of resilience: A critical evaluation and guidelines for future work. *Child Development, 71*(3), 543–562.

Macy, R. D., Macy, D. J., Gross, S. I., & Brighton, P. (2003). Healing in familiar settings: Support for children and youth in the classroom and community. *New Directions for Youth Development, 98*, 51–79.

Masten, A. S. (2011). Resilience in children threatened by extreme adversity: Frameworks for research, practice, and translational synergy. *Development and Psychopathology, 23*(2), 493–506.

Mels, C., Derluyn, I., Broekaert, E., & Rosseel, Y. (2010). The psychological impact of forced displacement and related risk factors on Eastern Congolese adolescents affected by war. *Journal of Child Psychology and Psychiatry, and Allied Disciplines, 51*(10), 1096–1104.

Morgos, D., Worden, J. W., & Gupta, L. (2007). Psychosocial effects of war experiences among displaced children in southern Darfur. *Omega*, *56*(3), 229–253.

Nielsen, S. S., Norredam, M., Christiansen, K. L., Obel, C., Hilden, J., & Krasnik, A. (2008). Mental health among children seeking asylum in Denmark—the effect of length of stay and number of relocations: a cross-sectional study. *BMC Public Health*, *8*, 293.

Panter-Brick, C., Goodman, A., Tol, W. A, & Eggerman, M. (2011). Mental health and childhood adversities: a longitudinal study in Kabul, Afghanistan. *Journal of the American Academy of Child and Adolescent Psychiatry*, *50*(4), 349–363.

Peltonen, K., & Punamäki, R.-L. (2010). Preventive interventions among children exposed to trauma of armed conflict: A literature review. *Aggressive Behavior*, *36*(2), 95–116.

Punamäki, R.-L. (1988). Historical-political and individualistic determinants of coping modes and fears among Palestinian children. *International Journal of Psychology*, *23*(1–6), 721–739.

Pynoos, R. S., Goenjian, A. K., & Steinberg, A. M. (1998). A public mental health approach to the postdisaster treatment of children and adolescents. *Child and Adolescent Psychiatric Clinics of North America*, *7*(1), 195–210, x.

Qouta, S., Punamäki, R.-L., Montgomery, E., & El Sarraj, E. (2007). Predictors of psychological distress and positive resources among Palestinian adolescents: Trauma, child, and mothering characteristics. *Child Abuse & Neglect*, *31*(7), 699–717.

Reed, R. V., Fazel, M., Jones, L., Panter-Brick, C., & Stein, A. (2012). Mental health of displaced and refugee children resettled in low-income and middle-income countries: Risk and protective factors. *Lancet*, *379*(9812), 250–265.

Rothe, E. M., Lewis, J., Castillo-Matos, H., Martinez, O., Busquets, R., & Martinez, I. (2002). Posttraumatic stress disorder among Cuban children and adolescents after release from a refugee camp. *Psychiatric Services (Washington, D.C.)*, *53*(8), 970–976.

Rousseau, C., Drapeau, A., & Platt, R. (2004). Family environment and emotional and behavioural symptoms in adolescent Cambodian refugees: Influence of time, gender, and acculturation. *Medicine, Conflict and Survival*, *20*(2), 151–165.

Rutter, M. (1987). Psychosocial resilience and protective mechanisms. *The American Journal of Orthopsychiatry*, *57*(3), 316–331.

Servan-Schreiber, D., Le Lin, B., & Birmaher, B. (1998). Prevalence of posttraumatic stress disorder and major depressive disorder in Tibetan refugee children. *Journal of the American Academy of Child and Adolescent Psychiatry*, *37*(8), 874–879.

Sphere Project (2011). *Humanitarian charter and minimum standards in humanitarian response* (2011 ed.). Rugby, Warwickshire, England: Practical Action Publishing.

Sujoldzić, A., Peternel, L., Kulenović, T., & Terzić, R. (2006). Social determinants of health—a comparative study of Bosnian adolescents in different cultural contexts. *Collegium Antropologicum*, *30*(4), 703–711.

Thabet, A. A., Abed, Y., & Vostanis, P. (2004). Comorbidity of PTSD and depression among refugee children during war conflict. *Journal of Child Psychology and Psychiatry, and Allied Disciplines*, *45*(3), 533–542.

Thabet, A. A., & Vostanis, P. (1998). Social adversities and anxiety disorders in the Gaza Strip. *Archives of Disease in Childhood*, *78*(5), 439–442.

Themnér, L., & Wallensteen, P. (2011). Armed conflict, 1946–2010. *Journal of Peace Research*, *48*(4), 525–536.

Tol, W. A., Barbui, C., Galappatti, A., Silove, D., Betancourt, T. S., Souza, R. et al. (2011). Mental health and psychosocial support in humanitarian settings: Linking practice and research. *Lancet*, *378*(9802), 1581–1591.

Tol, W. A, Jordans, M. J. D., Kohrt, B. A., Betancourt, T. S., & Komproe, I. H. (2013 a). Promoting mental health and psychosocial well-being in children affected by political violence: Part I—Current evidence for an ecological resilience approach. In M. Ferrari & C. Fernando, *Handbook of resilience in children of war*. New York, NY: Springer.

Tol, W. A, Jordans, M. J. D., Kohrt, B. A., Betancourt, T. S., & Komproe, I. H. (2013 b). Promoting mental health and psychosocial well-being in children affected by political violence: Part II—Expanding the evidence base. In M. Ferrari & C. Fernando. *Handbook of resilience in children of war*. New York, NY: Springer.

Tol, W. A., Jordans, M. J. D., Reis, R., & de Jong, J. T. V. M. (2009). Ecological resilience: Working with child-related psychosocial resources in war-affected communities. In D. Brom, R. Pat-Horenczyk & J. Ford (Eds.), *Treating traumatized children: Risk, resilience and recovery* (chap. 10). New York, NY: Springer.

Tol, W. A., Komproe, I. H., Jordans, M. J. D., Gross, A. L., Susanty, D., & Macy, R. D. (2010). Mediators and moderators of a psychosocial intervention for children affected by political violence. *Journal of Consulting and Clinical Psychology*, *78*(6), 818–828.

Tol, W. A., Komproe, I. H., Jordans, M. J. D., Vallipuram, A., Sipsma, H., Sivayokan, S. et al. (2012). Outcomes and moderators of a preventive school-based mental health intervention for children affected by war in Sri Lanka: A cluster randomized trial. *World Psychiatry*, *11*(2), 114–122.

Tol, W. A., Komproe, I. H., Susanty, D., Jordans, M. J. D., Macy, R. D., & de Jong, J. T. V. M. (2008). School-based mental health intervention for children affected by political violence in Indonesia: a cluster randomized trial. *Journal of the American Medical Association*, *300*(6), 655–662.

Tol, W. A., Patel, V., Tomlinson, M., Baingana, F., Galappatti, A., Panter-Brick, C. et al. (2011). Research priorities for mental health and psychosocial support in humanitarian settings. *PLoS Medicine*, *8*(9), e1001096.

Tol, W. A, Song, S., & Jordans, M. J. D. (2013). Annual research review: Resilience and mental health in children and adolescents living in areas of armed conflict—A systematic review of findings in low- and middle-income countries. *Journal of Child Psychology and Psychiatry*, *54*(4), 445–460.

Ungar, M. (2012). Researching and theorizing resilience across cultures and contexts. *Preventive Medicine*, 55(5), 387–389.

Van Ommeren, M., Sharma, B., Komproe, I., Poudyal, B. N., Sharma, G. K., Cardeña, E. et al. (2001). Trauma and loss as determinants of medically unexplained epidemic illness in a Bhutanese refugee camp. *Psychological Medicine*, *31*(7), 1259–1267.

Yurtbay, T., Alyanak, B., Abali, O., Kaynak, N., & Durukan, M. (2003). The psychological effects of forced emigration on Muslim Albanian children and adolescents. *Community Mental Health Journal*, *39*(3), 203–212.

Chapter 13

Developing a theoretical model of children's responses to disaster and conflict in the context of Islam

Katie Dawson and Richard A. Bryant

Since the introduction of posttraumatic stress disorder (PTSD) as a diagnosis, attention has been increasingly given to understanding what factors contribute to the development and maintenance of the disorder. In the West, cognitive models of PTSD have received substantial attention within the adult and child literatures. In an attempt to delineate the cardinal features of PTSD, these conceptualizations emphasize the role of memory and maladaptive cognitions attributed to the traumatic event and/or its sequelae. This chapter addresses the extent to which these models have relevance in non-Western contexts to explain traumatic stress responses in children.

The role of memory in traumatic stress

PTSD is often characterized by repeated and intrusive re-experiencing of the traumatic event (Brewin, Gregory, Lipton, & Burgess, 2010). According to prevailing cognitive theories (Brewin, Dalgleish, & Joseph, 1996; Ehlers & Clark, 2000), pervasive disturbances in the encoding of the traumatic event result in the memory being poorly elaborated and inadequately integrated into the person's autobiographical memory knowledge base. Going beyond earlier single-level theories, Brewin and colleagues (1996) proposed the dual representational theory of PTSD, which addresses these features of memory. The model posits that trauma memories are encoded in a situationally accessible memory store, which comprises perceptually based memories that are not contextualized in normal autobiographical memory. A similar process is described by Ehlers and Clark (2000), who propose that trauma memories often lack an episodic context because of the elevated arousal experienced at the time of encoding. Across theories, it is presumed that the nature of the encoding of trauma memories is important in the development and maintenance of PTSD, and particularly of intrusive and re-experiencing symptoms.

Analogous to adults, children with PTSD, even very young children, can suffer enduring re-experiencing symptoms (see Meiser-Stedman, 2002). The manifestation of these symptoms is, however, heavily influenced by a child's cognitive development; specifically, whether a child's language is sufficiently developed to convey their experiences, their memory retrieval capacity and their ability to be cognizant of these experiences can influence the nature of trauma memories (Salmon & Bryant, 2002; Sprung, 2008).

Emerging research in the adult PTSD literature has also focused on how people perceive trauma memories. Some researchers have postulated that taking the role of an observer when recalling the traumatic event may act as a form of cognitive avoidance that minimizes distress, but may potentially limit the emotional processing of the event (Kenny et al., 2009). McIsaac and Eich (2004) found that individuals with PTSD who recalled the traumatic event from an observer's perspective, as opposed to a field perspective (i.e., one's own perspective), reported less emotional content and experienced less anxiety. Eighty-nine percent of individuals who adopted an observer perspective reported doing so to avoid re-experiencing the horror of the event through their own eyes. Similar findings were reported in a prospective study completed with 947 adults who had been admitted to hospital following a traumatic injury (Kenny et al., 2009). The authors found that adopting an observer perspective shortly after the traumatic event was significantly associated with PTSD symptom severity during their hospitalization. Moreover, individuals who adopted an observer vantage point were twice as likely to receive a PTSD diagnosis 12 months later. To date, these processes in children's memory for traumatic events have not been investigated in culturally diverse populations.

Conway and Pleydell-Pearce's (2000) model of the self-memory system proposes that, when an individual retrieves an autobiographical memory, it is influenced by and consistent with one's current self-image and personal goals (the "working self"). According to this model, trauma survivors with PTSD should selectively retrieve memories associated with their trauma because the disorder is characterized by concerns about the effects of trauma. Consistent with this proposal, several studies have investigated self-defining memories following traumatic experience. Self-defining memories are those memories that are perceived by a person as seminal in shaping their current identity. Specifically, people with PTSD (Sutherland & Bryant, 2005) and complicated grief (Maccallum & Bryant, 2010) report self-defining memories involving trauma or loss-related events.

Few studies have sought to explore how similar memory processes are applied in a child population, but emerging data suggest similar findings. For instance, depressed adolescents and children with a history of maltreatment have demonstrated memory phenomena similar to those of adults with depression and PTSD, such as memory-specific deficits and preferential retrieval of negative autobiographical memories (Greenhoot, Johnson, Legerski, & McCloskey, 2009). Similarly, Valentino, Toth and Cicchetti (2009) found that abused children reported more negative self-representations when asked to recall memories in response to positive and negative cue words than in response to control words.

Cognitions and PTSD

Ehlers and Clark's (2000) cognitive model highlights the role of the idiosyncratic meaning an individual assigns to the traumatic event and/or its sequelae that gives rise to a sense of ongoing threat and heightened distress. These cognitions and metacognitions might include a range of judgments pertaining to the traumatic event (e.g., "Bad things always happen to me"); their reactions following the event, which evoke a sense of permanent change (e.g., "I'm going crazy"); others' perceived reactions to them (e.g., "They think I am too weak to cope on my own"); and changes in beliefs about one's future (e.g., "I cannot trust anyone"). According to this perspective, such appraisals, by maintaining a sense of current threat, motivate dysfunctional behaviors and coping strategies, including thought suppression, cognitive, emotional and/or behavioral avoidance and rumination.

The validity of the model has been confirmed in cross-sectional and prospective longitudinal studies of adult trauma survivors (Dunmore, Clark, & Ehlers, 2001; Foa, Ehlers, Clark, Tolin, & Orsillo, 1999). While the volume of data available in the child literature is meager by comparison, research pertaining to the applicability of the model to children has demonstrated similar findings. In a study conducted with 5- to 16-year-olds following a motor vehicle accident, Ehlers, Mayou and Bryant (2003) found that cognitive factors—specifically, negative appraisals of the trauma and its aftermath (i.e., negative interpretation of intrusive memories, perceived alienation of others and anger)—significantly predicted PTSD symptom severity three and six months later. More recent studies have applied the "child posttraumatic cognitions inventory" (CPTCI) (Meiser-Stedman, Smith, et al., 2009) to explore the effect of different types of appraisals. The CPTCI is a child version of a standardized measure originally developed as an assessment of maladaptive appraisals in trauma-exposed adults. Evaluation of the model's validity yielded a two-component structure. The first—"permanent and disturbing change" (CPTCI-PC)—pertains to negative appraisals about a child's sense of self and future, while the second—"fragile person in a scary world" (CPTCI-SW)—refers to appraisals alluding to a sense of personal weakness and vulnerability (Meiser-Stedman, Smith, et al., 2009).

Bryant, Salmon, Sinclair and Davidson (2007) investigated cognitive predictors of PTSD in 7- to 13-year-old children following a traumatic injury. Children who formulated unfavorable appraisals of their vulnerability immediately after the traumatic event were significantly more likely to develop PTSD. Such appraisals accounted for 13% of the variance in PTSD after controlling for a child's injury severity score, age, the presence of acute stress disorder (ASD) and parental ASD. A non-significant association was found between PTSD and unfavorable appraisals about permanent change, which constitutes the second subscale of the CPTCI (Meiser-Stedman, Smith, et al., 2009). The authors suggested that younger children may be at greater risk of formulating unfavorable appraisals about their vulnerability, whereas adolescents may be more vulnerable to holding unfavorable appraisals about permanent change, due to their developing cognitive skills, which allow them to reflect more about their personal identity. Meiser-Stedman, Dalgleish, Glucksman, Yule and Smith (2009) found evidence for an association between both subscales of the CPTCI, on the one hand, and PTSD, on the other, in 10- to 16-year-olds six months following a motor vehicle accident. Furthermore, unfavorable appraisals were found to be a significant mediating variable between initial posttraumatic stress reactions and chronic posttraumatic stress symptoms, suggesting that such appraisals play a causal function in the development and maintenance of child PTSD.

Role of spirituality

Several studies that have investigated the role of spirituality and religion following traumatic events have assessed faith-based behaviors, such as prayer, as a coping strategy in the wake of trauma or adversity. For instance, Ai, Tice, Huang and Ishisaka (2005) found that Muslim refugees from Kosovo and Bosnia relied on prayer to cope with their experiences of war trauma in their home country. Specific to children, Fernando (2007) reported that meditation and recitation of Buddhist chants was associated with better coping in Sri Lankan orphans affected by civil conflict. However, to date, no studies have explored how identification with a religion may mediate or influence the manifestation of PTSD features in children.

Attempts to explore posttraumatic stress reactions in non-Western cultures have sometimes been criticized for their failure to appreciate culturally specific constructs and language. Barenbaum and colleagues (Barenbaum, Ruchkin, & Schwab-Stone, 2004) argued that assessment of posttraumatic stress responses in non-Western cultures should recognize cultural manifestations of distress that incorporate spiritual beliefs and values as well as political and social histories.

While these criticisms are valid and have led to the appreciation of culture-specific syndromes and symptoms, Western constructs appear to function in diverse cultural settings. The adult cross-cultural literature has produced a considerable amount of evidence suggesting core similarities in posttraumatic stress symptoms (de Jong, 2005; Marsella, Friedman, & Spain, 1992; Silove, 1999). Emerging evidence in child populations has replicated findings from the adult literature. In a recent study, Betancourt, Speelman, Onyango and Bolton (2009) applied ethnographic methodology to explore local idioms of distress in youths from the Acholi ethnic group displaced by the war in northern Uganda. Results revealed five syndromes that reflect two Western nosological categories: anxiety/depression-type disorders and conduct problems. While there were some culturally specific symptoms, the authors also discovered that many of the symptoms of these culture-specific syndromes also shared features of Western child psychiatric disorders of anxiety, depression and conduct problems. For instance, low mood, diminished interest in activities, fatigue, feelings of worthlessness, disturbed concentration and suicidal ideation were common features of the mood-related cultural syndrome.

Childhood reactions in the context of Islam

This chapter attempts to illustrate the need to extend current cognitive models of childhood traumatic stress to accommodate cross-cultural issues by discussing the example of children in a strictly Islamic, non-Western setting: Aceh, Indonesia. Aceh is the northernmost province of Indonesia, where approximately 4 million people reside (Reid, 2006). It is thought to be the place where Islam was first established in Southeast Asia in the twelfth century. Since this time, it has proved exemplary in religious practice and teaching and has hence been regarded as the "Veranda of Mecca." Muslims make up more than 75% of the Indonesian population, with the most conservative followers of Islam living in Aceh ("Indonesia," 2010).

Islam permeates all aspects of Acehnese life, including cultural norms and values, and competence in religious involvement is highly valued. Following the 2004 Indonesian tsunami, a number of Islamic leaders concluded that the disaster was punishment for insufficient piety, which led to intensified concentration on adherence to Islamic law (United Nations High Commissioner for Refugees, 2007). As a result, changes were made to Aceh's religious laws, the most notable of these being the implementation of Sharia law (strict Islamic law, involving civil and criminal law as well as regulating individual, personal and moral conduct) and the introduction of Sharia police into Aceh.

Aceh's history is marked by a fierce and protracted conflict aiming for political independence and the control of Islamic law, initiated by the secessionist Free Aceh Movement (*Gerakan Aceh Merdeka* or GAM). The heaviest counterinsurgency was seen in the 1990s and human rights abuses were rampant. According to a Human Rights Watch report (2001), an estimated 871 people were killed directly by the army, 387 people were identified as missing and were later found dead, more than 500 others were listed as "disappeared" and never found, tens of thousands were imprisoned and tortured in military camps and there were 102 documented cases of rape. However, most non-government organizations' estimates are significantly higher. Schulze (2003) estimated between 1,000 and 3,000 people killed and a further 900–1400 disappeared. According to Renner (2006), approximately 120, 000 people were forced to evacuate their homes.

On December 26, 2004, this conflict was brought to a halt when a 9.3 magnitude underwater earthquake occurred approximately 100 km (62 miles) from the west coast of Aceh, triggering a devastating tsunami that hit the coastline. More than 225,000 people were estimated to have been killed in eleven countries. In Indonesia alone, over 126,960 people, approximately 2% of Indonesia's population, were confirmed dead by the World Health Organization (Doocy, 2005). However, Reid's (2006) estimates are significantly higher, citing a death toll of over 160,000, more than 4% of Aceh's population. Most Indonesian fatalities occurred in Aceh and Sumatra. Within Aceh, the hardest-hit cities in Aceh were the capital, Banda Aceh, Calang and Meulaboh. According to Tan (2007), 35,000 children in Aceh alone were left homeless, orphaned or separated from their parents. These rates are significantly higher than those in other countries impacted by the tsunami, demonstrating the vast devastation suffered by Aceh. By comparison, Tan documented that, in Sri Lanka and Thailand, 200 and 300 children, respectively, had lost one or both their parents

Research project

To explore the utility of cognitive models in a non-Western Islamic setting, we initiated a relationship with a local non-government organization in Aceh, Centre Mulia Hati (CMH), which was established following the tsunami to provide the local community with vocational training and psychosocial support. The initial steps of community engagement involved having CMH introduce the research team to influential figures within the community, including government officials, religious and community leaders and academic heads. Support and permission was offered for the research to be conducted by the community leaders. A Memorandum of Understanding was signed between CMH, representatives of Meulaboh's local government and the University of New South Wales, outlining a set of regulations that the research was to uphold in regard to the culture and the community at large.

Over the period from August 2009 to October 2010, a series of qualitative and quantitative studies were conducted with children (aged between 7 and 12 years old) already participating in CMH's afterschool development program. Children residing closer to the coastline were, in most cases, only affected by the tsunami, while children from schools further inland were generally only exposed to the civil conflict, thus creating two distinct samples of children.

The first phase of the research project involved a series of focus groups conducted with children (four groups) and adult key informants (i.e., teachers and health workers; three groups) to explore the similarities and differences in symptoms commensurate with Western notions of PTSD, prolonged grief, anger and depression.

The second phase of the project applied quantitative research methodology to corroborate findings from the qualitative studies as well as explore the applicability of Western cognitive models of PTSD in Aceh.

Primary posttraumatic stress reactions in children

The aim of the initial quantitative studies was to investigate the symptomatology of a range of chronic posttraumatic stress reactions. In these studies, the prevalence of PTSD, prolonged grief and depression was investigated through self-report measures. The "children's revised impact of event scale-13" (CRIES-13) (Smith, Perrin, Dyregrov, & Yule, 2003), which has validity across different cultural groups (Perrin, Meiser-Stedman, & Smith, 2005), was adapted to index PTSD. Some amendments were made to the CRIES-13 to reflect the cultural responses provided in the ethnographic pilot study. For item four (*"Do you have waves of strong feelings about it?"*), a literal translation of "waves of strong feelings" was found to be semantically and linguistically inappropriate. It was therefore changed to refer more literally to experiencing negative feelings when thinking about the tsunami.

Overall, children exposed to the tsunami experienced elevated rates of PTSD (48%). Similarly, all the children exposed to the civil conflict reported clinically significant levels of PTSD. Compared to previous studies, the reported prevalence rates were exceptionally high, particularly given the time that had elapsed since the conflict and the tsunami (Fletcher, 1996; La Greca, Silverman, Vernberg, & Roberts, 2002; Salmon & Bryant, 2002). These rates may reflect the ongoing difficulties and stressors in the posttrauma environment, such as high rates of unemployment and poverty. However, methodological limitations may also have contributed to the inflated prevalence rates, such as lack of validation of the measures utilized in the current context and lack of parent or teacher reports. Most importantly, this study sampled children who were attending an afterschool program and may not represent general levels of distress. In spite of these limitations, it is evident that the children claimed to have experienced ongoing psychological difficulties as a result of either the civil conflict or the tsunami.

Issues influencing children's responses

Appraisals

According to cognitive models of trauma, maladaptive appraisals play a pivotal role in the development and maintenance of posttraumatic stress reactions (Ehlers & Clark, 2000; Meiser-Stedman, 2002). The study in Aceh revealed that the belief that honoring Allah will keep them safe from traumatic events was positively correlated with PTSD severity. It is possible that children who perceive themselves as vulnerable to harm are more likely to endorse the belief that Allah can protect them because they are motivated to seek ways to protect themselves. By endorsing the belief that their safety is maintained by honoring Allah, children who feel vulnerable may be enhancing their sense of safety by reassuring themselves of a buffer against potential threat. Consistent with this interpretation, prior research in Western settings has shown that appraisals reflecting a sense of vulnerability are predictive of posttraumatic stress (Bryant et al., 2007; Meiser-Stedman, Dalgleish, et al., 2009; Meiser-Stedman, Dalgleish, Smith, Yule, & Glucksman, 2007). Alternatively, it is possible also that commitment to the belief that Allah can protect them from future disaster heightens their sense of vulnerability because it introduces an element that is beyond their control, which leads to an increased sense of threat. The nature of the association precludes drawing causal inferences about this relationship.

Moreover, boys endorsing the belief that they should have recovered from their posttraumatic stress symptoms were significantly more likely to report anger and aggression. Although this specific appraisal did not seem to influence girls' anger, this was likely because most girls endorsed the belief that they should have recovered, and so there was little variance between girls. Girls' mean rating for the appraisal that they should have accepted the experience and managed their distress was six times that of boys. These findings are consistent with the profile of girls based on reports from the ethnographic study and the tenaciously endorsed view that respectable Muslim girls should accept their destiny, including negative life stressors and emotional states, and inhibit emotional expression.

Western models of thought suppression have reliably shown that cognitive avoidance and suppression have paradoxical effects that lead to an increase in the occurrence of unwanted thoughts (Morgan, Matthews, & Winton, 1995; Wegner, Schneider, Carter, & White, 1987). In the trauma literature, the use of cognitive avoidance has been consistently associated with poorer psychological adjustment (Dempsey, Overstreet, & Moely, 2000; Stallard & Smith, 2007). The finding that children who are avoiding thoughts about the disaster and their experiences of loss suffer stronger stress and grief reactions supports the hypothesis that this avoidance impedes emotional processing and resolution. In addition, the fact that cognitive avoidance was a common strategy relied on by children was consistent with qualitative findings where children identified avoidance of trauma reminders as a common and helpful strategy. This also accords with culturally sanctioned beliefs about accepting negative life events that will be further addressed below.

Memory

We found that a third of the children did not personally recall the tsunami, but, nonetheless, had mental representations of the event. This is understandable, since people can reconstruct events even when they were not encoded, via the use of other sources of information (Bryant, 1996). Many children reported hearing stories of the tsunami directly from another person, and it appears that these secondhand accounts formed the basis of the children's trauma memories. Most of these children reported viewing their memories from an observer's perspective. That is, they recalled the event as if looking at it from the outside or from another person's perspective. Adopting this perspective was associated with less distressing memories in boys. Previous work has shown that trauma survivors who adopt the observer perspective typically report less distress (McIsaac & Eich, 2004), and that manipulating one's vantage point towards an observer perspective also results in reduced distress associated with the memory (Williams & Moulds, 2008). The smaller amount of distress observed in Acehnese boys accords with the proposal that adopting an observer's vantage point is associated with less posttraumatic distress, possibly because it serves an avoidance function. Although other research has shown that this vantage point can lead to impaired adjustment because it impedes emotional processing (Kenny & Bryant, 2007; Kenny et al., 2009), it is unknown whether this also occurs in the Acehnese children.

When children in Aceh were asked to report important memories, their free recall of seminal memories partly predicted their posttraumatic stress adjustment six months later. Controlling for initial levels of depression, the degree to which children's seminal memories were experienced as negative significantly predicted the severity of their depression six months later. However, this association was only found in boys. This pattern accords with previous studies with adults and children that have demonstrated that selective retrieval of negatively valenced memories is involved in the continuation of depressive symptoms (Williams et al., 2007).

These memory findings provide preliminary evidence for the applicability of Western notions of memory disturbance and posttraumatic stress severity. In addition, they highlight the possible influence of cultural dynamics, in that these findings occurred only in boys. In Western studies, the evidence overwhelmingly demonstrates that women are more likely to develop PTSD (Olff, Langeland, Draijer, & Gersons, 2007) and also show enhanced emotional memories (Fujita, Diener, & Sandvik, 1991; Seidlitz & Diener, 1998). It is possible that the Acehnese culture's deterrence of negative emotional expression in girls may have led to the lack of reported emotional disturbance in association with memory patterns in Acehnese girls.

Summary

Cognitive models, such as those proposed by Ehlers and Clark (2000) and Meiser-Stedman (2002), have been very influential in acquiring knowledge about the development and persistence of posttraumatic stress reactions in adults and children. These models stipulate that maladaptive appraisals and memory deficits play a pivotal role in determining whether individuals will develop persistent emotional disturbance following trauma. In addition, Conway and Pleydell-Pearce's (2000) conceptualization of autobiographical memory highlights the role of such memories and how they can shape one's self-identity.

While these models remain vital to the understanding and treatment of posttraumatic stress reactions in the West, the evidence emerging from Aceh highlights several factors that impinge on the applicability of these models in an Eastern, Muslim context. First, the findings did replicate some previous Western research by highlighting the role of maladaptive appraisals in predicting PTSD. However, to date, few studies have explored the role of appraisals in a strict Islamic context. Religion forms the social fabric of Aceh's society and, as evidenced in the qualitative phase of the above-detailed research project, religious practices offered strategies that children reported heavily relying on to cope with trauma. Attributing the tsunami to Allah's will appears to provide children with a perception that future harm can be avoided; the observation that this belief is linked to more severe posttraumatic stress suggests that children who feel at risk are more likely to engage in this appraisal.

Western cognitive models of PTSD do not distinguish between the genders, and empirical evidence demonstrates that in the West the same mechanisms that affect posttraumatic adjustment occur in males and females. However, the Aceh experience indicates the critical role of gender in constructing a sense of self, determining levels of emotional experience and expression and managing trauma memories. It is possible that culturally and religiously sanctioned beliefs contribute to these differences, in that, since Aceh is a patriarchal society, girls are discouraged from expressing negative emotions in the wake of stressful or traumatic events. It is likely these messages encourage girls to suppress negative emotions, which has the paradoxical effect of increasing them, as evidenced in prolonged grief and posttraumatic anger reactions.

In regard to Conway and Pleydell-Pearce's (2000) model, which stipulates that how people think about their past is affected by their self-construct, including their self-image and personal goals, caution needs to be taken when applying these principles to collective cultures, such as Aceh. The construct of self in Acehnese children, which seems to be defined collectively, relies on an amalgamation of social, cultural and religious identities. Previous research has consistently demonstrated significant cultural differences in aspects of children's and adults' autobiographical and trauma memories (Jobson & O'Kearney, 2006; Wang, 2001; Wang & Conway, 2004; Wang & Leichtman, 2000). It is very likely that the cultural and religious values that predominate in collectivist societies such as Aceh strongly determine trauma appraisals, coping strategies and beliefs about recovery. In this sense, cognitive models that are predominantly individualistic need to be adapted to accommodate the collectivist nature of self and socially shared appraisals that characterize many non-Western settings.

One of the lessons to be learned from the initial work conducted in Aceh is that there is an urgent need for more rigorous research that tests the applicability of Western models of trauma response in non-Western settings. Most children in the world who suffer trauma live in non-Western cultures, and many live in Muslim societies. If optimal intervention programs are to be initiated that meet the specific needs of these children, it is important to identify the mechanisms that promote recovery. These mechanisms can be explored using the building blocks of established Western models, but also need to be critically evaluated in light of cultural processes. As noted earlier, it is important to not impose Western constructs and models on other contexts, but it is useful to identify the shared and distinct processes that children use in managing trauma. The ultimate goal of understanding the mechanisms of recovery from trauma in children in non-Western settings is to improve treatment and management programs. The current gold standard for the treatment of childhood trauma is trauma-focused cognitive behavioral therapy, which emphasizes the role of maladaptive appraisals, seeking to modify them, while also addressing the trauma memories through prolonged imaginal exposure (Cohen, Mannarino, & Deblinger, 2006). Given the significance of religious and cultural factors, applying this Western type of intervention in non-Western settings may require adaptation. Specifically, cognitive strategies need to be sensitive in addressing religiously sanctioned trauma appraisals and potentially offer more adaptive appraisals that are consonant with Islamic values. For example, it can be unacceptable to challenge certain thoughts if this is perceived as not accepting one's destiny. Encouragement of religious practices, such as mediation and recitation of Buddhist tenets, was found in a previous study to be associated with better posttraumatic coping and well-being in Buddhist orphans affected by war in Sri Lanka (Fernando, 2007). To increase the effectiveness and validity of psychological interventions in Aceh, explicit recognition of religious issues is mandatory if the interventions are to be successful and acceptable.

References

Ai, A. L., Tice, T. N., Huang, B., & Ishisaka, A. (2005). Wartime faith-based reactions among traumatized Kosovar and Bosnian refugees in the United States. *Mental Health, Religion & Culture, 8*(4), 291–308.

Barenbaum, J., Ruchkin, V., & Schwab-Stone, M. (2004). The psychosocial aspects of children exposed to war: Practice and policy initiatives. *Journal of Child Psychology and Psychiatry, 45*(1), 41–62.

Betancourt, T. S., Speelman, L., Onyango, G., & Bolton, P. (2009). A qualitative study of mental health problems among children displaced by war in northern Uganda. *Transcultural Psychiatry, 46*(2), 238–256. doi:46/2/238 [pii] 10.1177/1363461509105815

Brewin, C. R., Dalgleish, T., & Joseph, S. (1996). A dual representation theory of posttraumatic stress disorder. *Psychological Review, 103*(4), 670–686.

Brewin, C. R., Gregory, J. D., Lipton, M., & Burgess, N. (2010). Intrusive images in psychological disorders: characteristics, neural mechanisms, and treatment implications. *Psychological Review, 117*(1), 210–232. doi: 10.1037/a0018113

Bryant, R., Salmon, K., Sinclair, E., & Davidson, P. (2007). A prospective study of appraisals in childhood posttraumatic stress disorder. *Behaviour Research and Therapy, 45*(10), 2502–2507.

Bryant, R. A. (1996). Posttraumatic stress disorder, flashbacks, and pseudomemories in closed head injury. *Journal of Traumatic Stress, 9*(3), 621–629.

Cohen, J. A., Mannarino, A. P., & Deblinger, E. (2006). *Treating trauma and traumatic grief in children and adolescents*. New York, NY: Guilford Press.

Conway, M. A., & Pleydell-Pearce, C. W. (2000). The construction of autobiographical memories in the self-memory system. *Psychological Review, 107*(2), 261–288.

Dempsey, M., Overstreet, S., & Moely, B. (2000). "Approach" and "avoidance" coping and PTSD symptoms in inner-city youth. *Current Psychology: Developmental, Learning, Personality, Social, 19*(1), 28–45.

Doocy, S. (2005). *Assessing tsunami related mortality in Aceh province*. Paper presented at the World Health Organization (WHO) Conference on the Health Aspects of the Tsunami Disaster in Asia, Phuket, Thailand, May 4–6, 2005.

Dunmore, E., Clark, D. M., & Ehlers, A. (2001). A prospective investigation of the role of cognitive factors in persistent posttraumatic stress disorder (PTSD) after physical or sexual assault. *Behaviour Research and Therapy, 39*(9), 1063–1084.

Ehlers, A., & Clark, D. M. (2000). A cognitive model of posttraumatic stress disorder. *Behaviour Research and Therapy, 38*(4), 319–345.

Ehlers, A., Mayou, R. A., & Bryant, R. (2003). Cognitive predictors of posttraumatic stress disorder in children: Results of a prospective longitudinal study. *Behaviour Research and Therapy, 41*(1), 1–10.

Fernando, C. (2007). *Children of war in Sri Lanka: Promoting resilience through faith development*. Doctoral dissertation, University of Toronto, Ontario, Canada.

Fletcher, K. E. (1996). Childhood posttraumatic stress disorder. In E. J. Marsh & R. Barkley (Eds.), *Child psychopathology* (pp. 242–276). New York, NY: Guildford Press.

Foa, E. B., Ehlers, A., Clark, D. M., Tolin, D. F., & Orsillo, S. M. (1999). The Posttraumatic Cognitions Inventory (PTCI): Development and validation. *Psychological Assessment, 11*(3), 303–314.

Fujita, F., Diener, E., & Sandvik, E. (1991). Gender differences in negative affect and well-being: The case for emotional intensity. *Journal of Personality and Social Psychology, 61*(3), 427–434.

Greenhoot, A. F., Johnson, R. J., Legerski, J.-P., & McCloskey, L. A. (2009). Stress and autobiographical memory functioning. In J. A. Quas & R. Fivush (Eds.), *Emotion and memory in development: Biological, cognitive, and social considerations* (pp. 86–117). New York, NY: Oxford University Press.

Human Rights Watch. (2001). *Indonesia: The war in Aceh* (Human Rights Watch, Asia Division, Vol. 13, No. 4). New York, NY: Author.

Indonesia. (2010) Retrieved from http://www.britannica.com/EBchecked/topic/286480/Indonesia

Jobson, L., & O'Kearney, R. (2006). Cultural differences in autobiographical memory of trauma. *Clinical Psychologist, 10*(3), 89–98.

de Jong, J. T. V. M. (2005). Commentary: Deconstructing critiques of the internationalization of PTSD. *Culture, Medicine and Psychiatry, 29*(3), 361–370.

Kenny, L. M., & Bryant, R. A. (2007). Keeping memories at an arm's length: Vantage point of trauma memories. *Behaviour Research and Therapy, 45*(8), 1915–1920.

Kenny, L. M., Bryant, R. A., Silove, D., Creamer, M., O'Donnell, M., & McFarlane, A. C. (2009). Distant memories: A prospective study of vantage point of trauma memories. *Psychological Science, 20*(9), 1049–1052.

La Greca, A., Silverman, W. K., Vernberg, E. M., & Roberts, M. C. (2002). *Helping children cope with disaster and terrorism*. Washington, D.C.: American Psychological Association.

Maccallum, F., & Bryant, R. A. (2010). Impaired autobiographical memory in complicated grief. *Behaviour Research and Therapy, 48*(4), 328–334.

Marsella, A. J., Friedman, M. J., & Spain, E. H. (1992). Ethnocultural aspects of PTSD: An overview of issues and research directions. In A. J. Marsella, M. J. Friedman, E. T. Gerrity, & R. M. Scurfield (Eds.), *Ethnocultural aspects of posttraumatic stress disorder: Issues, research and clinical applications* (pp. 105–129). Washington D.C.: American Psychological Association.

McIsaac, H. K., & Eich, E. (2004). Vantage point in traumatic memory. *Psychological Science, 15*(4), 248–253.

Meiser-Stedman, R. (2002). Towards a cognitive-behavioral model of PTSD in children and adolescents. *Clinical Child and Family Psychology Review, 5*(4), 217–232.

Meiser-Stedman, R., Dalgleish, T., Glucksman, E., Yule, W., & Smith, P. (2009). Maladaptive cognitive appraisals mediate the evolution of posttraumatic stress reactions: A 6-month follow-up of child and adolescent assault and motor vehicle accident survivors. *Journal of Abnormal Psychology, 118*(4), 778–787.

Meiser-Stedman, R., Dalgleish, T., Smith, P., Yule, W., & Glucksman, E. (2007). Diagnostic, demographic, memory quality, and cognitive variables associated with acute stress disorder in children and adolescents. *Journal of Abnormal Psychology, 116*(1), 65–79.

Meiser-Stedman, R., Smith, P., Bryant, R., Salmon, K., Yule, W., Dalgleish, T., & Nixon, R. D. V. (2009). Development and validation of the Child Post-traumatic Cognitions Inventory (CPTCI). *Journal of Child Psychology and Psychiatry, 50*(4), 432–440.

Morgan, I. A., Matthews, G., & Winton, M. (1995). Coping and personality as predictors of post-traumatic intrusions, numbing, avoidance, and general distress: A study of victims of the Perth flood. *Behavioural and Cognitive Psychotherapy, 23*(3), 251–264.

Olff, M., Langeland, W., Draijer, N., & Gersons, B. P. R. (2007). Gender differences in posttraumatic stress disorder. *Psychological Bulletin, 133*(2), 183–204.

Perrin, S., Meiser-Stedman, R., & Smith, P. (2005). The Children's Revised Impact of Event Scale (CRIES): Validity as a screening instrument for PTSD. *Behavioural and Cognitive Psychotherapy, 33*(4), 487–498.

Reid, A. (2006). *Verandah of violence: The background to the Aceh problem.* Singapore; Seattle, WA: Singapore University Press (in association with University of Washington Press).

Renner, M. (2006). Unexpected promise: Disaster creates an opportunity for peace in a conflict-riven land. *World Watch, 19*(6), 10–16.

Salmon, K., & Bryant, R. A. (2002). Posttraumatic stress disorder in children: The influence of developmental factors. *Clinical Psychology Review, 22*(2), 163–188.

Schulze, K. (2003). Ceasefire or more? *The World Today, 59*(1), 24–25.

Seidlitz, L., & Diener, E. (1998). Sex differences in the recall of affective experiences. *Journal of Personality and Social Psychology, 74*(1), 262–271.

Silove, D. (1999). The psychosocial effects of torture, mass human rights violations, and refugee trauma: Toward an integrated conceptual framework. *The Journal of Nervous and Mental Disease, 187*(4), 200–207.

Smith, P., Perrin, S., Dyregrov, A., & Yule, W. (2003). Principal components analysis of the impact of event scale with children in war. *Personality and Individual Differences, 34*(2), 315–322.

Sprung, M. (2008). Unwanted intrusive thoughts and cognitive functioning in kindergarten and young elementary school-age children following Hurricane Katrina. *Journal of Clinical Child & Adolescent Psychology, 37*(3), 575–587.

Stallard, P., & Smith, E. (2007). Appraisals and cognitive coping styles associated with chronic post-traumatic symptoms in child road traffic accident survivors. *Journal of Child Psychology and Psychiatry, 48*(2), 194–201.

Sutherland, K., & Bryant, R. A. (2005). Self-defining memories in post-traumatic stress disorder. *British Journal of Clinical Psychology, 44*(Pt 4), 591–598.

Tan, N. (2007). Impact of the Indian Ocean tsunami on the well-being of children. *Journal of Social Work in Disability and Rehabilitation, 5*(3), 43–56.

United Nations High Commissioner for Refugees. (2007). *2006 Global Trends: Refugees, asylum-seekers, returnees, internally displaced and stateless persons.* Geneva, Switzerland: Author.

Valentino, K., Toth, S. L., & Cicchetti, D. (2009). Autobiographical memory functioning among abused, neglected and nonmaltreated children: The overgeneral memory effect. *Journal of Child Psychology and Psychiatry, 50*(8), 1029–1038.

Wang, Q. (2001). Culture effects on adults' earliest childhood recollection and self-description: Implications for the relation between memory and the self. *Journal of Personality and Social Psychology, 81*(2), 220–233.

Wang, Q., & Conway, M. A. (2004). The stories we keep: Autobiographical memory in American and Chinese middle-aged adults. *Journal of Personality, 72*(5), 911–938.

Wang, Q., & Leichtman, M. D. (2000). Same beginnings, different stories: A comparison of American and Chinese children's narratives. *Child Development, 71*(5), 1329–1346.

Wegner, D. M., Schneider, D. J., Carter, S. R., III, & White, T. L. (1987). Paradoxical effects of thought suppression. *Journal of Personality and Social Psychology, 53*(1), 5–13.

Williams, A. D., & Moulds, M. L. (2008). Manipulating recall vantage perspective of intrusive memories in dysphoria. *Memory, 16*(7), 742–750.

Williams, J. M., Barnhofer, T., Crane, C., Herman, D., Raes, F., Watkins, E., et al. (2007). Autobiographical memory specificity and emotional disorder. *Psychological Bulletin, 133*(1), 122–148.

Chapter 14

Being a parent and a helping professional in the ongoing shared traumatic reality in southern Israel

Rachel Dekel and Orit Nuttman-Shwartz

Introduction

Most of the literature on helping professionals who work with trauma survivors has investigated the impact of the clients' trauma on the professionals; that is, secondary traumatization (Figley, 1995) or vicarious traumatization (McCann & Pearlman, 1990). However, when the whole community is exposed to terrorism and the helping professionals live and work in the same community as the people they serve, they are exposed to and threatened by the same traumatizing circumstances as their clients. Thus, they not only help survivors cope with the trauma, but also cope with the same traumatic experiences as their clients. The experience has been referred to in the literature as "shared traumatic reality" (STR) (Nuttman-Shwartz & Dekel, 2009a).

This chapter explores the unique challenges faced by helping professionals who live and work in the southern region of Israel, which has been the target of more than 12,500 Qassam rocket and Grad missile attacks over the past decade. We discuss how these professionals have coped with the threat that has plagued their region for so many years. More specifically, we explore the dynamics of the dual role they have to perform in their traumatized community: as parents who bear the responsibility of caring for their own children, and as professional clinicians who have responsibilities to their clients. The pertinent background for our study is provided by literature concerning patterns of parenting in times of war and terrorism, experiences of being a clinician during such periods and clinicians' perceptions of the challenges they face in performing both of these roles.

Parenting in times of war and terrorism

Parents play a major role in shaping their children's experience of the world. For families exposed to ongoing violence or terror, parenting is an especially challenging task. Parents' reactions affect their children's interpretations of the safety of situations. Moreover, parents' symptoms can impact negatively on their own functioning—their ability to parent effectively and to be sensitive to their children's needs (Appleyard & Osofsky, 2003; for review, see Gewirtz, Forgatch, &

Wieling, 2008). Research findings have revealed a strong positive association between parents' and children's posttraumatic stress disorder (Chemtob et al., 2010; Wickrama & Kaspar, 2008). Whereas parents' stress reactions may increase the risk of distress in their children, a supportive family environment may contribute to a better adjustment in children (e.g., Gil-Rivas, Holman, & Silver, 2004; Kronenberg et al., 2010).

Several additional themes have been documented in studies on the responses of parents during and after exposure to war and terror. The first theme involves basic survival, including the parents' need to keep their children safe and protect their lives (Dekel, 2004; Hafstad, Haavind, & Jensen, 2012; Robertson & Duckett, 2007). The second theme involves feelings of guilt, helplessness and frustration, which some parents experience as a result of their decision to raise their children in dangerous and insecure areas. In this context, there are parents who feel that they are unable to protect their children (Osofsky, 1995) and who fear for their children's current and future mental health (Litvak-Hirsch & Lazar, 2012). Alongside these difficulties, some parents have also reported favorable developments, such as feeling stronger, less vulnerable, more capable of taking responsibility and more prepared to manage future adverse situations (Itzhaky & Dekel, 2008).

Being a clinician in times of terrorism and war

Interventions in times of terrorism and war demand flexibility and commitment. In the acute phase of a traumatic situation, mental health workers are often required to go to their clients' homes, their clients' schools or the site of the traumatic incident itself. At that time, the workers need to be flexible and adapt their usual professional role to the circumstances of the traumatic situation.

These interventions sometimes lead mental health professionals to feel a sense of helplessness. These feelings derive from the challenges involved in dealing with large numbers of people who are trying to cope with intense pain (Eidelson, D'Alessio, & Eidelson, 2003), a feeling that their ability to help the clients cope with the magnitude of their suffering is limited (Cohen, Gagin, & Peled-Avram, 2006; Lev-Wiesel, Goldblatt, Eisikovits, & Admi, 2009) as well as their own sense of physical danger and lack of resources to protect themselves (Shamai, 2005).

In recent years, more attention has been given to the situation of shared trauma. The challenges of shared trauma have been explored during and after several traumatic events. Some studies have investigated one-time events, such as the September 11th attacks on the United States in 2001 (e.g., Tosone, 2006), and Hurricane Katrina (e.g., Faust, Black, Abrahams, Warner, & Bellando, 2008). Other studies have investigated situations of war and ongoing terrorism, such as the first Gulf War (e.g., Granot, 1995), the second Lebanon war (Lev-Wiesel et al., 2009) and suicide bombings in Israel (e.g., Shamai & Ron, 2009).

The need to function simultaneously as a helping professional and as a member of a threatened community creates conflicts of loyalty between professionals' personal and professional worlds (Dekel & Baum, 2010). These conflicts are reflected in questions such as: *"Is it right for me to leave my family when there might be another missile attack?"* and *"What kind of mother leaves her young children when they are frightened and confused by the events of the past hours?"* (Loewenberg, 1992; Somer, Buchbinder, Peled-Avram, & Ben-Yizhack, 2004). These conflicts tend to emerge more intensively in the acute phases of the events (Baum, 2010). In a recent study conducted among social workers who live and work under ongoing threat in southern Israel, participants used the term "emergency routine" to capture their constant preparedness and alertness in the face of danger, and their availability to deal simultaneously with their private and professional worlds (Baum, 2012).

When the therapist and client are "in the same boat" (Tosone & Bialkin, 2003), the nature of the standard psychotherapeutic relationship is also altered. Not only does the therapist take care of the client, but the client may also start taking care of the therapist and become involved in the therapist's world. In these situations, therapists are likely to be more stressed, preoccupied and defensive than under ordinary circumstances. Clients who perceive this change may lose confidence in the therapist's ability to provide assistance and contain the situation (Baum, 2010), and might even temporarily exchange roles with the therapist.

The current study

Notwithstanding existing knowledge about the concept of STR, not enough is known about the effects of prolonged shared trauma, such as the situation in southern Israel. The frequent random firings at all hours of the day and night, which have gone on for more than a decade, have led to a heightened state of physical and emotional alertness. Because the interval between the time a missile is fired and the time it lands is very short, there is little opportunity to protect oneself.

Social service agencies throughout the area have developed emergency and resilience centers in addition to regular municipal social services. Employees in these services are professionals from a variety of mental health disciplines who are trained to provide both emergency and long-term assistance in accordance with the circumstances. The study detailed here focused on the unique challenges of being both a parent and a clinician in such centers during such ongoing STR.

Method

Data were collected during three semi-structured, in-depth focus group interviews, each of which lasted around two hours. The researchers prepared a manual with several questions and issues they planned to address. These issues involved being a professional in situations of ongoing threat, being a parent in these situations and combining the two roles. The researchers used the manual as a basis for presenting similar questions to the professionals in the respective groups. The participants were asked to introduce themselves and then describe their experiences as helping professionals working in such "ongoing threat" situations. The participants were not asked directly about their personal lives. In every group, the participants were invited to respond to one another so as to clarify their comments and add their own ideas, associations and comments. The group interview was conducted in Hebrew, videotaped, and later transcribed and translated into English.

Participants

Thirty helping professionals (5 men and 25 women) participated in the groups. The participants ranged from 30 to 60 years of age, and they were in a variety of helping professions: 18 social workers (60%), 6 psychologists (20%) and 6 art therapists, animal therapists and physical therapists (20%). The duration of their employment in the region ranged from 1 month to 20 years, although most of the workers had been employed in the field for more than 5 years. All the workers were parents of children ranging in age from infants to adolescents. A few of them (3%) also had children who were already married and had families of their own. More than 75% of the professionals (23) lived in the region. The participants were employed by three agencies: two regional resilience centers (12 workers at one center, 9 workers at the other) and one municipal social service agency (9 workers), which had different levels of exposure to threat.

Procedures

The directors of the social agencies were contacted and asked to devote a staff meeting to discussing the implications of the security situation on therapeutic relationships. The authors came to the meeting, introduced themselves and described their research. They invited the staff members to participate in the study, and asked for permission to record the interviews. The groups were led by two therapists, both of whom were researchers and social workers. One lives and works outside of the confrontation zone; the second lives outside the area, but has worked there regularly over the last eight years. The authors were careful to ensure that all the interviewees had an opportunity to express themselves to a reasonable extent.

Ethical considerations

All the participants voluntarily consented to participate in the study after having received a brief explanation of the general aims of the research. Confidentiality was maintained by changing the participants' names and identifying details in all the reports. The results of the study were shared with the participants.

Data analysis

Content analysis was conducted as follows. First, the recordings were transcribed. Each researcher read the transcripts of the three groups. After identifying the participants' voices, they examined the main units of meaning in each of the individual's narratives in each of the groups (Patton, 1990; Unrau & Coleman, 1997). Finally, each of the researchers integrated the units into main themes after careful consideration and reconsideration of the texts. Subsequently, the authors compared their individual analyses. They discussed differences and looked for areas of agreement. The comparison involved both the content of the themes and interpretations of their meaning. The researchers derived similar interpretations of most of the themes. A few themes were found by only one researcher. In those cases, the researchers engaged in an open discussion and determined whether the theme would be considered a new one or would be ascribed to some other theme that had already been identified.

Findings

This section focuses on several themes. It begins by presenting the participants' descriptions of their extensive exposure to rocket attacks. We then explore how this situation affected their ability to function, their feelings of fear and their narrowed focus of concerns. Afterwards, we present the participants' multiple ways of coping with the two worlds. The presentation of findings concludes with descriptions that reflect the participants' sense of professional growth and competence.

Exposure to extensive missile attacks

The participants described high levels of direct exposure to missile attacks in their roles as residents of the region, parents and clinicians. For example, one of the participants mentioned that a missile had hit his home, causing a block of cement to fall on his daughter's bed and hitting her leg in the exact place where she usually rests her head. Other participants described situations in which they were driving with their children when a siren went off, warning them of a missile attack. They also described many occasions, almost routine events, in which they were in the middle of a therapeutic session with an individual client, a couple or a group when the siren went off and they had to run to a sheltered space with their clients, but continued with the session afterwards.

The effects of ongoing threat

FEAR AND FUNCTIONING

Several workers reported posttraumatic stress symptoms. In their personal role, they experienced emotional distress, confusion and difficulty in functioning (e.g., they avoided going shopping and had difficulty sleeping). Of these, two workers reported that they had experienced such high levels of distress and difficulties in functioning at home that they needed professional help. Nonetheless, it appears that most of the workers succeeded in coping with the ongoing threat.

Regarding their parental role, the participants mentioned the need to function and pull themselves together to help their children. When their children were not with them, sometimes the opportunity to focus on their personal lives and take a break from their professional roles allowed them to express fear.

> It's funny that I'm actually a bit scared when there's a red alert at my house and I go into the shelter. I'm a little scared there, but, at work, I detach myself. I find that I'm most scared in the personal domain, even now that I have two little girls. But I was even more afraid before they were born. It's as if I'm both on duty and living the situation.

The same worker mentioned the importance of professional functioning, which forces her to pull herself together and enables her to feel strong and competent:

> There's something about being on duty. There's fear, but there's something about it that makes you get organized.

In the therapeutic domain, despite the ongoing threat, most of the participants reported a high sense of professional competence. The participants described how they went into the protected space, pulled themselves together in front of their client and quickly returned to the therapeutic discussion. It appears that, even if fear existed, and even if it was intense at times, it occurred mostly in the personal domain. On the whole, in both the personal and professional domains, the participants described how they pulled themselves together quickly and felt that they could cope successfully.

CONSTRICTING ONE'S FOCUS

The constriction of one's focus was a theme that emerged in relation to both the participants' personal and professional lives. In their personal lives, the constriction of the participants' focus was evident at both the concrete and the emotional levels. At the concrete level, it involved the need to cope, function and get several young children into a protected room within a short time after the alarm. It also involved the constriction of experience and the need to spend hours with the children in the protected indoor space without engaging in outdoor activities. At the emotional level, the participants asked themselves how they could raise children in a setting characterized by ongoing threat. They were focused on the question of the price their children were paying, and the extent to which their children's childhood had been adversely affected or diminished. They compared the situation of their older children, who had been raised in a different setting, with the way that their younger children were growing up.

> I always see the gaps between my fourth daughter, who's six years old, and the rest of the family. She was born into this reality. It's so different raising her compared to what it was like raising the other three kids: she's a trauma child. It's hard for her to go places alone. I go with her to the bus station, and tell her that I'm driving away, and she says, "What if there's a red alert? What if I'm shaking? Who will I hold on to?" It's not easy for me to deal with that as a parent.

The participants raised the same questions in regard to their professional role: *"To what extent are the issues dealt with in therapy related to the security situation?"*, *"Are there other life events and developmental challenges that are relevant to my clients?"*, *"Do the perspectives I adopt as a result of my exposure to the security situation help me deal with other issues?"* Most of the participants indicated that, despite their wish to deal with other issues, and despite their professional knowledge, this was difficult, if not impossible.

> Even if people come to me for a different reason, the first thing I ask them is how they feel about where they're living, how they feel about the threat surrounding them. It's something you have to talk about. You have to ask what happens when there's an alert, how you should behave. . .

Only the new worker, who had just arrived in the region, was able to see how narrow the perspective was that the other workers had:

> There is too much emphasis on trauma, and that narrows possibilities. I started meeting with patients, and I could hear their trauma. I could deal with it, but I was also able to hear other things. Now, I'm preoccupied with these questions: *To what extent has the trauma taken over, and does it dominate the therapist's mind? What is the therapist looking for, and what does he or she hear?*

Other workers mentioned that, in their professional judgment, their clients' distress was almost always related to the security situation. For example, when children come for treatment of fear resulting from other traumatic events, the therapists believe that the fear reaction and sense of threat are a result of exposure to the security situation. When the clients are unable to see this connection, the therapists integrate it into their professional evaluations and the therapeutic process.

> I've often asked myself: *If this person had been born in Tel Aviv and experienced this problem, would he be seeing things the same way as someone*

from our area who has experienced the same problem? They don't connect the trauma of living with missile attacks to the problems they have today. But, when you listen to their stories, there's no doubt that for this person, with all of the troubles in his life, there is a connection.

Coping with the shared traumatic reality

The participants described a range of coping patterns they used to try and maintain both roles. These attempts can be conceptualized on a continuum. Attempts to disconnect the two worlds would be at one extreme, followed by choosing between the two worlds and merging the two worlds; finally, acknowledging the mutual effects of the two worlds would be at the other extreme.

DISCONNECTING THE TWO WORLDS

The first way of negotiating between the two worlds is to try to disconnect them from each other, both consciously and unconsciously.

Parents' fears for their children lead to various attempts to protect them. The participants described situations in which they sent their children to members of their extended family who live outside of the danger zone in order to protect them. This allowed the therapists to perform their professional tasks, relieved by the knowledge that the children were not exposed to the danger. There were other workers who described their sense of relief when their children grew up and left the region.

Another way of trying to disconnect the two worlds was reflected in the therapy sessions. One worker mentioned that, in light of her daughter's distress, she decided that she wouldn't treat other children. She only wanted to treat her own ("personal") daughter, and didn't want to treat other people's daughters.

The participants also gave examples of unconscious attempts to disconnect the two worlds. One worker mentioned that she rushed to the scene after a missile fell on her son's school. During the session with her client, she hadn't contacted her son. Only after she finished her professional duties did she "remember" that her son had been at the school that was hit, and check on him. Examples of this kind of "forgetting" were also provided in the participants' narratives about other family members, such as spouses and elderly parents.

However, such attempts to disconnect the personal and professional worlds were not always helpful. Although many of the narratives describe situations in which the workers functioned and carried out their professional duties, there were workers who reported intense distress and had difficulty functioning or detached themselves from the outside situation when they returned home.

Then I walked home, and I couldn't do anything. I just lay down on the sofa and said: "I have to relax a bit, that's what will help me." Then the missiles started falling and didn't stop. Over the next two hours, there were maybe

20 missiles, but I didn't move from my couch. I was in this *"How do I keep the missiles away from my mind?"* mode, just lying on the sofa doing relaxation exercises.

Another worker described how she became dependent on her spouse when she was home. She was unable to function, had anxiety attacks while she was driving to work and needed professional treatment. While all of this was happening, she continued functioning in the professional world.

CHOOSING BETWEEN THE TWO WORLDS

As mentioned in the literature, the need to choose between two worlds often causes a conflict of loyalties. Participants mentioned that they had experienced this kind of conflict when the threatening security situation began.

There was a very clear statement [at my workplace] that "you have to be there for the client." But it was really hard for me, and I felt the pressure. I also felt that staying with my kids was the best decision. Maybe my employer had a hard time understanding my situation, that I had nowhere to leave the kids. But I believe that, if I don't know my kids are in a safe place, I can't help anyone.

Sometimes, workers are asked to stay at the scene of the incident. Some of them feel that this obligation is forced on them, and that it doesn't show respect or empathy for their personal situation. For example, one participant described constant phone calls that she received from her father while she was at a professional meeting:

Wow, he's so agitated. He's alone, and no one's with him. I should have told them that I'm leaving, that the meeting is over, but I didn't. Instead, I went outside for a second and took a deep breath. Then I came back inside and said, "Okay, let's continue." They asked what had happened and I told them that the kibbutz was on fire. They said "Okay, let's go back to business, let's continue the meeting." There was no empathy, nothing. That's all it was: Come on, come back to the meeting, let's go.

However, the participants' responses in the focus group discussions revealed that, in most cases, they gave clear priority to their professional role, even if this choice caused tension.

I was in the house, and my family was supposed to come. I was taking food out and heating it. Then, all of a sudden, they announced what was happening. I told myself, *"Okay, my family will have to deal with the meal without me."* I explained everything to my mother so that she would know what to do.

But then my daughter came to me, absolutely panicked about my leaving to go to the place where people had been killed. She cried, "Maybe there were more missiles, maybe you won't be safe." She was begging me not to drive there. I told her, "This is my job, dear, I have to go." She was sobbing, and I drove off anyway.

The workers described several situations like that, where they believed they had to continue performing their professional duties. They expected it of themselves, even if their children were in distress, even if their children asked them to stay home and help and even if going to work caused them personal distress.

MERGING THE TWO WORLDS

Some of the texts described merging of the personal and professional worlds. This merging was manifested in the way the participants told the story and in the content of the narrative. That is, it was not always clear who they were talking about—the parent, the worker or the professional.

I'm driving to work. I'm supposed to meet a patient at eight whose daughter died in a missile attack . . . So I give a ride to my two kids and a friend of theirs from the neighborhood. While we're driving, my daughter says, "Mom, Mom!" Her friend has started panicking and shaking because her father texted her that a siren had sounded. We haven't heard the siren because it's winter and the car windows are closed. I know that this girl is in therapy, and my kids also know she's anxious. My daughter tells me to pull the car over and do breathing exercises with her friend. But I can't pull over because we're in the middle of the road. So my daughter says, "Okay, okay, you continue driving, and I'll do the breathing exercises with her."

The narrative clearly shows how the narrator's professional and personal lives have merged. During the incident, the mother and daughter helped each other provide emergency treatment and became partners in that process. Beyond that, the daughter assumed the role of therapist to her friend when her mother was unable to stop the car. This was a case in which the mother and daughter merged roles on both the personal and professional levels.

ACKNOWLEDGING THE TWO WORLDS

This coping pattern involves a clear differentiation between the personal and professional worlds, with continuous movement between them. There is recognition that professionals are also human beings with fears and limitations, and that a professional who personally experiences a situation can gain deeper insights into it than one who had never had that experience.

We can't erase our existence as people when we're treating others. Just because we're therapists, that doesn't mean that we're less sensitive or less scared. I don't separate the two. I don't know how to. Whatever happens to me will happen, and that's part of the treatment, whether I analyze it or not. It's part of the interaction between me and the patient. I'm not a hero, nor are they.

The next excerpt describes acknowledgment of the two worlds and recognition that both worlds exist. The participant indicated that sometimes an individual has to pay a price for these double or triple identities (person, parent and therapist) and multiple missions. She describes her experience in doing therapy under these circumstances:

Maybe my place there was mixed up . . . It's not that I bring my own experiences into the therapeutic sessions without any restraint, but I can't say that I don't sometimes think about my daughters during treatment, or that I don't have flashbacks in the house. I can't really separate these things.

Professional competence and growth

Despite the long-term, ongoing threat, the participants in all three focus groups reported that they felt a strong sense of professional competence. They described their deep commitment to their work, which they found to be highly meaningful. They felt that they had acquired knowledge and developed intervention skills unique to the ongoing threat situation. The meaning and importance they attributed to their work also derived, in part, from the help and support provided by family members and neighbors, who often stepped in to take over the parenting role when their work took them away from home.

In addition, most therapists felt that they were "seen" and cared for by their colleagues and by their professional supervisors and managers. They felt that both their emotional and instrumental needs were provided for. Some of them used the term "parental regulation" to describe the role of their supervisor in their lives. They also mentioned personal resources, such as belief in God, optimism and sports, which helped them cope with the tension and anxiety surrounding the ongoing security situation. In addition, they benefited from professional skills that they used in their work with clients, such as relaxation and breathing techniques.

Discussion

The present chapter is focused on personal, parental and professional functioning of therapists who experience ongoing STR. Even though we asked the participants in the study about their experiences as therapists in the face of an ongoing threat, most of their narratives involved the need to maneuver between their personal and professional worlds. This validates the concept of STR and highlights the need to continue exploring the unique difficulties and challenges of these situations.

It seems that the family domain was the vulnerable space for the participants in the study discussed here. In the parental role, they were concerned with the extent to which their children's lives had been adversely affected by the traumatic reality. This finding is consistent with the results of other studies conducted among mothers living in the region, which revealed that the mothers felt guilty about raising their children in a war zone (e.g., Hirsch & Lazar, 2011). Moreover, although the participants' professional role served as a shield that allowed them to continue functioning, there was more evidence of fear and functional difficulties in their personal role.

With regard to their professional role as therapists, some of the workers felt that the entire therapeutic process was dominated by the traumatic events, and that the possibility of considering other issues was limited. Other workers indicated that, in light of the ongoing traumatic reality, their clients' current situation of distress was undoubtedly an outcome of exposure to traumatic events. Consistent with the results of previous studies, the present research findings indicate that STR impaired the therapists' ability to create a safe space in which clients could make spontaneous transitions between the internal and external worlds. The therapeutic space was inevitably connected with the traumatic reality outside it, so that both the therapist and client were forced to address concrete issues, including the destructive consequences of the ongoing threat (Kretsch, Benyakar, Baruch, & Roth, 1997).

The study considered in this chapter documented a continuum of strategies for handling the demands of personal and professional spheres in the context of STR. The first strategy is splitting or separating the two worlds from each other. According to this idea, it is too difficult for therapists to function simultaneously in two worlds that both require a full investment of resources. As a result, they dissociate themselves or put aside certain aspects of one world. In most of the narratives, the detachment was unconscious. The participants "remembered" the components of their personal world that they had forgotten, such as children or elderly parents, only when they looked back at the event. These responses are consistent with findings cited in the literature that indicate that the ability to engage in splitting at the time of an event allows one to continue functioning effectively (Bryant, 2007).

The literature on STR indicates that blurring of the personal and professional worlds leads to a conflict of loyalties (Dekel & Baum, 2010), and that workers find it difficult to function in their professional roles as long as they are not sure that their own family members are safe (Faust et al., 2008; Shamai & Ron, 2009). Their decision to choose the professional world was clear, and they showed great commitment to their professional role.

There are several possible reasons for the clear choice of the professional world. First, the threat situation has persisted for many years, and the workers might have become accustomed to it. Second, their choice of the professional world might represent their loyalty to the workplace and colleagues. It is also possible that, when the direct supervisor not only assumes an administrative role, but also acknowledges the complexity of the situation, and helps regulate the workers' anxiety, it helps them perform their professional role. In addition, it is possible that this choice gave the participants a strong sense of meaning and professional contribution, which served as resilience factors that facilitate coping (Tosone, McTighe, Bauwens, & Naturale, 2011). However, in some cases, it seems that there was no process of making a choice or deliberating between the two worlds. Notably, many of the participants who worked in rural areas are known to have a strong ideological connection and sense of belonging to the region, and this might have reinforced their preference for the professional world (Dekel & Nuttman-Shwartz, 2009).

The texts of the interviews revealed two coping patterns in which the personal and professional worlds were more integrated. The first pattern is integration, to the point of merging and enmeshment of the two worlds, where enmeshment means blurring boundaries and minimizing interpersonal distance. Rapid transitions between the two worlds are often seen in the narratives. Although, in some cases, it was not clear which world they were referring to and who performed what roles, this pattern is not always dysfunctional (Bograd, 1984).

The second pattern recognizes the existence of two worlds and the difficulty entailed in separating them. In addition, the workers attempt to use one world as a basis for learning how to function in the other, and vice versa. This finding has been supported by Bonanno (2004), who revealed that successful adaptation is associated with the ability to move flexibly between emotional states.

Earlier descriptions of the blurring of the boundaries between personal and professional roles have described the dynamics between the two worlds as penetration (Baum, 2010). Our findings indicate that, in light of the ongoing threat, the manifestations of blurring were more varied, subtle and persistent, and the attempt to maneuver between the two worlds created a new identity. Moreover, while it is difficult to assess this in a qualitative study, it seems that workers use various coping patterns in different situations, and over a lengthy period. This is consistent with our earlier study on coping with the ongoing threat in this area, which documented the use of multiple ways of coping (Nuttman-Shwartz & Dekel, 2009b). Further research is needed to document these coping patterns and understand their frequency of use among workers over an extended period of time. In addition, it is important to study the contribution of each of these coping methods to people's adaptation.

Despite the need for intensive, ongoing professional work in situations of STR, the findings of the current study and others (Bauwens & Tosone, 2010) indicate that the participants felt a sense of professional competence and growth, and that they were confident of their ability to continue helping the residents of their locality. Several factors contributed to this feeling, including personal recognition of their professional knowledge and practice wisdom, which led to professional growth. The workers felt that they had appropriate knowledge and professional skills for work in the region. Their knowledge was based mainly on the experience they had gained as a result of their ongoing work in the region.

Consistent with previous research (Shamai & Ron, 2009; Tosone, Minami, Bettmann, & Jasperson, 2010), the participants also highlighted the importance of the professional and emotional guidance provided by their direct supervisor as an additional supporting factor. The supervisor deals with the concrete task of dividing the burden of work and assists with the emotional regulation of staff members, which gives them a sense of security. Support from family members and neighbors, who help out when the therapists need to work, is also important (Dekel & Baum, 2010).

Limitations of the current study

As mentioned, one of the researchers also worked in the region. Hence, there may have been some bias in the collection and analysis of the data because that investigator was involved in the traumatic reality just like the participants. To offset the potential bias, the second investigator was an expert in the field from another region of the country. In addition, conducting the sessions in focus groups and asking the workers to discuss their feelings in the presence of their work colleagues might have led them to minimize their expression of distress and dysfunction at work. Although this limitation cannot be ruled out, the participants in the groups seemed open and shared personal stories. Additionally, the professional literature suggests that focus groups actively facilitate the discussion of sensitive topics, because the less inhibited members of the group break the ice for the shyer participants. Participants can also provide mutual support by expressing feelings that are shared by other members of the group, but have not been brought into the discussion (Kitzinger, 1995).

The study included a smaller percentage of male than female participants, which reflects the distribution in the field. A comparison between the genders could add to an understanding of the STR phenomena and could be a subject for further study.

Finally, the study investigated the participants at only one point in time, after many of them had lived in the STR for 10 years. Hence, it is important to conduct a longitudinal study that investigates long-term changes and development in professional functioning. In addition, it would be worthwhile to investigate whether differences in the workers' personal and professional variables, such as place of residence and years of work experience, affect their patterns of coping and reactions to STR. The finding that STR impeded the parental role highlights the need to continue investigating the implications of STR for family relations.

The findings of the present study indicate that supervisors and professional workers should be aware of the complexity of STR. Rather than focusing exclusively on secondary traumatization, or on providing insights into the specific intervention, it is important to provide solutions that address the workers' dual parental and professional roles. In that context, the parallel processes involving personal and professional roles should be explored further, both at the personal level of each worker and at the team/service level. This can facilitate the formulation of policies for the benefit of the workers.

References

Appleyard, K., & Osofsky, J. (2003). Parenting after trauma: Supporting parents and caregivers in the treatment of children impacted by violence. *Infant Mental Health Journal, 24*(2), 111–125.

Baum, N. (2010). Shared traumatic reality in communal disasters: Toward a conceptualization. *Psychotherapy: Theory, Research, Practice and Training, 47*(2), 249–259.

Baum, N. (2012). Emergency routine: The experience of professionals in a shared traumatic reality of war. *British Journal of Social Work, 42*(3), 424–442.

Bauwens, J., & Tosone, C. (2010). Professional posttraumatic growth after a shared traumatic experience: Manhattan clinicians' perspectives on post-9/11 practice. *Journal of Loss and Trauma, 15*(6), 498–517.

Bograd, M. (1984). Family systems approaches to wife battering: A feminist critique. *American Journal of Orthopsychiatry, 54*(4), 558–568.

Bonanno, G. A. (2004). Loss, trauma, and human resilience: Have we underestimated the human capacity to thrive after extremely aversive events? *American Psychologist, 59*(1), 20–28.

Bryant, R. (2007). Does dissociation further our understanding of PTSD? *Journal of Anxiety Disorders, 21*(2), 183–191.

Chemtob, C. M., Nomura, Y., Rajendran, K., Yehuda, R., Schwarz, D., & Abramovitz, R. (2010). Impact of maternal posttraumatic stress disorder and depression following exposure to the September 11 attacks on preschool children's behavior. *Child Development, 81*(4), 1129–1141.

Cohen, M., Gagin, R. & Peled-Avram, M. (2006). Multiple terrorist attacks: Compassion fatigue in Israeli social workers. *Traumatology, 12*(4), 293–301.

Dekel, R. (2004). Motherhood in a time of terror: Subjective experiences and responses of Israeli mothers. *Affilia, 19*(1), 24–38.

Dekel, R., & Baum, N. (2010). Intervention in a shared traumatic reality: A new challenge for social workers. *British Journal of Social Work, 40*(6), 1927–1944.

Dekel, R., & Nuttman-Shwartz, O. (2009). Posttraumatic stress and growth: The contribution of cognitive appraisal and sense of belonging to the country. *Health and Social Work, 34*(2), 87–96.

Eidelson, R. J., D'Alessio, G. R., & Eidelson, J. I. (2003). The impact of September 11 on psychologists. *Professional Psychology: Research and Practice, 34*(2), 144–150.

Faust, D. S., Black, F. W., Abrahams, J. P., Warner, M. S., & Bellando, B. J. (2008). After the storm: Katrina's impact on psychological practice in New Orleans. *Professional Psychology: Research and Practice, 39*(1), 1–6.

Figley, C. R. (1995). Compassion fatigue as secondary traumatic stress disorder: An overview. In C. R. Figley (Ed.), *Compassion fatigue: Coping with secondary traumatic stress disorder in those who treat the traumatized* (pp. 1–20). New York, NY: Brunner/Mazel.

Gewirtz, A., Forgatch, M., & Wieling, E. (2008). Parenting practices as potential mechanisms for child adjustment following mass trauma. *Journal of Marital and Family Therapy, 34*(2), 177–193.

Gil-Rivas, V., Holman, E. A., & Silver, R. C. (2004). Adolescent vulnerability following the September 11th terrorist attacks: A study of parents and their children. *Applied Developmental Science, 8*(3), 130–142.

Granot, H. (1995). Israeli emergency social and mental health services in the Gulf War: Observations and experiences of a mental health professional. *Journal of Mental Health Counseling, 17*(3), 336–346.

Hafstad, G. S., Haavind, H., & Jensen, T. K. (2012). Parenting after a natural disaster: A qualitative study of Norwegian families surviving the 2004 tsunami in Southeast Asia. *Journal of Child and Family Studies, 21*(2), 293–302.

Itzhaky, H., & Dekel, R. (2008). Community intervention with Jewish Israeli mothers in times of terror. *British Journal of Social Work, 38*(3), 462–475.

Kitzinger, J. (1995). Qualitative research: Introducing focus groups. *British Medical Journal, 311*(7000), 299–302.

Kretsch, R., Benyakar, M., Baruch, E., & Roth, M. (1997). A shared reality of therapists and survivors in a national crisis as illustrated by the Gulf War. *Psychotherapy: Theory, Research, Practice, Training, 34*(1), 28–33.

Kronenberg, M. E., Hansel, T. C., Brennan, A. M., Osofsky, H. J., Osofsky, J. D., & Lawrason, B. (2010). Children of Katrina: Lessons learned about postdisaster symptoms and recovery patterns. *Child Development, 81*(4), 1241–1259.

Lev-Wiesel, R., Goldblatt, H., Eisikovits, Z., & Admi, H. (2009). Growth in the shadow of war: The case of social workers and nurses working in a shared war reality. *British Journal of Social Work, 39*(6), 1154–1174.

Litvak-Hirsch, T., & Lazar, A. (2011). Experiencing processes of growth: Coping and PTG among mothers who were exposed to rocket attacks. *Traumatology, 18*(2), 50–60.

Loewenberg, F. M. (1992). Notes on ethical dilemmas in wartime: Experiences of Israeli social workers during Operation Desert Shield. *International Social Work, 35*(4), 429–439.

McCann, I. L., & Pearlman, L. A. (1990). Vicarious traumatization: A framework for understanding the psychological effects of working with victims. *Journal of Traumatic Stress, 3*(1), 131–149.

Nuttman-Shwartz, O., & Dekel, R. (2009a). Challenges for students working in a shared traumatic reality. *British Journal of Social Work, 37*(3), 1247–1261.

Nuttman-Shwartz, O., & Dekel, R. (2009b). Ways of coping and sense of belonging in the face of a continuous threat. *Journal of Traumatic Stress, 22*(6), 667–670.

Osofsky, J. D. (1995). The effects of exposure to violence on young children. *American Psychologist, 50*(9), 782–788.

Patton, M. Q. (1990). *Qualitative evaluation and research methods* (2nd ed.). Newbury Park, CA: Sage.

Robertson, C. L., & Duckett, L. (2007). Mothering during war and postwar in Bosnia. *Journal of Family Nursing, 13*(4), 461–483.

Shamai, M. (2005). Personal experience in professional narratives: The role of helpers' families in their work with terror victims. *Family Process, 44*(2), 203–215.

Shamai, M., & Ron, P. (2009). Helping direct and indirect victims of national terror: Experiences of Israeli social workers. *Qualitative Health Research, 19*(1), 42–54.

Somer, E., Buchbinder, E., Peled-Avram, M., & Ben-Yizhack, Y. (2004). The stress and coping of Israeli emergency room social workers following terrorist attacks. *Qualitative Health Research, 14*(8), 1077–1093.

Tosone, C. (2006). Therapeutic intimacy: A post-9/11 perspective. *Smith College Studies in Social Work*, *76*(4), 89–98.

Tosone, C., & Bialkin, L. (2003). Mass violence and secondary trauma: Issues for the clinician. In S. L. Ashenberg Straussner & N. K. Phillips (Eds.), *Understanding mass violence: A social work perspective* (pp. 157–167). New York, NY: Pearson.

Tosone, C., McTighe, J. P., Bauwens, J., & Naturale, A. (2011). Shared traumatic stress and the long-term impact of 9/11 on Manhattan clinicians, *Journal of Traumatic Stress*, *24*(5), 546–552.

Tosone, C., Minami, T., Bettmann, J. E., & Jasperson, R. A. (2010). New York City social workers after 9/11: Their attachment, resiliency, and compassion fatigue. *International Journal of Emergency Mental Health*, *12*(2), 103–116.

Unrau, Y., & Coleman, H. (1997). Qualitative data analysis. In R. M. Grinnell (Ed.), *Social work research and evaluation: Quantitative and qualitative approaches* (pp. 512–514). Itasca, IL: F. E. Peacock Publishers.

Wickrama, K. A. S., & Kaspar, V. (2008). Family context of mental health risk in tsunami-exposed adolescents: Findings from a pilot study in Sri Lanka. *Social Science & Medicine*, *64*(3), 713–723.

Concluding comments

Chapter 15

Thoughts about survival mode theory of posttraumatic reactions

Danny Brom

Threat and trauma are abundantly present in society. In the past 40 years, interest in human responses to life-threatening situations and their psychopathological consequences has grown tremendously. The literature on posttraumatic stress disorder (PTSD) from the behavioral, cognitive, emotional, interpersonal and neurobiological perspectives has advanced the efficacy of treatment models. A variety of phenomena, perspectives and theories are presented on how people survive life-threatening situations and recover from such experiences. Survival mechanisms are being mentioned more and more as a way to understand responses to trauma (Valent, 1998). An overarching concept that can give a consistent theoretical frame for the wide array of posttraumatic phenomena has been proposed by Claude Chemtob and colleagues (Chemtob, Roitblat, Hamada, Carlson, & Twentyman, 1988; Chemtob, Novaco, Hamada, Gross, & Smith, 1997). They proposed the concept of "survival mode," which can help us understand individual, group and societal responses to threat—both healthy reactions and psychopathology.

"Survival mode" is conceptualized by Chemtob as a mechanism that rules human functioning when people perceive existential danger. The term refers to a complex interaction among neurobiological processes, attentional processes, cognitive tendencies, emotional biases, social orientation and behavioral responses. Processing potentially traumatic events means finding a way out of survival mode. PTSD can be seen as the failure of a person to let go of the survival mode. But PTSD is only one of the possible trajectories of adaptation after people have been in survival mode. There are also a variety of partially resilient ways of coping, which represent different levels of processing threat and trauma (Layne et al., 2009).

Human beings are mostly wired for survival. Efficient reactions to threat are essential for survival. The classical model of human response to threat consists of three phases: (a) recognition of the threat, (b) appraisal of the danger and its risks and (c) appraisal and deployment of one's coping resources. Extreme threat appears to create a qualitatively different response from daily stresses. Soldiers on the battlefield, for example, have immediate and overwhelming physiological responses, coming from the limbic system and interpreted by cortical structures. The appraisal of a life-threatening situation is instinctual, and the consequent behavioral responses are almost immediate. The conscious experience of fear is overruled by the demands of the acute life threat, replacing higher level brain functions by instinctive functioning through more primitive parts of the brain. Price (2005) goes so far as to call his article about the functioning of brain systems under threat "Free will versus survival." Under threat, the functioning of the organism's neurophysiological system rearranges itself to free up energy for immediate action (Perry, 1998).

The goal of instinctual reactions is to counter dangers and reestablish safety. There are many parts of the nervous system involved in the threat response. Attention narrows down to detecting the source of the danger and assessing its impact; emotional awareness diminishes; behavioral responses are quick, smooth and goal oriented; and, people often do not feel like themselves during these moments. Cognitive functioning is also quick and efficient, with people reporting that they had a clear and focused mind (Greene, Grasso & Ford, this volume).

Early on in the trauma literature, the notion was expressed that existential threats lead to biological changes. Kardiner (1941) saw veterans of World War I and maintained that traumatic neurosis (what we now would call PTSD) is a "physioneurosis,"; that is, a biological dysregulation: "This is present on the battlefield and . . . ever present and unchanged" (p. 95). Modern research has been able to elucidate the degree to which PTSD is indeed a "physioneurosis," a mental disorder based on the persistence of biological emergency responses (e.g., van der Kolk & Saporta, 1991). As can be seen from these citations, trauma researchers claim that there is a relationship between trauma and nervous system functioning. Also, it seems clear that immediate responses to an emergency may be associated with later psychopathology.

The effects of threat on cognitive functioning have been studied extensively by researchers in the field of terror management theory (Pyszczynski, Greenberg, Solomon, Arndt, & Schimel, 2004). They have shown that existential threats have both immediate and long-term effects on thought processes and contents. Human beings live with a cognitive map that is constantly being formed by experience. The cognitive map tells us what is dangerous and what is not; that is, how we can survive in a world full of dangers. As negative or threatening information is more powerful than positive, this cognitive map is based mostly on information derived from threatening experiences. The negative experiences form our cognitive map that functions as a defense system to keep us safe. In other words, serious threats challenge our assumptions about the world (Janoff-Bulman, 1989). The challenge after extreme events is to re-adapt our cognitive map so that we can continue functioning and avoid the fear of the threat's recurrence. We have proposed the concept of minimal learning (Brom & Kleber, 2009), indicating that adapting the cognitive map requires a learning process that can be ended when the map supports a feeling of safety despite the event that has occurred.

Characteristics of survival mode

The central claim of this chapter, which is heavily based on the work of Chemtob and colleagues (1988; 1997), is the existence of a "survival mode" of human functioning. The trigger of this mode of functioning is basically external, although cues that have been learned and that trigger the expectation of serious threats can also evoke this mode. The activation of survival mode is mainly automatic, although learning processes shape what type of trigger, and what intensity of the trigger, activates it.

Survival mode is characterized by a cascade of neurobiological responses that are interrelated in complex ways (Van Horn, 2011). The release of cortisol, epinephrine and oxytocin make the organism ready for the fight–flight response, but also prepare for relaxation and bonding, which are responses that release tension. Strong bonding is also one of the features of survival mode. Parallel to early attachment strategies that are activated due to primary needs such as hunger and fatigue, later attachment strategies are activated when threat is perceived (Mikulincer, Shaver, & Pereg, 2003). Attachment has been recognized as a survival mechanism, both during early development and in emergency situations. In particular, at times of serious threats, people have a clear tendency to engage in immediate strong bonding with a perceived benevolent authority, as well as with other people they perceive as sharing their fate. In parallel, there is a tendency to reject people perceived to be hostile or not part of the in-group.

This mechanism is also highly relevant for what happens in families during and after disasters. Parents living under existential threat lose part of their natural parenting skills, because their focus changes away from the emotional and developmental needs of their children and towards the security needs of survival. This might partly explain the association that has been found between posttraumatic responses in parents and in their children (Dekel & Nuttman-Shwartz, this volume; Scheeringa & Zeanah, 2001).

Survival mode is not only automatic, it also overrules other processes, whether cognitive, emotional or neurophysiological. This means that people in survival mode do not have all of their cognitive and emotional abilities available, as they are not relevant for the most important task at hand: survival. In this situation, the many everyday processes are subordinated to the demands of the situation.

If we want the concept of survival mode to guide us in helping children or adults after traumatic events, we should give special attention to the necessary conditions for the termination or deactivation of this mode. Greene, Grasso and Ford (this volume) call this the "shift from survival to learning mode." Some of the conditions for this shift away from survival mode are (a) the perception that the actual threat has passed; (b) the expectation that the threat will not return without prior warning; (c) arousal regulation has been re-established to a degree that allows cognitive flexibility; and (d) a subjective narrative of the occurrence of the threat has been established, supporting the notion that future threat can be avoided or effectively coped with.

A forum of trauma experts led by Hobfoll (Hobfoll et al., 2007) has defined five main principles for how to support people immediately after traumatic incidences. Looking at these principles from the perspective of survival mode theory, we can easily see how most of the principles promote the deactivation of survival mode. The five principles include the recommendations to promote a sense of safety, calming, a sense of self- and collective efficacy, connectedness and hope. The first four principles address the need of people to self-regulate and experience safety so as to deactivate the survival mode.

When people have difficulty terminating the survival mode, and continue their exclusive focus and investment in safety and survival even in safe circumstances, we see these as posttraumatic symptoms. Full-fledged symptoms of PTSD indicate that the person is still experiencing, consciously or unconsciously, the past traumatic event as ongoing or feeling that the event might recur any moment. Defenses such as avoidance and numbing are necessary to maintain balance, and self-regulation is under pressure and often gives way. The symptoms of hyperarousal are another sign of the person's perception that the traumatic event is ongoing and survival is still the primary task.

Dissociation is another key concept for understanding survival, trauma and coping, and is often seen as a marker of a pathological response. Following the French psychologist Pierre Janet, dissociation is described as "undue division of the personality" and that it is "at the heart of trauma-related disorders" (van der Hart, Nijenhuis, & Steele, 2006). Dissociation is clearly one of the processes that occur during major threats. Van der Hart and colleagues maintain that, under severe stress, the personality is divided into two psychobiological systems: the one responsible for approaching attractive stimuli, such as food and companionship, and the ones that is geared to avoid or escape from aversive or dangerous stimuli. During an event that is perceived as life threatening, the latter systems takes precedence, and action systems connected to fight–flight–freeze responses are activated. Once the danger has abated, the personality division should be re-evaluated and integration attempted. Dissociation is most common and most severe in people who have experienced the need for survival mode at times they were developmentally unready for it. When children go into survival mode and are not buffered from the threat by their environment, the more primary form of defense prevails. Severe deficits in regulatory abilities and an ongoing inclination to resort to dissociative defenses are noted consequences (van Dijke et al. 2011)

Different models of individual therapy for posttraumatic states now seem to be coming together in a three-phase consensus model. The first phase focuses on stabilization, the re-establishment of a sense of safety and re-organization of daily life; this is seen as a necessary condition for processing traumatic memories, which is the second phase. The family interventions in the second section of this book all focus on enhancing the protection of children through attachment, safety and co-regulation, thus allowing them to integrate their experiences. The second phase of the consensus model is directed at processing the traumatic experiences/

memories. This includes facing what has happened, confronting the memories that lead to so much emotion and arousal, and creating a consistent personal narrative. The third phase consists of reintegration into social life, as well as work on repairing the client's self-image so that one can start seeing oneself as a result of all of one's life experiences and not as defined by the traumatic experience. The consensus model explains how to help people first regulate their arousal system and deactivate survival mode and then integrate the experience into the individual's life and narrative. Community interventions, such as those described in the third section of this book, ideally integrate interventions that help people get out of survival mode so as to prevent difficulties later on, with interventions that assess the persistence of partial or full survival mode, in the form of posttraumatic symptoms, and offer appropriate treatment. An ongoing concern in the field of psychotraumatology in general, but even more so for traumatized children, is the enormous amount of non-psychopathological consequences of trauma and survival mode. Posttraumatic phenomena may include partial symptoms or changes in attitudes and worldviews that are based on the expectation that traumatic events will reoccur or that the evil they have experienced exclusively defines the world we live in. These consequences have been largely neglected and deserve our attention, as they are a major influence in societies coping with massive trauma.

References

Brom, D., & Kleber R. J. (2009). Resilience as the capacity for processing traumatic experiences. In D. Brom, R. Pat-Horenczyk & J. D. Ford (Eds.), *Treating traumatized children: Risk, resilience and recovery* (pp. 133–149). New York, NY: Routledge.

Chemtob, C. M., Novaco, R. W., Hamada, R. S., Gross, D. M., & Smith, G. (1997). Anger regulation deficits in combat-related posttraumatic stress disorder. *Journal of Traumatic Stress*, *10*(1), 17–36.

Chemtob, C. M., Roitblat, H. L, Hamada, R. S., Carlson, J. G., & Twentyman, C. T (1988). A cognitive action theory of post-traumatic stress disorder. *Journal of Anxiety Disorders*, *2*(3), 257–275.

Hobfoll, S. E., Watson, P., Bell, C. C., Bryant, R. A., Brymer, M. J., Friedman, M. J., et al. (2007). Five essential elements of immediate and mid-term mass trauma intervention: Empirical evidence. *Psychiatry*, *70*(4), 283–315.

Janoff-Bulman, R. (1989). Assumptive worlds and the stress of traumatic events: Applications of the schema construct. *Social Cognition* (Special Issue: Social Cognition and Stress), *7*(2), 113–136.

Kardiner, A. (1941). *The traumatic neuroses of war*. Washington, D.C.: National Research Council.

Layne, C. M., Beck, C. J., Rimmasch, H., Southwick, J. S., Moreno, M. A., & Hobfoll, S. E. (2009). Promoting "resilient" posttraumatic adjustment in childhood and beyond: "Unpacking" life events, adjustment trajectories, resources and interventions. In D. Brom, R. Pat-Horenczyk & J. D. Ford (Eds.), *Treating traumatized children: Risk, resilience and recovery* (pp. 13–40). New York, NY: Routledge.

Mikulincer, M., Shaver, P. R., & Pereg, D. (2003). Attachment theory and affect regulation: The dynamics, development, and cognitive consequences of attachment-related strategies. *Motivation and Emotion, 27*(2), 77–102.

Perry, B. D. (1998). Anxiety disorders. In C. E. Coffey & R. A. Brumback (Eds.), *Textbook of pediatric neuropsychiatry* (pp. 580–594). Washington, D.C.: American Psychiatric Press.

Price, J. L. (2005). Free will versus survival: Brain systems that underlie intrinsic constraints on behavior. *Journal of Comparative Neurology, 493*(1), 132–139.

Pyszczynski, T., Greenberg, J., Solomon, S., Arndt, J., & Schimel, J. (2004). Why do people need self-esteem? A theoretical and empirical review. *Psychological Bulletin, 130*(3): 435–468.

Scheeringa, M. S., & Zeanah, C. H. (2001). A relational perspective on PTSD in early childhood. *Journal of Traumatic Stress, 14*(4), 799–815.

Valent, P. (1998). *From survival to fulfillment: A framework for the life-trauma dialectic.* Philadelphia, PA: Brunner/Mazel.

Van der Hart, O., Nijenhuis, E. R. S., & Steele, K. (2006). *The haunted self: Structural dissociation and the treatment of chronic traumatization.* New York: Norton.

van der Kolk, B. A., & Saporta, J. (1991). The biological response to psychic trauma: Mechanisms and treatment of intrusion and numbing. *Anxiety, Stress & Coping, 4*(3), 199–212.

van Dijke, A., Ford, J. D., van der Hart, O., Van Son, M. J. M., Van der Heijden, P. G. M., & Bühring, M. (2011). Childhood traumatization by primary caretaker and affect dysregulation in patients with borderline personality disorder and somatoform disorder. *European Journal of Psychotraumatology, 2*, 5628, doi: 10.3402/ejpt.v2i0.5628

Van Horn, P. (2011). The impact of trauma on the developing social brain: Development and regulation in relationship. In J. D. Osofsky (Ed.), *Clinical work with traumatized young children* (chap. 2). New York, NY: Guilford Press.

Index

ABC-X model 83
ACTH 4, 5, 6
acute stress disorder 212
adaptation 4, 83, 84, 88–90, 94, 96, 151, 166; FAAR model 84–5, 86; *see also* coping
adaptive communication 93
adaptive coping 174
adolescents: aggression in 41–65; bereavement 69; group social identity 51
adrenocorticotrophic hormone *see* ACTH
adult PTSD 3; clinical implications 10–11; and HPA dysfunction 6–7; neuroendocrine alterations 4–5
adults traumatized in childhood 6
aggression: beliefs about 50–1; community interventions 55–6; emotional expression 43; escalation of 50; and exposure to violence 41–65; hostile intent 46–7; individual and family level interventions 54–5; national level interventions 56–7; social learning 49–50; threat perception 27, 46
aggressive scripts 47, 49, 50
alcohol abuse 26, 27, 28, 53, 57, 69, 141
alexithymia 25–6
allostatic load 26
ambiguous loss 90–1
anger 22, 26, 30, 44, 46, 48, 54, 56, 123, 126, 141, 150, 181, 212, 215, 216, 219
asylum seekers *see* refugees
attachment theory 143
attribution of meaning 183, 184, 185, 187–8, 189
avoidant behavior 27, 246

balance, restoration of 94
behavioral response 46, 47
belief systems 83, 89, 90, 91–2, 94, 95, 96
bereavement 66–78; adolescents 69; grief *see* grief; magical thinking 68; school-age children 68–9; sibling loss 72–4; symptoms of 70; very young children 68
Blueprints for Healthy Youth Development initiative 53–4
brain: development 19, 23, 42–3; dysregulation by trauma 19, 25; effects of exposure to violence 43; learning mode 29–30, 31; right hemisphere 43; in suicide victims 10; *see also* neuroendocrine alterations; survival mode
brain stem 43
Building Emotion and Affect Regulation (BEAR) program 54–5

caregivers 19–20; role in fostering resilience 67, 106; support from 23–5; *see also* family resilience; parents; parent-child relationship
Child FIRST 134
child posttraumatic cognitions inventory (CPTCI) 212–13
child psychosocial distress screener 202–3
child safety 139, 141–2
child thematic program 202
Child-Parent Psychotherapy 133–45; history 134–5
child-parent relationship therapy 107
children's revised impact of event scale-13 (CRIES-13) 215–16
Children's Room project 74–5
City Without Violence initiative 56–7